# Praise for *High Performance MySQL*, 4th Edition

I love that this new edition shifts the book's emphasis to a modern, pragmatic mindset of team players delivering business value. It moves past the previous editions' myopic focus on gnarly internals and theory to wring out diminishing returns, toward a more holistic perspective. The 'how databases work' material is still covered thoroughly, but now with a fresh, humanistic take that is greatly needed.

—*Baron Schwartz, Lead author of* High Performance MySQL, *2nd and 3rd editions*

*High Performance MySQL* has been a staple of the MySQL world since the first edition 17 years ago. MySQL moves ever onward, and Silvia and Jeremy have done an excellent job bringing this essential work up to date with modern MySQL.

—*Jeremy Cole*

Updated to meet modern practices, this latest edition is rich with solid advice for MySQL administrators and developers.

—*Shlomi Noach, Database Engineer, PlanetScale*

**FOURTH EDITION**

# High Performance MySQL

*Proven Strategies for Operating at Scale*

*Silvia Botros and Jeremy Tinley*
*Foreword by Jeremy Cole*

Beijing · Boston · Farnham · Sebastopol · Tokyo

**High Performance MySQL**

by Silvia Botros and Jeremy Tinley

Published by O'Reilly Media, Inc., 1005 Gravenstein Highway North, Sebastopol, CA 95472.

O'Reilly books may be purchased for educational, business, or sales promotional use. Online editions are also available for most titles (*http://oreilly.com*). For more information, contact our corporate/institutional sales department: 800-998-9938 or *corporate@oreilly.com*.

| | |
|---|---|
| **Editors:** Virginia Wilson and Andy Kwan | **Indexer:** Judith McConville |
| **Production Editor:** Elizabeth Faerm | **Interior Designer:** David Futato |
| **Copyeditor:** Shannon Turlington | **Cover Designer:** Karen Montgomery |
| **Proofreader:** Kim Cofer | **Illustrator:** Kate Dullea |

November 2021:     Fourth Edition

**Revision History for the Fourth Edition**
2021-11-17:   First Release

See *http://oreilly.com/catalog/errata.csp?isbn=9781492080510* for release details.

978-1-492-08051-0

[LSI]

# Table of Contents

# Foreword

A fresh copy of *High Performance MySQL* has been the first book to get plopped down on the desk of every newly-hired DBA, systems engineer, or database-minded developer since it came out nearly two decades ago.

When Jeremy Zawodny and Derek Balling set out to write a book about running MySQL at scale, to bring clarity and structure to years of mystery, it was destined to become an instant classic in the MySQL world. Through the years and several updates, some of the content of the original and the subsequent updates has held up, and some not so much.

MySQL itself has advanced, the MySQL community has changed a lot, and the ways in which we use MySQL have changed. Now in the 4th edition, Silvia and Jeremy undertake a thankless and gargantuan task to update this classic for the modern era—and they are just the pair for the task.

In my time (now more than 20 years!) in the MySQL community, the one consistent thing has been, well, inconsistency. Everyone uses MySQL (and databases in general) in slightly different ways, and they each have different expectations of it. Everyone makes some good decisions, some well-intentioned but questionable decisions, and, always, their share of bad ones. Sometimes, progress is easy, but sometimes it takes sage advice and a new way of thinking about the problem learned straight from an expert.

Silvia and Jeremy are just such experts. Everything from MySQL architecture, optimization, replication, backups, and more, stood to benefit from them sharing their extensive experience in the trenches with MySQL. In this new 4th edition, many subjects got new treatment, a lot of outdated material was removed, errors were corrected, and a new and fresh style was brought to the material.

Like the original (now vintage, and quaintly small) 1st edition, the 4th edition promises to help carry the newest generation of developers, DBAs, and their bosses into the new world of MySQL; sometimes with excitement, but perhaps sometimes kicking and screaming.

Thanks, Silvia and Jeremy, for your hard work to nurture the next generation of MySQL geeks who will be keeping the world's data safe and the world's top websites and other data-driven systems performing at their peak.

Congratulations on getting this done through COVID and everything else. The rest of us will make sure to get all the new DBAs a copy.

*— Jeremy Cole*
*near Reno, Nevada*
*October 2021*

# Preface

The official documentation maintained by Oracle gives you the knowledge necessary to install, configure, and interact with MySQL. This book serves as a companion to that documentation, helping you understand how best to leverage MySQL as a powerful data platform for your use case.

This edition also expands on the growing role of compliance and security as parts of operating a database footprint. New realities such as privacy laws and data sovereignty have changed how companies build their products, and that naturally introduces new complexities in how the technical architecture evolves.

## Who This Book Is For

This book is first and foremost for engineers looking to grow their expertise in running MySQL. This edition assumes its audience is familiar with the basic principles of why you want to use a relational database management system (RDBMS). We also assume some experience with general system administration, networking, and operating systems.

We will offer you proven strategies for running MySQL at scale with a modern architecture and more up-to-date tooling and practices.

Ultimately, we hope that the knowledge you gain from this book of MySQL's internals and scaling strategies will help you in scaling the data storage layer at your organization. And we hope that your newfound insight will help you to learn and practice a methodical approach to designing, maintaining, and troubleshooting an architecture that is built on MySQL.

# What Is Different in This Edition

*High Performance MySQL* has been a part of the database engineering community for years, with past editions released in 2004, 2008, and 2012. In these previous editions, the goal was always to teach developers and administrators how to optimize MySQL for every drop of performance by focusing on deep internal design, explaining what various tuning settings mean, and arming the user with the knowledge to be effective in changing these settings. This edition maintains the same goal but with a different focus.

Since the third edition, the MySQL ecosystem has seen a lot of changes. Three new major versions have been released. The tooling landscape expanded significantly beyond Perl and Bash scripts and into full-fledged tooling solutions. Entirely new open source projects have been built that change how organizations manage scaling MySQL.

Even the traditional database administrator (DBA) role has evolved. There's an old joke in the industry that says that DBA stands for "Don't Bother Asking." DBAs had a reputation for being speed bumps in the software development life cycle (SDLC), not explicitly because of any curmudgeonly attitude, but simply because databases weren't evolving as fast as the rest of the SDLC around them.

With books like *Database Reliability Engineering: Designing and Operating Resilient Database Systems* by Laine Campbell and Charity Majors (O'Reilly), it has become the new reality that technical organizations look to database engineers more as enablers of business growth and less as the sole operators of all databases. Where once a DBA's primary day-to-day involved schema design and query optimization, they now are responsible for teaching those skills to developers and managing systems that allow developers to deploy their own schema changes quickly and safely.

With these changes, the focus should no longer be on optimizing MySQL to get a few percentage points faster. We think that *High Performance MySQL* is now about giving people the information they need to make educated decisions about how to best use MySQL. This begins by understanding how MySQL is designed, which gives way to understanding what MySQL is and is not good at.[1] Modern releases of MySQL offer reasonably sane defaults, and there's very little tuning you need to do unless you're experiencing a very specific scaling problem. Modern teams are now dealing with schema changes, compliance issues, and sharding. We want *High Performance MySQL* to be a comprehensive guide to how modern companies run MySQL at scale.

---

[1] Famously, people often used MySQL as a queue and then learned the hard way why it was bad. The most cited reasons were the overhead of polling for new queue actions, the management of locking records for processing, and the unwieldy size of queue tables as data grows over time.

# Conventions Used in This Book

The following typographical conventions are used in this book:

*Italic*

Indicates new terms, URLs, email addresses, filenames, and file extensions.

`Constant width`

Used for program listings, as well as within paragraphs to refer to program elements such as variable or function names, databases, data types, environment variables, statements, and keywords.

**`Constant width bold`**

Shows commands or other text that should be typed literally by the user.

*`Constant width italic`*

Shows text that should be replaced with user-supplied values or by values determined by context.

This icon signifies a tip or suggestion.

This icon signifies a general note.

This icon indicates a warning or caution.

# O'Reilly Online Learning

 For more than 40 years, O'Reilly Media (*http://oreilly.com*) has provided technology and business training, knowledge, and insight to help companies succeed.

Our unique network of experts and innovators share their knowledge and expertise through books, articles, and our online learning platform. O'Reilly's online learning platform gives you on-demand access to live training courses, in-depth learning paths, interactive coding environments, and a vast collection of text and video from O'Reilly and 200+ other publishers. For more information, visit *http://oreilly.com*.

# How to Contact Us

Please address comments and questions concerning this book to the publisher:

O'Reilly Media, Inc.
1005 Gravenstein Highway North
Sebastopol, CA 95472
800-998-9938 (in the United States or Canada)
707-829-0515 (international or local)
707-829-0104 (fax)

We have a web page for this book, where we list errata, examples, and any additional information. You can access this page at *https://oreil.ly/hiperfmysql_2e*.

Email *bookquestions@oreilly.com* to comment or ask technical questions about this book.

For news and information about our books and courses, visit *http://oreilly.com*.

Find us on Facebook: *http://facebook.com/oreilly*

Follow us on Twitter: *http://twitter.com/oreillymedia*

Watch us on YouTube: *http://www.youtube.com/oreillymedia*

# Acknowledgments for the Fourth Edition

## From Silvia

First and foremost, I'd like to thank my family. My parents, who sacrificed stable jobs and lives in Egypt to bring me and my brother to the United States. My husband, Armea, for supporting me through this and all the past years of my career as I took on one challenge after the next, culminating in this accomplishment.

I started off in tech as an immigrant who left her college years in the Middle East to achieve her dream of moving to the United States. After earning my degree in a state university in California, I took a job in New York City, and I remember the second edition of this book being the very first tech book I bought with my own money that was not a college book. I owe the authors of the previous editions teaching me a lot of fundamental lessons that prepared me to manage databases during my career.

I am grateful for the support of so many people I have worked with in my career. Their encouragement has gotten me to write this edition of this book that taught me so much earlier in my career. I'd like to thank Tim Jenkins, the former CTO of Send-Grid, for hiring me for the job of a lifetime even though I told him in my interview that he was using MySQL replication the wrong way, and for trusting me with what turned out to be a rocket ship.

I'd like to thank all the amazing women in tech who have been my support network and cheerleaders. Special thanks to Camille Fournier and Dr. Nicole Forsgren for writing the two books that have influenced the past few years of my career and changed my view on my day-to-day work.

Thank you to my team at Twilio. To Sean Kilgore for making me a much better engineer who cares about a lot more than just the databases. To John Martin for being the most optimistic human I ever worked with. Thanks to Laine Campbell and her Palo-minoDB team (later acquired by Pythian) who helped support me and taught me so much during the toughest years, and to Baron Schwartz for encouraging me to write about my experiences.

Finally, thanks to Virginia Wilson for being an excellent editor, for helping turn my stream of ideas into sentences that make sense and for helping me through this process with so much support and grace.

## From Jeremy

When Silvia approached me to help with this book, it was in the middle of an extraordinarily stressful period of most people's lives—the global pandemic, which started in 2020. I was unsure that I wanted to add any more stress to my life. My wife, Selena, told me that I would regret it if I didn't accept, and I know better than to argue with her. She has always supported me and encouraged me to be the best human being I can be. I will forever love her for all that she does for me.

To my family, coworkers, and community friends: I would have never gotten to this point without you. You all taught me how to be who I am today. My career is the sum of my experiences with you all. You taught me how to accept criticism, how to lead by example, how to fail and recover, and most importantly, that the sum is better than the individual.

Lastly, I want to thank Silvia, who trusted me to bring a shared understanding but different perspective to this book. I hope I met your expectations.

## A Thank You to Tech Reviewers

The authors also want to recognize the tech reviewers who helped get this book to where it is today: Aisha Imran, Andrew Regner, Baron Schwartz, Daniel Nichter, Hayley Anderson, Ivan Mora Perez, Jam Leoni, Jaryd Remillard, Jennifer Davis, Jeremy Cole, Keith Wells, Kris Hamoud, Nick Vyzas, Shubheksha Jalan, Tom Krouper, and Will Gunty. Thank you all for your time and effort.

# CHAPTER 1

# MySQL Architecture

MySQL's architectural characteristics make it useful for a wide range of purposes. Although it is not perfect, it is flexible enough to work well in both small and large environments. These range from a personal website up to large-scale enterprise applications. To get the most from MySQL, you need to understand its design so that you can work with it, not against it.

This chapter provides a high-level overview of the MySQL server architecture, the major differences between the storage engines, and why those differences are important. We've tried to explain MySQL by simplifying the details and showing examples. This discussion will be useful for those new to database servers as well as readers who are experts with other database servers.

## MySQL's Logical Architecture

A good mental picture of how MySQL's components work together will help you understand the server. Figure 1-1 shows a logical view of MySQL's architecture.

The topmost layer, clients, contains the services that aren't unique to MySQL. They're services most network-based client/server tools or servers need: connection handling, authentication, security, and so forth.

The second layer is where things get interesting. Much of MySQL's brains are here, including the code for query parsing, analysis, optimization, and all the built-in functions (e.g., dates, times, math, and encryption). Any functionality provided across storage engines lives at this level: stored procedures, triggers, and views, for example.

The third layer contains the storage engines. They are responsible for storing and retrieving all data stored "in" MySQL. Like the various filesystems available for GNU/Linux, each storage engine has its own benefits and drawbacks. The server communicates with them through the storage engine API. This API hides differences between storage engines and makes them largely transparent at the query layer. It also contains a couple of dozen low-level functions that perform operations such as "begin a transaction" or "fetch the row that has this primary key." The storage engines don't parse SQL[1] or communicate with one another; they simply respond to requests from the server.

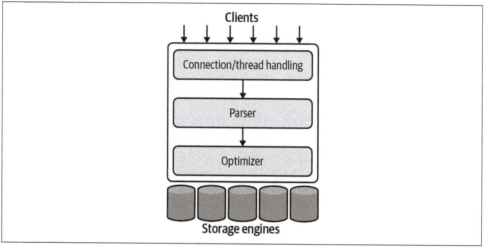

*Figure 1-1. A logical view of the MySQL server architecture*

## Connection Management and Security

By default, each client connection gets its own thread within the server process. The connection's queries execute within that single thread, which in turn resides on one core or CPU. The server maintains a cache of ready-to-use threads, so they don't need to be created and destroyed for each new connection.[2]

When clients (applications) connect to the MySQL server, the server needs to authenticate them. Authentication is based on username, originating host, and password. X.509 certificates can also be used across a Transport Layer Security (TLS) connection. Once a client has connected, the server verifies whether the client has privileges for each query it issues (e.g., whether the client is allowed to issue a SELECT statement that accesses the Country table in the world database).

---

1 One exception is InnoDB, which does parse foreign key definitions because the MySQL server doesn't yet implement them itself.

2 MySQL 5.5 and newer versions support an API that can accept thread-pooling plug-ins, though not commonly used. The common practice for thread pooling is done at access layers, which we discuss in Chapter 5.

## Optimization and Execution

MySQL parses queries to create an internal structure (the parse tree) and then applies a variety of optimizations. These can include rewriting the query, determining the order in which it will read tables, choosing which indexes to use, and so on. You can pass hints to the optimizer through special keywords in the query, affecting its decision-making process. You can also ask the server to explain various aspects of optimization. This lets you know what decisions the server is making and gives you a reference point for reworking queries, schemas, and settings to make everything run as efficiently as possible. There is more detail on this in Chapter 8.

The optimizer does not really care what storage engine a particular table uses, but the storage engine does affect how the server optimizes the query. The optimizer asks the storage engine about some of its capabilities and the cost of certain operations as well as for statistics on the table data. For instance, some storage engines support index types that can be helpful to certain queries. You can read more about schema optimization and indexing in Chapters 6 and 7.

In older versions, MySQL made use of an internal query cache to see if it could serve the results from there. However, as concurrency increased, the query cache became a notorious bottleneck. As of MySQL 5.7.20, the query cache was officially deprecated as a MySQL feature, and in the 8.0 release, the query cache is fully removed. Even though the query cache is no longer a core part of the MySQL server, caching frequently served result sets is a good practice. While outside the scope of this book, a popular design pattern is to cache data in memcached or Redis.

## Concurrency Control

Any time more than one query needs to change data at the same time, the problem of concurrency control arises. For our purposes in this chapter, MySQL has to do this at two levels: the server level and the storage-engine level. We will give you a simplified overview of how MySQL deals with concurrent readers and writers, so you have the context you need for the rest of this chapter.

To illustrate how MySQL handles concurrent work on the same set of data, we will use a traditional spreadsheet file as an example. A spreadsheet consists of rows and columns, much like a database table. Assume the file is on your laptop and only you have access to it. There are no potential conflicts; only you can make changes to the file. Now, imagine you need to collaborate with a coworker on that spreadsheet. It is now on a shared server that both of you have access to. What happens when both of you need to make changes to this file at the same time? What if we have an entire team of people actively trying to edit, add, and remove cells from this spreadsheet? We can say that they should take turns making changes, but that is not efficient. We need an approach for allowing concurrent access to a high-volume spreadsheet.

## Read/Write Locks

Reading from the spreadsheet isn't as troublesome. There's nothing wrong with multiple clients reading the same file simultaneously; because they aren't making changes, nothing is likely to go wrong. What happens if someone tries to delete cell number A25 while others are reading the spreadsheet? It depends, but a reader could come away with a corrupted or inconsistent view of the data. So, to be safe, even reading from a spreadsheet requires special care.

If you think of the spreadsheet as a database table, it's easy to see that the problem is the same in this context. In many ways, a spreadsheet is really just a simple database table. Modifying rows in a database table is very similar to removing or changing the content of cells in a spreadsheet file.

The solution to this classic problem of concurrency control is rather simple. Systems that deal with concurrent read/write access typically implement a locking system that consists of two lock types. These locks are usually known as *shared locks* and *exclusive locks*, or read locks and write locks.

Without worrying about the actual locking mechanism, we can describe the concept as follows. *Read locks* on a resource are shared, or mutually nonblocking: many clients can read from a resource at the same time and not interfere with one another. *Write locks*, on the other hand, are exclusive—that is, they block both read locks and other write locks—because the only safe policy is to have a single client writing to the resource at a given time and to prevent all reads when a client is writing.

In the database world, locking happens all the time: MySQL has to prevent one client from reading a piece of data while another is changing it. If a database server is performing in an acceptable manner, this management of locks is fast enough to not be noticeable to the clients. We will discuss in Chapter 8 how to tune your queries to avoid performance issues caused by locking.

## Lock Granularity

One way to improve the concurrency of a shared resource is to be more selective about what you lock. Rather than locking the entire resource, lock only the part that contains the data you need to change. Better yet, lock only the exact piece of data you plan to change. Minimizing the amount of data that you lock at any one time lets changes to a given resource occur simultaneously, as long as they don't conflict with each other.

Unfortunately, locks are not free—they consume resources. Every lock operation—getting a lock, checking to see whether a lock is free, releasing a lock, and so on—has overhead. If the system spends too much time managing locks instead of storing and retrieving data, performance can suffer.

A locking strategy is a compromise between lock overhead and data safety, and that compromise affects performance. Most commercial database servers don't give you much choice: you get what is known as row-level locking in your tables, with a variety of often complex ways to give good performance with many locks. Locks are how databases implement consistency guarantees. An expert operator of a database would have to go as far as reading the source code to determine the most appropriate set of tuning configurations to optimize this trade-off of speed versus data safety.

MySQL, on the other hand, does offer choices. Its storage engines can implement their own locking policies and lock granularities. Lock management is a very important decision in storage-engine design; fixing the granularity at a certain level can improve performance for certain uses yet make that engine less suited for other purposes. Because MySQL offers multiple storage engines, it doesn't require a single general-purpose solution. Let's have a look at the two most important lock strategies.

## Table locks

The most basic locking strategy available in MySQL, and the one with the lowest overhead, is table locks. A *table lock* is analogous to the spreadsheet locks described earlier: it locks the entire table. When a client wishes to write to a table (insert, delete, update, etc.), it acquires a write lock. This keeps all other read and write operations at bay. When nobody is writing, readers can obtain read locks, which don't conflict with other read locks.

Table locks have variations for improved performance in specific situations. For example, READ LOCAL table locks allow some types of concurrent write operations. Write and read lock queues are separate with the write queue being wholly of higher priority than the read queue.[3]

## Row locks

The locking style that offers the greatest concurrency (and carries the greatest overhead) is the use of row locks. Going back to the spreadsheet analogy, *row locks* would be the same as locking just the row in the spreadsheet. This strategy allows multiple people to edit different rows concurrently without blocking one another. This enables the server to take more concurrent writes, but the cost is more overhead in having to keep track of who has each row lock, how long they have been open, and what kind of row locks they are as well as cleaning up locks when they are no longer needed.

---

[3] We definitely recommend you read the documentation on exclusive versus shared locks, intention locking, and record locks (*https://oreil.ly/EPfwc*).

Row locks are implemented in the storage engine, not the server. The server is mostly[4] unaware of locks implemented in the storage engines, and as you'll see later in this chapter and throughout the book, the storage engines all implement locking in their own ways.

# Transactions

You can't examine the more advanced features of a database system for very long before transactions enter the mix. A *transaction* is a group of SQL statements that are treated atomically, as a single unit of work. If the database engine can apply the entire group of statements to a database, it does so, but if any of them can't be done because of a crash or other reason, none of them is applied. It's all or nothing.

Little of this section is specific to MySQL. If you're already familiar with ACID transactions, feel free to skip ahead to "Transactions in MySQL" on page 11.

A banking application is the classic example of why transactions are necessary.[5] Imagine a bank's database with two tables: checking and savings. To move $200 from Jane's checking account to her savings account, you need to perform at least three steps:

1. Make sure her checking account balance is greater than $200.
2. Subtract $200 from her checking account balance.
3. Add $200 to her savings account balance.

The entire operation should be wrapped in a transaction so that if any one of the steps fails, any completed steps can be rolled back.

You start a transaction with the START TRANSACTION statement and then either make its changes permanent with COMMIT or discard the changes with ROLLBACK. So the SQL for our sample transaction might look like this:

```
1 START  TRANSACTION;
2 SELECT balance FROM checking WHERE customer_id = 10233276;
3 UPDATE checking SET balance = balance - 200.00 WHERE customer_id = 10233276;
4 UPDATE savings SET balance = balance + 200.00 WHERE customer_id = 10233276;
5 COMMIT;
```

Transactions alone aren't the whole story. What happens if the database server crashes while performing line 4? Who knows? The customer probably just lost $200. What if

---

4 There are metadata locks, which are used when dealing with table name changes or changing schemas, and in 8.0 we are introduced to "application level locking functions." In the course of run-of-the-mill data changes, internal locking is left to the InnoDB engine.

5 Although this is a common academic exercise, most banks actually rely on daily reconciliation and not on strict transactional operations during the day.

---

another process comes along between lines 3 and 4 and removes the entire checking account balance? The bank has given the customer a $200 credit without even knowing it.

And there are a lot more failure possibilities in this sequence of operations. You could see connection drops, timeouts, or even a crash of the database server running them midway through the operations. This is typically why highly complex and slow two-phase-commit systems exist: to mitigate against all sorts of failure scenarios.

Transactions aren't enough unless the system passes the ACID test. ACID stands for atomicity, consistency, isolation, and durability. These are tightly related criteria that a data-safe transaction processing system must meet:

Atomicity
> A transaction must function as a single indivisible unit of work so that the entire transaction is either applied or never committed. When transactions are atomic, there is no such thing as a partially completed transaction: it's all or nothing.

Consistency
> The database should always move from one consistent state to the next. In our example, consistency ensures that a crash between lines 3 and 4 doesn't result in $200 disappearing from the checking account. If the transaction is never committed, none of the transaction's changes are ever reflected in the database.

Isolation
> The results of a transaction are usually invisible to other transactions until the transaction is complete. This ensures that if a bank account summary runs after line 3 but before line 4 in our example, it will still see the $200 in the checking account. When we discuss isolation levels later in this chapter, you'll understand why we said "usually invisible."

Durability
> Once committed, a transaction's changes are permanent. This means the changes must be recorded such that data won't be lost in a system crash. Durability is a slightly fuzzy concept, however, because there are actually many levels. Some durability strategies provide a stronger safety guarantee than others, and nothing is ever 100% durable (if the database itself were truly durable, then how could backups increase durability?).

ACID transactions and the guarantees provided through them in the InnoDB engine specifically are one of the strongest and most mature features in MySQL. While they come with certain throughput trade-offs, when applied appropriately they can save you from implementing a lot of complex logic in the application layer.

# Isolation Levels

Isolation is more complex than it looks. The ANSI SQL standard defines four isolation levels. If you are new to the world of databases, we highly recommend you get familiar with the general standard of ANSI SQL[6] before coming back to reading about the specific MySQL implementation. The goal of this standard is to define the rules for which changes are and aren't visible inside and outside a transaction. Lower isolation levels typically allow higher concurrency and have lower overhead.

 Each storage engine implements isolation levels slightly differently, and they don't necessarily match what you might expect if you're used to another database product (thus, we won't go into exhaustive detail in this section). You should read the manuals for whichever storage engines you decide to use.

Let's take a quick look at the four isolation levels:

READ UNCOMMITTED

In the READ UNCOMMITTED isolation level, transactions can view the results of uncommitted transactions. At this level, many problems can occur unless you really, really know what you are doing and have a good reason for doing it. This level is rarely used in practice because its performance isn't much better than the other levels, which have many advantages. Reading uncommitted data is also known as a *dirty read*.

READ COMMITTED

The default isolation level for most database systems (but not MySQL!) is READ COMMITTED. It satisfies the simple definition of isolation used earlier: a transaction will continue to see changes made by transactions that were committed after it began, and its changes won't be visible to others until it has committed. This level still allows what's known as a nonrepeatable read. This means you can run the same statement twice and see different data.

REPEATABLE READ

REPEATABLE READ solves the problems that READ UNCOMMITTED allows. It guarantees that any rows a transaction reads will "look the same" in subsequent reads within the same transaction, but in theory it still allows another tricky problem: phantom reads. Simply put, a phantom read can happen when you select some range of rows, another transaction inserts a new row into the range, and then you select the same range again; you will then see the new "phantom" row. InnoDB

---

6 For more information, read a summary of ANSI SQL (*https://oreil.ly/joikF*) by Adrian Coyler and an explanation of consistency models (*http://jepsen.io/consistency*) by Kyle Kingsbury.

and XtraDB solve the phantom read problem with multiversion concurrency control, which we explain later in this chapter.

REPEATABLE READ is MySQL's default transaction isolation level.

SERIALIZABLE

The highest level of isolation, SERIALIZABLE, solves the phantom read problem by forcing transactions to be ordered so that they can't possibly conflict. In a nutshell, SERIALIZABLE places a lock on every row it reads. At this level, a lot of timeouts and lock contention can occur. We've rarely seen people use this isolation level, but your application's needs might force you to accept the decreased concurrency in favor of the data safety that results.

Table 1-1 summarizes the various isolation levels and the drawbacks associated with each one.

*Table 1-1. ANSI SQL isolation levels*

| Isolation level | Dirty reads possible | Nonrepeatable reads possible | Phantom reads possible | Locking reads |
|---|---|---|---|---|
| READ UNCOMMITTED | Yes | Yes | Yes | No |
| READ COMMITTED | No | Yes | Yes | No |
| REPEATABLE READ | No | No | Yes | No |
| SERIALIZABLE | No | No | No | Yes |

# Deadlocks

A *deadlock* is when two or more transactions are mutually holding and requesting locks on the same resources, creating a cycle of dependencies. Deadlocks occur when transactions try to lock resources in a different order. They can happen whenever multiple transactions lock the same resources. For example, consider these two transactions running against a StockPrice table, which has a primary key of (stock_id, date):

Transaction 1

```
START TRANSACTION;
UPDATE StockPrice SET close = 45.50 WHERE stock_id = 4 and date = '2020-05-01';
UPDATE StockPrice SET close = 19.80 WHERE stock_id = 3 and date = '2020-05-02';
COMMIT;
```

Transaction 2

```
START TRANSACTION;
UPDATE StockPrice SET high = 20.12 WHERE stock_id = 3 and date = '2020-05-02';
UPDATE StockPrice SET high = 47.20 WHERE stock_id = 4 and date = '2020-05-01';
COMMIT;
```

Each transaction will execute its first query and update a row of data, locking that row in the primary key index and any additional unique index it is part of in the process. Each transaction will then attempt to update its second row, only to find that it is already locked. The two transactions will wait forever for each other to complete unless something intervenes to break the deadlock. We cover further in Chapter 7 how indexing can make or break the performance of your queries as your schema evolves.

To combat this problem, database systems implement various forms of deadlock detection and timeouts. The more sophisticated systems, such as the InnoDB storage engine, will notice circular dependencies and return an error instantly. This can be a good thing—otherwise, deadlocks would manifest themselves as very slow queries. Others will give up after the query exceeds a lock wait timeout, which is not always good. The way InnoDB currently handles deadlocks is to roll back the transaction that has the fewest exclusive row locks (an approximate metric for which will be the easiest to roll back).

Lock behavior and order are storage engine specific, so some storage engines might deadlock on a certain sequence of statements even though others won't. Deadlocks have a dual nature: some are unavoidable because of true data conflicts, and some are caused by how a storage engine works.[7]

Once they occur, deadlocks cannot be broken without rolling back one of the transactions, either partially or wholly. They are a fact of life in transactional systems, and your applications should be designed to handle them. Many applications can simply retry their transactions from the beginning, and unless they encounter another deadlock, they should be successful.

## Transaction Logging

Transaction logging helps make transactions more efficient. Instead of updating the tables on disk each time a change occurs, the storage engine can change its in-memory copy of the data. This is very fast. The storage engine can then write a record of the change to the transaction log, which is on disk and therefore durable. This is also a relatively fast operation, because appending log events involves sequential I/O in one small area of the disk instead of random I/O in many places. Then, at some later time, a process can update the table on disk. Thus, most storage engines that use this technique (known as *write-ahead logging*) end up writing the changes to disk twice.

---

[7] As you will see later in this chapter, some storage engines lock entire tables, and others implement more complex row-based locking. All that logic lives for the most part in the storage engine layer.

If there's a crash after the update is written to the transaction log but before the changes are made to the data itself, the storage engine can still recover the changes upon restart. The recovery method varies between storage engines.

# Transactions in MySQL

Storage engines are the software that drives how data will be stored and retrieved from disk. While MySQL has traditionally offered a number of storage engines that support transactions, InnoDB is now the gold standard and the recommended engine to use. Transaction primitives described here will be based on transactions in the InnoDB engine.

## Understanding AUTOCOMMIT

By default, a single INSERT, UPDATE, or DELETE statement is implicitly wrapped in a transaction and committed immediately. This is known as AUTOCOMMIT mode. By disabling this mode, you can execute a series of statements within a transaction and, at conclusion, COMMIT or ROLLBACK.

You can enable or disable the AUTOCOMMIT variable for the current connection by using a SET command. The values 1 and ON are equivalent, as are 0 and OFF. When you run with AUTOCOMMIT=0, you are always in a transaction until you issue a COMMIT or ROLLBACK. MySQL then starts a new transaction immediately. Additionally, with AUTOCOMMIT enabled, you can begin a multistatement transaction by using the keyword BEGIN or START TRANSACTION. Changing the value of AUTOCOMMIT has no effect on nontransactional tables, which have no notion of committing or rolling back changes.

Certain commands, when issued during an open transaction, cause MySQL to commit the transaction before they execute. These are typically DDL commands that make significant changes, such as ALTER TABLE, but LOCK TABLES and some other statements also have this effect. Check your version's documentation for the full list of commands that automatically commit a transaction.

MySQL lets you set the isolation level using the SET TRANSACTION ISOLATION LEVEL command, which takes effect when the next transaction starts. You can set the isolation level for the whole server in the configuration file or just for your session:

```
SET SESSION TRANSACTION ISOLATION LEVEL READ COMMITTED;
```

It is preferable to set the isolation you use most at the server level and only change it in explicit cases. MySQL recognizes all four ANSI standard isolation levels, and InnoDB supports all of them.

## Mixing storage engines in transactions

MySQL doesn't manage transactions at the server level. Instead, the underlying storage engines implement transactions themselves. This means you can't reliably mix different engines in a single transaction.

If you mix transactional and nontransactional tables (for instance, InnoDB and MyISAM tables) in a transaction, the transaction will work properly if all goes well. However, if a rollback is required, the changes to the nontransactional table can't be undone. This leaves the database in an inconsistent state from which it might be difficult to recover and renders the entire point of transactions moot. This is why it is really important to pick the right storage engine for each table and to avoid mixing storage engines in your application logic at all costs.

MySQL will usually not warn you or raise errors if you do transactional operations on a nontransactional table. Sometimes rolling back a transaction will generate the warning, "Some nontransactional changed tables couldn't be rolled back," but most of the time, you'll have no indication you're working with nontransactional tables.

 It is best practice to not mix storage engines in your application. Failed transactions can lead to inconsistent results as some parts can roll back and others cannot.

## Implicit and explicit locking

InnoDB uses a two-phase locking protocol. It can acquire locks at any time during a transaction, but it does not release them until a COMMIT or ROLLBACK. It releases all the locks at the same time. The locking mechanisms described earlier are all implicit. InnoDB handles locks automatically, according to your isolation level.

However, InnoDB also supports explicit locking, which the SQL standard does not mention at all:[8, 9]

```
SELECT ... FOR SHARE
SELECT ... FOR UPDATE
```

MySQL also supports the LOCK TABLES and UNLOCK TABLES commands, which are implemented in the server, not in the storage engines. If you need transactions, use a transactional storage engine. LOCK TABLES is unnecessary because InnoDB supports row-level locking.

---

8  These locking hints are frequently abused and should usually be avoided.

9  SELECT...FOR SHARE is a MySQL 8.0 feature that replaces SELECT...LOCK IN SHARE MODE of previous versions.

---

The interaction between LOCK TABLES and transactions is complex, and there are unexpected behaviors in some server versions. Therefore, we recommend that you never use LOCK TABLES unless you are in a transaction and AUTOCOMMIT is disabled, no matter what storage engine you are using.

# Multiversion Concurrency Control

Most of MySQL's transactional storage engines don't use a simple row-locking mechanism. Instead, they use row-level locking in conjunction with a technique for increasing concurrency known as *multiversion concurrency control (MVCC)*. MVCC is not unique to MySQL: Oracle, PostgreSQL, and some other database systems use it too, although there are significant differences because there is no standard for how MVCC should work.

You can think of MVCC as a twist on row-level locking; it avoids the need for locking at all in many cases and can have much lower overhead. Depending on how it is implemented, it can allow nonlocking reads while locking only the necessary rows during write operations.

MVCC works by using snapshots of the data as it existed at some point in time. This means transactions can see a consistent view of the data, no matter how long they run. It also means different transactions can see different data in the same tables at the same time! If you've never experienced this before, it might be confusing, but it will become easier to understand with familiarity.

Each storage engine implements MVCC differently. Some of the variations include optimistic and pessimistic concurrency control. We illustrate one way MVCC works by explaining InnoDB's behavior[10] in the form of a sequence diagram in Figure 1-2.

InnoDB implements MVCC by assigning a transaction ID for each transaction that starts. That ID is assigned the first time the transaction reads any data. When a record is modified within that transaction, an undo record that explains how to revert that change is written to the undo log, and the rollback pointer of the transaction is pointed at that undo log record. This is how the transaction can find the way to roll back if needed.

---

10 We recommend reading this blog post (*https://oreil.ly/jbljq*) by Jeremy Cole to get a deeper understanding of records structure in InnoDB.

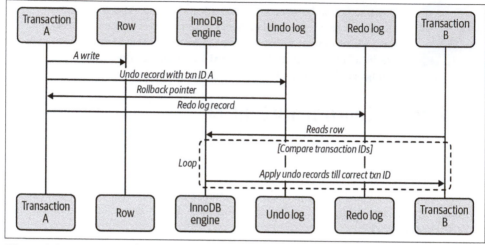

*Figure 1-2. A sequence diagram of handling multiple versions of a row across different transactions*

When a different session reads a cluster key index record, InnoDB compares the record's transaction ID versus the read view of that session. If the record in its current state should not be visible (the transaction that altered it has not yet committed), the undo log record is followed and applied until the session reaches a transaction ID that is eligible to be visible. This process can loop all the way to an undo record that deletes this row entirely, signaling to the read view that this row does not exist.

Records in a transaction are deleted by setting a "deleted" bit in the "info flags" of the record. This is also tracked in the undo log as a "remove delete mark."

It is also worth noting that all undo log writes are also redo logged because the undo log writes are part of the server crash recovery process and are transactional.[11] The size of these redo and undo logs also plays a large part in how transactions at high concurrency perform. We cover their configuration in more detail in Chapter 5.

The result of all this extra record keeping is that most read queries never acquire locks. They simply read data as fast as they can, making sure to select only rows that meet the criteria. The drawbacks are that the storage engine has to store more data with each row, do more work when examining rows, and handle some additional housekeeping operations.

---

11 For a lot more detail on how InnoDB handles multiple versions of its records, see this blog post (*https:// oreil.ly/exaaL*) by Jeremy Cole.

MVCC works only with the REPEATABLE READ and READ COMMITTED isolation levels. READ UNCOMMITTED isn't MVCC compatible[12] because queries don't read the row version that's appropriate for their transaction version; they read the newest version, no matter what. SERIALIZABLE isn't MVCC compatible because reads lock every row they return.

# Replication

MySQL is designed for accepting writes on one node at any given time. This has advantages in managing consistency but leads to trade-offs when you need the data written in multiple servers or multiple locations. MySQL offers a native way to distribute writes that one node takes to additional nodes. This is referred to as *replication*. In MySQL, the source node has a thread per replica that is logged in as a replication client that wakes up when a write occurs, sending new data. In Figure 1-3, we show a simple example of this setup, which is usually called a *topology tree* of multiple MySQL servers in a source and replica setup.

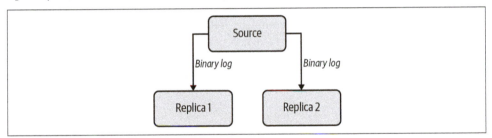

*Figure 1-3. A simplified view of a MySQL server replication topology*

For any data you run in production, you should use replication and have at least three more replicas, ideally distributed in different locations (in cloud-hosted environments, known as *regions*) for disaster-recovery planning.

Over the years, replication in MySQL gained more sophistication. Global transaction identifiers, multisource replication, parallel replication on replicas, and semisync replication are some of the major updates. We cover replication in great detail in Chapter 9.

---

12 There is no formal standard that defines MVCC, so different engines and databases implement it very differently, and no one can say any of them is wrong.

# Datafiles Structure

In version 8.0, MySQL redesigned table metadata into a data dictionary that is included with a table's *.ibd* file. This makes information on the table structure support transactions and atomic data definition changes. Instead of relying only on `informa tion_schema` for retrieving table definition and metadata during operations, we are introduced to the dictionary object cache, which is a least recently used (LRU)-based in-memory cache of partition definitions, table definitions, stored program definitions, charset, and collation information. This major change in how the server accesses metadata about tables reduces I/O and is efficient, especially if a subset of tables is what sees the most activity and therefore is in the cache most often. The *.ibd* and *.frm* files are replaced with serialized dictionary information (*.sdi*) per table.

# The InnoDB Engine

InnoDB is the default transactional storage engine for MySQL and the most important and broadly useful engine overall. It was designed for processing many short-lived transactions that usually complete rather than being rolled back. Its performance and automatic crash recovery make it popular for nontransactional storage needs too. If you want to study storage engines, it is well worth your time to study InnoDB in depth to learn as much as you can about it, rather than studying all storage engines equally.

 It is best practice to use the InnoDB storage engine as the default engine for any application. MySQL made that easy by making InnoDB the default engine a few major versions ago.

InnoDB is the default MySQL general-purpose storage engine. By default, InnoDB stores its data in a series of datafiles that are collectively known as a *tablespace*. A tablespace is essentially a black box that InnoDB manages all by itself.

InnoDB uses MVCC to achieve high concurrency, and it implements all four SQL standard isolation levels. It defaults to the REPEATABLE READ isolation level, and it has a next-key locking strategy that prevents phantom reads in this isolation level: rather than locking only the rows you've touched in a query, InnoDB locks gaps in the index structure as well, preventing phantoms from being inserted.

InnoDB tables are built on a clustered index, which we will cover in detail in Chapter 8 when we discuss schema design. InnoDB's index structures are very different from those of most other MySQL storage engines. As a result, it provides very fast primary key lookups. However, secondary indexes (indexes that aren't the primary key) contain the primary key columns, so if your primary key is large, other indexes will also be large. You should strive for a small primary key if you'll have many indexes on a table.

InnoDB has a variety of internal optimizations. These include predictive read-ahead for prefetching data from disk, an adaptive hash index that automatically builds hash indexes in memory for very fast lookups, and an insert buffer to speed inserts. We cover these in Chapter 4 of this book.

InnoDB's behavior is very intricate, and we highly recommend reading the "InnoDB Locking and Transaction Model" (*https://oreil.ly/AfuTi*) section of the MySQL manual if you're using InnoDB. Because of its MVCC architecture, there are many subtleties you should be aware of before building an application with InnoDB. Working with a storage engine that maintains consistent views of the data for all users, even when some users are changing data, can be complex.

As a transactional storage engine, InnoDB supports truly "hot" online backups through a variety of mechanisms, including Oracle's proprietary MySQL Enterprise Backup and the open source Percona XtraBackup. We'll dive into backup and restore in detail in Chapter 10.

Beginning with MySQL 5.6, InnoDB introduced online DDL, which at first had limited use cases that expanded in the 5.7 and 8.0 releases. In-place schema changes allow for specific table changes without a full table lock and without using external tools, which greatly improve the operationality of MySQL InnoDB tables. We will be covering options for online schema changes, both native and external tools, in Chapter 6.

## JSON Document Support

First introduced to InnoDB as part of the 5.7 release, the JSON type arrived with automatic validation of JSON documents as well as optimized storage that allows for quick read access, a significant improvement to the trade-offs of old-style binary large object (BLOB) storage engineers used to resort to for JSON documents. Along with the new data type support, InnoDB also introduced SQL functions to support rich operations on JSON documents. A further improvement in MySQL 8.0.7 adds the ability to define multivalued indexes on JSON arrays. This feature can be a powerful way to even further speed up read-access queries to JSON types by matching the common access patterns to functions that can map the JSON document values. We go over the use and performance implications of the JSON data type in "JSON Data" on page 139 in Chapter 6.

## Data Dictionary Changes

Another major change in MySQL 8.0 is removing file-based table metadata storage and moving to a data dictionary using InnoDB table storage. This change brings all of InnoDB's crash-recovery transactional benefits to operations like changes to tables.

This change, while much improving the management of data definitions in MySQL, does also require major changes in operating a MySQL server. Most notably, back-up processes that used to rely on the table metadata files now have to query the new data dictionary to extract table definitions.

## Atomic DDL

Finally, MySQL 8.0 introduced atomic data definition changes. This means that data definition statements now can either wholly finish successfully or be wholly rolled back. This becomes possible through creating a DDL-specific undo and redo log that InnoDB relies on to track the change—another place where InnoDB's proven design has been expanded to the operations of MySQL server.

# Summary

MySQL has a layered architecture, with server-wide services and query execution on top and storage engines underneath. Although there are many different plug-in APIs, the storage engine API is the most important. If you understand that MySQL executes queries by handing rows back and forth across the storage engine API, you've grasped the fundamentals of the server's architecture.

In the past few major releases, MySQL has settled on InnoDB as its primary development focus and has even moved its internal bookkeeping around table metadata, authentication, and authorization after years in MyISAM. This increased investment from Oracle in the InnoDB engine has led to major improvements such as atomic DDLs, more robust online DDLs, better resilience to crashes, and better operability for security-minded deployments.

InnoDB is the default storage engine and the one that should cover nearly every use case. As such, the following chapters focus heavily on the InnoDB storage engine when talking about features, performance, and limitations, and only rarely will we touch on any other storage engine from here on out.

# CHAPTER 2
# Monitoring in a Reliability Engineering World

Monitoring systems is an extensive topic that has been heavily shaped in the past few years by the seminal work in *Site Reliability Engineering: How Google Runs Production Systems* (O'Reilly) and its followup, *The Site Reliability Workbook: Practical Ways to Implement SRE* (O'Reilly). Since these two books came out, site reliability engineering (SRE) has become a popular trend in open job listings. Some companies have gone as far as retitling existing staff as some flavor of "reliability engineering."

Site reliability engineering has changed how teams think about operational work. This is because it consists of a set of principles that allow us to more easily answer questions like:

- Are we providing an acceptable customer experience?
- Should we focus on reliability and resilience work?
- How do we balance new features against toil?

This chapter expects the reader to have an understanding of what these principles are. If you have not read either of the aforementioned books, we recommend these chapters from *The Site Reliability Workbook* as a crash course:

- Chapter 1 offers a deeper understanding of the philosophy behind moving toward service-level performance management in production.
- Chapter 2 covers how to implement service level objectives (SLOs).
- Chapter 5 covers alerting on SLOs.

Some may argue that SRE implementation isn't strictly a part of high performance MySQL, but we disagree. In her book, *Accelerate*,[1] Dr. Nicole Forsgren says, "Our measure should focus on outcomes, not outputs." A key aspect of effective MySQL management is good monitoring of the health of your databases. Traditional monitoring is a relatively well-paved path. As SRE is a new space, it's less understood how to implement SRE principles against MySQL. As SRE principles continue to gain acceptance, the traditional role of a DBA will evolve, and that includes how DBAs think about monitoring their systems.

# The Impact of Reliability Engineering on DBA Teams

For many years, monitoring database performance relied on deep dives into single-server performance. That still has a lot of value but tends to be more about reactive measurements, like profiling a server that is performing poorly. This was the standard operating procedure in the days of the gatekeeping DBA teams when no one else was allowed to know how the database operated.

Enter Google's introduction of reliability engineering. The role of a DBA became more complex and turned into more of a site reliability engineer (SRE) or database reliability engineer (DBRE). Teams had to optimize for their time. Service levels help you define when customers are unhappy and allow you to better balance your time between addressing things like performance issues and scaling challenges against working on internal tooling. Let's discuss the different ways you need to monitor MySQL to ensure a successful customer experience.

# Defining Service Level Goals

Before going into how to measure whether customers are happy with the performance of your database clusters, we must first know what our goals are and align on a common language to describe these goals. Here are some questions that can serve as conversation starters in your organization to define these goals:

- What are the metrics appropriate for measuring success?
- What values for these metrics are acceptable to the customers and our business needs?
- At what point are we considered in a degraded state?
- When are we in an altogether failed state and need to remediate as soon as possible?

---

1 Nicole Forsgren, *Accelerate: The Science of Lean Software and DevOps* (IT Revolution Press, 2018). *https://oreil.ly/Bfvda*

There are scenarios with obvious answers to these questions (e.g., the source database is down, we are not taking any writes, and therefore, business is halted). Some are less obvious, such as a periodic task is sometimes hogging all the database disk I/O and suddenly everything else is slower. Having a shared understanding across the organization of what we are measuring and why can help guide prioritization conversations. Reaching that shared understanding through ongoing conversations across the organization helps guide whether you can spend engineering effort on new features or if there needs to be more investment in performance improvement or stability.

In SRE practices, these discussions about customer satisfaction will align the team on what is healthy for the business in terms of service level indicators (SLIs), SLOs, and service level agreements (SLAs). Let's start by defining what these terms mean:

*Service level indicator (SLI)*
> In very simple terms, an SLI answers the question, "How do I measure whether my customers are happy?" The answer represents a healthy system from the users' perspective. SLIs can be business-level indicators, such as "response time for a customer-facing API," or a more fundamental "service is up." You may find you need different indicators or metrics depending on the data's context and how it relates to the product.

*Service level objective (SLO)*
> An SLO answers the question, "What is the minimum I can allow my SLI to be to ensure that my customers are happy?" SLO is the objective range we want to be in for a given SLI to be considered a healthy service. If you think uptime is the SLI, then the number of nines you want to be up for a given time span is the SLO. SLOs have to be defined as a value *over a given time frame* to ensure that everyone is aligned on what the SLO means. An SLI plus an SLO forms the basic equation for knowing if your customers are happy.

*Service level agreement (SLA)*
> SLAs provide the answer to the question, "What SLO am I willing to agree to that has consequences?" An SLA is an SLO that has been included in an agreement with one or more customers of the business (paying customers, not internal stakeholders), with financial or other penalties if that SLA is not met. It is important to note that SLAs are optional.

> We will not cover SLAs much in this chapter as they tend to require more of a business discussion than an engineering one. This sort of decision hinges mostly on what sales the business expects to get if they promise an SLA in contracts and if that is worth the risk to revenue if the SLA were to be broken. Hopefully, such a decision is informed by what we do cover here around choosing both SLIs and matching SLOs.

Defining these SLIs, SLOs, and SLAs guide not only the business's health but also planning within engineering teams. If a team is not hitting its agreed-upon SLOs, it should not proceed with new feature work. The same is true for database-engineering teams. If one of the potential SLOs we discuss in this chapter is not being met, that should spur the conversation of why not. When you come armed with the data to explain why customer experience is suboptimal, you can have more meaningful conversations about team priorities.

## What Does It Take to Make Customers Happy?

After choosing a set of metrics as your SLIs, it may be tempting to set the goals to 100%. You must fight that urge, though. Remember that the goal of picking indicators and objectives is to evaluate at any time, with an objective metric, whether your team can innovate with new features or if stability is at risk of dropping below acceptable levels for customers and therefore needs more attention and resources. The goal is to define what is the *absolute minimum* you need to do to make customers happy. If a customer is happy with your pages loading in two seconds, there's no need to set a target for pages to load in 750 milliseconds. This can create an unreasonable burden for engineering teams.

Taking an example of uptime as an indicator and objective values for it, we can declare that "we will not have any downtime," but what does that mean when implementing and tracking if we are meeting goals? Reaching three nines of availability is no small feat. Three nines over a whole year amount to just over eight hours, translating to only 10 minutes in a given week. The more nines you promise, the harder this gets, and the more expensive engineering hours the team will have to spend to deliver on such a promise. Table 2-1 is a helpful chart from Amazon Web Services showing the challenge in raw numbers.

*Table 2-1. Availability time by nines*

| Availability | Downtime per year | Downtime per month | Downtime per week | Downtime per day |
|---|---|---|---|---|
| 99.999% | 5 mins, 15.36 secs | 26.28 secs | 6.06 secs | 0.14 secs |
| 99.995% | 26 mins, 16.8 secs | 2 mins, 11.4 secs | 30.3 secs | 4.32 secs |
| 99.990% | 52 mins, 33.6 secs | 4 mins, 22.8 secs | 1 mins, 0.66 secs | 8.64 secs |
| 99.950% | 4 hrs, 22 mins, 48 secs | 31 mins, 54 secs | 5 mins, 3 secs | 43 secs |
| 99.900% | 8 hrs, 45 mins, 36 secs | 43 mins, 53 secs | 10 mins, 6 secs | 1 min, 26 secs |
| 99.500% | 43 hrs, 48 mins, 36 secs | 3 hrs, 39 mins | 50 hrs, 32 mins, 17 secs | 7 mins, 12 secs |
| 99.250% | 65 hrs, 42 mins | 5 hrs, 34 mins, 30 secs | 1 hr, 15 mins, 48 secs | 10 mins, 48 secs |
| 99.000% | 3 days, 15 hrs, 54 mins | 7 hrs, 18 mins | 1 hr, 41 mins, 5 secs | 14 mins, 24 secs |

Because engineering time is a finite resource, you must be careful not to strive for perfection when choosing SLOs. Not all the features in your product require all these nines to keep customers satisfied, so you will find that as your product's feature set grows, you will have varying SLIs and SLOs depending on the specific feature impact or the revenue being driven by it. That is to be expected and is a sign of a thoughtful process. You have a critical task here: detecting when a data set becomes a bottleneck for very different query profiles by different stakeholders, jeopardizing performance. This also means finding a way to separate those different stakeholder needs so that you can provide them reasonable SLIs and SLOs.

These indicators and objectives are also an effective way to have a uniform language between product and engineering that guides making decisions between "spend engineering time on new features" versus "spend time on resilience and fixing issues." It is also a way to decide, from the list of things we would like to accomplish, which is the most important based on customer experience. You can use SLIs and SLOs to guide work-prioritization conversations that are otherwise hard to align on.

# What to Measure

Let's imagine a company whose product is an online store. The company is seeing a lot more traffic due to increased online shopping, and there is demand on the infrastructure group to ensure that the database layer can handle the increased demand. Throughout this section we will talk about what to measure as if we are that fictional infrastructure team.

## Defining SLIs and SLOs

Defining a good SLI and a matching SLO is centered around explaining succinctly how to provide a delightful user experience for your customers. We will not spend a ton of time explaining in the abstract how to create meaningful SLIs and SLOs.[2] In the context of MySQL, it needs to be a representation that defines three major themes: availability, latency, and lack of critical errors.

For our online store example, this means pages that load quickly, faster than a few hundred milliseconds at least 99.5% of the time, measured across a month. It also means a reliable checkout process where intermittent failures are allowed only 1% of the time in a given calendar month. Note how these indicators and objectives are defined. We don't define 100% as a requirement because we operate in a world where failure is inevitable. We do use a time span so that the team can accurately balance its work between new features and resilience.

"I expect 99.5% of my database requests to be served in less than two milliseconds with no errors" is both a sufficient SLI with a clear SLO and not simple. You can't confirm all of this in one metric. It's a single-sentence representation of how you

---

2 We highly recommend *Implementing Service Level Objectives* by Alex Hidalgo (O'Reilly).

expect the database layer to behave in order to provide an acceptable customer experience.

So what is a good example in our online store for metrics that can build this customer experience picture? Start with synthetic tests such as page loads in production that sample load rate. This is useful as a consistent signal that "things are OK." But it's just the beginning. Let's discuss different facets of signals to track to build a picture. As we move through these examples, we will tie it with our online store to help you visualize how these different metrics create a picture of a good customer experience. First, let's talk about tracking query response time.

## Monitoring Solutions

Query analysis and monitoring query latency in the context of SLIs and SLOs need to focus on customer experience. This means relying on tooling that can alert you as soon as possible when query response times are growing longer than an agreed-upon threshold. Let's discuss a few paths you can take to achieve that level of monitoring.

### Commercial options

This is one of the examples where paying a vendor whose competitive advantage is this specific task of profiling MySQL performance can pay your organization back in dividends. Tools like SolarWinds Database Performance Management (*https://oreil.ly/ v5wSR*) can go a long way toward making profiling query performance both automated and accessible to a large cohort of your engineering organization.

### Open source options

A well-established open source option is Percona Monitoring and Management (*https://oreil.ly/e4l9A*), known as PMM. It operates as a client/server pair. You install a client on your database instances, which collects and sends metrics to the server portion. The server side also has a set of dashboards that allow you to view graphs relating to performance. One of the major benefits of PMM is that the organization of the dashboards is guided by long-time experience in the Percona community around monitoring MySQL performance. This makes it an excellent resource to get engineers new to MySQL familiar with how to monitor MySQL performance.

Another route you can take is shipping your database slow logs and MySQL Performance Schema outputs to a centralized location where you can use well-known tools like *pt-query-digest*, part of the Percona Toolkit package, to analyze the logs and gain more insight into what your database instances are spending their time on. While effective, this process can be slow and possibly affect customers if not properly used. You ideally want to discover issues before customers notice them. By reactively checking logs after that happens, you run the risk of eroding customer trust because of how long it takes to discover performance regressions and the process of digging into all sorts of postfact artifacts to determine what happened.

Lastly, using Performance Schema to profile MySQL performance can be very helpful as you will see in more detail in Chapter 3. You can use it to find bottlenecks to make your instances do more with the same specification, save in infrastructure costs, or answer the question, "Why is this taking this long?" This is not a tool to determine solely if you are meeting your service reliability promises, as it is far deep in the internals of MySQL. For service level performance evaluation, we need a new way of thinking about performance.

---

### A Note on "Testing in Production"

We often hear the drumbeat of "test in production," and it makes a lot of folks cringe. The reality is that testing in production can have a lot of value. Production is where you discover how that change interacts with the rest of the system, at scale, with real customer traffic. It allows you to see the impact on the adjacent systems.

By using the basic "are customers happy" question, you can see:

- When the feedback loop from production is quick and tied strongly to a change, it becomes much faster to roll back the change and reinspect the specific change that was being deployed.

- This method fosters stronger collaboration between feature teams and the database engineers. When all parties involved are aligned on the specific metrics to watch and what values they should be, the task of measuring performance becomes a team effort.

- In the case of a regression, the effort spent outside production to look into "what happened" is far more specific than trying to re-create a benchmark suite that emulates a larger footprint of code paths. Engineering time spent to debug becomes far better targeted.

---

Now let's dive into additional metrics that help you further understand the experience of the customers of your online store. You should think about the metrics you can get from MySQL in the frame of outcomes, not outputs. We will also cover examples of things you cannot measure through MySQL metrics alone.

## Monitoring Availability

An online store that is intermittently offline risks eroding shopper confidence. This is why availability as a standalone metric, and as part of your view of the customer experience, is so important.

*Availability* is being able to respond to customer requests without an error. To frame this in standard HTTP terms, it may be a response that is a clear-cut success, like a 200 response code, or a successful acceptance of a request with a promise to finish the related work asynchronously, like a 202 accepted. Availability used to be a simple metric in the days of monolithic single-host systems. Nowadays, most architectures are a lot more complicated. The concept of availability has also evolved into a more nuanced reflection of how distributed systems fail. When attempting to turn availability into an SLI and SLO for your database architecture, consider discussing further details (along with examples from our online store), such as the following:

- When dealing with inevitable catastrophic failures, what features are nonnegotiable and what features are "nice to have" (e.g., can customers continue with existing shopping carts and check those out but maybe not add new items during this failure)?
- What types of failures do we define as "catastrophic" (e.g., failure of listing search might not be catastrophic, but failure of checkout operations would be)?
- What does "degraded functionality" look like (e.g., can we load generic recommendations instead of customized ones based on past purchase history when needed)?
- What is the shortest possible mean time to recovery (MTTR) we can promise for our core features given a set of probable failure scenarios (e.g., if the database powering a shopping cart checkout system is failing writes, how fast can we safely pivot to a new source node)?

When choosing a set of metrics to represent availability, you want to set expectations with your customer support team that "100% uptime" is not reasonable and that the focus here is to provide the best customer experience possible in a world *understanding and accepting* that component failures are inevitable.

The preferred method to verify availability is from a client or remote endpoint. This can be done passively if you have access to a client's logs for database access. Explicitly, this means that if your application is PHP and you run under Apache, you need access to the Apache logs to determine if PHP is emitting any errors for connecting to your database. You can also verify availability actively. If your environment is segregated and you cannot get access to client logs, consider setting up remote code that performs an action on your database to ensure it is available. This could be something simple, like a `SELECT 1` query, which verifies that MySQL is receiving and parsing your query but does not access the storage layer. Or this could be more complex, like reading actual data from a table or executing a write and subsequent read to verify the write was successful. This kind of synthetic transaction from elsewhere in the network can give you perspective into whether your application is available.

Remote validation of availability is useful for tracking an availability objective. It does not help you gain insight *before* a problem arises. One MySQL metric that can be used as a leading indicator for availability issues is the MySQL status counter `Threads_running`. It tracks how many queries are currently in flight on a given database host. When threads running are growing at a fast rate and not showing any signs of decline, that indicates queries are not finishing fast enough and are therefore stacking and consuming resources. Allowing this metric to grow usually results in a database host causing either a full CPU lockup or intense memory load that can lead to the entire MySQL process being shut down by the operating system. This is obviously a major outage if it happens on a source node and something you should strive to have leading indicators for. A starting point to monitor this is to inspect how many CPU cores you have and, if `Threads_running` is exceeding that, that can be a sign that your server is hitting that precarious state. In conjunction with that, you can monitor how close you get to `max_connections` as another data point to check for an overload of work in progress.

The section "Safety Settings" on page 120 in Chapter 5 gives insight into how you can set the brakes on runaway MySQL threads.

## Monitoring Query Latency

MySQL has introduced a number of long-needed enhancements to track how long queries take to run (*https://oreil.ly/h9cDB*), and you should definitely use your monitoring stack to track these trends as your application code changes. However, this is still not a full picture of the customer experience, especially given how modern software architecture is designed. In addition to internally tracked latency, you also need a view on how latency is perceived by your applications and what happens when that perceived latency increases. This means that besides tracking query latency from the database server directly, you would also be well served by tooling the clients to report on time to query completion, so you can get as close to the customer experience as possible. Digesting all of these sample metrics from clients (especially when your infrastructure footprint grows) can be done with paid tools like Datadog or Solar-Winds Database Performance Monitor, or even by using open source tools like PMM. This is an area where close collaboration with your organization's application developers is paramount. You need to be aware of how the application team measures this from the application perspective and add more insight to the outliers using tracing tools like Honeycomb or Lightstep.

## Monitoring for Errors

Do you need to track and alert on every error that ever happens? It depends.

The sheer existence of errors for a MySQL client in a running service is not an indication of something being definitely broken. In a world of distributed systems, there are many scenarios where clients can encounter errors that are intermittent and, in many cases, resolved with a simple retry of the failed query. The *rate* of errors happening, though, across the fleet of services handling database queries in your infrastructure can be a crucial indicator of brewing trouble. Here are some examples of client-side errors that might normally be just noise but are a sign of trouble if their rate accelerates:

*Lock wait timeout*
> Your clients reporting a sharp increase of this error can be a sign of an escalating row-lock contention on your source node that transactions keep retrying and still failing. It can be a precursor for write downtime.

*Aborted connections*
> Clients reporting a sudden surge of aborted connections can be an indicator of issues in any access layer you have between the clients and the database instances. Not tracking that down can lead to a lot of client-side retries, which consumes resources.

One thing MySQL server tracks that can help you is the set of server variables named Connection_errors_xxx (*https://oreil.ly/F4VUw*) where *xxx* is different kinds of connection errors. A sudden increase of any of these counters can be a strong indicator telling you that something new and unusual is currently broken.

Are there errors where a single instance means there is trouble and needs to be handled? Yes.

For example, getting errors that the MySQL instance is running in read-only mode is a sign of issues even if these errors do not happen very often. This can mean that you just had a replica promoted to source, but it is still running in read-only mode (you run replicas in read-only mode, don't you?), which is downtime of writes for your cluster. Or it can mean there is some issue in your access layer sending write traffic to a replica. In either of those cases, it is not a sign of an intermittent issue solved with a retry.

Another server-side error that is a flag for a major problem is either "too many connections" or an OS-level "cannot create new thread." These are signs that your application layer has created and left open more connections than your database server is configured to allow, either in the server `max_connections` variable or the number of threads the MySQL process is allowed to open. These errors translate immediately as 5xx errors to your application and, depending on your application design, can also be impactful to your customers.

As you can see, measuring performance and choosing which errors to frame your SLIs around is as much a communication and social problem as it is a technical one, so you should be prepared for that.

## Proactive Monitoring

As we've said, SLO monitoring is focused on whether or not your customers are happy. This helps keep you focused on improving their experience when they are not happy and on other tasks, like toil reduction, when they are. This misses out on a key area: proactive monitoring.

If we return to our online store example and how we envision monitoring our customers' experience, we can elaborate further. Imagine you aren't experiencing any major failures of any components, but you note that there is a rising tide of customer support tickets reporting "slowness" or occasional errors that seem to disappear on their own. How do you track down behavior like this? This can be a very difficult task if you do not already have a good idea what the baseline performance of a number of signals is. The dashboards and scripts that you use to trigger on-call alerts can be referred to as *steady state monitoring*. These let you know something unexpected is happening with a given system whether or not there was a change. They are an important tool for giving you leading indicators *before* your customers experience failure.

The balance you need to strike with monitoring is that it always needs to be actionable while also being a true leading indicator. Alerting on disk space for a database at 100% full is too late as the service is already down, but alerting on 80% might be too slow or not as actionable if the growth rate is not that fast.

Let's talk about useful signals you can monitor that are not directly tied to actual customer impact.

### Disk growth

Tracking disk growth is the sort of metric that you might not think about until it becomes a problem. When it does become a problem, solving the issue can be time consuming and affect your business. It is definitely better to understand how you track it, have a plan to mitigate it, and know what alerting thresholds are appropriate.

There are a number of strategies you can use to monitor disk growth. Let's break them down from most ideal to bare minimum.

If your monitoring tooling can allow it, tracking the rate of growth of disk space usage can be remarkably useful. There are always scenarios where available disk space can burn down relatively quickly, putting your availability at risk. Operations like long-running transactions with large undo logs or alter tables are examples of why you might approach full disk too fast. There are many incident stories out there where excessive logging or a change in insert pattern for a given data set went undetected until "the database" ran out of disk space. Only then did all sorts of alerts fire.

If tracking the rate of growth is not feasible (not all monitoring tools provide this ability), you can set multiple thresholds with lower warnings that only fire during business hours and a higher, more critical value as an alert to off-hours on call. This allows the team to have a heads-up warning during business hours before things get dire enough to wake someone up.

If you can neither monitor the rate of growth nor define multiple thresholds for the same metric, then you have to at least determine a single-value threshold for disk space used at which you page your on-call engineers. This threshold needs to be low enough to allow some action and free disk space as the team assesses the reasons it fired and consider longer-term mitigation. Consider evaluating the maximum throughput your disk can write (MB/s) and using that to help calculate how long at max traffic throughput it would take to fill the disk. You need that much lead time to avoid an event.

We discuss in Chapter 4 operating system and hardware configurations that relate to how MySQL uses disk space and what trade-offs to consider in those decisions in relation to disk space growth. It should be expected that at some point, hopefully, your business will have grown so that you cannot store all of your data in one cluster of servers. Even if you run in a cloud environment that can expand volumes for you, you still need to do planning around this, so you always want to have a threshold for free disk space that allows you the time to plan and do the needed expansion without a panic.

The takeaway here is to make sure you have some monitor for disk space growth, even if you think it is early days and too soon to need one. This is one of the growth axes that catches almost everyone unprepared.

### Connection growth

As your business grows, a common layer that grows linearly is your application layer. You will need more instances to support login, shopping carts, processing requests, or whatever the context of the product may be. All of these added instances start opening more and more connections to your database hosts. You may mitigate that growth for some time by adding replicas, using replication as a scale-out measure, or even using middleware layers like ProxySQL to decouple the growth of your frontend from connection load directly on the database.

While your traffic is growing, the database server can support a finite pool of connections, which is configured as the server setting `max_connections`. Once the total number of connections to the server reaches that maximum, your database will not allow any new ones, which is a common contributing cause to incidents where you can no longer open new connections to the database, leading to increased errors for your users.

Monitoring connection growth is about making sure your resources are not exhausted to the point of risking your database availability. This risk can come in two different ways:

- The application layer is opening lots of connections it's not using and creating the risk of maxing out connections for no good reason. A clear sign of this is seeing connections count (`threads_connected`) as high but `threads_running` is still low.
- The application layer is actively using lots of connections and risking overloading the database. You can distinguish this state by seeing that both `threads_connected` *and* `threads_running` are at high values (hundreds? thousands?) and increasing.

A useful thing to consider when setting up monitoring for connection count is relying on percentages and not absolute numbers. A percentage of `threads_connected/max_connections` shows you how close the growth of your application node count is taking you to the maximum connection pool the database can allow. This helps you monitor for the first state of connection growth trouble.

Separately, you should be tracking and alerting on how busy a database host is, which, as we explained earlier, is seen in the value of `threads_running`. Typically, if this value is growing north of one hundred threads, you start to see elevated CPU usage and increased memory use, which is a general sign of high load on the database host. This is an immediate concern for your database availability, as it can escalate to the MySQL process getting killed by the operating system. A common quick solution is to use the kill process command or a tool that automates using it, such as *pt-kill*, tactically to relieve load, then look into why the database got into this state using query analysis, which we described earlier.

 Connection storms are situations in production systems where the application layer perceives increases in query latency and responds with opening more connections to the database layer. This can result in adding significant load on the database as it handles the large influx of new connections, which takes away resources from fulfilling query requests. Connection storms can cause a sudden decrease in available connections in `max_connections` and increase the risk of your database availability.

### Replication lag

MySQL has a native replication feature that sends data from one server, the *source*, to one or more additional servers, referred to as *replicas*. The delay between data being written on the source and being available on the replicas is referred to as *replication lag*. If your application reads data from the replicas, lag can make it seem as if your data has inconsistencies as you send reads to replicas not yet caught up on all the changes. In a social media example, a user may comment on something someone else has posted. This data is written to the source and then replicated out to the replicas. When the user attempts to view their reply, if the application sends the request to a server that is lagged, the replica may not have the data yet. This can create confusion for the user, thinking their comment was not saved. We cover strategies to fight replication lag in more detail in Chapter 9.

Lag is one of those metrics that can be an acute SLI that can trigger incidents. It is also a longer-term trend indicating the need for more architectural change. In the longer-term context, even if you never hit replication lag that is affecting the customer experience, it is still a sign that, at least intermittently, the volume of writes from source nodes is surpassing what replicas can write at current configuration. It can be a canary in the coal mine for your write capacity. If listened to, it can prevent future full-blown incidents.

 Be wary of alerting someone to replication lag. Immediate actionable remediation may not always be possible. Likewise, if you don't read from replicas, consider how aggressively your monitoring system alerts someone to this condition. Alerts that someone receives, especially off hours, should always be actionable.

Replication lag is one of those metrics that can affect both immediate and tactical decisions, but also keeping an eye on its trends long term can help save you the hassle of larger business impact and keep you ahead of the growth curve.

### I/O utilization

One of the never-ending endeavors of a database engineer is "do as much of the work as possible in memory because it is faster." While that is certainly accurate, we also know that we cannot possibly accomplish that 100% of the time because that would mean our data entirely fits in memory, in which case "scale" is not yet a thing we need to expend energy on.

As your database infrastructure scales and your data does not fit in memory anymore, you come to realize that the next best thing is to not read so much data from disk that queries are stuck waiting their turn for those precious I/O cycles. This remains true even in this era of almost everything running on solid-state drives. As the size of your data grows and your queries need to scan more of it to fulfill requests, you will find that I/O wait can become a bottleneck for your traffic growth.

Monitoring your disk I/O activity helps you get ahead of performance degradation before it becomes customer facing. There are a few things you can monitor to achieve this goal. Tools like *iostat* can help you monitor for I/O wait. You want to monitor and alert if your database server has a lot of threads sitting in IOwait, an indication that they are in queue waiting on some disk resources to be available. You find this by tracking IOutil as a running graph for a meaningful period of time, such as a day or two, or even a week. IOutil is reported as a percentage of the overall system's disk access capacity. Having that be close to 100% for sustained periods on a host that is not running backups can be an indication of full table scans and inefficient queries. You also want to monitor the overall utilization of your disk I/O capacity as a percentage since that can forewarn you of disk access becoming a future bottleneck for your database performance.

### Auto-increment space

One of the less well-known landmines in using MySQL is that auto-increment primary keys are by default created as signed integers and can run out of key space. This happens when you have done enough inserts that the auto-increment key has reached the maximum possible value for its data type. When planning what metrics you should monitor on a long-term basis, monitoring remaining integer space for any tables that use auto increments as the primary key is a simple action that will almost certainly save you some major incident pain in the future because you can predict the need for a larger key space in advance.

How do you monitor this key space? You have a few options. If you already use PMM and its Prometheus exporter, this comes baked in and all you need to do is turn on the flag -collect.auto_increment.columns. If your team does not use Prometheus, you can use the following query, which can be modified either as a metrics producer or an alert to tell you when any of your tables are approaching the maximum key space possible (*https://oreil.ly/xfypm*). This query relies on information_schema, which has all the metadata about the tables in your database instance:

```
SELECT
    t.TABLE_SCHEMA AS `schema`,
    t.TABLE_NAME AS `table`,
    t.AUTO_INCREMENT AS `auto_increment`,
    c.DATA_TYPE AS `pk_type`,
    (
        t.AUTO_INCREMENT /
        (CASE DATA_TYPE
            WHEN 'tinyint'
                THEN IF(COLUMN_TYPE LIKE '%unsigned',
                    255,
                    127
                )
            WHEN 'smallint'
                THEN IF(COLUMN_TYPE LIKE '%unsigned',
                    65535,
                    32767
                )
```

```
          WHEN 'mediumint'
              THEN IF(COLUMN_TYPE LIKE '%unsigned',
                  16777215,
                  8388607
              )
          WHEN 'int'
              THEN IF(COLUMN_TYPE LIKE '%unsigned',
                  4294967295,
                  2147483647
              )
          WHEN 'bigint'
              THEN IF(COLUMN_TYPE LIKE '%unsigned',
                  18446744073709551615,
                  9223372036854775807
              )
      END / 100)
) AS `max_value`
FROM information_schema.TABLES t
INNER JOIN information_schema.COLUMNS c
    ON t.TABLE_SCHEMA = c.TABLE_SCHEMA
    AND t.TABLE_NAME = c.TABLE_NAME
WHERE
    t.AUTO_INCREMENT IS NOT NULL
    AND c.COLUMN_KEY = 'PRI'
    AND c.DATA_TYPE LIKE '%int'
;
```

There is a lot of nuance and context that you have to think about when picking a primary key in general and for managing auto increments specifically, and we will cover that in Chapter 6.

### Backup creation/restore time

Long-term planning is not only about growth while the business is running as usual but also recovery in an acceptable time frame. We will discuss how to think about disaster recovery in more depth in Chapter 10, and how it is part of your compliance control duties in Chapter 13, but we bring it up here to note that a good disaster recovery plan only works when you revisit it and adjust its goals.

---

## Functional Sharding and Horizontal Sharding

In this chapter and other sections throughout this book, you will see us mention sharding or partitioning as different ways to split your data on separate instances in order to scale. We want to define what we mean by these and how they differ to avoid confusion as you read the rest of this book.

*Functional sharding* means splitting specific tables that serve a specific business function into a dedicated cluster in order to manage separately this data set's uptime, performance, or even access controls.

---

*Horizontal sharding* is when you have a data set that has grown past the size you can reliably serve out of a single cluster, so you split it into multiple clusters and serve the data from several nodes, relying on some look-up mechanism to locate the subset you need.

If your databases are reaching a size where restoring from a backup will take longer than what is acceptable for restoring critical functionality of the business, then even if everything else is running fine, you need to examine adjusting that MTTR target, changing the definition of "critical functionality," or finding a way to make the backup-restore time shorter. Here are some things to think about when planning for disaster recovery:

- Be *very specific* what functionality falls into this recovery target, and if needed, look into whether the data that powers that functionality subset needs to be in a separate cluster to actually make that expectation realistic.
- If functionally partitioning that data into multiple and smaller instances is not feasible, the entire data set is now under that target for recovering via backups. The data set that takes the longest to restore from backups will be what drives this recovery process completion time.
- Make sure to have automated methods for testing (we will cover some examples in Chapter 10). Monitor how long it takes to restore a backup from a file to a running database that has also caught up on replicating all changes since the backup was created, and store that metric somewhere with enough retention to see long-term (at least a year) trends. This is one of those indicators that can slip by and become surprisingly long if monitoring it is not automated.

You will see that in many of the example long-term metrics we describe shortly, we almost always point out the need for either functional sharding or horizontal sharding of your data. The goal here is to point explicitly to the fact that if you consider sharding when you have incidents where capacity issues are a major contributing cause, then you likely have considered it too late. The work of breaking down your data into manageable pieces doesn't start when your data is too large for one cluster but well before that, when you are still determining what your goals for providing a successful customer experience are.

Understanding how long it takes you to recover your data can help set expectations for what to do in a real disaster. It can also make you aware of when it might take longer than the business wants it to. This is a precursor to needing to shard.

# Measuring Long-Term Performance

Choosing SLIs and SLOs for day-to-day operations is only the beginning. You need to make sure you are not mistaking the forest for the trees and focusing on specific host metrics instead of inspecting the overall system performance and the customer-experience outcomes. In this section, we cover strategies you can use to think about overall long-term health of the system.

## Learning Your Business Cadence

It is important to be aware of the traffic cadence of your business, as that will always be the time when all your SLOs are both the most tested and receiving the most scrutiny from your most important customers. The business cadence can mean peak traffic times are orders of magnitude larger than "average," and that has plenty of consequences if your database infrastructure is not prepared. In the context of the database infrastructure, this can translate to orders of magnitude more requests per second to fulfill, a lot more connection load from your application servers, or larger revenue impact if you were to have an intermittent failure of write operations. Here are some examples of business cadence that should help you understand what business cycle your company operates within:

*Ecommerce site*
> Late November through the end of the year is the busiest time for many countries, and online stores can see orders of magnitude more sales. This means a lot more shopping carts, a lot more concurrent sales, and a lot more revenue impact for the same failures any other time of the year.

*Human resources software*
> In the United States, November is typically when a lot of employees are making benefits elections during a time known as "open enrollment," which will create a lot more traffic.

*Online fresh-flowers vendor*
> Valentine's Day will be the busiest time of the year, with a lot more folks ordering deliveries of bouquets.

As you can see, these business cycles can vary widely depending on the customer needs that the business is filling. It is crucial for you to be aware of the cycle for your business and the implications that has on the business's revenue, its reputation, and therefore how much preparation you should make to meet the demand without affecting the stability of the systems you are tasked to run.

When it comes to measuring the performance of the database infrastructure underpinning the business, it is important not to measure performance in a bubble separate from the other important metrics that your engineering organization is tracking.

Database performance should be part of the larger conversation about tech-stack performance and not handled as a special case. Start by using the same tools as the rest of your engineering organization as much as possible. You want the metrics and dashboard you rely on to determine how the database layer is performing to be equally as accessible as the application-layer metrics or even in the same dashboards. This mindset, regardless of what tech or vendor you use, will go a long way toward creating an environment where everyone is invested in the performance of the full stack and reducing the proverbial wall engineers can feel between the features they write and the databases that support them.

## Tracking Your Metrics Effectively

There are a number of things to be concerned with when it comes to long-term planning for a business, which includes but is not limited to:

- Planning for future capacity
- Foreseeing when major improvements are needed and when incremental changes are enough
- Planning for the increased costs of running your infrastructure

You need to be able to not just measure the health of the data-store infrastructure at a certain point in time but also trend performance improvement or degradation on a long-term basis. This means not just identifying SLIs and SLOs but also finding which SLIs and SLOs remain valuable, high-signal metrics for long-term trends as well. You will likely find that not all metrics that can be used in short-term on-call decision making are also appropriate for long-term business planning.

Before we dive into which metrics are important for long-term planning, let's talk about some tools that empower that long-term trend monitoring.

## Using Monitoring Tools to Inspect the Performance

Measuring performance is important in both the immediate "are we currently in an incident" sense and the long-term tracking and trending sense. The tool that holds the metrics you care about is as important a decision as what the metrics themselves are. What is the use of choosing a good SLI if you then cannot properly see its trend over time in a manner that is relatable to the rest of the organization metrics?

The field of monitoring tools is rapidly growing, and there are lots of strong opinions on how it should be done. The goal here is increased transparency and a focus on tracking outcomes rather than outputs. In the field of making an infrastructure stack successful, tracking success is a team sport.

Instead of talking about specific tools here, we will instead list some important features and aspects to think about when considering if a tool is good for this kind of long-term trending.

### Say no to averages

Whether you are self-managing your metrics solution as an engineering organization or using a software as a service (SaaS), be careful how your metrics solution normalizes data for long-term storage. A lot of solutions aggregate long-term data into averages by default (Graphite is one of the first to do that), and that is a big problem. If you need to look at the trend of a metric over a period longer than a few weeks, the average will smooth *down* peaks, which means if you are looking to see if your disk I/O utilization can double for the next year, a graph of average data points will very likely give you a false sense of security. Always look at peaks when trending months' data, so you can keep the fidelity of occasional spikes in your view.

### Percentiles are your friend

Percentiles rely on ordering the data points in a given time span and removing the highest value ones depending on the target percentile (i.e., if you are looking for 95th, remove the top 5%). This is an excellent way to make the data you are looking at get visually more similar to how we look at SLIs and SLOs. If you can make the graph showing your query response time show the 95th percentile, you can far more easily match that to the SLO you want to achieve for application-request completion and make the database metrics make sense to folks like your customer support team and your engineers, not just your database-engineering team.

### Long retention period and performance

This may seem obvious, but the performance of a monitoring tool when trying to display long time spans is important. If you are evaluating solutions for business-metric trending, you need to make sure to test out how the user experience changes when asking for longer and longer time spans of data. A metrics solution is only as good as it can be at making that data available, not just the speed of ingestion or how long it keeps it.

Now that we have described what a long-term monitoring tool should look like, let's discuss how all we've covered so far in choosing SLIs and SLOs can guide your data architecture.

## Using SLOs to Guide Your Overall Architecture

Keeping a consistent and good customer experience while your business is also growing is no small feat. As the size of the business grows, keeping even the same SLOs, much less setting more ambitious ones, becomes harder and harder. Take something like availability, for example: everyone wants as many nines as possible of uptime for both reads and writes for all their data. But the more stringent the SLOs you want to achieve, the more expensive the work becomes, as your peak database transactions per second or its size also grows by orders of magnitude.

Using the SLIs and SLOs we already discussed, you can find the points in growth where it makes sense to start splitting your data into either functional shards or data partitions. We will discuss scaling MySQL using sharding in Chapter 11 in more detail, but the important point to make here is that the same SLIs and SLOs that tell you how the system is performing now can also guide you to knowing when it is time to invest in scaling MySQL so that the individual clusters remain manageable within the boundaries of the SLOs that preserve your customers' experience.

Having a metrics solution that can handle both short- and long-term metrics and can trend changes for you in a useful manner is a very important part of tracking tactical performance metrics along with the longer-term, business-impacting trends of how your database infrastructure is doing.

## Summary

It is important during your journey of applying reliability engineering concepts to monitoring your database infrastructure that you constantly improve and revisit your indicators and objectives. They are not meant to be set in stone after the first time you define some SLIs and SLOs. As the business grows, you will gain a deeper understanding of the customers' experience, and that should drive improvements to your SLIs and SLOs.

Be conscious as you choose metrics and assign goals to them that you are always focused on representing customer experience. Also, do not focus all your effort on metrics that show you when an incident is happening, but spend some time on monitoring things that can help you *prevent* incidents. This is all about proactive activity to protect the customer experience.

We recommend setting goals up front on three key areas: latency, availability, and errors. These three areas can provide a great signal as to whether your customers are happy. Beyond that, make sure you're also doing proactive monitoring in the areas of connection growth, disk space, and disk I/O and latency.

We hope this chapter helps frame for you how to apply reliability engineering to monitoring MySQL successfully as your company scales.

# CHAPTER 3

# Performance Schema

*Contributed by Sveta Smirnova*

Tuning the performance of databases under high load is an iterative cycle. Every time you make a change to tune the performance of the database, you need to understand if the change had any effect. Are your queries running faster than before? Are locks slowing down the application, or are they entirely gone? Did memory usage change? Did the time spent waiting on disk change? Once you understand how to answer these questions, you'll be able to evaluate and respond to day-to-day situations faster and with more confidence.

Performance Schema is a database that stores the data required to answer these questions. This chapter will help you understand how Performance Schema works, what its limitations are, and how to best go about using it—along with its companion sys schema—to uncover common information about what is going on inside MySQL.

## Introduction to Performance Schema

Performance Schema provides low-level metrics on operations running inside MySQL server. To explain how Performance Schema works, there are two concepts I need to introduce early.

The first is an *instrument*. An instrument refers to any portion of the MySQL code that we want to capture information about. For example, if we want to collect information about metadata locks, we would need to enable the `wait/lock/meta data/sql/mdl` instrument.

The second concept is a *consumer*, which is simply a table that stores the information about what code was instrumented. If we instrument queries, the consumer will record information like the total number of executions, how many times no index was used, the time spent, and so forth. The consumer is what most people closely associate with Performance Schema.

The general function of Performance Schema is shown in Figure 3-1.

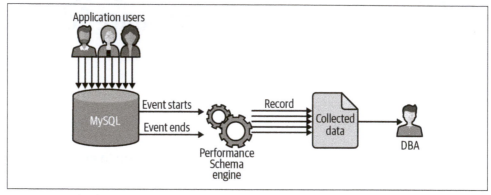

*Figure 3-1. The flow of queries running on a database, showing how perfor mance_schema collects and aggregates the data and then presents it to the DBA*

When application users connect to MySQL and execute an instrumented instruction, performance_schema encapsulates each examined call into two macros, then records the results in the corresponding consumer table. The takeaway here is that enabling instruments calls additional code, which in turn means instruments consume CPU.

## Instrument Elements

In performance_schema, the setup_instruments table contains a list of all supported instruments. All instruments' names consist of parts separated by a slash. I'll use the following examples to help you understand how these are named:

- statement/sql/select
- wait/synch/mutex/innodb/autoinc_mutex

The leftmost part of the instrument name indicates the type of the instrument. Thus, statement indicates that the instrument is a statement, wait indicates it is a wait, and so on.

The rest of the elements in the name field, from left to right, indicate the subsystem from general to specific. In the preceding example, select is a part of the sql subsystem, which is of type statement. Or autoinc_mutex belongs to innodb, which is part of the more generic instrument class mutex, which, in turn, is part of the more generic instrument sync of instrument type wait.

Most of the instrument names are self-descriptive. As in the examples, `statement/sql/select` is a SELECT query, and `wait/synch/mutex/innodb/auto inc_mutex` is a mutex that InnoDB sets on the auto-increment column. There is also a `DOCUMENTATION` column in the `setup_instruments` table that may contain more details:

```
mysql> SELECT * FROM performance_schema.setup_instruments
    -> WHERE DOCUMENTATION IS NOT NULL LIMIT 5, 5\G
*************************** 1. row ***************************
       NAME: statement/sql/error
    ENABLED: YES
      TIMED: YES
 PROPERTIES:
 VOLATILITY: 0
DOCUMENTATION: Invalid SQL queries (syntax error).
*************************** 2. row ***************************
       NAME: statement/abstract/Query
    ENABLED: YES
      TIMED: YES
 PROPERTIES: mutable
 VOLATILITY: 0
DOCUMENTATION: SQL query just received from the network. At this point, the
real statement type is unknown, the type will be refined after SQL parsing.
*************************** 3. row ***************************
       NAME: statement/abstract/new_packet
    ENABLED: YES
      TIMED: YES
 PROPERTIES: mutable
 VOLATILITY: 0
DOCUMENTATION: New packet just received from the network. At this point,
the real command type is unknown, the type will be refined after reading
the packet header.
*************************** 4. row ***************************
       NAME: statement/abstract/relay_log
    ENABLED: YES
      TIMED: YES
 PROPERTIES: mutable
 VOLATILITY: 0
DOCUMENTATION: New event just read from the relay log. At this point, the
real statement type is unknown, the type will be refined after parsing the event.
*************************** 5. row ***************************
       NAME: memory/performance_schema/mutex_instances
    ENABLED: YES
      TIMED: NULL
 PROPERTIES: global_statistics
 VOLATILITY: 1
DOCUMENTATION: Memory used for table performance_schema.mutex_instances
5 rows in set (0,00 sec)
```

Unfortunately, the DOCUMENTATION column may be NULL for many instruments, so you need to use the instrument name, your intuition, and knowledge of the MySQL source code to understand what the particular instrument examines.

## Consumer Organization

As I mentioned before, a consumer is the destination where an instrument sends its information. Performance Schema stores instrument results in many tables; in fact, MySQL Community 8.0.25 contains 110 tables in performance_schema. To understand what they are intended for, it is easier to put them into groups.

### Current and historical data

Events are put into tables whose names end as follows:

\*_current
Events that are occurring on the server at present

\*_history
Last 10 completed events per thread

\*_history_long
Last 10,000 completed events per thread, globally

The sizes of the \*_history and \*_history_long tables are configurable.

Current and historical data are available for the following:

events_waits
Low-level server waits, such as acquiring mutexes

events_statements
SQL statements

events_stages
Profile information, such as creating temporary tables or sending data

events_transactions
Transactions

### Summary tables and digests

A summary table holds aggregated information about whatever the table suggests. For example, the memory_summary_by_thread_by_event_name table holds aggregated memory usage per MySQL thread for user connections or any background thread.

Digests are a way to aggregate queries by removing the variations in them. Take the following query examples:

```
SELECT user,birthdate FROM users WHERE user_id=19;
SELECT user,birthdate FROM users WHERE user_id=13;
SELECT user,birthdate FROM users WHERE user_id=27;
```

The digest for this query would be:

```
SELECT user,birthdate FROM users WHERE user_id=?
```

This allows Performance Schema to keep track of metrics like latency for the digest without needing to retain each variation of the query separately.

### Instances

Instances refer to object instances, available for the MySQL installation. For example, the `file_instances` table contains filenames and the number of threads that access these files.

### Setup

Setup tables are used for runtime setup of `performance_schema`.

### Other tables

There are other tables whose names do not follow a strict pattern. For example, the `metadata_locks` table holds data about metadata locks. I will introduce a few of them later in the chapter when discussing issues that `performance_schema` can help solve.

## Resource Consumption

The data collected by Performance Schema is kept in memory. You can limit the amount of memory it uses by setting the maximum size of the consumers. Some tables in `performance_schema` support autoscaling. This means that they allocate a minimal amount of memory at startup and adjust their size as needed. However, this memory is never freed once allocated, even if you disabled specific instrumentation and truncated the table.

As I mentioned earlier, every instrumented call adds two more macro calls to store data in `performance_schema`. This means that the more you instrument, the higher the CPU usage will be. The actual impact on CPU utilization depends on the specific instrument. For example, a statement-related instrument could be called only once during the query while a wait instrument could be called much more often. To scan an InnoDB table with one million rows, for instance, the engine will need to set and release one million row locks. If you instrument locks, CPU usage may increase significantly. However, the same query will require a single call to figure out if it is a `statement/sql/select`. Therefore, you would not notice any increase in CPU load if you enable statement instrumentation. The same is true for memory or metadata lock instrumentation.

# Limitations

Before discussing how to set up and use performance_schema, it is important to understand its limitations:

*It must be supported by a MySQL component.*
> For example, let's say you are using memory instrumentation to calculate which MySQL component or thread uses most of the memory. You discover that the component that uses the most memory is a storage engine, which does not support memory instrumentation. In this case, you would not be able to find where the memory has gone.

*It collects data only after the specific instrument and consumer are enabled.*
> For example, if you started a server with all instrumentation disabled then decided to instrument memory usage, you would not be able to know the exact amount allocated by a global buffer such as an InnoDB buffer pool because it was already allocated before you enabled memory instrumentation.

*It is difficult to free memory.*
> You can limit the size of consumers at startup or leave them autosized. In the latter case, they do not allocate memory at the startup but only when enabled data is collected. However, even if you disable specific instruments or consumers later, memory would not be freed unless you restart the server.

In the rest of the chapter, I will assume you are aware of these limitations, so I will not specifically focus on them.

# sys Schema

Since version 5.7, standard MySQL distribution includes a companion schema for performance_schema data called sys schema. This schema consists only of views and stored routines over performance_schema. While it is designed to make your experience with performance_schema smoother, it does not store any data by itself.

> The sys schema is very convenient, but you need to remember that it only accesses data stored in the performance_schema tables. If you need data not available in the sys schema, check if it exists in the underlying table in performance_schema.

# Understanding Threads

MySQL server is multithreaded software. Each of its components uses threads. It could be a background thread created, for example, by a main thread or a storage engine, or a foreground thread created for a user connection. Each of the threads has at least two unique identifiers: an operating system thread ID that is visible, for example, in the output of the Linux `ps -eLf` command, and an internal MySQL thread ID. This internal MySQL thread ID is called THREAD_ID in most of the perfor mance_schema tables. Additionally, each foreground thread has an assigned PROCESS LIST_ID: connection identifier, visible in the SHOW PROCESSLIST command output or in the "Your MySQL connection id is" string when you connect with the MySQL command-line client.

 THREAD_ID is not equal to PROCESSLIST_ID!

The threads table in performance_schema contains all the threads existing in the server:

```
mysql> SELECT NAME, THREAD_ID, PROCESSLIST_ID, THREAD_OS_ID
    -> FROM performance_schema.threads;
+-----------------------+-----------+----------------+--------------+
| NAME                  | THREAD_ID | PROCESSLIST_ID | THREAD_OS_ID |
+-----------------------+-----------+----------------+--------------+
| thread/sql/main       |         1 |           NULL |       797580 |
| thread/innodb/io_ib...|         3 |           NULL |       797583 |
| thread/innodb/io_lo...|         4 |           NULL |       797584 |
...
| thread/sql/slave_io   |        42 |              5 |       797618 |
| thread/sql/slave_sql  |        43 |              6 |       797619 |
| thread/sql/event_sc...|        44 |              7 |       797620 |
| thread/sql/signal_h...|        45 |           NULL |       797621 |
| thread/mysqlx/accep...|        46 |           NULL |       797623 |
| thread/sql/one_conn...|     27823 |          27784 |       797695 |
| thread/sql/compress...|        48 |              9 |       797624 |
+-----------------------+-----------+----------------+--------------+
44 rows in set (0.00 sec)
```

Besides thread number information, the threads table contains the same data as the SHOW PROCESSLIST output and a few additional columns, such as RESOURCE_GROUP or PARENT_THREAD_ID.

 Performance Schema uses THREAD_ID everywhere while PROCESS LIST_ID is available only in the threads table. If you need to get PROCESSLIST_ID—for example, to kill a connection holding the lock—you need to query the threads table to obtain its value.

The `threads` table could be joined to the many other tables to provide additional information about the running query (e.g., query data, locks, mutexes, or table instances open).

In the rest of the chapter, I expect you to be familiar with this table and the meaning of `THREAD_ID`.

# Configuration

A few portions of Performance Schema can only be changed at server startup: enabling or disabling of Performance Schema itself and variables relating to memory usage and limits for data collected. The Performance Schema instruments and consumers can be enabled or disabled dynamically.

 You can start Performance Schema with all consumers and instruments disabled and enable only those that are needed to resolve specific issues right before you expect the issue to happen. This way, you will not spend any resources on Performance Schema where you do not need to or run the risk of starving your system because of overinstrumentation.

## Enabling and Disabling Performance Schema

To enable or disable Performance Schema, set the variable `performance_schema` to `ON` or `OFF` correspondingly. This is a read-only variable that can be changed only in the configuration file or via a command-line parameter when MySQL server starts.

## Enabling and Disabling Instruments

Instruments can be either enabled or disabled. To see the state of an instrument, you can query the `setup_instruments` table:

```
mysql> SELECT * FROM performance_schema.setup_instruments
    -> WHERE NAME='statement/sql/select'\G
*************************** 1. row ***************************
  NAME: statement/sql/select
  ENABLED: NO
  TIMED: YES
  PROPERTIES:
  VOLATILITY: 0
  DOCUMENTATION: NULL
1 row in set (0.01 sec)
```

As we see, `ENABLED` is `NO`; this tells us that we are not currently instrumenting `SELECT` queries.

There are three options for enabling or disabling `performance_schema` instruments:

- Use the `setup_instruments` table.
- Call the `ps_setup_enable_instrument` stored procedure in the `sys` schema.
- Use the startup parameter `performance-schema-instrument`.

## UPDATE statement

The first method is to use an UPDATE statement to change the column value:

```
mysql> UPDATE performance_schema.setup_instruments
    -> SET ENABLED='YES' WHERE NAME='statement/sql/select';
Query OK, 1 rows affected (0.00 sec)
Rows matched: 1 Changed: 1 Warnings: 0
```

Since this is standard SQL, you can also use wildcards to enable all SQL statement instruments:

```
mysql> UPDATE performance_schema.setup_instruments
    -> SET ENABLED='YES' WHERE NAME LIKE statement/sql/%';
Query OK, 167 rows affected (0.00 sec)
Rows matched: 167 Changed: 167 Warnings: 0
```

This method does not persist between restarts.

## sys stored procedure

The `sys` schema provides two stored procedures—`ps_setup_enable_instrument` and `ps_setup_disable_instrument`—that enable and disable instruments, passed as their parameters. Both routines support wildcards. If you want to enable or disable all supported instruments, use wildcard `'%'`:

```
mysql> CALL sys.ps_setup_enable_instrument('statement/sql/select');
+----------------------+
| summary              |
+----------------------+
| Enabled 1 instrument |
+----------------------+
1 row in set (0.01 sec)
```

This method is effectively the exact same as the previous one, including that it does not persist between restarts.

## Startup options

As mentioned before, both methods allow you to change the `performance_schema` configuration online but do not store that change between server restarts. If you want to save options for particular instruments between restarts, use the configuration parameter `performance-schema-instrument`.

This variable supports the `performance-schema-instrument='instrument_name=value'` syntax, where `instrument_name` is the name of the instrument and `value` is either `ON`, `TRUE`, or `1` for enabled instruments; `OFF`, `FALSE`, or `0` for disabled; and `COUNTED` for those that are counted instead of `TIMED`. You can specify this option several times to enable or disable different instruments. The option also supports wildcards:

```
performance-schema-instrument='statement/sql/select=ON'
```

 If multiple options are specified, the longer instrument string has precedence over the shorter regardless of the order.

## Enabling and Disabling Consumers

Like instruments, consumers can be enabled or disabled by:

- Updating the `setup_consumers` table in Performance Schema
- Using the stored procedures `ps_setup_enable_consumer` and `ps_setup_disable_consumer` in `sys` schema
- Setting the `performance-schema-consumer` configuration parameter

There are 15 possible consumers. Some of them have rather self-explanatory names, but there are a few consumers whose names need more explanation, listed in Table 3-1.

*Table 3-1. Consumers and their purposes*

| Consumer | Description |
|---|---|
| `events_stages_[current\|history\|history_long]` | Profiling details, such as "Creating tmp table", "statistics", or "buffer pool load" |
| `events_statements_[current\|history\|history_long]` | Statements statistics |
| `events_transactions_[current\|history\|history_long]` | Transactions |
| `events_waits_[current\|history\|history_long]` | Waits |
| `global_instrumentation` | Enables or disables global instrumentation. If disabled, no individual parameters are checked and no global or per-thread data is maintained. No individual event is collected. |
| `thread_instrumentation` | Per-thread instrumentation. Only checked if global instrumentation is enabled. If disabled, no per-thread or individual event data is collected. |
| `statements_digest` | Statement digests |

The examples given for instruments are repeatable for consumers, using the methods noted.

## Tuning Monitoring for Specific Objects

Performance Schema allows you to enable and disable monitoring for specific object types, schemas, and names. This is done in the setup_objects table.

The OBJECT_TYPE column may have one of five values: EVENT, FUNCTION, PROCEDURE, TABLE, and TRIGGER. Additionally, you can specify OBJECT_SCHEMA and OBJECT_NAME. Wildcards are supported.

For example, to disable performance_schema for triggers in the test database, use the following statement:

```
mysql> INSERT INTO performance_schema.setup_objects
    -> (OBJECT_TYPE, OBJECT_SCHEMA, OBJECT_NAME, ENABLED)
    -> VALUES ('TRIGGER', 'test', '%', 'NO');
```

If you want to make an exception for a trigger called my_trigger, add it with the statement:

```
mysql> INSERT INTO performance_schema.setup_objects
    -> (OBJECT_TYPE, OBJECT_SCHEMA, OBJECT_NAME, ENABLED)
    -> VALUES ('TRIGGER', 'test', 'my_trigger', 'YES');
```

When performance_schema decides if a specific object needs to be instrumented, it first searches for the more specific rule, then falls back to the less specific. For example, if a user runs a query on a table that fires test.my_trigger, it will examine the statements fired by the trigger. But if a user runs a query on a table that fires a trigger called test.some_other_trigger, the trigger will not be examined.

There is no configuration file option for the objects. If you need to persist changes in this table during restarts, you will need to write these INSERT statements in a SQL file and use the init_file option to load the SQL file on startup.

## Tuning Threads Monitoring

The setup_threads table contains a list of background threads that could be monitored. The ENABLED column specifies if the instrumentation for the specific thread is enabled. The HISTORY column specifies if the instrumented events for the specific thread should also be stored in the _history and _history_long tables.

For example, to disable history logging for the event scheduler (thread/sql/event_scheduler), run:

```
mysql> UPDATE performance_schema.setup_threads SET HISTORY='NO'
    -> WHERE NAME='thread/sql/event_scheduler';
```

The `setup_threads` table does not store settings for the user threads. For this purpose, the `setup_actors` table exists, which contains the columns described in Table 3-2.

*Table 3-2. Columns contained in table `setup_actors`*

| Column name | Description |
| --- | --- |
| HOST | Host, such as localhost, %, my.domain.com, or 199.27.145.65 |
| USER | Username, such as `sveta` or % |
| ROLE | Not used |
| ENABLED | If the thread is enabled |
| HISTORY | If storing data in the `_history` and `_history_long` tables is enabled |

To specify rules for specific accounts, use a command like this:

```
mysql> INSERT INTO performance_schema.setup_actors
    -> (HOST, USER, ENABLED, HISTORY)
    -> VALUES ('localhost', 'sveta', 'YES', 'NO'),
    -> ('example.com', 'sveta', 'YES', 'YES'),
    -> ('localhost', '%', 'NO', 'NO');
```

This statement enables instrumentation for `sveta@localhost` and `sveta@exam ple.com`, disables history for `sveta@localhost`, and disables both instrumentation and history for all other users connected from the `localhost`.

Like the object monitoring, there is no configuration file option for the threads and actors. If you need to persist changes in this table during restarts, you will need to write these `INSERT` statements in a SQL file and use the `init_file` option to load the SQL file on startup.

## Adjusting Memory Size for Performance Schema

Performance Schema stores data in tables that use the `PERFORMANCE_SCHEMA` engine. This engine stores data in memory. Some of the `performance_schema` tables are auto-sized by default; others have a fixed number of rows. You can adjust these options by changing startup variables. The names of the variables follow the pattern `perform ance_schema_object_[size|instances|classes|length|handles]`, where the `object` is either a consumer, a setup table, or an instrumented instance of the specific event. For example, the configuration variable `perform ance_ schema_ events_ stages_history_size` defines the number of stages per thread that the `performance_ schema_events_stages_history` table will store. The variable `perform ance_ schema_max_memory_classes` defines the maximum number of memory instruments that could be used.

# Defaults

Default values for different parts of MySQL change from version to version; therefore, it is better to consult the user reference manual prior to relying on values described here. However, for Performance Schema, they affect overall performance of the server, so I want to cover the important ones.

Since version 5.7, Performance Schema is enabled by default with most of the instruments disabled. Only global, thread, statements, and transaction instrumentation is enabled. Since version 8.0, metadata lock and memory instrumentation are additionally enabled by default.

The `mysql`, `information_schema`, and `performance_schema` databases are not instrumented. All other objects, threads, and actors are instrumented.

Most of the instances, handles, and setup tables are autosized. For the `_history` tables, the last 10 events per thread are stored. For the `_history_long` tables, the latest 10,000 events per thread are stored. The maximum stored SQL text length is 1,024 bytes. The maximum SQL digest length is also 1,024 bytes. Everything that is larger is right-trimmed.

# Using Performance Schema

Now that I've covered how Performance Schema is configured, I want to provide examples to help you solve common troubleshooting cases.

## Examining SQL Statements

As I mentioned in "Instrument Elements" on page 42, Performance Schema supports a rich set of instruments to examine performance of SQL statements. You will find tools for the standard prepared statements and stored routines. With `perfor mance_schema` you can easily find which query causes performance issues and for what reason.

To enable statements instrumentation, you need to enable instruments of type `state ment`, as described in Table 3-3.

*Table 3-3. Statement instruments and their descriptions*

| Instrument class | Description |
|---|---|
| `statement/sql` | SQL statements, such as SELECT or CREATE TABLE |
| `statement/sp` | Stored procedures control |
| `statement/scheduler` | Event scheduler |
| `statement/com` | Commands, such as quit, KILL, DROP DATABASE, or Binlog Dump. Some are not available for users and are called by the *mysqld* process itself. |

| Instrument class | Description |
| --- | --- |
| statement/abstract | Class of four commands: clone, Query, new_packet, and relay_log |

## Regular SQL statements

Performance Schema stores statement metrics in the events_statements_current, events_statements_history, and events_statements_history_long tables. All three tables have the same structure.

**Using performance_schema directly.** Here's an example of an event_statement_history entry:

```
THREAD_ID: 3200
EVENT_ID: 22
END_EVENT_ID: 23
EVENT_NAME: statement/sql/select
SOURCE: init_net_server_extension.cc:94
TIMER_START: 878753511280779000
TIMER_END: 878753544491277000
TIMER_WAIT: 33210498000
LOCK_TIME: 657000000
SQL_TEXT: SELECT film.film_id, film.description FROM sakila.film INNER JOIN
( SELECT film_id FROM sakila.film ORDER BY title LIMIT 50, 5 )
AS lim USING(film_id)
DIGEST: 2fdac27c4a9434806da3b216b9fa71aca738f70f1e8888a581c4fb00a349224f
DIGEST_TEXT: SELECT `film` . `film_id` , `film` . `description` FROM `sakila` .
`film` INNER JOIN ( SELECT `film_id` FROM `sakila` . `film` ORDER BY
`title` LIMIT?, ... ) AS `lim` USING ( `film_id` )
CURRENT_SCHEMA: sakila
OBJECT_TYPE: NULL
OBJECT_SCHEMA: NULL
OBJECT_NAME: NULL
OBJECT_INSTANCE_BEGIN: NULL
MYSQL_ERRNO: 0
RETURNED_SQLSTATE: NULL
MESSAGE_TEXT: NULL
ERRORS: 0
WARNINGS: 0
ROWS_AFFECTED: 0
ROWS_SENT: 5
ROWS_EXAMINED: 10
CREATED_TMP_DISK_TABLES: 0
CREATED_TMP_TABLES: 1
SELECT_FULL_JOIN: 0
SELECT_FULL_RANGE_JOIN: 0
SELECT_RANGE: 0
SELECT_RANGE_CHECK: 0
SELECT_SCAN: 2
SORT_MERGE_PASSES: 0
SORT_RANGE: 0
SORT_ROWS: 0
```

```
SORT_SCAN: 0
NO_INDEX_USED: 1
NO_GOOD_INDEX_USED: 0
NESTING_EVENT_ID: NULL
NESTING_EVENT_TYPE: NULL
NESTING_EVENT_LEVEL: 0
STATEMENT_ID: 25
```

These columns are explained in the official documentation (*https://oreil.ly/FROLv*), so I won't cover each and every one of them. Table 3-4 lists the columns that could be used as indicators for identifying queries that require optimization. Not all such columns are equal. For example, CREATED_TMP_DISK_TABLES in most cases is a sign of a badly optimized query, while four sort-related columns may just indicate that query results require sorting. Column importance indicates how severe the indicator is.

*Table 3-4. Columns in* event_statement_history *that can be used as indicators for optimization*

| Column | Description | Importance |
|---|---|---|
| CREATED_TMP_DISK_TABLES | The query created this number of disk-based temporary tables. You have two options to resolve this issue: optimize the query or increase maximum size for in-memory temporary tables. | High |
| CREATED_TMP_TABLES | The query created this number of memory-based temporary tables. Use of in-memory temporary tables is not bad per se. However, if the underlying table grows, they may be converted into disk-based tables. It is good to be prepared for such situations in advance. | Medium |
| SELECT_FULL_JOIN | The JOIN performed a full table scan because there is no good index to resolve the query otherwise. You need to reconsider your indexes unless the table is very small. | High |
| SELECT_FULL_RANGE_JOIN | If the JOIN used a range search of the referenced table. | Medium |
| SELECT_RANGE | If the JOIN used a range search to resolve rows in the first table. This is usually not a big issue. | Low |
| SELECT_RANGE_CHECK | If the JOIN is without indexes, which checks for keys after each row. This is a very bad symptom, and you need to reconsider your table indexes if this value is greater than zero. | High |
| SELECT_SCAN | If the JOIN did a full scan of the first table. This is an issue if the table is large. | Medium |
| SORT_MERGE_PASSES | The number of merge passes that the sort has to perform. If the value is greater than zero and the query performance is slow, you may need to increase sort_buffer_size. | Low |
| SORT_RANGE | If the sort was done using ranges. | Low |

| Column | Description | Importance |
|---|---|---|
| SORT_ROWS | The number of sorted rows. Compare with the value of the returned rows. If the number of sorted rows is higher, you may need to optimize your query. | Medium (see Description) |
| SORT_SCAN | If the sort was done by scanning a table. This is a very bad sign unless you purposely select all rows from the table without using an index. | High |
| NO_INDEX_USED | No index was used to resolve the query. | High, unless tables are small |
| NO_GOOD_INDEX_USED | Index used to resolve the query is not the best. You need to reconsider your indexes if this value is greater than zero. | High |

To find out which statements require optimization, you can choose any of said columns and compare it with zero. For example, to find all the queries that do not use a good index, run the following:

```
SELECT THREAD_ID, SQL_TEXT, ROWS_SENT, ROWS_EXAMINED, CREATED_TMP_TABLES,
NO_INDEX_USED, NO_GOOD_INDEX_USED
FROM performance_schema.events_statements_history_long
WHERE NO_INDEX_USED > 0 OR NO_GOOD_INDEX_USED > 0;
```

To find all the queries that created temporary tables, run:

```
SELECT THREAD_ID, SQL_TEXT, ROWS_SENT, ROWS_EXAMINED, CREATED_TMP_TABLES,
CREATED_TMP_DISK_TABLES
FROM performance_schema.events_statements_history_long
WHERE CREATED_TMP_TABLES > 0 OR CREATED_TMP_DISK_TABLES > 0;
```

You can use values in these columns to show potential problems individually. For example, to find all queries that returned errors, use the condition `WHERE ERRORS > 0`; to find all queries executed for more than five seconds, use the condition `WHERE TIMER_WAIT > 5000000000`; and so on.

Alternatively, you can create a query that will find all the statements with problems using long conditions, as follows:

```
WHERE ROWS_EXAMINED > ROWS_SENT
OR ROWS_EXAMINED > ROWS_AFFECTED
OR ERRORS > 0
OR CREATED_TMP_DISK_TABLES > 0
OR CREATED_TMP_TABLES > 0
OR SELECT_FULL_JOIN > 0
OR SELECT_FULL_RANGE_JOIN > 0
OR SELECT_RANGE > 0
OR SELECT_RANGE_CHECK > 0
OR SELECT_SCAN > 0
OR SORT_MERGE_PASSES > 0
OR SORT_RANGE > 0
```

```
OR SORT_ROWS > 0
OR SORT_SCAN > 0
OR NO_INDEX_USED > 0
OR NO_GOOD_INDEX_USED > 0
```

**Using sys schema.**   The sys schema provides views that could be used to find problematic statements. For example, `statements_with_errors_or_warnings` lists all statements with errors and warnings, and `statements_with_full_table_scans` lists all statements that required a full table scan. The sys schema uses digest text instead of query text, so you will get the digest query text instead of either SQL or digest text like you do when accessing the raw performance_schema tables:

```
mysql> SELECT query, total_latency, no_index_used_count, rows_sent,
    -> rows_examined
    -> FROM sys.statements_with_full_table_scans
    -> WHERE db='employees' AND
    -> query NOT LIKE '%performance_schema%'\G
*********************** 1. row ***********************
 query: SELECT COUNT ( 'emp_no' ) FROM ... 'emp_no' )
WHERE 'title' = ?
total_latency: 805.37 ms
no_index_used_count: 1
rows_sent: 1
rows_examined: 397774
...
```

Other views that could be used to find statements that require optimizations are described in Table 3-5.

*Table 3-5. Views that can be used to find statements requiring optimization*

| View | Description |
|---|---|
| statement_analysis | A normalized statement view with aggregated statistics, ordered by the total execution time per the normalized statement. Similar to the events_statements_summary_by_digest table but less detailed. |
| statements_with_errors_or_warnings | All normalized statements that raised errors or warnings. |
| statements_with_full_table_scans. | All normalized statements that have done a full table scan. |
| statements_with_runtimes_in_95th_percentile | All normalized statements whose average execution time is in the top 95th percentile. |
| statements_with_sorting | All normalized statements that have done sorts. The view includes all kinds of sorts. |
| statements_with_temp_tables | All normalized statements that used temporary tables. |

## Prepared statements

The `prepared_statements_instances` table contains all prepared statements existing in the server. It has the same statistics as in the `events_statements_[current|his tory|history_long]` tables and, additionally, information about the thread that owns the prepared statement and how many times the statement was executed. Unlike in the `events_statements_[current|history|history_long]` tables, statistics data is summed, and the table contains the total amount of all statement executions.

 The `COUNT_EXECUTE` column contains the number of times the statement was executed, so you can get average statistics per statement by dividing the total value by the number in this column. Note, however, that any average statistics could be inaccurate. For example, if you executed a statement 10 times and the value in the column `SUM_SELECT_FULL_JOIN` is 10, the average would be one full join per statement. If you then add an index and execute the statement one more time, `SUM_SELECT_FULL_JOIN` will remain 10, so the average will be $10/11 = 0.9$. This does not show that the issue is now resolved.

To enable prepared statements instrumentation, you need to enable the instruments described in Table 3-6.

*Table 3-6. Instruments to enable for prepared statements instrumentation*

| Instrument class | Description |
| --- | --- |
| `statement/sql/prepare_sql` | PREPARE statement in the text protocol (when run via MySQL CLI) |
| `statement/sql/execute_sql` | EXECUTE statement in the text protocol (when run via MySQL CLI) |
| `statement/com/Prepare` | PREPARE statement in the binary protocol (if accessed via MySQL C API) |
| `statement/com/Execute` | EXECUTE statement in the binary protocol (if accessed via MySQL C API) |

Once enabled, you can prepare a statement and execute it a few times:

```
mysql> PREPARE stmt FROM
    -> 'SELECT COUNT(*) FROM employees WHERE hire_date > ?';
Query OK, 0 rows affected (0.00 sec)
Statement prepared

mysql1> SET @hd='1995-01-01';
Query OK, 0 rows affected (0.00 sec)

mysql1> EXECUTE stmt USING @hd;
+----------+
| count(*) |
+----------+
| 34004    |
+----------+
```

```
1 row in set (1.44 sec)

-- Execute a few more times with different values
```

Then you can check the diagnostics:

```
mysql2> SELECT statement_name, sql_text, owner_thread_id,
    -> count_reprepare, count_execute, sum_timer_execute
    -> FROM prepared_statements_instances\G
*************************** 1. row ***************************
  statement_name: stmt
        sql_text: select count(*) from employees where hire_date > ?
 owner_thread_id: 22
 count_reprepare: 0
   count_execute: 3
sum_timer_execute: 4156561368000
1 row in set (0.00 sec)
```

Note that you will see the statements in the `prepared_statements_instances` table only when they exist in the server. Once they are dropped, you cannot access their statistics anymore:

```
mysql1> DROP PREPARE stmt;
Query OK, 0 rows affected (0.00 sec)

mysql2> SELECT * FROM prepared_statements_instances\G
Empty set (0.00 sec)
```

### Stored routines

With `performance_schema` you can retrieve information about how your stored routines were executed: for example, which of the branches of the `IF … ELSE` flow control statement has been chosen or if an error handler was called.

To enable stored routines instrumentation, you need to enable instruments that follow the pattern `'statement/sp/%'`. The instrument `statement/sp/stmt` is responsible for the statements, called inside the routine, while other instruments are responsible for tracking events, such as entering or leaving the procedure, loop, or any other control instruction.

To demonstrate how stored routines instrumentation works, use the stored procedure:

```
CREATE DEFINER='root'@'localhost' PROCEDURE 'sp_test'(val int)
BEGIN
  DECLARE CONTINUE HANDLER FOR 1364, 1048, 1366
  BEGIN
    INSERT IGNORE INTO t1 VALUES('Some string');
    GET STACKED DIAGNOSTICS CONDITION 1 @stacked_state = RETURNED_SQLSTATE;
    GET STACKED DIAGNOSTICS CONDITION 1 @stacked_msg = MESSAGE_TEXT;
  END;
```

```
        INSERT INTO t1 VALUES(val);
    END
```

Then call it with different values:

```
mysql> CALL sp_test(1);
Query OK, 1 row affected (0.07 sec)

mysql> SELECT THREAD_ID, EVENT_NAME, SQL_TEXT
    -> FROM EVENTS_STATEMENTS_HISTORY
    -> WHERE EVENT_NAME LIKE 'statement/sp%';
+-----------+-------------------------+-----------------------------+
| THREAD_ID | EVENT_NAME              | SQL_TEXT                    |
+-----------+-------------------------+-----------------------------+
|        24 | statement/sp/hpush_jump | NULL                        |
|        24 | statement/sp/stmt       | INSERT INTO t1 VALUES(val)  |
|        24 | statement/sp/hpop       | NULL                        |
+-----------+-------------------------+-----------------------------+
3 rows in set (0.00 sec)
```

In this case, the error handler was not called, and the procedure inserted the argument value (1) into the table:

```
mysql> CALL sp_test(NULL);
Query OK, 1 row affected (0.07 sec)

mysql> SELECT THREAD_ID, EVENT_NAME, SQL_TEXT
    -> FROM EVENTS_STATEMENTS_HISTORY
    -> WHERE EVENT_NAME LIKE 'statement/sp%';
+-----------+-------------------------+-----------------------------+
| THREAD_ID | EVENT_NAME              | SQL_TEXT                    |
+-----------+-------------------------+-----------------------------+
|        24 | statement/sp/hpush_jump | NULL                        |
|        24 | statement/sp/stmt       | INSERT INTO t1 VALUES(val)  |
|        24 | statement/sp/stmt       | INSERT IGNORE INTO t1       |
|                                     |     VALUES('Some str... |
|        24 | statement/sp/stmt       | GET STACKED DIAGNOSTICS     |
|                                     |     CONDITION 1 @s...   |
|        24 | statement/sp/stmt       | GET STACKED DIAGNOSTICS     |
|                                     |     CONDITION 1 @s...   |
|        24 | statement/sp/hreturn    | NULL                        |
|        24 | statement/sp/hpop       | NULL                        |
+-----------+-------------------------+-----------------------------+
7 rows in set (0.00 sec)
```

In the second call, however, the content of the events_statements_history table is different: it contains calls from the error handler and the SQL statement that replaced the erroneous one.

While the return value of the procedure itself did not change, we clearly see that it has been executed differently. Understanding such differences in the routine execution flow can help to understand why the same routine can finish almost immediately if called once and can take much longer when called another time.

## Statements profiling

The `events_stages_[current|history|history_long]` table contains profiling information, such as how much time MySQL spent while creating a temporary table, updating, or waiting for a lock. To enable profiling, you need to enable said consumers and also instruments that follow the pattern `'stage/%'`. Once enabled, you can find answers to such questions as "Which stage of the query execution took a critically long time?" The following example searches for stages that took more than one second:

```
mysql> SELECT eshl.event_name, sql_text,
    ->        eshl.timer_wait/10000000000 w_s
    -> FROM performance_schema.events_stages_history_long eshl
    -> JOIN performance_schema.events_statements_history_long esthl
    -> ON (eshl.nesting_event_id = esthl.event_id)
    -> WHERE eshl.timer_wait > 1*10000000000\G
*************************** 1. row ***************************
event_name: stage/sql/Sending data
sql_text: SELECT COUNT(emp_no) FROM employees JOIN salaries
USING(emp_no) WHERE hire_date=from_date
w_s: 81.7
1 row in set (0.00 sec)
```

Another technique for using `events_stages_[current|history|history_long]` tables is to pay attention to those statements that spent more than a certain threshold in stages known to cause performance issues. Table 3-7 lists these stages.

*Table 3-7. Stages that are indicators of performance issues*

| Stage class(es) | Description |
|---|---|
| stage/sql/%tmp% | Everything related to the temporary tables. |
| stage/sql/%lock% | Everything related to locks. |
| stage/%/Waiting for% | Everything waiting for a resource. |
| stage/sql/Sending data | This stage should be compared to the number of ROWS_SENT in the statements statistics. If ROWS_SENT is small, a statement spending a lot of time in this stage could mean that it has to create a temporary file or table to resolve intermediary results. This is often followed by filtering the rows before sending data to the client. This is usually a symptom of a badly optimized query. |
| stage/sql/freeing items<br>stage/sql/cleaning up<br>stage/sql/closing tables<br>stage/sql/end | These are stages that clean resources. Unfortunately, they are not detailed enough, and each of them includes more than a single task. If you see that your queries spend a long time in these stages, you most likely hit resource contention due to high concurrency. You need to check your CPU, I/O, and memory usage as well as whether your hardware and MySQL options can handle concurrency that your application creates. |

It is very important to note that profiling is available only for the general server stages. Storage engines do not support profiling with performance_schema. As a result, stages such as stage/sql/update mean that the job is inside the storage engine and may include not only the update itself, but also waits for the engine-specific locks or other contention issues.

## Examining Read Versus Write Performance

Statement instrumentation in Performance Schema could be very useful to understand if your workload is read or write bound. You may start by counting types of statements:

```
mysql> SELECT EVENT_NAME, COUNT(EVENT_NAME)
    -> FROM events_statements_history_long
    -> GROUP BY EVENT_NAME;
+----------------------+-------------------+
| EVENT_NAME           | COUNT(EVENT_NAME) |
+----------------------+-------------------+
| statement/sql/insert |               504 |
| statement/sql/delete |               502 |
| statement/sql/select |              6987 |
| statement/sql/update |              1007 |
| statement/sql/commit |               500 |
| statement/sql/begin  |               500 |
+----------------------+-------------------+
6 rows in set (0.03 sec)
```

In this example, the number of SELECT queries is larger than the number of any other queries. This shows that most of the queries in this setup are read queries.

If you want to know the latency of your statements, aggregate by the LOCK_TIME column:

```
mysql> SELECT EVENT_NAME, COUNT(EVENT_NAME),
    -> SUM(LOCK_TIME/1000000) AS latency_ms
    -> FROM events_statements_history
    -> GROUP BY EVENT_NAME ORDER BY latency_ms DESC;
+--------------------------------+-------------------+------------+
| EVENT_NAME                     | COUNT(EVENT_NAME) | latency_ms |
+--------------------------------+-------------------+------------+
| statement/sql/select           |               194 |  7362.0000 |
| statement/sql/update           |                33 |  1276.0000 |
| statement/sql/insert           |                16 |   599.0000 |
| statement/sql/delete           |                16 |   470.0000 |
| statement/sql/show_status      |                 2 |   176.0000 |
| statement/sql/begin            |                 4 |     0.0000 |
| statement/sql/commit           |                 2 |     0.0000 |
| statement/com/Ping             |                 2 |     0.0000 |
| statement/sql/show_engine_status |               1 |     0.0000 |
+--------------------------------+-------------------+------------+
9 rows in set (0.01 sec)
```

You may also want to know the amount of bytes and rows read and written. For this purpose, use the global status variables `Handler_*`:

```
mysql> WITH rows_read AS (SELECT SUM(VARIABLE_VALUE) AS rows_read
    -> FROM global_status
    -> WHERE VARIABLE_NAME IN ('Handler_read_first', 'Handler_read_key',
    -> 'Handler_read_next', 'Handler_read_last', 'Handler_read_prev',
    -> 'Handler_read_rnd', 'Handler_read_rnd_next')),
    -> rows_written AS (SELECT SUM(VARIABLE_VALUE) AS rows_written
    -> FROM global_status
    -> WHERE VARIABLE_NAME IN ('Handler_write'))
    -> SELECT * FROM rows_read, rows_written\G
*************************** 1. row ***************************
rows_read: 169358114082
rows_written: 33038251685
1 row in set (0.00 sec)
```

## Examining Metadata Locks

Metadata locks are used to protect database object definitions from modification. Shared metadata locks are set for any SQL statement: `SELECT`, `UPDATE`, and so on. They do not affect other statements that require shared metadata locks. However, they prevent those statements that change the database object definition, such as `ALTER TABLE` or `CREATE INDEX`, from starting until the lock is freed. While most of the issues caused by metadata lock conflicts affect tables, the locks themselves are set for any database object, such as `SCHEMA`, `EVENT`, `TABLESPACE`, and so on.

Metadata locks are held until the transaction finishes. This makes troubleshooting them harder if you use multiple statement transactions. Which statement is waiting for the lock is usually clear: DDL statements implicitly commit transactions, so they are the only statement in the new transaction, and you will find them in the process list in the `"Waiting for a metadata lock"` status. However, the statement that holds the lock may vanish from the process list if it is part of the multiple statement transaction that is still open.

The `metadata_locks` table in `performance_schema` holds information about locks that are currently set by different threads, and it also holds information about lock requests that are waiting for the lock. This way, you can easily identify which thread does not allow your DDL request to start and decide if you want to kill this statement or wait until it finishes executing.

To enable metadata lock instrumentation, you need to enable the `wait/lock/meta data/sql/mdl` instrument.

The following example shows that a thread, visible in the process list with ID 5, holds the lock that the thread with processlist_id=4 is waiting for:

```
mysql> SELECT processlist_id, object_type,
    -> lock_type, lock_status, source
    -> FROM metadata_locks JOIN threads ON (owner_thread_id=thread_id)
    -> WHERE object_schema='employees' AND object_name='titles'\G
*************************** 1. row ***************************
 processlist_id: 4
    object_type: TABLE
      lock_type: EXCLUSIVE
    lock_status: PENDING -- waits
         source: mdl.cc:3263
*************************** 2. row ***************************
 processlist_id: 5
    object_type: TABLE
      lock_type: SHARED_READ
    lock_status: GRANTED -- holds
         source: sql_parse.cc:5707
```

# Examining Memory Usage

To turn on memory instrumentation in performance_schema, enable instruments of the class memory. Once enabled, you can find details on exactly how memory is used by the internal MySQL structures.

## Using performance_schema directly

Performance Schema stores memory usage statistics in the digest tables, whose names start with the memory_summary_ prefix. Memory use aggregation is described in Table 3-8.

*Table 3-8. Aggregation parameters for memory use*

| Aggregation parameter | Description |
| --- | --- |
| global | Globally per event name |
| thread | Per thread: includes both background and user threads |
| account | User account |
| host | Host |
| user | Username |

For example, to find InnoDB structures that use most of the memory, issue the following query:

```
mysql> SELECT EVENT_NAME,
    -> CURRENT_NUMBER_OF_BYTES_USED/1024/1024 AS CURRENT_MB,
    -> HIGH_NUMBER_OF_BYTES_USED/1024/1024 AS HIGH_MB
    -> FROM performance_schema.memory_summary_global_by_event_name
    -> WHERE EVENT_NAME LIKE 'memory/innodb/%'
```

```
    -> ORDER BY CURRENT_NUMBER_OF_BYTES_USED DESC LIMIT 10;
+------------------------------+--------------+--------------+
| EVENT_NAME                   | CURRENT_MB   | HIGH_MB      |
+------------------------------+--------------+--------------+
| memory/innodb/buf_buf_pool   | 130.68750000 | 130.68750000 |
| memory/innodb/ut0link_buf    |  24.00006104 |  24.00006104 |
| memory/innodb/buf0dblwr      |  17.07897949 |  24.96951294 |
| memory/innodb/ut0new         |  16.07891273 |  16.07891273 |
| memory/innodb/sync0arr       |   6.25006866 |   6.25006866 |
| memory/innodb/lock0lock      |   4.85086060 |   4.85086060 |
| memory/innodb/ut0pool        |   4.00003052 |   4.00003052 |
| memory/innodb/hash0hash      |   3.69776917 |   3.69776917 |
| memory/innodb/os0file        |   2.60422516 |   3.61988068 |
| memory/innodb/memory         |   1.23812866 |   1.42373657 |
+------------------------------+--------------+--------------+
10 rows in set (0,00 sec)
```

## Using sys schema

The sys schema has views that allow you to get memory statistics in a better way. They also support aggregation by host, user, thread, or global. The view mem ory_global_total contains a single value, displaying the total amount of the instrumented memory:

```
mysql> SELECT * FROM sys.memory_global_total;
+-----------------+
| total_allocated |
+-----------------+
| 441.84 MiB      |
+-----------------+
1 row in set (0,09 sec)
```

Aggregation views convert bytes into kilobytes, megabytes, and gigabytes as needed. The view memory_by_thread_by_current_bytes has a user column that may take one of the following values:

NAME@HOST
  Regular user account, such as sveta@oreilly.com.

*System users, such as* sql/main *or* innodb/*
  Data for such "usernames" is taken from the threads table and is handy when you need to understand what the particular thread is doing.

Rows in the view memory_by_thread_by_current_bytes are sorted by the currently allocated memory in descending order, so you will easily find which thread takes most of the memory:

```
mysql> SELECT thread_id tid, user,
    -> current_allocated ca, total_allocated
    -> FROM sys.memory_by_thread_by_current_bytes LIMIT 9;
+-----+-----------------------------+------------+-----------------+
```

```
| tid | user                         | ca         | total_allocated |
+-----+------------------------------+------------+-----------------+
|  52 | sveta@localhost              | 1.36 MiB   | 10.18 MiB       |
|   1 | sql/main                     | 1.02 MiB   | 4.95 MiB        |
|  33 | innodb/clone_gtid_thread     | 525.36 KiB | 24.04 MiB       |
|  44 | sql/event_scheduler          | 145.72 KiB | 4.23 MiB        |
|  43 | sql/slave_sql                | 48.74 KiB  | 142.46 KiB      |
|  42 | sql/slave_io                 | 20.03 KiB  | 232.23 KiB      |
|  48 | sql/compress_gtid_table      | 13.91 KiB  | 17.06 KiB       |
|  25 | innodb/fts_optimize_thread   | 1.92 KiB   | 2.00 KiB        |
|  34 | innodb/srv_purge_thread      | 1.56 KiB   | 1.64 KiB        |
+-----+------------------------------+------------+-----------------+
9 rows in set (0,03 sec)
```

The preceding example is taken on a laptop; therefore, numbers are not descriptive of a production server. It is still clear that a local connection uses most of the memory, followed by the main server process.

The memory instrumentation is handy when you need to find a user thread that takes the most memory. In the following example, a user connection allocated 36 GB of RAM, which is quite huge even in modern high-memory systems:

```
mysql> SELECT * FROM sys.memory_by_thread_by_current_bytes
    -> ORDER BY current_allocated desc\G
*************************** 1. row ***************************
      thread_id: 152
           user: lj@127.0.0.1
current_count_used: 325
current_allocated: 36.00 GiB
current_avg_alloc: 113.43 MiB
current_max_alloc: 36.00 GiB
total_allocated: 37.95 GiB
...
```

## Examining Variables

Performance Schema brings variable instrumentation to a new level. It provides instrumentation for:

- Server variables
  - Global
  - Session, for all currently opened sessions
  - Source, from which all current variable values originate
- Status variables
  - Global
  - Session, for all currently open sessions
  - Aggregations by

— Host

— User

— Account

— Thread

• User variables

 Prior to version 5.7, server and status variables were instrumented in information_schema. This instrumentation was limited: it allowed tracking of only global and current session values. Information about variables and status in other sessions, as well as information about the user variables, was not accessible. However, for backward-compatibility reasons, MySQL 5.7 uses informa tion_schema to track variables. To enable performance_schema support for variables, you need to set the configuration variable show_compatibility_56 to 0. This requirement, as well as variable tables in information_schema, no longer exists in version 8.0.

Global variable values are stored in the table global_variables. Session variables for the current session are stored in the table session_variables. Both tables have only two columns with self-explanatory names: VARIABLE_NAME and VARIABLE_VALUE.

The variables_by_thread table has an additional column, THREAD_ID, indicating the thread to which the variable belongs. This allows you to find threads that set session variable values to be different than specified by the default configuration.

In the following example, the thread with THREAD_ID=84 sets the variable tx_isola tion to SERIALIZABLE, which may lead to situations when transactions acquire more locks than if the default level is used:

```
mysql> SELECT * FROM variables_by_thread
    -> WHERE VARIABLE_NAME='tx_isolation';
+-----------+---------------+----------------+
| THREAD_ID | VARIABLE_NAME | VARIABLE_VALUE |
+-----------+---------------+----------------+
|        71 | tx_isolation  | REPEATABLE-READ |
|        83 | tx_isolation  | REPEATABLE-READ |
|        84 | tx_isolation  | SERIALIZABLE   |
+-----------+---------------+----------------+
3 rows in set, 3 warnings (0.00 sec)
```

The following example finds all threads with session variable values that are different from the current active session:

```
mysql> SELECT vt2.THREAD_ID AS TID, vt2.VARIABLE_NAME,
    -> vt1.VARIABLE_VALUE AS MY_VALUE,
```

```
    -> vt2.VARIABLE_VALUE AS OTHER_VALUE
    -> FROM performance_schema.variables_by_thread vt1
    -> JOIN performance_schema.threads t USING(THREAD_ID)
    -> JOIN performance_schema.variables_by_thread vt2
    -> USING(VARIABLE_NAME)
    -> WHERE vt1.VARIABLE_VALUE != vt2.VARIABLE_VALUE
    -> AND t.PROCESSLIST_ID=@@pseudo_thread_id;
+-----+--------------------+-------------------+--------------------+
| TID | VARIABLE_NAME      | MY_VALUE          | OTHER_VALUE        |
+-----+--------------------+-------------------+--------------------+
|  42 | max_allowed_packet | 67108864          | 1073741824         |
|  42 | pseudo_thread_id   | 22715             | 5                  |
|  42 | timestamp          | 1626650242.678049 | 1626567255.695062  |
|  43 | gtid_next          | AUTOMATIC         | NOT_YET_DETERMINED |
|  43 | pseudo_thread_id   | 22715             | 6                  |
|  43 | timestamp          | 1626650242.678049 | 1626567255.707031  |
+-----+--------------------+-------------------+--------------------+
6 rows in set (0,01 sec)
```

Global and current session status values are stored in the tables global_status and session_status, respectively. They also have only two columns: VARIABLE_NAME and VARIABLE_VALUE.

Status variables can be aggregated by user account, host, user, and thread. In my opinion, the most interesting aggregation is by thread because it allows you to identify quickly which connection is creating most of the resource pressure on the server. For example, the following snippet clearly shows that the connection with THREAD_ID=83 is doing most of the writes:

```
mysql> SELECT * FROM status_by_thread
    -> WHERE VARIABLE_NAME='Handler_write';
+-----------+---------------+----------------+
| THREAD_ID | VARIABLE_NAME | VARIABLE_VALUE |
+-----------+---------------+----------------+
|        71 | Handler_write | 94             |
|        83 | Handler_write | 4777777777     | -- Most writes
|        84 | Handler_write | 101            |
+-----------+---------------+----------------+
3 rows in set (0.00 sec)
```

User-defined variables are created as SET @my_var = 'foo' and are tracked in the table user_variables_by_thread:

```
mysql> SELECT * FROM user_variables_by_thread;
+-----------+---------------+----------------+
| THREAD_ID | VARIABLE_NAME | VARIABLE_VALUE |
+-----------+---------------+----------------+
|        71 | baz           | boo            |
|        84 | foo           | bar            |
+-----------+---------------+----------------+
2 rows in set (0.00 sec)
```

This instrumentation is useful when you need to find sources of memory consumption because each variable takes bytes to hold its values. You may also use this information to solve tricky issues with persistence connections, using user-defined variables. And, last but not least, this table is the only way to find out which variables you defined in your own session.

The table `variables_info` does not contain any variable values. Rather, it has information about where server variables originated and other documentation, such as the variable default minimum and maximum values. The `SET_TIME` column contains the timestamp of the latest variable change. The `SET_HOST` and `SET_USER` columns identify the user account that set the variable. For example, to find all the variables that were changed dynamically since the server started, run:

```
mysql> SELECT * FROM performance_schema.variables_info
    -> WHERE VARIABLE_SOURCE = 'DYNAMIC'\G
*************************** 1. row ***************************
  VARIABLE_NAME: foreign_key_checks
VARIABLE_SOURCE: DYNAMIC
  VARIABLE_PATH:
      MIN_VALUE: 0
      MAX_VALUE: 0
       SET_TIME: 2021-07-18 03:14:15.560745
       SET_USER: NULL
       SET_HOST: NULL
*************************** 2. row ***************************
  VARIABLE_NAME: sort_buffer_size
VARIABLE_SOURCE: DYNAMIC
  VARIABLE_PATH:
      MIN_VALUE: 32768
      MAX_VALUE: 18446744073709551615
       SET_TIME: 2021-07-19 02:37:11.948190
       SET_USER: sveta
       SET_HOST: localhost
2 rows in set (0,00 sec)
```

Possible `VARIABLE_SOURCE` values include:

`COMMAND_LINE`
Variable set on the command line

`COMPILED`
Compiled-in default value

`PERSISTED`
Set from a server-specific *mysqld-auto.cnf* option file

There are also many options for variables, set in different option files. I will not discuss them all: they are either self-descriptive or could be easily checked in the User Reference Manual. The number of details is also increasing from version to version.

# Examining Most Frequent Errors

In addition to the specific error information, performance_schema provides digest tables, aggregating errors by user, host, account, thread, and globally by the error number. All aggregation tables have a structure similar to that used in the events_errors_summary_global_by_error table:

```
mysql> USE performance_schema;
mysql> SHOW CREATE TABLE events_errors_summary_global_by_error\G
*************************** 1. row ***************************
    Table: events_errors_summary_global_by_error
Create Table: CREATE TABLE `events_errors_summary_global_by_error` (
 `ERROR_NUMBER` int DEFAULT NULL,
 `ERROR_NAME` varchar(64) DEFAULT NULL,
 `SQL_STATE` varchar(5) DEFAULT NULL,
 `SUM_ERROR_RAISED` bigint unsigned NOT NULL,
 `SUM_ERROR_HANDLED` bigint unsigned NOT NULL,
 `FIRST_SEEN` timestamp NULL DEFAULT '0000-00-00 00:00:00',
 `LAST_SEEN` timestamp NULL DEFAULT '0000-00-00 00:00:00',
 UNIQUE KEY `ERROR_NUMBER` (`ERROR_NUMBER`)
) ENGINE=PERFORMANCE_SCHEMA DEFAULT CHARSET=utf8mb4 COLLATE=utf8mb4_0900_ai_ci
1 row in set (0,00 sec)
```

The columns ERROR_NUMBER, ERROR_NAME, and SQL_STATE identify the error. SUM_ERROR_RAISED is the number of times the error was raised. SUM_ERROR_HANDLED is the number of times the error was handled. FIRST_SEEN and LAST_SEEN are timestamps when the error was first and last seen.

Specific aggregate tables have additional columns. Thus, the table events_errors_summary_by_thread_by_error has a column named THREAD_ID, which identifies the thread that raised the error, the table events_errors_summary_by_host_by_error has a column named HOST, and so on.

For example, to find all accounts that ran statements that caused errors more than 10 times, run:

```
mysql> SELECT * FROM
    -> performance_schema.events_errors_summary_by_account_by_error
    -> WHERE SUM_ERROR_RAISED > 10 AND USER IS NOT NULL
    -> ORDER BY SUM_ERROR_RAISED DESC\G
*************************** 1. row ***************************
    USER: sveta
    HOST: localhost
    ERROR_NUMBER: 3554
    ERROR_NAME: ER_NO_SYSTEM_TABLE_ACCESS
    SQL_STATE: HY000
    SUM_ERROR_RAISED: 60
    SUM_ERROR_HANDLED: 0
    FIRST_SEEN: 2021-07-18 03:14:59
    LAST_SEEN: 2021-07-19 02:50:13
1 row in set (0,01 sec)
```

Error digest tables can be useful for finding out which user accounts, hosts, users, or threads send the most erroneous queries and perform an action. They could also help with errors like ER_DEPRECATED_UTF8_ALIAS, which may show that some of the frequently used queries were written for previous MySQL versions and need to be updated.

## Examining Performance Schema Itself

You can examine Performance Schema itself using the same instruments and consumers as you do for your own schemas. Just note that by default, if performance_schema is set as the default database, queries to it are not tracked. If you need to examine queries to performance_schema, you need to update the setup_actors table first.

Once the setup_actors table is updated, all instruments can be used. For example, to find the 10 consumers in performance_schema that allocated most of the memory, run:

```
mysql> SELECT SUBSTRING_INDEX(EVENT_NAME, '/', -1) AS EVENT,
    -> CURRENT_NUMBER_OF_BYTES_USED/1024/1024 AS CURRENT_MB,
    -> HIGH_NUMBER_OF_BYTES_USED/1024/1024 AS HIGH_MB
    -> FROM performance_schema.memory_summary_global_by_event_name
    -> WHERE EVENT_NAME LIKE 'memory/performance_schema/%'
    -> ORDER BY CURRENT_NUMBER_OF_BYTES_USED DESC LIMIT 10;
+------------------------------------------+-------------+-------------+
| EVENT                                    | CURRENT_MB  | HIGH_MB     |
+------------------------------------------+-------------+-------------+
| events_statements_summary_by_digest      | 39.67285156 | 39.67285156 |
| events_statements_history_long           | 13.88549805 | 13.88549805 |
| events_errors_summary_by_thread_by_...   | 11.81640625 | 11.81640625 |
| events_statements_summary_by_thread...   |  9.79296875 |  9.79296875 |
| events_statements_history_long.dige...   |  9.76562500 |  9.76562500 |
| events_statements_summary_by_digest...   |  9.76562500 |  9.76562500 |
| events_statements_history_long.sql_...   |  9.76562500 |  9.76562500 |
| memory_summary_by_thread_by_event_name   |  7.91015625 |  7.91015625 |
| events_errors_summary_by_host_by_error   |  5.90820313 |  5.90820313 |
| events_errors_summary_by_account_by...   |  5.90820313 |  5.90820313 |
+------------------------------------------+-------------+-------------+
10 rows in set (0,00 sec)
```

Or use sys schema:

```
mysql> SELECT SUBSTRING_INDEX(event_name, '/', -1), current_alloc
    -> FROM sys.memory_global_by_current_bytes
    -> WHERE event_name LIKE 'memory/performance_schema/%' LIMIT 10;
+------------------------------------------+---------------+
| SUBSTRING_INDEX(event_name, '/', -1)     | current_alloc |
+------------------------------------------+---------------+
| events_statements_summary_by_digest      | 39.67 MiB     |
| events_statements_history_long           | 13.89 MiB     |
```

```
| events_errors_summary_by_thread_by_error             | 11.82 MiB  |
| events_statements_summary_by_thread_by_event_name    | 9.79 MiB   |
| events_statements_history_long.digest_text           | 9.77 MiB   |
| events_statements_summary_by_digest.digest_text      | 9.77 MiB   |
| events_statements_history_long.sql_text              | 9.77 MiB   |
| memory_summary_by_thread_by_event_name               | 7.91 MiB   |
| events_errors_summary_by_host_by_error               | 5.91 MiB   |
| events_errors_summary_by_account_by_error            | 5.91 MiB   |
+------------------------------------------------------+------------+
10 rows in set (0,00 sec)
```

performance_schema also supports the SHOW ENGINE PERFORMANCE_SCHEMA STATUS
statement:

```
mysql> SHOW ENGINE PERFORMANCE_SCHEMA STATUS\G
*************************** 1. row ***************************
  Type: performance_schema
  Name: events_waits_current.size
Status: 176
*************************** 2. row ***************************
  Type: performance_schema
  Name: events_waits_current.count
Status: 1536
*************************** 3. row ***************************
  Type: performance_schema
  Name: events_waits_history.size
Status: 176
*************************** 4. row ***************************
  Type: performance_schema
  Name: events_waits_history.count
Status: 2560
…
*************************** 244. row ***************************
  Type: performance_schema
  Name: (pfs_buffer_scalable_container).count
Status: 17
*************************** 245. row ***************************
  Type: performance_schema
  Name: (pfs_buffer_scalable_container).memory
Status: 1904
*************************** 246. row ***************************
  Type: performance_schema
  Name: (max_global_server_errors).count
Status: 4890
*************************** 247. row ***************************
  Type: performance_schema
  Name: (max_session_server_errors).count
Status: 1512
*************************** 248. row ***************************
  Type: performance_schema
  Name: performance_schema.memory
Status: 218456400
248 rows in set (0,00 sec)
```

In its output, you will find such details as how many specific events are stored in the consumers or the maximum values of the specific metrics. The last row contains the number of bytes that Performance Schema currently takes.

## Summary

Performance Schema is a feature that has often been criticized. Earlier versions of MySQL had less than optimal implementations, leading to high resource consumption. It was common advice to simply turn it off.

It was also considered difficult to understand. Enabling an instrument is just enabling an additional bit of code in the server that records data and submits it to the consumers. The consumers are just tables that live in memory, and you need to use standard SQL to ask the table the right questions to find what you are looking for. Understanding how Performance Schema manages its own memory will help you realize that MySQL is not leaking memory; it's just keeping consumer data in memory, and it only releases that memory on restart.

My advice here is simple: you should keep Performance Schema enabled, dynamically enabling the instruments and consumers that will help you address whatever concerns you might have—query performance, locking, disk I/O, errors, and more. You should also leverage the sys schema as a shortcut to addressing the most common questions. Doing this will give you an accessible way to measure performance directly from within MySQL.

# CHAPTER 4

# Operating System and Hardware Optimization

Your MySQL server can perform only as well as its weakest link, and the operating system and hardware on which it runs are often limiting factors. The disk size, the available memory and CPU resources, the network, and the components that link them all limit the system's ultimate capacity. Thus, you need to choose your hardware carefully and configure the hardware and operating system appropriately. For example, if your workload is I/O bound, one approach is to design your application to minimize MySQL's I/O workload. However, it's often smarter to upgrade the I/O subsystem, install more memory, or reconfigure existing disks. If you're running in a cloud-hosted environment, the information in this chapter can still be very useful, especially for understanding filesystem limitations and Linux I/O schedulers.

## What Limits MySQL's Performance?

Many different hardware components can affect MySQL's performance, but the most frequent bottleneck we see is CPU exhaustion. CPU saturation can happen when MySQL tries to execute too many queries in parallel or when a smaller number of queries runs for too long on the CPU.

I/O saturation can still happen but much less frequently than CPU exhaustion. This is largely because of the transition to using solid-state drives (SSDs). Historically, the performance penalty of no longer working in memory and going to the hard disk drive (HDD) was extreme. SSDs are generally 10 to 20 times faster than SSH. Nowadays, if queries need to hit disk, you're still going to see decent performance from them.

Memory exhaustion can still happen but usually only when you try to allocate too much memory to MySQL. We talk about optimal configuration settings to prevent this in "Configuring Memory Usage" on page 109 in Chapter 5.

# How to Select CPUs for MySQL

You should consider whether your workload is CPU bound when upgrading current hardware or purchasing new hardware. You can identify a CPU-bound workload by checking the CPU utilization, but instead of looking only at how heavily your CPUs are loaded overall, look at the balance of CPU usage and I/O for your most important queries, and notice whether the CPUs are loaded evenly.

Broadly speaking, you have two goals for your server:

*Low latency (fast response time)*
> To achieve this, you need fast CPUs because each query will use only a single CPU.

*High throughput*
> If you can run many queries at the same time, you might benefit from multiple CPUs to service the queries.

If your workload doesn't utilize all of your CPUs, MySQL can still use the extra CPUs for background tasks such as purging InnoDB buffers, network operations, and so on. However, these jobs are usually minor compared to executing queries.

# Balancing Memory and Disk Resources

The main reason to have a lot of memory isn't so you can hold a lot of data in memory: it's ultimately so you can avoid disk I/O, which is orders of magnitude slower than accessing data in memory. The trick is to balance the memory and disk size, speed, cost, and other qualities so you get good performance for your workload.

## Caching, Reads, and Writes

If you have enough memory, you can insulate the disk from read requests completely. If all your data fits in memory, every read will be a cache hit once the server's caches are warmed up. There will still be logical reads from memory but no physical reads from disk. Writes are a different matter, though. A write can be performed in memory just as a read can, but sooner or later it has to be written to the disk so it's permanent. In other words, a cache can delay writes, but caching cannot eliminate writes as it can for reads.

In fact, in addition to allowing writes to be delayed, caching can permit them to be grouped together in two important ways:

*Many writes, one flush*

A single piece of data can be changed many times in memory without all of the new values being written to disk. When the data is eventually flushed to disk, all the modifications that happened since the last physical write are permanent. For example, many statements could update an in-memory counter. If the counter is incremented one hundred times and then written to disk, one hundred modifications have been grouped into one write.

*I/O merging*

Many different pieces of data can be modified in memory, and the modifications can be collected together, so the physical writes can be performed as a single disk operation.

This is why many transactional systems use a write-ahead logging strategy. Write-ahead logging lets them make changes to the pages in memory without flushing the changes to disk, which usually involves random I/O and is very slow. Instead, they write a record of the changes to a sequential logfile, which is much faster. A background thread can flush the modified pages to disk later; when it does, it can optimize the writes.

Writes benefit greatly from buffering because it converts random I/O into more sequential I/O. Asynchronous (buffered) writes are typically handled by the operating system and are batched so they can be flushed to disk more optimally. Synchronous (unbuffered) writes have to be written to disk before they finish. That's why they benefit from buffering in a Redundant Array of Inexpensive Disks (RAID) controller's battery-backed write-back cache (we discuss RAID a bit later).

## What's Your Working Set?

Every application has a "working set" of data—that is, the data that it really needs to do its work. A lot of databases also have plenty of data that is not in the working set. You can imagine the database as a desk with filing drawers. The working set consists of the papers you need to have on the desktop to get your work done. The desktop represents main memory in this analogy, while the filing drawers are the hard disks. Just as you don't need to have *every* piece of paper on the desktop to get your work done, you don't need the whole database to fit in memory for optimal performance— just the working set.

When dealing with HDDs, it was good practice to try to find an effective memory-to-disk ratio. This was largely due to the slower latency and low input/output operations per second (IOPS) of HDDs. With SSDs, the memory-to-disk ratio becomes far less important.

# Solid-State Storage

Solid-state (flash) storage is the standard for most database systems, especially online transaction processing (OLTP). Only on very large data warehouses or legacy systems would you typically find HDDs. This shift came as the price of SSDs dropped significantly around 2015.

Solid-state storage devices use nonvolatile flash memory chips composed of cells instead of magnetic platters. They're also called *nonvolatile random access memory (NVRAM)*. They have no moving parts, which makes them behave very differently than hard drives.

Here's a quick summary of flash performance. High-quality flash devices have:

*Much better random read and write performance compared to hard drives*
Flash devices are usually slightly better at reads than writes.

*Better sequential read and write performance than hard drives*
However, it's not as dramatic an improvement as that of random I/O because hard drives are much slower at random I/O than they are at sequential I/O.

*Much better support for concurrency than hard drives*
Flash devices can support many more concurrent operations, and in fact, they don't really achieve their top throughput until you have lots of concurrency.

The most important things are improvements in random I/O and concurrency. Flash memory gives you very good random I/O performance at high concurrency.

## An Overview of Flash Memory

Hard drives with spinning platters and oscillating heads had inherent limitations and characteristics that are consequences of the physics involved. The same is true of solid-state storage, which is built on top of flash memory. Don't get the idea that solid-state storage is simple. It's actually more complex than a hard drive in some ways. The limitations of flash memory are pretty severe and hard to overcome, so the typical solid-state device has an intricate architecture with lots of abstractions, caching, and proprietary "magic."

The most important characteristic of flash memory is that it can be read many times rapidly and in small units, but writes are much more challenging. A cell can't be rewritten without a special erase operation and can only be erased in large blocks—for example, 512 KB. The erase cycle is slow and eventually wears out the block. The number of erase cycles a block can tolerate depends on the underlying technology it uses—more about this later.

The limitations on writes are the reason for the complexity of solid-state storage. This is why some devices provide stable, consistent performance and others don't. The magic is all in the proprietary firmware, drivers, and other bits and pieces that make a solid-state device run. To make write operations perform well and avoid wearing out the blocks of flash memory prematurely, the device must be able to relocate pages and perform garbage collection and so-called *wear leveling*. The term *write amplification* is used to describe the additional writes caused by moving data from place to place, writing data and metadata multiple times due to partial block writes.

## Garbage Collection

Garbage collection is important to understand. To keep some blocks fresh and ready for new writes, the device reclaims blocks. This requires some free space on the device. Either the device will have some reserved space internally that you can't see or you will need to reserve space yourself by not filling it up all the way; this varies from device to device. Either way, as the device fills up, the garbage collector has to work harder to keep some blocks clean, so the write amplification factor increases.

As a result, many devices get slower as they fill up. How much slower is different for every vendor and model and depends on the device's architecture. Some devices are designed for high performance even when they are pretty full, but in general, a 100 GB file will perform differently on a 160 GB SSD than on a 320 GB SSD. The slow-down is caused by having to wait for erases to complete when there are no free blocks. A write to a free block takes a couple of hundred microseconds, but an erase is much slower—typically a few milliseconds.

# RAID Performance Optimization

Storage engines often keep their data and/or indexes in single large files, which means RAID is usually the most feasible option for storing a lot of data. RAID can help with redundancy, storage size, caching, and speed. But as with the other optimizations we've been looking at, there are many variations on RAID configurations, and it's important to choose one that's appropriate for your needs.

We won't cover every RAID level here, or go into the specifics of exactly how the different RAID levels store data. Instead, we focus on how RAID configurations satisfy a database server's needs. These are the most important RAID levels:

*RAID 0*

RAID 0 is the cheapest and highest-performance RAID configuration, at least when you measure cost and performance simplistically (if you include data recovery, for example, it starts to look more expensive). Because it offers no redundancy, we do not think RAID 0 is ever appropriate on a production database, but if you were truly looking to save costs, it can be a choice in development environments where a full server failure does not turn into an incident.

Again, note that *RAID 0 does not provide any redundancy*, even though "redundant" is the R in the RAID acronym. In fact, the probability of a RAID 0 array failing is actually *higher* than the probability of any single disk failing, not lower!

*RAID 1*

RAID 1 offers good read performance for many scenarios, and it duplicates your data across disks, so there's good redundancy. RAID 1 is a little bit faster than RAID 0 for reads. It's good for servers that handle logging and similar workloads because sequential writes rarely need many underlying disks to perform well (as opposed to random writes, which can benefit from parallelization). It is also a typical choice for low-end servers that need redundancy but have only two hard drives.

RAID 0 and RAID 1 are very simple, and they can often be implemented well in software. Most operating systems will let you create software RAID 0 and RAID 1 volumes easily.

*RAID 5*

RAID 5 used to be quite scary for database systems, largely due to the performance implications. With SSDs becoming commonplace, it's now a viable option. It spreads the data across many disks with distributed parity blocks so that if any one disk fails, the data can be rebuilt from the parity blocks. If two disks fail, the entire volume will fail unrecoverably. In terms of cost per unit of storage, it's the most economical redundant configuration because you lose only one disk's worth of storage space across the entire array.

The biggest "gotcha" with RAID 5 is how the array performs if a disk fails. This is because the data has to be reconstructed by reading all the other disks. This affected performance severely on HDD, which is why it was generally discouraged. It was even worse if you had lots of disks. If you try to keep the server online during the rebuild, don't expect either the rebuild or the array's performance to be good. Other performance costs included limited scalability because of the parity blocks—RAID 5 doesn't scale well past 10 disks or so—and caching issues. Good RAID 5 performance depends heavily on the RAID controller's cache, which can conflict with the database server's needs. As we mentioned earlier, SSDs offer substantially improved performance in terms of IOPS and throughput, and the issues of poorly performing random read/write performance are also gone.

One of the mitigating factors for RAID 5 is that it's so popular. As a result, RAID controllers are often highly optimized for RAID 5, and despite the theoretical limits, smart controllers that use caches well can sometimes perform nearly as well as RAID 10 controllers for some workloads. This might actually reflect that the RAID 10 controllers are less highly optimized, but regardless of the reason, this is what we've seen.

*RAID 6*

The largest issue with RAID 5 was that the loss of two disks was catastrophic. The more disks you have in your array, the higher the probability of disk failure. RAID 6 helps to curb the failure possibility by adding a second parity disk. This allows you to sustain two disk failures and still rebuild the array. The downside is that calculating the additional parity will make writes slower than RAID 5.

*RAID 10*

RAID 10 is a very good choice for data storage. It consists of mirrored pairs that are striped, so it scales both reads and writes well. It is fast and easy to rebuild, in comparison to RAID 5. It can also be implemented in software fairly well.

The performance loss when one hard drive goes out can still be significant because that stripe can become a bottleneck. Performance can degrade by up to 50%, depending on the workload. One thing to watch out for is RAID controllers that use a "concatenated mirror" implementation for RAID 10. This is suboptimal because of the absence of striping: your most frequently accessed data might be placed on only one pair of disks instead of being spread across many, so you'll get poor performance.

*RAID 50*

RAID 50 consists of RAID 5 arrays that are striped, and it can be a good compromise between the economy of RAID 5 and the performance of RAID 10 if you have many disks. This is mainly useful for very large data sets, such as data warehouses or extremely large OLTP systems.

Table 4-1 summarizes the various RAID configurations.

*Table 4-1. Comparison of RAID levels*

| Level | Synopsis | Redundancy | Disks required | Faster reads | Faster writes |
|---|---|---|---|---|---|
| RAID 0 | Cheap, fast, dangerous | No | N | Yes | Yes |
| RAID 1 | Fast reads, simple, safe | Yes | 2 (usually) | Yes | No |
| RAID 5 | Cheap, fast with SSDs | Yes | N + 1 | Yes | Depends |
| RAID 6 | Like RAID 5 but more resilient | Yes | N + 2 | Yes | Depends |
| RAID 10 | Expensive, fast, safe | Yes | 2N | Yes | Yes |
| RAID 50 | For very large data stores | Yes | 2(N + 1) | Yes | Yes |

# RAID Failure, Recovery, and Monitoring

RAID configurations (with the exception of RAID 0) offer redundancy. This is important, but it's easy to underestimate the likelihood of concurrent disk failures. You shouldn't think of RAID as a strong guarantee of data safety.

RAID doesn't eliminate—or even reduce—the need for backups. When there is a problem, the recovery time will depend on your controller, the RAID level, the array size, the disk speed, and whether you need to keep the server online while you rebuild the array.

There is a chance of disks failing at exactly the same time. For example, a power spike or overheating can easily kill two or more disks. What's more common, however, is two disk failures happening close together. Many such issues can go unnoticed. A common cause is corruption on the physical media holding data that is seldom accessed. This might go undetected for months, until either you try to read the data or another drive fails and the RAID controller tries to use the corrupted data to rebuild the array. The larger the hard drive is, the more likely this is.

That's why it's important to monitor your RAID arrays. Most controllers offer some software to report on the array's status, and you need to keep track of this because you might otherwise be totally ignorant of a drive failure. You might miss your opportunity to recover the data and discover the problem only when a second drive fails, and then it's too late. You should configure a monitoring system to alert you when a drive or volume changes to a degraded or failed status.

You can mitigate the risk of latent corruption by actively checking your arrays for consistency at regular intervals. Background Patrol Read, a feature of some controllers that checks for damaged media and fixes it while all the drives are online, can also help avert such problems. As with recovery, extremely large arrays can be slow to check, so make sure you plan accordingly when you create large arrays.

You can also add a hot spare drive, which is unused and configured as a standby for the controller to automatically use for recovery. This is a good idea if you depend on every server. It's expensive with servers that have only a few hard drives because the cost of having an idle disk is proportionately higher, but if you have many disks, it's almost foolish not to have a hot spare. Remember that the probability of a drive failure increases rapidly with more disks.

In addition to monitoring your drives for failures, you should monitor the RAID controller's battery backup unit and write cache policy. If the battery fails, by default most controllers will disable write caching by changing the cache policy to write-through instead of write-back. This can cause a severe drop in performance. Many controllers will also periodically cycle the battery through a learning process, during which time the cache is also disabled. Your RAID controller's management utility should let you view and configure when the learning cycle is scheduled so that it doesn't catch you off guard. Newer RAID controllers avoid this by using a flash-backed cache that uses NVRAM to store uncommitted writes instead of a battery-backed cache. This avoids the entire pain of the learning cycle.

You might also want to benchmark your system with the cache policy set to write-through so you'll know what to expect. The preferred approach is to schedule your battery learning cycles at low traffic periods, typically at night or during the weekend. If performance suffers badly enough with write-through at any time, you could also failover to another server before your learning cycle begins. As a very last resort, you could reconfigure your servers by changing the `innodb_flush_log_at_trx_commit` and `sync_binlog` variables to lower durability settings. This will reduce the disk utilization during write-through and may offer acceptable performance; however, this should really be done as a last resort. Reducing durability has a big impact on how much data you may lose during a database crash and your ability to recover it.

## RAID Configuration and Caching

You can usually configure the RAID controller itself by entering its setup utility during the machine's boot sequence or by running it from the command prompt. Although most controllers offer a lot of options, the two we focus on are the *chunk size* for striped arrays and the *on-controller cache* (also known as the *RAID cache*; we use the terms interchangeably).

### The RAID stripe chunk size

The optimal stripe chunk size is workload and hardware specific. In theory, it's good to have a large chunk size for random I/O because that means more reads can be satisfied from a single drive.

To see why this is so, consider the size of a typical random I/O operation for your workload. If the chunk size is at least that large and the data doesn't span the border between chunks, only a single drive needs to participate in the read. But if the chunk size is smaller than the amount of data to be read, there's no way to avoid involving more than one drive in the read.

So much for theory. In practice, many RAID controllers don't work well with large chunks. For example, the controller might use the chunk size as the cache unit in its cache, which could be wasteful. The controller might also match the chunk size, cache size, and read-unit size (the amount of data it reads in a single operation). If the read unit is too large, its cache might be less effective, and it might end up reading a lot more data than it really needs, even for tiny requests.

It's also hard to know whether any given piece of data will span multiple drives. Even if the chunk size is 16 KB, which matches InnoDB's page size, you can't be certain all of the reads will be aligned on 16 KB boundaries. The filesystem might fragment the file, and it will typically align the fragments on the filesystem block size, which is often 4 KB. Some filesystems might be smarter, but you shouldn't count on it.

## The RAID cache

The RAID cache is a (relatively) small amount of memory that is physically installed on a hardware RAID controller. It can be used to buffer data as it travels between the disks and the host system. Here are some of the reasons a RAID card might use the cache:

*Caching reads*

> After the controller reads some data from the disks and sends it to the host system, it can store the data; this will enable it to satisfy future requests for the same data without having to go to disk again.

> This is usually a very poor use of the RAID cache. Why? Because the operating system and the database server have their own much larger caches. If there's a cache hit in one of these caches, the data in the RAID cache won't be used. Conversely, if there's a miss in one of the higher-level caches, the chance that there'll be a hit in the RAID cache is vanishingly small. Because the RAID cache is so much smaller, it will almost certainly have been flushed and filled with other data, too. Either way you look at it, it's a waste of memory to cache reads in the RAID cache.

*Caching read-ahead data*

> If the RAID controller notices sequential requests for data, it might decide to do a read-ahead read—that is, to prefetch data it predicts will be needed soon. It has to have somewhere to put the data until it's requested, though. It can use the RAID cache for this. The performance impact of this can vary widely, and you should check to ensure it's actually helping. Read-ahead operations might not help if the database server is doing its own smart read-ahead (as InnoDB does), and it might interfere with the all-important buffering of synchronous writes.

*Caching writes*

> The RAID controller can buffer writes in its cache and schedule them for a later time. The advantage to doing this is twofold: first, it can return "success" to the host system much more quickly than it would be able to if it had to actually perform the writes on the physical disks, and second, it can accumulate writes and do them more efficiently.

*Internal operations*

> Some RAID operations are very complex—especially RAID 5 writes, which have to calculate parity bits that can be used to rebuild data in the event of a failure. The controller needs to use some memory for this type of internal operation. This is one reason why RAID 5 can perform poorly on some controllers: it needs to read a lot of data into the cache for good performance. Some controllers can't balance caching writes with caching for the RAID 5 parity operations.

In general, the RAID controller's memory is a scarce resource that you should try to use wisely. Using it for reads is usually a waste, but using it for writes is an important way to speed up your I/O performance. Many controllers let you choose how to allocate the memory. For example, you can choose how much of it to use for caching writes and how much for reads. For RAID 0, RAID 1, and RAID 10, you should probably allocate 100% of the controller's memory for caching writes. For RAID 5, you should reserve some of the controller's memory for its internal operations. This is generally good advice, but it doesn't always apply—different RAID cards require different configurations.

When you're using the RAID cache for write caching, many controllers let you configure how long it's acceptable to delay the writes (one second, five seconds, and so on). A longer delay means more writes can be grouped together and flushed to the disks optimally. The downside is that your writes will be more "bursty." That's not a bad thing, unless your application happens to make a bunch of write requests just as the controller's cache fills up, when it's about to be flushed to disk. If there's not enough room for your application's write requests, it'll have to wait. Keeping the delay shorter means you'll have more write operations and they'll be less efficient, but it smooths out the spikiness and helps keep more of the cache free to handle bursts from the application. (We're simplifying here—controllers often have complex, vendor-specific balancing algorithms, so we're just trying to cover the basic principles.)

The write cache is very helpful for synchronous writes, such as issuing `fsync()` calls on the transaction logs and creating binary logs with `sync_binlog` enabled, but you shouldn't enable it unless your controller has a battery backup unit (BBU) or other nonvolatile storage. Caching writes without a BBU is likely to corrupt your database, and even your transactional filesystem, in the event of power loss. If you have a BBU, however, enabling the write cache can increase performance by a factor of 20 or more for workloads that do a lot of log flushes, such as flushing the transaction log when a transaction commits.

A final consideration is that many hard drives have write caches of their own, which can "fake" `fsync()` operations by lying to the controller that the data has been written to physical media. Hard drives that are attached directly (as opposed to being attached to a RAID controller) can sometimes let their caches be managed by the operating system, but this doesn't always work either. These caches are typically flushed for an `fsync()` and bypassed for synchronous I/O, but again, the hard drive can lie. You should either ensure that these caches are flushed on `fsync()` or disable them because they are not battery-backed. Hard drives that aren't managed properly by the operating system or RAID firmware have caused many instances of data loss.

For this and other reasons, it's always a good idea to do genuine crash testing (literally pulling the power plug out of the wall) when you install new hardware. This is often the only way to find subtle misconfigurations or sneaky hard drive behaviors. A handy script for this can be found online (*https://oreil.ly/2Lume*).

To test whether you can really rely on your RAID controller's BBU, make sure you leave the power cord unplugged for a realistic amount of time. Some units don't last as long without power as they're supposed to. Here again, one bad link can render your whole chain of storage components useless.

## Network Configuration

Just as latency and throughput are limiting factors for a hard drive, latency and bandwidth are limiting factors for a network connection. The biggest problem for most applications is latency; a typical application does a lot of small network transfers, and the slight delay for each transfer adds up.

A network that's not operating correctly is a major performance bottleneck, too. Packet loss is a common problem. Even 1% loss is enough to cause significant performance degradation because various layers in the protocol stack will try to fix the problems with strategies such as waiting a while and then resending packets, which adds extra time. Another common problem is broken or slow DNS resolution.[1]

DNS is enough of an Achilles' heel that enabling `skip_name_resolve` is a good idea for production servers. Broken or slow DNS resolution is a problem for lots of applications, but it's particularly severe for MySQL. When MySQL receives a connection request, it does both a forward and a reverse DNS lookup. There are lots of reasons this could go wrong. When it does, it will cause connections to be denied, slow down the process of connecting to the server, and generally wreak havoc, up to and including denial-of-service attacks. If you enable the `skip_name_resolve` option, MySQL won't do any DNS lookups at all. However, this also means that your user accounts must have only IP addresses, "localhost," or IP address wildcards in the host column. Any user account that has a hostname in the host column will not be able to log in.

It's usually more important, though, to adjust your settings to deal efficiently with a lot of connections and small queries. One of the more common tweaks is to change your local port range. Linux systems have a range of local ports that can be used. When the connection is made back to a caller, it uses a local port. If you have many simultaneous connections, you can run out of local ports.

Here's a system that is configured to default values:

```
$ cat /proc/sys/net/ipv4/ip_local_port_range
32768 61000
```

---

1 Popular haiku: It's not DNS. There's no way it's DNS. It was DNS.

---

Sometimes you might need to change these values to a larger range. For example:

```
$ echo 1024 65535 > /proc/sys/net/ipv4/ip_local_port_range
```

The TCP protocol allows a system to queue up incoming connections, like a bucket. If the bucket fills up, clients won't be able to connect. You can allow more connections to queue up as follows:

```
$ echo 4096 > /proc/sys/net/ipv4/tcp_max_syn_backlog
```

For database servers that are used only locally, you can shorten the timeout that comes after closing a socket in the event that the peer is broken and doesn't close its side of the connection. The default is one minute on most systems, which is rather long:

```
$ echo <value> > /proc/sys/net/ipv4/tcp_fin_timeout
```

Most of the time, these settings can be left at their defaults. You'll typically need to change them only when something unusual is happening, such as extremely poor network performance or very large numbers of connections. An Internet search for "TCP variables" will turn up lots of good reading about these and many more variables.

# Choosing a Filesystem

Your filesystem choices are pretty dependent on your operating system. In many systems, such as Windows, you really have only one or two choices, and only one (NTFS) is really viable. GNU/Linux, on the other hand, supports many filesystems.

Many people want to know which filesystems will give the best performance for MySQL on GNU/Linux or, even more specifically, which of the choices is best for InnoDB. The benchmarks actually show that most of them are very close in most respects, but looking to the filesystem for performance is really a distraction. The filesystem's performance is very workload specific, and no filesystem is a magic bullet. Most of the time, a given filesystem won't perform significantly better or worse than any other filesystem. The exception is if you run into some filesystem limit, such as how it deals with concurrency, working with many files, fragmentation, and so on.

Overall, you're best off using a journaling filesystem, such as ext4, XFS, or ZFS. If you don't, a filesystem check after a crash can take a long time.

If you use ext3 or its successor, ext4, you have three options for how the data is journaled, which you can place in the /etc/fstab mount options:

data=writeback

>   This option means only metadata writes are journaled. Writes to the metadata are not synchronized with the data writes. This is the fastest configuration, and it's *usually* safe to use with InnoDB because it has its own transaction log. The

exception is that a crash at just the right time could cause corruption in a *.frm* file on a pre-8.0 version of MySQL.

Here's an example of how this configuration could cause problems. Say a program decides to extend a file to make it larger. The metadata (the file's size) will be logged and written before the data is actually written to the (now larger) file. The result is that the file's tail—the newly extended area—contains garbage.

data=ordered

This option also journals only the metadata, but it provides some consistency by writing the data before the metadata so it stays consistent. It's only slightly slower than the writeback option, and it's much safer when there's a crash. In this configuration, if we suppose again that a program wants to extend a file, the file's metadata won't reflect the file's new size until the data that resides in the newly extended area has been written.

data=journal

This option provides atomic journaled behavior, writing the data to the journal before it's written to the final location. It is usually unnecessary and has much higher overhead than the other two options. However, in some cases it can improve performance because the journaling lets the filesystem delay the writes to the data's final location.

Regardless of the filesystem, there are some specific options that it's best to disable because they don't provide any benefit and can add quite a bit of overhead. The most famous is recording access time, which requires a write even when you're reading a file or directory. To disable this option, add the noatime,nodiratime mount options to your */etc/fstab*; this can sometimes boost performance by as much as 5%–10%, depending on the workload and the filesystem (although it might not make much difference in other cases). Here's a sample */etc/fstab* line for the ext3 options we mentioned:

```
/dev/sda2 /usr/lib/mysql ext3 noatime,nodiratime,data=writeback 0 1
```

You can also tune the filesystem's read-ahead behavior because it might be redundant. For example, InnoDB does its own read-ahead prediction. Disabling or limiting read-ahead is especially beneficial on Solaris's UFS. Using innodb_ flush_ method= O_DIRECT automatically disables read-ahead.

Some filesystems don't support features you might need. For example, support for direct I/O might be important if you're using the O_DIRECT flush method for InnoDB. Also, some filesystems handle a large number of underlying drives better than others; XFS is often much better at this than ext3, for instance. Finally, if you plan to use Logical Volume Manager (LVM) snapshots for initializing replicas or taking backups, you should verify that your chosen filesystem and LVM version work well together.

Table 4-2 summarizes the characteristics of some common filesystems.

*Table 4-2. Common filesystem characteristics*

| Filesystem | Operating system | Journaling | Large directories |
|---|---|---|---|
| ext3 | GNU/Linux | Optional | Optional/partial |
| ext4 | GNU/Linux | Yes | Yes |
| Journaled File System (JFS) | GNU/Linux | Yes | No |
| NTFS | Windows | Yes | Yes |
| ReiserFS | GNU/Linux | Yes | Yes |
| UFS (Solaris) | Solaris | Yes | Tunable |
| UFS (FreeBSD) | FreeBSD | No | Optional/partial |
| UFS2 | FreeBSD | No | Optional/partial |
| XFS | GNU/Linux | Yes | Yes |
| ZFS | GNU/Linux, Solaris, FreeBSD | Yes | Yes |

We usually recommend using the XFS filesystem. The ext3 filesystem just has too many serious limitations, such as its single mutex per inode, and bad behavior, such as flushing all dirty blocks in the whole filesystem on fsync() instead of just one file's dirty blocks. The ext4 filesystem is an acceptable choice, although there have been performance bottlenecks in specific kernel versions that you should investigate before committing to it.

When considering any filesystem for a database, it's good to consider how long it has been available, how mature it is, and how proven it has been in production environments. The filesystem bits are the very lowest level of data integrity you have in a database.

## Choosing a Disk Queue Scheduler

On GNU/Linux, the queue scheduler determines the order in which requests to a block device are actually sent to the underlying device. The default is Completely Fair Queuing, or cfq. It's okay for casual use on laptops and desktops, where it helps *prevent* I/O starvation, but it's terrible for servers. It causes very poor response times under the types of workload that MySQL generates because it stalls some requests in the queue needlessly.

You can see which schedulers are available and which one is active with the following command:

```
$ cat /sys/block/sda/queue/scheduler
noop deadline [cfq]
```

You should replace *sda* with the device name of the disk you're interested in. In our example, the square brackets indicate which scheduler is in use for this device. The other two choices are suitable for server-class hardware, and in most cases they work about equally well. The `noop` scheduler is appropriate for devices that do their own scheduling behind the scenes, such as hardware RAID controllers and storage area networks (SANs), and `deadline` is fine for both RAID controllers and disks that are directly attached. Our benchmarks show very little difference between these two. The main thing is to use anything but `cfq`, which can cause severe performance problems.

## Memory and Swapping

MySQL performs best with a large amount of memory allocated to it. As we learned in Chapter 1, InnoDB uses memory as a cache to avoid disk access. This means that the performance of the memory system can have a direct impact on how fast queries are served. Even today, one of the best ways to ensure faster memory access has been to replace the built-in memory allocator (`glibc`) with an external one such as `tcmalloc` or `jemalloc`. Numerous benchmarks[2] have shown that both of these offer improved performance and reduced memory fragmentation when compared with `glibc`.

Swapping occurs when the operating system writes some virtual memory to disk because it doesn't have enough physical memory to hold it. Swapping is transparent to processes running on the operating system. Only the operating system knows whether a particular virtual memory address is in physical memory or on disk.

When using SSDs, the performance penalty isn't nearly as sharp as it used to be with HDDs. You should still actively avoid swapping—even if just to avoid unnecessary writes that may shorten the overall life span of the disk. You may also consider taking the approach of using no swap, which forgoes the potential altogether but does put you in a situation where running out of memory may lead to process termination.

On GNU/Linux, you can monitor swapping with *vmstat* (we show some examples in the next section). You need to look at the swap I/O activity, reported in the `si` and `so` columns, rather than the swap usage, which is reported in the `swpd` column. The `swpd` column can show processes that have been loaded but aren't being used, which are not really problematic. We like the `si` and `so` column values to be 0, and they should definitely be less than 10 blocks per second.

In extreme cases, too much memory allocation can cause the operating system to run out of swap space. If this happens, the resulting lack of virtual memory can crash MySQL. But even if it doesn't run out of swap space, very active swapping can cause the entire operating system to become unresponsive, to the point that you can't even log in and kill the MySQL process. Sometimes the Linux kernel can even hang

---

2 See the blog posts "Impact of Memory Allocators on MySQL Performance" (*https://oreil.ly/AAJHX*) and "MySQL (or Percona) Memory Usage Tests" (*https://oreil.ly/slp7v*) for comparisons.

completely when it runs out of swap space. We recommend you run your databases without using swap space at all. Disk is still an order of magnitude slower than RAM, and this avoids all of the headaches mentioned here.

Another thing that frequently happens under extreme virtual memory pressure is that the out-of-memory (OOM) killer process will kick in and kill something. This is frequently MySQL, but it can also be another process such as SSH, which can leave you with a system that's not accessible from the network. You can prevent this by setting the SSH process's `oom_adj` or `oom_score_adj` value. When working with dedicated database servers, we highly recommend that you identify any key processes like MySQL and SSH and proactively adjust the OOM killer score to prevent those from being selected first for termination.

You can solve most swapping problems by configuring your MySQL buffers correctly, but sometimes the operating system's virtual memory system decides to swap MySQL anyway, sometimes related to how nonuniform memory access (NUMA) works[3] in Linux. This usually happens when the operating system sees a lot of I/O from MySQL, so it tries to increase the file cache to hold more data. If there's not enough memory, something must be swapped out, and that something might be MySQL itself. Some older Linux kernel versions also have counterproductive priorities that swap things when they shouldn't, but this has been alleviated a bit in more recent kernels.

Operating systems usually allow some control over virtual memory and I/O. We mention a few ways to control them on GNU/Linux. The most basic is to change the value of */proc/sys/vm/swappiness* to a low value, such as 0 or 1. This tells the kernel not to swap unless the need for virtual memory is extreme. For example, here's how to check the current value:

```
$ cat /proc/sys/vm/swappiness
60
```

The value shown, 60, is the default swappiness setting (the range is from 0 to 100). This is a very bad default for servers. It's only appropriate for laptops. Servers should be set to 0:

```
$ echo 0 > /proc/sys/vm/swappiness
```

Another option is to change how the storage engines read and write data. For example, using `innodb_flush_method=O_DIRECT` relieves I/O pressure. Direct I/O is not cached, so the operating system doesn't see it as a reason to increase the size of the file cache. This parameter works only for InnoDB.

---

3 See this blog post (*https://oreil.ly/VGW65*) for more.

Another option is to use MySQL's `memlock` configuration option, which locks MySQL in memory. This will avoid swapping, but it can be dangerous: if there's not enough lockable memory left, MySQL can crash when it tries to allocate more memory. Problems can also be caused if too much memory is locked and there's not enough left for the operating system.

Many of the tricks are specific to a kernel version, so be careful, especially when you upgrade. In some workloads, it's hard to make the operating system behave sensibly, and your only recourse might be to lower the buffer sizes to suboptimal values.

## Operating System Status

Your operating system provides tools to help you find out what the operating system and hardware are doing. In this section, we'll show you examples of how to use two widely available tools, *iostat* and *vmstat*. If your system doesn't provide either of these tools, chances are it will provide something similar. Thus, our goal isn't to make you an expert at using *iostat* or *vmstat* but simply to show you what to look for when you're trying to diagnose problems with tools such as these.

In addition to these tools, your operating system might provide others, such as *mpstat* or *sar*. If you're interested in other parts of your system, such as the network, you might want to use tools such as *ifconfig* (which shows how many network errors have occurred, among other things) or *netstat* instead.

By default, *vmstat* and *iostat* produce just one report showing the average values of various counters since the server was started, which is not very useful. However, you can give both tools an interval argument. This makes them generate incremental reports showing what the server is doing right now, which is much more relevant. (The first line shows the statistics since the system was started; you can just ignore this line.)

### How to read vmstat output

Let's look at an example of *vmstat* first. To make it print out a new report every five seconds, reporting sizes in megabytes, use the following command:

```
$ vmstat -SM 5
procs -------memory------- -swap- -----io---- ---system---- ------cpu-----
 r  b swpd free buff cache  si so    bi    bo      in     cs us sy id wa st
11  0    0 2410    4 57223   0  0  9902 35594 122585 150834 10  3 85  1  0
10  2    0 2361    4 57273   0  0 23998 35391 124187 149530 11  3 84  2  0
```

You can stop *vmstat* with Ctrl-C. The output you see depends on your operating system, so you might need to read the manual page to figure it out.

As stated earlier, even though we asked for incremental output, the first line of values shows the averages since the server was booted. The second line shows what's happening right now, and subsequent lines will show what's happening at five-second intervals. The columns are grouped by one of the following headers:

*procs*

> The r column shows how many processes are waiting for CPU time. The b column shows how many are in uninterruptible sleep, which generally means they're waiting for I/O (disk, network, user input, and so on).

*memory*

> The swpd column shows how many blocks are swapped out to disk (paged). The remaining three columns show how many blocks are free (unused), how many are being used for buffers (buff), and how many are being used for the operating system's cache.

*swap*

> These columns show swap activity: how many blocks per second the operating system is swapping in (from disk) and out (to disk). They are much more important to monitor than the swpd column. We like to see si and so at 0 most of the time, and we definitely don't like to see more than 10 blocks per second. Bursts are also bad.

*io*

> These columns show how many blocks per second are read in from (bi) and written out to (bo) block devices. This usually reflects disk I/O.

*system*

> These columns show the number of interrupts per second (in) and the number of context switches per second (cs).

*cpu*

> These columns show the percentages of total CPU time spent running user (non-kernel) code, running system (kernel) code, idle, and waiting for I/O. A possible fifth column (st) shows the percent "stolen" from a virtual machine if you're using virtualization. This refers to the time during which something was runnable on the virtual machine, but the hypervisor chose to run something else instead. If the virtual machine doesn't want to run anything and the hypervisor runs something else, that doesn't count as stolen time.

The *vmstat* output is system dependent, so you should read your system's vmstat(8) manpage if yours looks different from the sample we've shown.

## How to read iostat output

Now let's move on to *iostat*. By default, it shows some of the same CPU usage information as *vmstat*. We're usually interested in just the I/O statistics, though, so we use the following command to show only extended device statistics:

```
$ iostat -dxk 5
Device: rrqm/s wrqm/s r/s w/s rkB/s wkB/s
sda 0.00 0.00 1060.40 3915.00 8483.20 42395.20

avgrq-sz avgqu-sz await r_await w_await svctm %util
 20.45 3.68 0.74 0.57 0.78 0.20 98.22
```

As with *vmstat*, the first report shows averages since the server was booted (we generally omit it to save space), and the subsequent reports show incremental averages. There's one line per device.

There are various options that show or hide columns. The official documentation is a bit confusing, and we had to dig into the source code to figure out what was really being shown. Here's what each column is showing:

rrqm/s *and* wrqm/s
> The number of merged read and write requests queued per second. *Merged* means the operating system took multiple logical requests from the queue and grouped them into a single request to the actual device.

r/s *and* w/s
> The number of read and write requests sent to the device per second.

rkB/s *and* wkB/s
> The number of kilobytes read and written per second.

avgrq-sz
> The request size in sectors.

avgqu-sz
> The number of requests waiting in the device's queue.

await
> The number of milliseconds spent in the disk queue.

r_await *and* w_await
> The average time in milliseconds for read requests issued to the device to be served, for both reads and writes, respectively. This includes the time spent by the requests in queue and the time spent servicing them.

svctm
> The number of milliseconds spent servicing requests, excluding queue time.

`%util`[4]

The percentage of time during which at least one request was active. This is very confusingly named. It is *not* the device's utilization, if you're familiar with the standard definition of *utilization* in queuing theory. A device with more than one hard drive (such as a RAID controller) should be able to support a higher concurrency than 1, but `%util` will never exceed 100% unless there's a rounding error in the math used to compute it. As a result, it is *not* a good indication of device saturation, contrary to what the documentation says, except in the special case where you're looking at a single physical hard drive.

You can use the output to deduce some facts about a machine's I/O subsystem. One important metric is the number of requests served concurrently. Because the reads and writes are per second and the service time's unit is thousandths of a second, you can use Little's law to derive the following formula for the number of concurrent requests the device is serving:

```
concurrency = (r/s + w/s) * (svctm/1000)
```

Plugging the preceding sample numbers into the concurrency formula gives a concurrency of about 0.995. This means that on average, the device was serving less than one request at a time during the sampling interval.

## Other Helpful Tools

We've shown *vmstat* and *iostat* because they're widely available, and *vmstat* is usually installed by default on many Unix-like operating systems. However, each of these tools has its limitations, such as confusing units of measurement, sampling at intervals that don't correspond to when the operating system updates the statistics, and the inability to see all of the metrics at once. If these tools don't meet your needs, you might be interested in *dstat* (*http://dag.wieers.com/home-made/dstat*) or *collectl* (*https://oreil.ly/DSvmM*).

We also like to use *mpstat* to watch CPU statistics; it provides a much better idea of how the CPUs are behaving individually, instead of grouping them all together. Sometimes this is very important when you're diagnosing a problem. You might find *blktrace* to be helpful when you're examining disk I/O usage, too.

Percona wrote its own replacement for *iostat* called *pt-diskstats*. It's part of Percona Toolkit. It addresses some of the complaints about *iostat*, such as the way it presents reads and writes in aggregate and the lack of visibility into concurrency. It is also interactive and keystroke driven, so you can zoom in and out, change the aggregation, filter out devices, and show and hide columns. It is a great way to slice and dice a

---

4 Software RAID, like MD/RAID, may not show utilization for the RAID array itself.

sample of disk statistics, which you can gather with a simple shell script even if you don't have the tool installed. You can capture samples of disk activity and email or save them for later analysis.

Lastly, *perf*, the Linux profiler, is an invaluable tool for inspecting what is going on at the operating system level. You can use *perf* to inspect general information about the operating system, such as why the kernel is using CPU so much. You can also inspect specific process IDs, allowing you to see how MySQL is interacting with the operating system. Inspecting system performance is a very deep dive, so we recommend *Systems Performance, Second Edition* by Brendan Gregg (Pearson) as excellent follow-up reading.

# Summary

Choosing and configuring hardware for MySQL, and configuring MySQL for the hardware, is not a mystical art. In general, you need the same skills and knowledge that you need for most other purposes. However, there are some MySQL-specific things you should know.

What we commonly suggest for most people is to find a good balance between performance and cost. First, we like to use commodity servers, for many reasons. For example, if you're having trouble with a server and you need to take it out of service while you try to diagnose it, or if you simply want to try swapping it with another server as a form of diagnosis, this is a lot easier to do with a $5,000 server than one that costs $50,000 or more. MySQL is also typically a better fit—both in terms of the software itself and in terms of the typical workloads it runs—for commodity hardware.

The four fundamental resources MySQL needs are CPU, memory, disk, and network resources. The network doesn't tend to show up as a serious bottleneck very often, but CPUs, memory, and disks certainly do. The balance of speed and quantity really depends on the workload, and you should strive for a balance of fast and many as your budget allows. The more concurrency you expect, the more you should lean on more CPUs to accommodate your workload.

The relationship between CPUs, memory, and disks is intricate, with problems in one area often showing up elsewhere. Before you throw resources at a problem, ask yourself whether you should be throwing resources at a different problem instead. If you're I/O bound, do you need more I/O capacity, or just more memory? The answer hinges on the working set size, which is the set of data that's needed most frequently over a given duration.

Solid-state devices are great for improving server performance overall and should generally be the standard for databases now, especially OLTP workloads. The only reason to continue using HDDs is in extremely budget-constrained systems or ones where you need a staggeringly high amount of disk space—on the order of petabytes in a data-warehousing situation.

In terms of the operating system, there are just a few Big Things that you need to get right, mostly related to storage, networking, and virtual memory management. If you use GNU/Linux, as most MySQL users do, we suggest using the XFS filesystem and setting the swappiness and disk queue scheduler to values that are appropriate for a server. There are some network parameters that you might need to change, and you might wish to tweak a number of other things (such as disabling SELinux), but those changes are a matter of preference.

# CHAPTER 5

# Optimizing Server Settings

In this chapter, we'll explain a process by which you can create a suitable configuration file for your MySQL server. It is a roundabout trip, with many points of interest and side trips to scenic overlooks. These side trips are necessary. Determining the shortest path to a suitable configuration doesn't start with studying configuration options and asking which ones you should set or how you should change them. Nor does it begin with examining server behavior and asking whether any configuration options can improve it. It's best to start with an understanding of MySQL's internals and behavior. You can then use that knowledge as a guide for how to configure MySQL. Finally, you can compare the desired configuration to the current configuration and correct any significant and worthwhile differences.

People often ask, "What's the optimal configuration file for my server with 32 GB of RAM and 12 CPU cores?" Unfortunately, it's not that simple. You should configure the server for the workload, data, and application requirements, not just the hardware. MySQL has scores of settings that you can change—but you shouldn't. It's usually better to configure the basic settings correctly (and there are only a few that matter in most cases) and spend more time on schema optimization, indexes, and query design. After you've set MySQL's basic configuration options correctly, the potential gains from further changes are usually small.

On the other hand, the potential downside of fiddling with the configuration can be great. The MySQL defaults are there with good reason. Changing them without understanding the impact can lead to crashes, constant stalls, or slow performance. As such, you should never blindly trust what someone reports as an optimal configuration from popular help sites like the MySQL forums or Stack Overflow.[1] Always review any changes by reading the associated manual entry and test carefully.

So what *should* you do? You should make sure the basics such as the InnoDB buffer pool and logfile size are appropriate. Then you should set a few safety options if you want to prevent undesired behavior (but note that these usually won't improve performance—they'll only avoid problems). Then leave the rest of the settings alone. If you experience a problem, begin by diagnosing it carefully. If your problem is caused by a part of the server whose behavior can be corrected with a configuration option, then you might need to change it.

Sometimes you might also need to set specific configuration options that can have a significant performance impact in special cases. However, these should not be part of a basic server configuration file. You should set them only when you find the specific performance problems they address. That's why we don't suggest that you approach configuration options by looking for bad things to improve. If something needs to be improved, it should show up in query response times. It's best to start your search with queries and their response times, not with configuration options. This could save you a lot of time and prevent many problems.

Another good way to save time and trouble is to use the defaults unless you know you shouldn't. There is safety in numbers, and a lot of people are running with default settings. That makes them the most thoroughly tested settings. Unexpected bugs can arise when you change things needlessly.

## How MySQL's Configuration Works

We'll begin by explaining MySQL's configuration mechanisms before covering what you should configure in MySQL. MySQL is generally pretty forgiving about its configuration, but following these suggestions may save you a lot of work and time.

The first thing to know is where MySQL gets configuration information: from command-line arguments and settings in its configuration file. On Unix-like systems, the configuration file is typically located at */etc/my.cnf* or */etc/mysql/my.cnf*. If you use your operating system's startup scripts, this is typically the only place you'll specify configuration settings. If you start MySQL manually, which you might do when you're running a test installation, you can also specify settings on the command line. The server actually reads the contents of the configuration file, removes any comment lines and newlines, and then processes it together with the command-line options.

---

1 For example, MySQL can run incredibly fast if you turn off durability settings, but it will also leave your data vulnerable to loss during a crash.

Any settings you decide to use permanently should go into the global configuration file instead of being specified at the command line. Otherwise, you risk accidentally starting the server without them. It's also a good idea to keep all of your configuration files in a single place so that you can inspect them easily.

Be sure you know where your server's configuration file is located! We've seen people try unsuccessfully to configure a server with a file it doesn't read, such as */etc/my.cnf* on Debian servers, which look in */etc/mysql/my.cnf* for their configuration. Sometimes there are files in several places, perhaps because a previous system administrator was confused as well. If you don't know which files your server reads, you can ask it:

```
$ which mysqld
/usr/sbin/mysqld
$ /usr/sbin/mysqld --verbose --help | grep -A 1 'Default options'
Default options are read from the following files in the given order:
/etc/mysql/my.cnf ~/.my.cnf /usr/etc/my.cnf
```

The configuration file is in the standard INI format and is divided into sections, each of which begins with a line that contains the section name in square brackets. A MySQL program will generally read the section that has the same name as that program, and many client programs also read the `client` section, which gives you a place to put common settings. The server usually reads the `mysqld` section. Be sure you place your settings in the correct section in the file, or they will have no effect.

## Syntax, Scope, and Dynamism

Configuration settings are written in all lowercase, with words separated by underscores or dashes. The following are equivalent, and you might see both forms in command lines and configuration files:

```
/usr/sbin/mysqld --auto-increment-offset=5
/usr/sbin/mysqld --auto_increment_offset=5
```

We suggest that you pick a style and use it consistently. This makes it easier to search for settings in your files.

Configuration settings can have several scopes. Some settings are server-wide (global scope), others are different for each connection (session scope), and others are per-object. Many session-scoped variables have global equivalents, which you can think of as defaults. If you change the session-scoped variable, it affects only the connection from which you changed it, and the changes are lost when the connection closes. Here are some examples of the variety of behaviors of which you should be aware:

- The `max_connections` variable is globally scoped.
- The `sort_buffer_size` variable has a global default, but you can set it per session as well.
- The `join_buffer_size` variable has a global default and can be set per session, but a single query that joins several tables can allocate one join buffer *per join*, so there might be several join buffers per query.

In addition to setting variables in the configuration files, you can change many (but not all) of them while the server is running. MySQL refers to these as *dynamic* configuration variables. The following statements show different ways to change the session and global values of `sort_buffer_size` dynamically:

```
SET sort_buffer_size = <value>;
SET GLOBAL sort_buffer_size = <value>;
SET @@sort_buffer_size := <value>;
SET @@session.sort_buffer_size := <value>;
SET @@global.sort_buffer_size := <value>;
```

If you set variables dynamically, be aware that those settings will be lost when MySQL shuts down. If you want to keep the settings, you'll have to update your configuration file as well.

If you set a variable's global value while the server is running, the values for the current session and any other existing sessions are not affected. Keep this in mind if your clients rely on persistent database connections. This is because the session values are initialized from the global value when the connections are created. You should inspect the output of SHOW GLOBAL VARIABLES after each change to make sure it's had the desired effect.

There is also a special value you can assign to variables with the SET command: the keyword DEFAULT. Assigning this value to a session-scoped variable sets that variable to the corresponding globally scoped variable's value. This is useful for resetting session-scoped variables back to the values they had when you opened the connection. We advise you not to use it for global variables because it probably won't do what you want—that is, it doesn't set the values back to what they were when you started the server or even the value specified in the configuration file; it sets the variable to the compiled-in default.

## Persisted System Variables

If all of this variable scoping and configuration business wasn't complicated enough, you also had to be aware that if MySQL was restarted, it would revert back to what you had in your configuration file—even if you had used SET GLOBAL to change a global variable. This meant that you had to manage a configuration file *and* the runtime configuration of MySQL as well as ensure they stayed in sync with each other. If you wanted to increase max_connections for your servers, you had to issue a SET GLOBAL max_connections command on each running instance and then follow up with editing the configuration file to reflect your new configuration.

MySQL 8.0 introduced a new feature called persisted system variables (*https://oreil.ly/ZDwXZ*), which helps to make this a little less complicated. The new syntax SET PERSIST now allows you to set the value once for runtime and MySQL will write this setting out to disk, enabling it to be used at the next restart.

## Side Effects of Setting Variables

Setting variables dynamically can have unexpected side effects, such as flushing dirty blocks from buffers. Be careful which settings you change online because this can cause the server to do a lot of work.

Sometimes you can infer a variable's behavior from its name. For example, max_heap_table_size does what it sounds like: it specifies the *maximum* size to which implicit in-memory temporary tables are allowed to grow. However, the naming conventions aren't completely consistent, so you can't always guess what a variable will do by looking at its name.

Let's take a look at some commonly used variables and the effects of changing them dynamically:

table_open_cache
: Setting this variable has no immediate effect: the effect is delayed until the next time a thread opens a table. When this happens, MySQL checks the variable's value. If the value is larger than the number of tables in the cache, the thread can insert the newly opened table into the cache. If the value is smaller than the number of tables in the cache, MySQL deletes unused tables from the cache.

thread_cache_size
: Setting this variable has no immediate effect: the effect is delayed until the next time a connection is closed. At that time, MySQL checks whether there is space in the cache to store the thread. If so, it caches the thread for future reuse by

another connection. If not, it kills the thread instead of caching it. In this case, the number of threads in the cache, and hence the amount of memory the thread cache uses, does not immediately decrease; it decreases only when a new connection removes a thread from the cache to use it. (MySQL adds threads to the cache only when connections close and removes them from the cache only when new connections are created.)

`read_buffer_size`
> MySQL doesn't allocate any memory for this buffer until a query needs it, but then it immediately allocates the entire chunk of memory specified here.

`read_rnd_buffer_size`
> MySQL doesn't allocate any memory for this buffer until a query needs it, and then it allocates only as much memory as needed. (The name `max_ read_ rnd_buffer_size` would describe this variable more accurately.)

The official MySQL documentation explains what these variables do in detail, and this isn't an exhaustive list. Our goal here is simply to show you what behavior to expect when you change a few common variables.

You should not raise the value of a per-connection setting globally unless you know it's the right thing to do. Some buffers are allocated all at once, even if they're not needed, so a large global setting can be a huge waste. Instead, you can raise the value when a query needs it.

## Planning Your Variable Changes

Be careful when setting variables. More is not always better, and if you set the values too high, you can easily cause problems: you might run out of memory or cause your server to swap.

Referring back to Chapter 2, monitor your SLOs to ensure that your changes don't affect the customer experience. Benchmarks aren't enough because they're not real. If you don't measure your server's actual performance, you might hurt performance without knowing it. We've seen many cases where someone changed a server's configuration and thought it improved performance, when in fact the server's performance worsened overall because of a different workload at a different time of day or day of the week.

Ideally, you're using a version control system to track changes to your configuration files. This strategy can be very effective at correlating a performance change or SLO breach to a specific configuration change. Just be aware that changing the configuration file doesn't actually do anything by default—you have to change the runtime setting too.

Before you start changing your configuration, you should optimize your queries and your schema, addressing at least the obvious things such as adding indexes. If you get deep into tweaking the configuration and then change your queries or schema, you might need to reevaluate the configuration. Keep in mind that unless your hardware, workload, and data are completely static, chances are you'll need to revisit your configuration later. And in fact, most people's servers don't even have a steady workload throughout the day—meaning that the "perfect" configuration for the middle of the morning is not right for midafternoon! Obviously, chasing the mythical "perfect" configuration is completely impractical. Thus, you don't need to squeeze every last ounce of performance out of your server; in fact, the return for such an investment of time will probably be very small. We suggest that you focus on optimizing for your peak workload and then stop at "good enough," unless you have reason to believe you're forgoing a significant performance improvement.

# What Not to Do

Before we get started with server configuration, we want to encourage you to avoid a few common practices that we've found to be risky or practically not worth the effort. Warning: rants ahead!

You might be expected (or believe that you're expected) to set up a benchmark suite and "tune" your server by changing its configuration iteratively in search of optimal settings. This usually is not something we advise most people to do. It requires so much work and research, and the potential payoff is so small in most cases, that it can be a huge waste of time. You are probably better off spending that time on other things such as checking your backups, monitoring changes in query plans, and so on.

You should not "tune by ratio." The classic "tuning ratio" is the rule of thumb that your InnoDB buffer pool hit ratio should be higher than some percentage, and you should increase the cache size if the hit rate is too low. This is very wrong advice. Regardless of what anyone tells you, *the cache hit ratio has nothing to do with whether the cache is too large or too small*. To begin with, the hit ratio depends on the workload —some workloads simply aren't cacheable no matter how big the cache is—and secondly, cache hits are meaningless, for reasons we'll explain later. It sometimes happens that when the cache is too small, the hit rate is low, and increasing the cache size increases the hit rate. However, this is an accidental correlation and does not indicate anything about performance or proper sizing of the cache.

The problem with correlations that sometimes appear to be true is that people begin to believe they will always be true. Oracle DBAs abandoned ratio-based tuning years ago, and we wish MySQL DBAs would follow their lead.[2] We wish even more fervently that people wouldn't write "tuning scripts" that codify these dangerous practices and teach them to thousands of people. This leads to our next suggestion of what not to do: don't use tuning scripts! There are several very popular ones that you can find on the internet. It's probably best to ignore them.

We also suggest that you avoid the word *tuning*, which we've used liberally in the past few paragraphs. We favor *configuration* or *optimization* instead (as long as that's what you're actually doing). The word *tuning* conjures up images of an undisciplined novice who tweaks the server and sees what happens. We suggested in the previous section that this practice is best left to those who are researching server internals. "Tuning" your server can be a stunning waste of time.

On a related topic, searching the internet for configuration advice is not always a great idea. You can find a lot of bad advice in blogs, forums, and so on. Although many experts contribute what they know online, it is not always easy to tell who is qualified. We can't give unbiased recommendations about where to find real experts, of course. But we can say that the credible, reputable MySQL service providers are a safer bet in general than what a simple internet search turns up because people who have happy customers are probably doing something right. Even their advice, however, can be dangerous to apply without testing and understanding because it might have been directed at a situation that differed from yours in a way you don't understand.

Finally, don't believe the popular memory consumption formula—yes, the very one that MySQL itself prints out when it crashes. (We won't repeat it here.) This formula is from an ancient time. It is not a reliable or even useful way to understand how much memory MySQL can use in the worst case. You might see some variations on this formula on the internet, too. These are similarly flawed, even though they add in more factors that the original formula doesn't have. The truth is that you can't put an upper bound on MySQL's memory consumption. It is not a tightly regulated database server that controls memory allocation.

# Creating a MySQL Configuration File

As we mentioned at the beginning of this chapter, we don't have a one-size-fits-all "best configuration file" for, say, a 4 CPU server with 16 GB of memory and 12 hard drives. You really do need to develop your own configurations because even a good starting point will vary widely depending on how you're using the server.

---

2 If you are not convinced that "tuning by ratio" is bad, please read *Optimizing Oracle Performance* by Cary Millsap and Jeff Holt (O'Reilly). They even devote an appendix to the topic, with a tool that can artificially generate any cache hit ratio you wish, no matter how badly your system is performing! Of course, it's all for the purpose of illustrating how useless the ratio is.

# Minimal Configuration

We've created a minimal sample configuration file for this book, which you can use as a good starting point for your own servers.[3] You must choose values for a few of the settings; we'll explain those later in this chapter. Our base file, built around MySQL 8.0, looks like this:

```
[mysqld]
# GENERAL
datadir                         = /var/lib/mysql
socket                          = /var/lib/mysql/mysql.sock
pid_file                        = /var/lib/mysql/mysql.pid
user                            = mysql
port                            = 3306
# INNODB
innodb_buffer_pool_size         = <value>
innodb_log_file_size            = <value>
innodb_file_per_table           = 1
innodb_flush_method             = O_DIRECT
# LOGGING
log_error                       = /var/lib/mysql/mysql-error.log
log_slow_queries                = /var/lib/mysql/mysql-slow.log
# OTHER
tmp_table_size                  = 32M
max_heap_table_size             = 32M
max_connections                 = <value>
thread_cache_size               = <value>
table_open_cache                = <value>
open_files_limit                = 65535
[client]
socket                          = /var/lib/mysql/mysql.sock
port                            = 3306
```

This might seem *too* minimal in comparison to what you're used to seeing, but it's actually more than many people need. There are a few other types of configuration options that you are likely to use as well, such as binary logging; we'll cover those later in this and other chapters.

The first thing we configured is the location of the data. We chose */var/lib/mysql* for this, because it's a popular location on many Unix variants. There is nothing wrong with choosing another location; you decide. We've put the *.pid* file in the same location, but many operating systems will want to place it in */var/run* instead. That's fine, too. We simply needed to have something configured for these settings. By the way, don't let the socket and *.pid* file be located according to the server's compiled-in defaults; there are some bugs in various MySQL versions that can cause problems with this. It's best to set these locations explicitly. (We're not advising you to choose

---

3 Please note that versions of MySQL remove, deprecate, and change some options; check the docs for details.

different locations; we're just advising you to make sure the *my.cnf* file mentions those locations explicitly, so they won't change and break things if you upgrade the server.)

We also specified that *mysqld* should run as the *mysql* user account on the operating system. You'll need to make sure this account exists and that it owns the data directory and all files within. The port is set to the default of 3306, but sometimes you'll want to change that.

In MySQL 8.0, a new configuration option, `innodb_dedicated_server`, was introduced. This option examines the available memory on the server and configures four additional variables (`innodb_buffer_pool_size`, `innodb_log_file_size`, `innodb_log_files_in_group`, and `innodb_flush_method`) appropriately for a dedicated database server, which simplifies calculating and changing these values. This can be especially useful in a cloud environment, where you might run a virtual machine (VM) with 128 GB of RAM and then reboot it to scale up to 256 GB RAM. MySQL here would be self-configuring, and you don't need to manage changing the values in the configuration file. This is often the best way to manage these four settings.

Most of the other settings in our sample file are pretty self-explanatory, and many of them are a matter of judgment. We'll explore several of them throughout the rest of this chapter. We'll also discuss some safety settings later in this chapter, which can be very helpful for making your server more robust and helping to prevent bad data and other problems. We don't show those settings here.

One setting to explain here is the `open_files_limit` option. We've set this as large as possible on a typical Linux system. Open file handles are very cheap on modern operating systems. If this setting isn't large enough, you'll see error 24, "too many open files."

Skipping all the way to the end, the last section in the configuration file is for client programs like *mysql* and *mysqladmin* and simply lets them know how to connect to the server. You should set the values for client programs to match those you chose for the server.

## Inspecting MySQL Server Status Variables

Sometimes you can use the output from `SHOW GLOBAL STATUS` as input to your configuration to help customize the settings better for your workload. For the best results, look both at absolute values and at how the values change over time, preferably with several snapshots at peak and off-peak times. You can use the following command to see incremental changes to status variables every 60 seconds:

```
$ mysqladmin extended-status -ri60
```

We will frequently refer to changes in status variables over time as we explain various configuration settings. We will usually expect you to be examining the output of a command such as the one we just showed. Other helpful tools that can provide a compact display of status counter changes are Percona Toolkit's *pt-mext* or *pt-mysql-summary*.

Now that we've shown you the preliminaries, we'll take you on a guided tour of some server internals, interleaved with advice on configuration. This will give you the background you'll need to choose appropriate values for configuration options when we return to the sample configuration file later.

# Configuring Memory Usage

Using `innodb_dedicated_server` will typically use 50%–75% of your RAM. This leaves you with at least 25% for per-connection memory allocations, operating system overhead, and other memory settings. We go over each of these in the following sections, and then we take a more detailed look at the various MySQL caches' requirements.

## Per-Connection Memory Needs

MySQL needs a small amount of memory just to hold a connection (typically with an associated dedicated thread) open. It also requires a base amount of memory to execute any given query. You'll need to set aside enough memory for MySQL to execute queries during peak load times. Otherwise, your queries will be starved for memory, and they will run poorly or fail.

It's useful to know how much memory MySQL will consume during peak usage, but some usage patterns can unexpectedly consume a lot of memory, which makes this hard to predict. Prepared statements are one example because you can have many of them open at once. Another example is the InnoDB data dictionary (more about this later).

You don't need to assume a worst-case scenario when trying to predict peak memory consumption. For example, if you configure MySQL to allow a maximum of one hundred connections, it theoretically might be possible to simultaneously run large queries on all one hundred connections, but in reality this probably won't happen. Queries that use many large temporary tables or complex stored procedures are the most likely causes of high per-connection memory consumption.

## Reserving Memory for the Operating System

Just as with queries, you need to reserve enough memory for the operating system to do its work. This involves running any local monitoring software, configuration management tooling, scheduled jobs, and so forth. The best indication that the operating system has enough memory is that it's not actively swapping (paging) virtual memory to disk.

# The InnoDB Buffer Pool

The InnoDB buffer pool needs more memory than anything else, as it's generally the most important variable for performance. The InnoDB buffer pool doesn't just cache indexes: it also holds row data, the adaptive hash index, the change buffer, locks, and other internal structures. InnoDB also uses the buffer pool to help it delay writes, so it can merge many writes together and perform them sequentially. In short, InnoDB relies *heavily* on the buffer pool, and you should be sure to allocate enough memory to it. You can use variables from SHOW commands or tools such as *innotop* to monitor your InnoDB buffer pool's memory usage.

If you don't have much data and you know that your data won't grow quickly, you don't need to overallocate memory to the buffer pool. It's not really beneficial to make it much larger than the size of the tables and indexes that it will hold. There's nothing wrong with planning ahead for a rapidly growing database, of course, but sometimes we see huge buffer pools with a tiny amount of data. This isn't necessary.

Large buffer pools come with some challenges, such as long shutdown and warm-up times. If there are a lot of dirty (modified) pages in the buffer pool, InnoDB can take a long time to shut down because it writes the dirty pages to the datafiles upon shutdown. You can force it to shut down quickly, but then it just has to do more recovery when it restarts, so you can't actually speed up the shutdown and restart cycle time. If you know in advance when you need to shut down, you can change the innodb_max_dirty_pages_pct variable at runtime to a lower value, wait for the flush thread to clean up the buffer pool, and then shut down once the number of dirty pages becomes small. You can monitor the number of dirty pages by watching the innodb_buffer_pool_pages_dirty server status variable or using *innotop* to monitor SHOW INNODB STATUS. You can also use the variable innodb_fast_shutdown to tweak how shutdown occurs.

Lowering the value of the innodb_max_dirty_pages_pct variable doesn't actually guarantee that InnoDB will keep fewer dirty pages in the buffer pool. Instead, it controls the threshold at which InnoDB stops being "lazy." InnoDB's default behavior is to flush dirty pages with a background thread, merging writes together and performing them sequentially for efficiency. This behavior is called "lazy" because it lets InnoDB delay flushing dirty pages in the buffer pool unless it needs to use the space for some other data. When the percentage of dirty pages exceeds the threshold, InnoDB will flush pages as quickly as it can to try to keep the dirty page count lower. These page cleaner operations have been greatly optimized (*https://oreil.ly/S8ong*) from previous behavior, including being able to configure multiple threads to perform flushing.

When MySQL starts back up again, the buffer pool cache is empty, also referred to as a *cold cache*. All of the benefits of having rows and pages in memory are now gone.

Thankfully, by default the configuration options `innodb_buffer_pool_dump_at_shut` `down` and `innodb_buffer_pool_load_at_startup` work together to warm the server at startup. The load at startup takes time, but it can speed up the performance of a server much faster than waiting for it to naturally populate.

## The Thread Cache

The thread cache holds threads that aren't currently associated with a connection but are ready to serve new connections. When there's a thread in the cache and a new connection is created, MySQL removes the thread from the cache and gives it to the new connection. When the connection is closed, MySQL places the thread back into the cache, if there's room. If there isn't room, MySQL destroys the thread. As long as MySQL has a free thread in the cache, it can respond rapidly to connection requests because it doesn't have to create a new thread for each connection.

The `thread_cache_size` variable specifies the number of threads MySQL can keep in the cache. You probably won't need to change this from the default value of -1 or auto-sized unless your server gets many connection requests. To check whether the thread cache is large enough, watch the `Threads_created` status variable. We generally try to keep the thread cache large enough that we see fewer than 10 new threads created each second, but it's often pretty easy to get this number lower than one per second.

A good approach is to watch the `Threads_connected` variable and try to set `thread_cache_size` large enough to handle the typical fluctuation in your workload. For example, if `Threads_connected` usually stays between 100 and 120, you can set the cache size to 20. If it stays between 500 and 700, a thread cache of 200 should be large enough. Think of it this way: at 700 connections, there are probably no threads in the cache; at 500 connections, there are 200 cached threads ready to be used if the load increases to 700 again.

Making the thread cache very large is probably not necessary for most uses, but keeping it small doesn't save much memory, so there's little benefit in doing so. Each thread that's in the thread cache or sleeping typically uses around 256 KB of memory. This is not very much compared to the amount of memory a thread can use when a connection is actively processing a query. In general, you should keep your thread cache large enough that `Threads_created` doesn't increase very often. If this is a very large number, however (e.g., many thousands of threads), you might want to set it lower because some operating systems don't handle very large numbers of threads well, even when most of them are sleeping.

# Configuring MySQL's I/O Behavior

A few configuration options affect how MySQL synchronizes data to disk and performs recovery. These can affect performance dramatically because they involve I/O operations. They also represent a trade-off between performance and data safety. In general, it's expensive to ensure that your data is written to disk immediately and consistently. If you're willing to risk the danger that a disk write won't really make it to permanent storage, you can increase concurrency and/or reduce I/O waits, but you'll have to decide for yourself how much risk you can tolerate.

InnoDB permits you to control not only how it recovers but also how it opens and flushes its data, which greatly affects recovery and overall performance. InnoDB's recovery process is automatic and always runs when InnoDB starts, although you can influence what actions it takes. Leaving aside recovery and assuming nothing ever crashes or goes wrong, there's still a lot to configure for InnoDB. It has a complex chain of buffers and files designed to increase performance and guarantee ACID properties, and each piece of the chain is configurable. Figure 5-1 illustrates these files and buffers.

A few of the most important things to change for normal usage are the InnoDB logfile size, how InnoDB flushes its log buffer, and how InnoDB performs I/O.

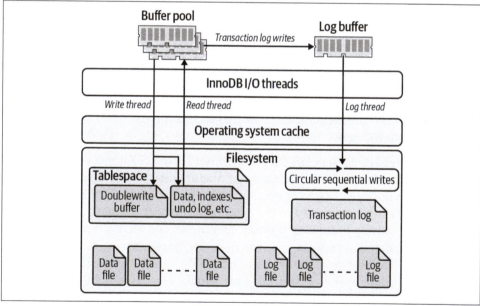

*Figure 5-1. InnoDB's buffers and files*

# The InnoDB Transaction Log

InnoDB uses its log to reduce the cost of committing transactions. Instead of flushing the buffer pool to disk when each transaction commits, it logs the transactions. The changes transactions make to data and indexes often map to random locations in the tablespace, so flushing these changes to disk would require random I/O. InnoDB assumes it's using conventional disks, where random I/O is much more expensive than sequential I/O because of the time it takes to seek to the correct location on disk and wait for the desired part of the disk to rotate under the head.

InnoDB uses its log to convert this random disk I/O into sequential I/O. Once the log is safely on disk, the transactions are permanent, even though the changes haven't been written to the datafiles yet. If something bad happens (such as a power failure), InnoDB can replay the log and recover the committed transactions.

Of course, InnoDB does ultimately have to write the changes to the datafiles because the log has a fixed size. It writes to the log in a circular fashion: when it reaches the end of the log, it wraps around to the beginning. It can't overwrite a log record if the changes contained there haven't been applied to the datafiles because this would erase the only permanent record of the committed transaction.

InnoDB uses a background thread to flush the changes to the datafiles intelligently. This thread can group writes together and make the data writes sequential for improved efficiency. In effect, the transaction log converts random datafile I/O into mostly sequential logfile and datafile I/O. Moving flushes into the background makes queries complete more quickly and helps cushion the I/O system from spikes in the query load.

The overall logfile size is controlled by `innodb_log_file_size` and `innodb_log_files_in_group`, and it's very important for write performance. If you took our earlier advice and used `innodb_dedicated_server`, these are managed for you based on how much memory your system has.

# Log Buffer

When InnoDB changes any data, it writes a record of the change into its *log buffer*, which it keeps in memory. InnoDB flushes the buffer to the logfiles on disk when the buffer gets full, when a transaction commits, or once per second, whichever comes first. Increasing the buffer size, which is 1 MB by default, can help reduce I/O if you have large transactions. The variable that controls the buffer size is called `innodb_log_buffer_size`.

You usually don't need to make the buffer very large. The recommended range is 1–8 MB, and this usually will be enough unless you write a lot of huge `BLOB` records. The log entries are very compact compared to InnoDB's normal data. They are not page based, so they don't waste space storing whole pages at a time. InnoDB also makes log entries as short as possible. They are sometimes even stored as a few integers, indicating the type of operation logged and any parameters needed by that operation!

### How InnoDB flushes the log buffer

When InnoDB flushes the log buffer to the logfiles on disk, it locks the buffer with a mutex, flushes it up to the desired point, and then moves any remaining entries to the front of the buffer. It is possible that more than one transaction will be ready to flush its log entries when the mutex is released. InnoDB uses a group commit feature that can commit all of them to the log in a single I/O operation.

The log buffer *must* be flushed to durable storage to ensure that committed transactions are fully durable. If you care more about performance than durability, you can change `innodb_flush_log_at_trx_commit` to control where and how often the log buffer is flushed.

Possible settings are as follows:

0

> Write the log buffer to the logfile and flush the logfile every second but do nothing at transaction commit.

1

> Write the log buffer to the logfile and flush it to durable storage every time a transaction commits. This is the default (and safest) setting; it guarantees that you won't lose any committed transactions unless the disk or operating system "fakes" the flush operation.

2

> Write the log buffer to the logfile at every commit but don't flush it. InnoDB schedules a flush once every second. The most important difference from the 0 setting is that 2 won't lose any transactions if the MySQL process crashes. If the entire server crashes or loses power, however, you can still lose transactions.

It's important to know the difference between *writing* the log buffer to the logfile and *flushing* the log to durable storage. In most operating systems, writing the buffer to the log simply moves the data from InnoDB's memory buffer to the operating system's cache, which is also in memory. It doesn't actually write the data to durable storage. Thus, settings 0 and 2 *usually* result in at most one second of lost data if there's a crash or a power outage because the data might exist only in the operating system's cache. We say "usually" because InnoDB tries to flush the logfile to disk about once per second no matter what, but it is possible to lose more than a second of transactions in some cases, such as when a flush gets stalled.

Sometimes the hard disk controller or operating system fakes a flush by putting the data into yet *another* cache, such as the hard disk's own cache. This is faster but very dangerous because the data might still be lost if the drive loses power. This is even worse than setting `innodb_flush_log_at_trx_commit` to something other than 1 because it can cause data corruption, not just lost transactions.

Setting `innodb_flush_log_at_trx_commit` to anything other than 1 can cause you to lose transactions. However, you might find the other settings useful if you don't care about durability (the D in ACID). Maybe you just want some of InnoDB's other features, such as clustered indexes, resistance to data corruption, and row-level locking.

The best configuration for high-performance transactional needs is to leave `innodb_flush_log_at_trx_commit` set to 1 and place the logfiles on a RAID volume with a battery-backed write cache and SSDs. This is both safe and very fast. In fact, we dare say that any production database server that's expected to handle a serious workload needs to have this kind of hardware.

### How InnoDB opens and flushes logfiles and datafiles

The `innodb_flush_method` option lets you configure how InnoDB actually interacts with the filesystem. Despite its name, it also affects how InnoDB reads data, not just how it writes it.

 Changing how InnoDB performs I/O operations can affect performance greatly, so be sure you understand what you're doing before you change anything!

This is a slightly confusing option because it affects both the logfiles and the datafiles, and it sometimes does different things to each kind of file. It would be nice to have one configuration option for the logs and another for the datafiles, but they're combined.

If you use a Unix-like operating system and your RAID controller has a battery-backed write cache, we recommend that you use O_DIRECT. If not, either the default or O_DIRECT will probably be the best choice, depending on your application. If you opted to use `innodb_dedicated_server`, as we mentioned earlier, this option is set automatically for you.

## The InnoDB Tablespace

InnoDB keeps its data in a *tablespace*, which is essentially a virtual filesystem spanning one or many files on disk. InnoDB uses the tablespace for many purposes, not just for storing tables and indexes. It keeps its undo log (information necessary to re-create old row versions), change buffer, doublewrite buffer, and other internal structures in the tablespace.

### Configuring the tablespace

You specify the tablespace files with the `innodb_data_file_path` configuration option. The files are all contained in the directory given by `innodb_data_home_dir`. Here's an example:

```
innodb_data_home_dir = /var/lib/mysql/
innodb_data_file_path = ibdata1:1G;ibdata2:1G;ibdata3:1G
```

That creates a 3 GB tablespace in three files. Sometimes people wonder whether they can use multiple files to spread load across drives, like this:

```
innodb_data_file_path = /disk1/ibdata1:1G;/disk2/ibdata2:1G;...
```

While that does indeed place the files in different directories, which represent different drives in this example, InnoDB concatenates the files end-to-end. Thus, you usually don't gain much this way. InnoDB will fill the first file, then the second when the first is full, and so on; the load isn't really spread in the fashion you need for higher performance. A RAID controller is a smarter way to spread load.

To allow the tablespace to grow if it runs out of space, you can make the last file auto-extend as follows:

```
...ibdata3:1G:autoextend
```

The default behavior is to create a single 10 MB auto-extending file. If you make the file auto-extend, it's a good idea to place an upper limit on the tablespace's size to keep it from growing very large because once it grows, it doesn't shrink. For example, the following limits the auto-extending file to 2 GB:

```
...ibdata3:1G:autoextend:max:2G
```

Managing a single tablespace can be a hassle, especially if it auto-extends and you want to reclaim the space (for this reason, we recommend disabling the auto-extend feature or at least setting a reasonable cap on the space). The only way to reclaim space is to dump your data, shut down MySQL, delete all the files, change the configuration, restart, let InnoDB create new empty files, and restore your data. InnoDB is completely unforgiving about its tablespace: you cannot simply remove files or change their sizes. It will refuse to start if you corrupt its tablespace. It is likewise very strict about its logfiles. If you're used to casually moving files around as you could do with MyISAM, take heed!

The `innodb_file_per_table` option lets you configure InnoDB to use one file per table. It stores the data in the database directory as *tablename.ibd* files. This makes it easier to reclaim space when you drop a table. However, placing the data in multiple files can actually result in more wasted space overall because it trades internal fragmentation in the single InnoDB tablespace for wasted space in the *.ibd* files.

Even if you enable the `innodb_file_per_table` option, you'll still need the main tablespace for the undo logs and other system data. It will be smaller if you're not storing all the data in it.

Some people like to use `innodb_file_per_table` just because of the extra manageability and visibility it gives you. For example, it's much faster to find a table's size by examining a single file than it is to use `SHOW TABLE STATUS`, which has to perform more complex work to determine how many pages are allocated to a table.

 There has always been a dark side to `innodb_file_per_table`: slow `DROP TABLE` performance. This can be severe enough to cause a noticeable server-wide stall for two reasons.

Dropping the table unlinks (deletes) the file at the filesystem level, which can be very slow on some filesystems (ext3, we're looking at you). You can shorten the duration of this with tricks on the filesystem: link the *.ibd* file to a zero-sized file, then delete the file manually instead of waiting for MySQL to do it.

When you enable this option, each table gets its own tablespace inside InnoDB. It turns out that removing the tablespace actually requires InnoDB to lock and scan the buffer pool while it looks for pages belonging to this tablespace, which is very slow on a server with a large buffer pool. This is improved if you break the buffer pool into many parts using `innodb_buffer_pool_instances`.

Several fixes have been applied to various versions of MySQL along the way. As of 8.0.23, this should no longer be an issue.

What's the final recommendation? We suggest that you use `innodb_file_per_table` and cap the size of your shared tablespace to make your life easier. If you run into any circumstances that make this painful, as noted previously, consider one of the fixes we suggested.

## Old row versions and the tablespace

InnoDB's tablespace can grow very large in a write-heavy environment. If transactions stay open for a long time (even if they're not doing any work) and they're using the default `REPEATABLE READ` transaction isolation level, InnoDB won't be able to remove old row versions because the uncommitted transactions will still need to be able to see them. InnoDB stores the old versions in the tablespace, so it continues to grow as more data is updated. The purge process is multithreaded but may need to be tuned for workloads if you experience problems with purge lag (`innodb_purge_threads` and `innodb_purge_batch_size`).

The output of SHOW INNODB STATUS can help you pinpoint the problem. Look at the history list length in the TRANSACTIONS section; it shows the size of the undo log:

```
------------
TRANSACTIONS
------------
Trx id counter 1081043769321
Purge done for trx's n:o < 1081041974531 undo n:o < 0 state: running but idle
History list length 697068
```

If you have a large undo log and your tablespace is growing because of it, you can force MySQL to slow down enough for InnoDB's purge thread to keep up. This might not sound attractive, but there's no alternative. Otherwise, InnoDB will keep writing data and filling up your disk until the disk runs out of space or the tablespace reaches the limits you've defined.

To throttle the writes, set the innodb_max_purge_lag variable to a value other than 0. This value indicates the maximum number of transactions that can be waiting to be purged before InnoDB starts to delay further queries that update data. You'll have to know your workload to decide on a good value. As an example, if your average transaction affects 1 KB of rows and you can tolerate 100 MB of unpurged rows in your tablespace, you could set the value to 100000.

Bear in mind that unpurged row versions affect all queries because they effectively make your tables and indexes larger. If the purge thread simply can't keep up, performance can decrease. Setting the innodb_max_purge_lag variable will slow down performance too, but it's the lesser of the two evils.

## Other I/O Configuration Options

The sync_binlog option controls how MySQL flushes the binary log to disk. Its default value is 1, which means MySQL will perform flushing and keep binary logs durable and safe. This is the recommended setting, and we caution you against setting this to any other value.

If you don't keep sync_binlog set at 1, it's likely that a crash will cause your binary log to be out of sync with your transactional data. This can easily break replication and make recovery impossible, especially if your databases are using global transaction IDs (more on this in Chapter 9). The safety provided by leaving this at 1 far outweighs the I/O performance penalty that is incurred.

We covered RAID in more depth in Chapter 4, but it's worth repeating here that good-quality RAID controllers, with battery-backed write caches set to use the write-back policy, can handle thousands of writes per second and still give you durable storage. The data gets written to a fast cache with a battery, so it will survive even if the system loses power. When the power comes back, the RAID controller will write the data from the cache to the disk before making the disk available for use. Thus, a good RAID controller with a large enough battery-backed write cache can improve performance dramatically and is a very good investment. Of course, solid-state storage is also the recommended solution at this point, which dramatically improves I/O performance as well.

# Configuring MySQL Concurrency

When you're running MySQL in a high-concurrency workload, you might run into bottlenecks you wouldn't otherwise experience. This section explains how to detect these problems when they happen and how to get the best performance possible under these workloads.

If you have problems with InnoDB concurrency and you are not running at least MySQL 5.7, the solution is usually to upgrade the server. Older versions still held a lot of high concurrency scalability challenges. Everything queued on global mutexes such as the buffer pool mutex, and the server practically ground to a halt. If you upgrade to one of the newer versions of MySQL, you don't need to limit concurrency in most cases.

If you find yourself hitting this bottleneck, your best option is to shard your data. If sharding is not a viable path forward, you may need to limit concurrency. InnoDB has its own "thread scheduler" that controls how threads enter its kernel to access data and what they can do once they're inside the kernel. The most basic way to limit concurrency is with the `innodb_thread_concurrency` variable, which limits how many threads can be in the kernel at once. A value of 0 means there is no limit on the number of threads. If you are having InnoDB concurrency problems in older MySQL versions, this variable is the most important one to configure.

MySQL's online documentation (*https://oreil.ly/ThOBP*) provides the best guide for configuration here. You will have to experiment to find the best value for your system, but our recommendation is to start with setting `innodb_thread_concurrency` to the same number of CPU cores you have available and then begin tuning up or down as needed.

If more than the allowed number of threads are already in the kernel, a thread can't enter the kernel. InnoDB uses a two-phase process to try to let threads enter as efficiently as possible. The two-phase policy reduces the overhead of context switches caused by the operating system scheduler. The thread first sleeps for `innodb_thread_sleep_delay` microseconds and then tries again. If it still can't enter, it goes into a queue of waiting threads and yields to the operating system.

The default sleep time in the first phase is 10,000 microseconds. Changing this value can help in high-concurrency environments, when the CPU is underused with a lot of threads in the "sleeping before entering queue" status. The default value can also be much too large if you have a lot of small queries because it adds to query latency.

Once a thread is inside the kernel, it has a certain number of "tickets" that let it back into the kernel for "free," without any concurrency checks. This limits how much work it can do before it has to get back in line with other waiting threads. The `innodb_concurrency_tickets` option controls the number of tickets. It rarely needs to be changed unless you have a lot of extremely long-running queries. Tickets are granted per query, not per transaction. Once a query finishes, its unused tickets are discarded.

In addition to the bottlenecks in the buffer pool and other structures, there's another concurrency bottleneck at the commit stage, which is largely I/O bound because of flush operations. The `innodb_commit_concurrency` variable governs how many threads can commit at the same time. Configuring this option might help if there's a lot of thread thrashing even when `innodb_thread_concurrency` is set to a low value.

## Safety Settings

After your basic configuration settings are in place, you may wish to enable a number of settings that make the server safer and more reliable. Some of them influence performance because safety and reliability are often more costly to guarantee. Some are just sensible, however: they prevent silly mistakes such as inserting nonsensical data into the server. And some don't make a difference in day-to-day operations but prevent bad things from happening in edge cases.

Let's look at a collection of useful options for general server behavior first:

max_connect_errors

 If something goes wrong with your networking for a moment, there is an application or configuration error, or there is another problem that prevents connections from completing successfully for a brief period of time, clients can get blocked and will be unable to connect again until you flush the host cache. The default setting for this option (100) is so small that this problem can happen too easily. You might want to increase it, and in fact, if you know that the server is adequately secured against brute-force attacks, you can just make it very large to effectively disable blocking of hosts due to connection errors. If `skip_name_resolve` is enabled, however, the `max_connect_errors` option will have no effect because its behavior depends on the *host* cache, which is disabled by `skip_name_resolve`.

max_connections

 This setting acts like an emergency brake to keep your server from being overwhelmed by a surge of connections from the application. If the application misbehaves or the server encounters a problem such as a stall, a lot of new connections can be opened. But opening a connection does no good if it can't execute queries, so being denied with a "too many connections" error is a way to fail fast and fail cheaply.

Set `max_connections` high enough to accommodate the usual load that you think you'll experience as well as a safety margin to permit logging in and administering the server. For example, if you think you'll have 300 or so connections in normal operations, you might set this to 500 or so. If you don't know how many connections you'll get, 500 is not an unreasonable starting point anyway. The default is 151, but that's not enough for a lot of applications.

Beware also of surprises that might make you hit the limit of connections. For example, if you restart an application server, it might not close its connections cleanly, and MySQL might not realize they've been closed. When the application server comes back up and tries to open connections to the database, it might be refused due to the dead connections that haven't timed out yet. This can also come into play if you do not use persistent connections and your application does not disconnect gracefully. The server will keep a connection around until it reaches a TCP timeout or, in the worst case, until the number of seconds configured with `wait_timeout`.

Watch the `max_used_connections` status variable over time. It is a high-water mark that shows you if the server has had a spike in connections at some point. If it reaches `max_connections`, chances are a client has been denied at least once.

`skip_name_resolve`
This setting disables another networking- and authentication-related trap: DNS lookups. DNS is one of the weak points in MySQL's connection process. When you connect to the server, by default it tries to determine the hostname from which you're connecting and uses that as part of the authentication credentials (that is, your credentials are your username, hostname, and password—not just your username and password). But to verify your hostname, the server needs to perform a forward-confirmed reverse DNS lookup (or "double reverse DNS lookup"), which involves both a reverse and a forward DNS lookup before accepting the connection. This is all fine until DNS starts to have problems, which is pretty much a certainty at some point in time. When that happens, everything piles up, and eventually the connection times out. To prevent this, we strongly recommend that you set this option, which disables DNS lookups during authentication. However, if you do this, you will need to convert all of your hostname-based grants to use IP addresses, wildcards, or the special hostname "localhost" because hostname-based accounts will be disabled.

`sql_mode`
This setting can accept a variety of options that modify server behavior. We don't recommend changing these just for the fun of it; it's better to let MySQL be

MySQL in most ways and not try to make it behave like other database servers. (Many client and GUI tools expect MySQL to have its own flavor of SQL, for example, so if you change it to speak more ANSI-compliant SQL some things might break.) However, several of the settings are very useful, and some might be worth considering in your specific cases. In the past, MySQL was generally very loose about sql_mode, but it is much more strict in later versions.

However, be aware that it might not be a good idea to change these settings for existing applications because doing so might make the server incompatible with the application's expectations. It's pretty common for people to unwittingly write queries that refer to columns not in the GROUP BY clause or use aggregate functions, for example, so if you want to enable the ONLY_FULL_GROUP_BY option, it's a good idea to do it in a development or staging server first and only deploy it in production once you're sure everything is working.

Also, be sure to check for changes to the default sql_mode as you plan upgrades to your databases. Changes to this variable may be incompatible with your existing application, and you need to preemptively test this beforehand. We talk more about upgrading in Appendix A.

sysdate_is_now

This is another setting that might be backward incompatible with applications' expectations. But if you don't explicitly desire the SYSDATE() function to have nondeterministic behavior, which can break replication and make point-in-time recovery from backups unreliable, you might want to enable this option and make its behavior deterministic.

read_only *and* super_read_only

The read_only option prevents unprivileged users from making changes on replicas, which should be receiving changes only via replication, not from the application. We strongly recommend setting replicas to read-only mode.

There is a more restrictive read-only option, super_read_only, which prevents even users with the SUPER privilege from being able to write data. With this enabled, the only thing that can write changes to your database is replication. We also *strongly* recommend enabling super_read_only. It will prevent you from accidentally using an administrator account to write data to a read-only replica, putting it out of sync.

# Advanced InnoDB Settings

Some of these InnoDB options are quite important for server performance, and there are also a couple of safety options:

`innodb_autoinc_lock_mode`

This option controls how InnoDB generates auto-incrementing primary key values, which can be a bottleneck in some cases, such as high-concurrency inserts. If you have many transactions waiting on the auto-increment lock (you can see this in `SHOW ENGINE INNODB STATUS`), you should investigate this setting. We won't repeat the manual's explanation of the options and their behaviors.

`innodb_buffer_pool_instances`

This setting divides the buffer pool into multiple segments in MySQL 5.5 and newer and is probably one of the most important ways to improve MySQL's scalability on multicore machines with a highly concurrent workload. Multiple buffer pools partition the workload so that some of the global mutexes are not such hot contention points.

`innodb_io_capacity`

InnoDB used to be hardcoded to assume that it ran on a single hard disk capable of one hundred I/O operations per second. This was a bad default. Now you can inform InnoDB how much I/O capacity is available to it. InnoDB sometimes needs this set quite high (tens of thousands on extremely fast storage such as PCIe flash devices) to flush dirty pages in a steady fashion, for reasons that are quite complex to explain.[4]

`innodb_read_io_threads` *and* `innodb_write_io_threads`

These options control how many background threads are available for I/O operations. The default in recent versions of MySQL is to have four read threads and four write threads, which is enough for a lot of servers, especially with the native asynchronous I/O available since MySQL 5.5. If you have many hard drives and a high-concurrency workload and you see that the threads are having a hard time keeping up, you can increase the number of threads, or you can simply set them to the number of physical spindles you have for I/O (even if they're behind a RAID controller).

`innodb_strict_mode`

This setting makes InnoDB throw errors instead of warnings for some conditions, especially invalid or possibly dangerous `CREATE TABLE` options. If you enable this option, be certain to check all of your `CREATE TABLE` options because it might not let you create some tables that used to be fine. Sometimes it's a bit

---

4 For follow-up reading, see the Percona blog posts "Give Love to Your SSDs—Reduce innodb_io_capacity_max" (*https://oreil.ly/aSGC6*), "InnoDB Flushing in Action for Percona Server for MySQL" (*https://oreil.ly/CdzsQ*), and "Tuning MySQL/InnoDB Flushing for a Write-Intensive Workload" (*https://oreil.ly/mnA8m*).

pessimistic and overly restrictive. You wouldn't want to find this out while trying to restore a backup.

innodb_old_blocks_time

> InnoDB has a two-part buffer pool LRU list, which is designed to prevent ad hoc queries from evicting pages that are used many times over the long term. One-off queries such as those issued by *mysqldump* will typically bring a page into the buffer pool LRU list, read the rows from it, and move on to the next page. In theory, the two-part LRU list will prevent this page from displacing pages that will be needed for a long time by placing it into the "young" sublist and only moving it to the "old" sublist after it has been accessed multiple times. But InnoDB is not configured to prevent this by default because the page has multiple rows, and thus the multiple accesses to read rows from the page will cause it to be moved to the "old" sublist immediately, placing pressure on pages that need a long lifetime. This variable specifies the number of milliseconds that must elapse before a page can move from the "young" part of the LRU list to the "old" part. It's set to 0 by default, and setting it to a small value such as 1000 (one second) has proven very effective in our benchmarks.

## Summary

After you've worked through this chapter, you should have a server configuration that is much better than the defaults. Your server should be fast and stable, and you should not need to tweak the configuration unless you run into an unusual circumstance.

To review, we suggest that you begin with our sample configuration file, set the basic options for your server and workload, and add safety options as desired. That's really all you need to do.

If you're running a dedicated database server, then the best option you can set is innodb_dedicated_server, which handles 90% of your performance configuration. If you are unable to use this option, then the most important options are these two:

- innodb_buffer_pool_size
- innodb_log_file_size

Congratulations—you just solved the vast majority of real-world configuration problems we've seen!

We've also made a lot of suggestions about what not to do. The most important of these are not to "tune" your server and not to use ratios, formulas, or "tuning scripts" as a basis for setting the configuration variables.

# CHAPTER 6

# Schema Design and Management

Good logical and physical design is the cornerstone of high performance, and you must design your schema for the specific queries you will run. This often involves trade-offs. For example, a denormalized schema can speed up some types of queries but slow down others. Adding counter and summary tables is a great way to optimize queries, but they can be expensive to maintain. MySQL's particular features and implementation details influence this quite a bit.

Likewise, your schema will evolve over time—as a result of what you learn about how you store and access data as well as how your business requirements change over time. This means that you should plan for schema changes as a frequent event. Later in this chapter, we help guide you through how to keep this activity from becoming an operational bottleneck for your organization.

This chapter—and the following one, which focuses on indexing—cover the MySQL-specific bits of schema design. We assume that you know how to design databases, so this is not an introductory chapter, or even an advanced chapter, on database design. As a chapter on MySQL database design, it's about what is different when designing databases with MySQL rather than other RDBMSs. If you need to study the basics of database design, we suggest Clare Churcher's book *Beginning Database Design* (Apress).

This chapter is preparation for the two that follow. In these three chapters, we will explore the interaction of logical design, physical design, and query execution. This requires a big-picture approach as well as attention to details. You need to understand the whole system to understand how each piece will affect others. You might find it useful to review this chapter after reading Chapter 7 on indexing and Chapter 8 on query optimization. Many of the topics discussed can't be considered in isolation.

# Choosing Optimal Data Types

MySQL supports a large variety of data types, and choosing the correct type to store your data is crucial to getting good performance. The following simple guidelines can help you make better choices, no matter what type of data you are storing:

*Smaller is usually better*

In general, try to use the smallest data type that can correctly store and represent your data. Smaller data types are usually faster because they use less space on the disk, in memory, and in the CPU cache. They also generally require fewer CPU cycles to process.

Make sure you don't underestimate the range of values you need to store, though, because increasing the data type range in multiple places in your schema can be a painful and time-consuming operation. If you're in doubt as to which is the best data type to use, choose the smallest one that you don't think you'll exceed. (If the system is not very busy or doesn't store much data, or if you're at an early phase in the design process, you can easily change it later.)

*Simple is good*

Fewer CPU cycles are typically required to process operations on simpler data types. For example, integers are cheaper to compare than characters because character sets and collations (sorting rules) make character comparisons complicated. Here are two examples: you should store dates and times in MySQL's built-in types instead of as strings, and you should use integers for IP addresses. We discuss these topics further later.

*Avoid NULL if possible*

A lot of tables include nullable columns even when the application does not need to store NULL (the absence of a value), merely because it's the default. It's usually best to specify columns as NOT NULL unless you intend to store NULL in them. It's harder for MySQL to optimize queries that refer to nullable columns because they make indexes, index statistics, and value comparisons more complicated. A nullable column uses more storage space and requires special processing inside MySQL. The performance improvement from changing NULL columns to NOT NULL is usually small, so don't make it a priority to find and change them on an existing schema unless you know they are causing problems.

The first step in deciding what data type to use for a given column is to determine what general class of types is appropriate: numeric, string, temporal, and so on. This is usually pretty straightforward, but we mention some special cases where the choice is unintuitive.

The next step is to choose the specific type. Many of MySQL's data types can store the same kind of data but vary in the range of values they can store, the precision they permit, or the physical space (on disk and in memory) they require. Some data types also have special behaviors or properties.

For example, a DATETIME and a TIMESTAMP column can store the same kind of data: date and time, to a precision of one second. However, TIMESTAMP uses only half as much storage space, is time zone aware, and has special auto-updating capabilities. On the other hand, it has a much smaller range of allowable values, and sometimes its special capabilities can be a handicap.

We discuss base data types here. MySQL supports many aliases for compatibility, such as INTEGER (maps to INT), BOOL (maps to TINYINT), and NUMERIC (maps to DECIMAL). These are only aliases. They can be confusing, but they don't affect performance. If you create a table with an aliased data type and then examine SHOW CREATE TABLE, you'll see that MySQL reports the base type, not the alias you used.

## Whole Numbers

There are two kinds of numbers: whole numbers and real numbers (numbers with a fractional part). If you're storing whole numbers, use one of the integer types: TINYINT, SMALLINT, MEDIUMINT, INT, or BIGINT. These require 8, 16, 24, 32, and 64 bits of storage space, respectively. They can store values from $-2^{(N - 1)}$ to $2^{(N - 1)} - 1$, where $N$ is the number of bits of storage space they use.

Integer types can optionally have the UNSIGNED attribute, which disallows negative values and approximately doubles the upper limit of positive values you can store. For example, a TINYINT UNSIGNED can store values ranging from 0 to 255 instead of from −128 to 127.

Signed and unsigned types use the same amount of storage space and have the same performance, so use whatever's best for your data range.

Your choice determines how MySQL *stores* the data, in memory and on disk. However, integer computations generally use 64-bit BIGINT integers. (The exceptions are some aggregate functions, which use DECIMAL or DOUBLE to perform computations.)

MySQL lets you specify a "width" for integer types, such as INT(11). This is meaningless for most applications: it does not restrict the legal range of values but simply specifies the number of characters MySQL's interactive tools (such as the command-line client) will reserve for display purposes. For storage and computational purposes, INT(1) is identical to INT(20).

## Real Numbers

Real numbers are numbers that have a fractional part. However, they aren't just for fractional numbers; you can also use DECIMAL to store integers that are so large they don't fit in BIGINT. MySQL supports both exact and inexact types.

The FLOAT and DOUBLE types support approximate calculations with standard floating-point math. If you need to know exactly how floating-point results are calculated, you will need to research your platform's floating-point implementation.

You can specify a floating-point column's desired precision in a couple of ways, which can cause MySQL to silently choose a different data type or to round values when you store them. These precision specifiers are nonstandard, so we suggest that you specify the type you want but not the precision.

Floating-point types typically use less space than DECIMAL to store the same range of values. A FLOAT column uses 4 bytes of storage. DOUBLE consumes 8 bytes and has greater precision and a larger range of values than FLOAT. As with integers, you're choosing only the storage type; MySQL uses DOUBLE for its internal calculations on floating-point types.

Because of the additional space requirements and computational cost, you should use DECIMAL only when you need exact results for fractional numbers—for example, when storing financial data. But in some high-volume cases, it actually makes sense to use a BIGINT instead and store the data as some multiple of the smallest fraction of currency you need to handle. Suppose you are required to store financial data to the ten-thousandth of a cent. You can multiply all dollar amounts by a million and store the result in a BIGINT, avoiding both the imprecision of floating-point storage and the cost of the precise DECIMAL math.

## String Types

MySQL supports quite a few string data types, with many variations on each. Each string column can have its own character set and set of sorting rules for that character set, or collation.

### VARCHAR and CHAR types

The two major string types are VARCHAR and CHAR, which store character values. Unfortunately, it's hard to explain exactly how these values are stored on disk and in memory because the implementations depend on the storage engine. We assume you are using InnoDB; if not, you should read the documentation for your storage engine.

Let's take a look at how VARCHAR and CHAR values are typically stored on disk. Be aware that a storage engine may store a CHAR or VARCHAR value differently in memory from how it stores that value on disk, and the server may translate the value into yet another storage format when it retrieves it from the storage engine. Here's a general comparison of the two types:

## VARCHAR

VARCHAR stores variable-length character strings and is the most common string data type. It can require less storage space than fixed-length types because it uses only as much space as it needs (i.e., less space is used to store shorter values).

VARCHAR uses 1 or 2 extra bytes to record the value's length: 1 byte if the column's maximum length is 255 bytes or less, and 2 bytes if it's more. Assuming the latin1 character set, a VARCHAR(10) will use up to 11 bytes of storage space. A VARCHAR(1000) can use up to 1,002 bytes, because it needs 2 bytes to store length information.

VARCHAR helps performance because it saves space. However, because the rows are variable length, they can grow when you update them, which can cause extra work. If a row grows and no longer fits in its original location, the behavior is storage engine dependent. For example, InnoDB may need to split the page to fit the row into it. Other storage engines may never update data in place at all.

It's usually worth using VARCHAR when the maximum column length is much larger than the average length; when updates to the field are rare, so fragmentation is not a problem; and when you're using a complex character set such as UTF-8, where each character uses a variable number of bytes of storage.

It's trickier with InnoDB, which can store long VARCHAR values as BLOBs. We will discuss this later.

## CHAR

CHAR is fixed-length: MySQL always allocates enough space for the specified number of characters. When storing a CHAR value, MySQL removes any trailing spaces. Values are padded with spaces as needed for comparisons.

CHAR is useful if you want to store very short strings or if all the values are nearly the same length. For example, CHAR is a good choice for MD5 values for user passwords, which are always the same length. CHAR is also better than VARCHAR for data that's changed frequently because a fixed-length row is not prone to fragmentation. For very short columns, CHAR is also more efficient than VARCHAR; a CHAR(1) designed to hold only Y and N values will use only 1 byte in a single-byte character set,[1] but a VARCHAR(1) would use 2 bytes because of the length byte.

---

1 Remember that the length is specified in characters, not bytes. A multibyte character set can require more than 1 byte to store each character.

This behavior can be a little confusing, so we'll illustrate with an example. First, we create a table with a single CHAR(10) column and store some values in it:

```
mysql> CREATE TABLE char_test( char_col CHAR(10));
mysql> INSERT INTO char_test(char_col) VALUES
    -> ('string1'), (' string2'), ('string3 ');
```

When we retrieve the values, the trailing spaces have been stripped away:

```
mysql> SELECT CONCAT("'", char_col, "'") FROM char_test;
+---------------------------+
| CONCAT("'", char_col, "'") |
+---------------------------+
| 'string1'                 |
| ' string2'                |
| 'string3'                 |
+---------------------------+
```

If we store the same values in a VARCHAR(10) column, we get the following result upon retrieval, where the trailing space on string3 has not been removed:

```
mysql> SELECT CONCAT("'", varchar_col, "'") FROM varchar_test;
+------------------------------+
| CONCAT("'", varchar_col, "'") |
+------------------------------+
| 'string1'                    |
| ' string2'                   |
| 'string3 '                   |
+------------------------------+
```

The sibling types for CHAR and VARCHAR are BINARY and VARBINARY, which store binary strings. Binary strings are very similar to conventional strings, but they store bytes instead of characters. Padding is also different: MySQL pads BINARY values with \0 (the zero byte) instead of spaces and doesn't strip the pad value on retrieval.[2]

These types are useful when you need to store binary data and want MySQL to compare the values as bytes instead of characters. The advantage of byte-wise comparisons is more than just a matter of case insensitivity. MySQL literally compares BINARY strings one byte at a time, according to the numeric value of each byte. As a result, binary comparisons can be much simpler than character comparisons, so they are faster.

---

2 Be careful with the BINARY type if the value must remain unchanged after retrieval. MySQL will pad it to the required length with \0s.

Storing the value `'hello'` requires the same amount of space in a `VARCHAR(5)` and a `VARCHAR(200)` column. Is there any advantage to using the shorter column?

As it turns out, there is a big advantage. The larger column can use much more memory, because MySQL often allocates fixed-size chunks of memory to hold values internally. This is especially bad for sorting or operations that use in-memory temporary tables. The same thing happens with filesorts that use on-disk temporary tables.

The best strategy is to allocate only as much space as you really need.

## BLOB and TEXT types

`BLOB` and `TEXT` are string data types designed to store large amounts of data as either binary or character strings, respectively.

In fact, they are each families of data types: the character types are `TINYTEXT`, `SMALLTEXT`, `TEXT`, `MEDIUMTEXT`, and `LONGTEXT`, and the binary types are `TINYBLOB`, `SMALLBLOB`, `BLOB`, `MEDIUMBLOB`, and `LONGBLOB`. `BLOB` is a synonym for `SMALLBLOB`, and `TEXT` is a synonym for `SMALLTEXT`.

Unlike all other data types, MySQL handles each `BLOB` and `TEXT` value as an object with its own identity. Storage engines often store them specially; InnoDB may use a separate "external" storage area for them when they're large. Each value requires from 1 to 4 bytes of storage space in the row and enough space in external storage to actually hold the value.

The only difference between the `BLOB` and `TEXT` families is that `BLOB` types store binary data with no collation or character set, but `TEXT` types have a character set and collation.

MySQL sorts `BLOB` and `TEXT` columns differently from other types: instead of sorting the full length of the string, it sorts only the first `max_sort_length` bytes of such columns. If you need to sort by only the first few characters, you can decrease the `max_sort_length` server variable.

MySQL can't index the full length of these data types and can't use the indexes for sorting.

## Images in a Database?

In the past, it was not uncommon for some applications to accept uploaded images and store them as BLOB data in a MySQL database. This method was convenient for keeping the data for an application together; however, as the size of the data grew, operations like schema changes got slower and slower due to the size of that BLOB data.

If you can avoid it, don't store data like images in a database. Instead, write them to a separate object data store and use the table to track the location or filename for the image.

### Using ENUM instead of a string type

Sometimes you can use an ENUM column instead of conventional string types. An ENUM column can store a predefined set of distinct string values. MySQL stores them very compactly, packed into 1 or 2 bytes depending on the number of values in the list. It stores each value internally as an integer representing its position in the field definition list. Here's an example:

```
mysql> CREATE TABLE enum_test(
    -> e ENUM('fish', 'apple', 'dog') NOT NULL
    -> );
mysql> INSERT INTO enum_test(e) VALUES('fish'), ('dog'), ('apple');
```

The three rows actually store integers, not strings. You can see the dual nature of the values by retrieving them in a numeric context:

```
mysql> SELECT e + 0 FROM enum_test;
+-------+
| e + 0 |
+-------+
|     1 |
|     3 |
|     2 |
+-------+
```

This duality can be terribly confusing if you specify numbers for your ENUM constants, as in ENUM('1', '2', '3'). We suggest you don't do this.

Another surprise is that an ENUM field sorts by the internal integer values, not by the strings themselves:

```
mysql> SELECT e FROM enum_test ORDER BY e;
+-------+
| e     |
+-------+
| fish  |
```

```
| apple |
| dog   |
+-------+
```

You can work around this by specifying ENUM members in the order in which you want them to sort. You can also use FIELD() to specify a sort order explicitly in your queries, but this prevents MySQL from using the index for sorting:

```
mysql> SELECT e FROM enum_test ORDER BY FIELD(e, 'apple', 'dog', 'fish');
+-------+
| e     |
+-------+
| apple |
| dog   |
| fish  |
+-------+
```

If we'd defined the values in alphabetical order, we wouldn't have needed to do that.

Because MySQL stores each value as an integer and has to do a lookup to convert it to its string representation, ENUM columns have some overhead. This is usually offset by their smaller size, but not always. In particular, it can be slower to join a CHAR or VARCHAR column to an ENUM column than to another CHAR or VARCHAR column.

To illustrate, we benchmarked how quickly MySQL performs such a join on a table in one of our applications. The table has a fairly wide primary key:

```
CREATE TABLE webservicecalls (
   day date NOT NULL,
   account smallint NOT NULL,
   service varchar(10) NOT NULL,
   method varchar(50) NOT NULL,
   calls int NOT NULL,
   items int NOT NULL,
   time float NOT NULL,
   cost decimal(9,5) NOT NULL,
   updated datetime,
   PRIMARY KEY (day, account, service, method)
) ENGINE=InnoDB;
```

The table contains about 110,000 rows and is only about 10 MB, so it fits entirely in memory. The service column contains 5 distinct values with an average length of 4 characters, and the method column contains 71 values with an average length of 20 characters.

We made a copy of this table and converted the service and method columns to ENUM, as follows:

```
CREATE TABLE webservicecalls_enum (
   ... omitted ...
   service ENUM(...values omitted...) NOT NULL,
   method ENUM(...values omitted...) NOT NULL,
```

```
      ... omitted ...
    ) ENGINE=InnoDB;
```

We then measured the performance of joining the tables by the primary key columns. Here is the query we used:

```
mysql> SELECT SQL_NO_CACHE COUNT(*)
    -> FROM webservicecalls
    -> JOIN webservicecalls USING(day, account, service, method);
```

We varied this query to join the VARCHAR and ENUM columns in different combinations. Table 6-1 shows the results.[3]

*Table 6-1. Speed of joining VARCHAR and ENUM columns*

| Test | Queries per second |
|---|---|
| VARCHAR joined to VARCHAR | 2.6 |
| VARCHAR joined to ENUM | 1.7 |
| ENUM joined to VARCHAR | 1.8 |
| ENUM joined to ENUM | 3.5 |

The join is faster after converting the columns to ENUM, but joining the ENUM columns to VARCHAR columns is slower. In this case, it looks like a good idea to convert these columns, as long as they don't have to be joined to VARCHAR columns. It's a common design practice to use "lookup tables" with integer primary keys to avoid using character-based values in joins.

However, there's another benefit to converting the columns: according to the Data_length column from SHOW TABLE STATUS, converting these two columns to ENUM made the table about one-third smaller. In some cases, this might be beneficial even if the ENUM columns have to be joined to VARCHAR columns. Also, the primary key itself is only about half the size after the conversion. Because this is an InnoDB table, if there are any other indexes on this table, reducing the primary key size will make them much smaller, too.

 While ENUM types are very efficient in how they store values, changes to the valid values that can be in an ENUM always require a schema change. If you do not yet have a robust system that automates schema changes as we describe later in this chapter, this operational need can be a major inconvenience if your ENUM changes often. We also refer to an antipattern of "too many ENUMs" in schema design later.

---

3 Times are for relative comparison, as the speed of CPUs, memory, and other hardware changes over time.

# Date and Time Types

MySQL has many types for various kinds of date and time values, such as YEAR and DATE. The finest granularity of time MySQL can store is microsecond. Most of the temporal types have no alternatives, so there is no question of which one is the best choice. The only question is what to do when you need to store both the date and the time. MySQL offers two very similar data types for this purpose: DATETIME and TIME STAMP. For many applications, either will work, but in some cases, one works better than the other. Let's take a look:

DATETIME

This type can hold a large range of values, from the year 1000 to the year 9999, with a precision of one microsecond. It stores the date and time packed into an integer in YYYYMMDDHHMMSS format, independent of time zone. This uses 8 bytes of storage space.

By default, MySQL displays DATETIME values in a sortable, unambiguous format, such as 2008-01-16 22:37:08. This is the ANSI standard way to represent dates and times.

TIMESTAMP

As its name implies, the TIMESTAMP type stores the number of seconds elapsed since midnight, January 1, 1970, Greenwich Mean Time (GMT)—the same as a Unix timestamp. TIMESTAMP uses only 4 bytes of storage, so it has a much smaller range than DATETIME: from the year 1970 to January 19, 2038. MySQL provides the FROM_UNIXTIME() and UNIX_TIMESTAMP() functions to convert a Unix time-stamp to a date and vice versa.

The value a TIMESTAMP displays also depends on the time zone. The MySQL server, operating system, and client connections all have time zone settings.

Thus, a TIMESTAMP that stores the value 0 actually displays it as 1969-12-31 19:00:00 in Eastern Standard Time (EST), which has a five-hour offset from GMT. It's worth emphasizing this difference: if you store or access data from multiple time zones, the behavior of TIMESTAMP and DATETIME will be very different. The former preserves values relative to the time zone in use, while the latter preserves the textual representation of the date and time.

TIMESTAMP also has special properties that DATETIME doesn't have. By default, MySQL will set the first TIMESTAMP column to the current time when you insert a row without specifying a value for the column.[4] MySQL also updates the first `TIMESTAMP` column's value by default when you update the row unless you assign a value explicitly in the `UPDATE` statement. You can configure the insertion and update behaviors for any `TIMESTAMP` column. Finally, `TIMESTAMP` columns are `NOT NULL` by default, which is different from every other data type.

---

### Storing Date and Time as an Integer?

Both `DATETIME` and `TIMESTAMP` force you to deal with time zones on the server and the client, and while a `TIMESTAMP` is more space efficient than a `DATETIME` (4 bytes versus 8 bytes, ignoring fractional second support), it also suffers from the year 2038 problem.

Ultimately, storing date and time comes down to a few things:

- How far forward or backward do you need to support date and time?
- How much does storage space matter for this data?
- Do you need fractional second support?
- Do you want to shift date, time, and time zone handling to MySQL or deal with it in code?

It is becoming increasingly popular to avoid the complexities of MySQL's handling by storing your date and time as the Unix epoch, or number of seconds since January 1, 1970, in Coordinated Universal Time (UTC). With a signed 32-bit `INT`, you get until the year 2038. With an unsigned 32-bit `INT`, you get until the year 2106. With 64-bit, you can go beyond that.

Much like popular discussions around operating systems, editors, and tabs versus spaces, how you store this particular set of data can be more of an opinion than best practice. Consider if this is a viable route for your use case.

---

## Bit-Packed Data Types

MySQL has a few storage types that use individual bits within a value to store data compactly. All of these types are technically string types, regardless of the underlying storage format and manipulations:

---

4 The rules for `TIMESTAMP` behavior are complex and have changed in various MySQL versions, so you should verify that you are getting the behavior you want. It's usually a good idea to examine the output of `SHOW CRE ATE TABLE` after making changes to `TIMESTAMP` columns.

## BIT

You can use a BIT column to store one or many true/false values in a single column. BIT(1) defines a field that contains a single bit, BIT(2) stores 2 bits, and so on; the maximum length of a BIT column is 64 bits. InnoDB stores each column as the smallest integer type large enough to contain the bits, so you don't save any storage space.

MySQL treats BIT as a string type, not a numeric type. When you retrieve a BIT(1) value, the result is a string, but the contents are the binary value 0 or 1, not the ASCII value "0" or "1". However, if you retrieve the value in a numeric context, the result is the number to which the bit string converts. Keep this in mind if you need to compare the result to another value. For example, if you store the value b'00111001' (which is the binary equivalent of 57) into a BIT(8) column and retrieve it, you will get the string containing the character code 57. This happens to be the ASCII character code for "9". But in a numeric context, you'll get the value 57:

```
mysql> CREATE TABLE bittest(a bit(8));
mysql> INSERT INTO bittest VALUES(b'00111001');
mysql> SELECT a, a + 0 FROM bittest;
+------+-------+
| a    | a + 0 |
+------+-------+
| 9    |    57 |
+------+-------+
```

This can be very confusing, so we recommend that you use BIT with caution. For most applications, we think it is a better idea to avoid this type.

If you want to store a true/false value in a single bit of storage space, another option is to create a nullable CHAR(0) column. This column is capable of storing either the absence of a value (NULL) or a zero-length value (the empty string). This works in practice, but it can be obtuse to others using data in the database and make it difficult to write queries. Unless you're hyper-focused on saving space, we still recommend using TINYINT.

## SET

If you need to store many true/false values, consider combining many columns into one with MySQL's native SET data type, which MySQL represents internally as a packed set of bits. It uses storage efficiently, and MySQL has functions such as FIND_IN_SET() and FIELD() that make it easy to use in queries.

### Bitwise operations on integer columns

An alternative to SET is to use an integer as a packed set of bits. For example, you can pack 8 bits in a TINYINT and manipulate them with bitwise operators. You can make this easier by defining named constants for each bit in your application code.

The major advantage of this approach over SET is that you can change the "enumeration" the field represents without an ALTER TABLE. The drawback is that your queries are harder to write and understand (what does it mean when bit 5 is set?). Some people are comfortable with bitwise manipulations and some aren't, so whether you'll want to try this technique is largely a matter of taste.

An example application for packed bits is an access control list (ACL) that stores permissions. Each bit or SET element represents a value such as CAN_READ, CAN_WRITE, or CAN_DELETE. If you use a SET column, you'll let MySQL store the bit-to-value mapping in the column definition; if you use an integer column, you'll store the mapping in your application code. Here's what the queries would look like with a SET column:

```
mysql> CREATE TABLE acl (
    -> perms SET('CAN_READ', 'CAN_WRITE', 'CAN_DELETE') NOT NULL
    -> );
mysql> INSERT INTO acl(perms) VALUES ('CAN_READ,CAN_DELETE');
mysql> SELECT perms FROM acl WHERE FIND_IN_SET('CAN_READ', perms);
+---------------------+
| perms               |
+---------------------+
| CAN_READ,CAN_DELETE |
+---------------------+
```

If you used an integer, you could write that example as follows:

```
mysql> SET @CAN_READ := 1 << 0,
    -> @CAN_WRITE := 1 << 1,
    -> @CAN_DELETE := 1 << 2;
mysql> CREATE TABLE acl (
    -> perms TINYINT UNSIGNED NOT NULL DEFAULT 0
    -> );
mysql> INSERT INTO acl(perms) VALUES(@CAN_READ + @CAN_DELETE);
mysql> SELECT perms FROM acl WHERE perms & @CAN_READ;
+-------+
| perms |
+-------+
| 5     |
+-------+
```

We've used variables to define the values, but you can use constants in your code instead.

# JSON Data

It is becoming increasingly common to use JSON as a format for interchanging data between systems. MySQL has a native JSON data type that makes it easy to operate on parts of the JSON structure directly within the table. Purists may suggest that storing raw JSON in a database is an antipattern because ideally, schemas are a representation of the fields in JSON. Newcomers may look at the JSON data type and see a short path by avoiding creating and managing independent fields. Which method is better is largely subjective, but we'll be objective by presenting a sample use case and comparing both query speed and data size.

Our sample data was a list of 202 near-Earth asteroids and comets discovered, courtesy of NASA (*https://oreil.ly/2oZX9*). Tests were performed under MySQL 8.0.22 on a four-core, 16 GB RAM virtual machine. An example of the data:

```
[
  {
    "designation":"419880 (2011 AH37)",
    "discovery_date":"2011-01-07T00:00:00.000",
    "h_mag":"19.7",
    "moid_au":"0.035",
    "q_au_1":"0.84",
    "q_au_2":"4.26",
    "period_yr":"4.06",
    "i_deg":"9.65",
    "pha":"Y",
    "orbit_class":"Apollo"
  }
]
```

This data represents a designation, date it was discovered, and data collected about the entity, including numeric and text fields.

First, we took the data set in JSON and converted it to be one row per entry. This resulted in a schema that looks relatively simple:

```
mysql> DESC asteroids_json;
+-----------+------+------+-----+---------+-------+
| Field     | Type | Null | Key | Default | Extra |
+-----------+------+------+-----+---------+-------+
| json_data | json | YES  |     | NULL    |       |
+-----------+------+------+-----+---------+-------+
```

Second, we took this JSON and converted the fields to columns using a suitable data type for the data. This resulted in the following schema:

```
mysql> DESC asteroids_sql;
+----------------+-------------+------+-----+---------+-------+
| Field          | Type        | Null | Key | Default | Extra |
+----------------+-------------+------+-----+---------+-------+
| designation    | varchar(30) | YES  |     | NULL    |       |
| discovery_date | date        | YES  |     | NULL    |       |
| h_mag          | float       | YES  |     | NULL    |       |
| moid_au        | float       | YES  |     | NULL    |       |
| q_au_1         | float       | YES  |     | NULL    |       |
| q_au_2         | float       | YES  |     | NULL    |       |
| period_yr      | float       | YES  |     | NULL    |       |
| i_deg          | float       | YES  |     | NULL    |       |
| pha            | char(3)     | YES  |     | NULL    |       |
| orbit_class    | varchar(30) | YES  |     | NULL    |       |
+----------------+-------------+------+-----+---------+-------+
```

The first comparison is on data size:

```
mysql> SHOW TABLE STATUS\G
*************************** 1. row ***************************
          Name: asteroids_json
        Engine: InnoDB
       Version: 10
    Row_format: Dynamic
          Rows: 202
Avg_row_length: 405
   Data_length: 81920
Max_data_length: 0
  Index_length: 0

*************************** 2. row ***************************
          Name: asteroids_sql
        Engine: InnoDB
       Version: 10
    Row_format: Dynamic
          Rows: 202
Avg_row_length: 243
   Data_length: 49152
Max_data_length: 0
  Index_length: 0
```

Our SQL version uses three 16 KB pages, and our JSON version uses five 16 KB pages. This doesn't come as much of a surprise. A JSON data type will use more space to store the additional characters for defining JSON (braces, brackets, colons, etc.) as well as the whitespace. In this small example, the size of data storage can be improved by converting JSON to specific data types.

There may be valid use cases where the data size is not that important. How does query latency measure up between the two?

To select all of a single column in SQL, our syntax is straightforward:

```
SELECT designation FROM asteroids_sql;
```

On our first run of this query, uncached by InnoDB's buffer pool, we got a result of 1.14 milliseconds (ms). The second execution, with it in memory, we got 0.44 ms.

For JSON, we are able to access a field inside of the JSON structure:

```
SELECT json_data->'$.designation' FROM asteroids_json
```

Similarly, our first execution, uncached, executed in 1.13 ms. Subsequent executions were at around 0.80 ms. At this execution speed, we expect that there will be a reasonable variation—we're talking about a difference of hundreds of microseconds in a VM environment. In our opinion, both queries executed reasonably quickly, although it's worth noting that the JSON query is still about twice as long.

What about accessing specific rows, though? For the single-row lookup, we take advantage of using indexes:

```
ALTER TABLE asteroids_sql ADD INDEX ( designation );
```

When we do a single-row lookup, our SQL version runs in 0.33 ms, and our JSON version runs in 0.58 ms, giving an edge to the SQL version. This is easily explained: our index is allowing InnoDB to return 1 row instead of 202 rows.

Comparing an indexed query to a full table scan is unfair, though. To level the playing field, we need to use the *generated columns* feature to extract the designation and then create an index against that virtual generated column:

```
ALTER TABLE asteroids_json ADD COLUMN designation VARCHAR(30) GENERATED ALWAYS AS
(json_data->"$.designation"), ADD INDEX ( designation );
```

This gives us a schema on our JSON table that looks like this:

```
mysql> DESC asteroids_json;
+-------------+-------------+------+-----+---------+-------------------+
| Field       | Type        | Null | Key | Default | Extra             |
+-------------+-------------+------+-----+---------+-------------------+
| json_data   | json        | YES  |     | NULL    |                   |
| designation | varchar(30) | YES  | MUL | NULL    | VIRTUAL GENERATED |
+-------------+-------------+------+-----+---------+-------------------+
```

Our schema now generates a virtual column for the designation from the `json_data` column and indexes it. Now, we rerun our single-row lookup to use the indexed column instead of the JSON column path operator (`->`). Since the field data is quoted in the JSON, we need to search for it quoted in our SQL as well:

```
SELECT * FROM asteroids_json WHERE designation='"(2010 GW62)"';
```

This query executed in 0.4 ms, fairly close to our SQL version of 0.33 ms.

From our preceding simple test case, the amount of used tablespace seems to be the primary driver for why you would use SQL columns rather than storing a raw JSON document. Speed is still better with SQL columns. Overall, the decision to use native SQL versus JSON comes down to whether the ease of storing JSON in the database outweighs the performance. If you're accessing this data millions or billions of times per day, the speed difference is going to add up.

## Choosing Identifiers

In general, an *identifier* is the way you refer to a row and often what makes it unique. For example, if you have a table about users, you might want to assign each user a numerical ID or a unique username. This field may be some or all of your PRIMARY KEY.

Choosing a good data type for an identifier column is very important. You're more likely to compare these columns to other values (for example, in joins) and to use them for lookups than other columns. You're also likely to use them in other tables as foreign keys, so when you choose a data type for an identifier column, you're probably choosing the type in related tables as well. (As we demonstrated earlier in this chapter, it's a good idea to use the same data types in related tables because you're likely to use them for joins.)

When choosing a type for an identifier column, you need to consider not only the storage type but also how MySQL performs computations and comparisons on that type. For example, MySQL stores ENUM and SET types internally as integers but converts them to strings when doing comparisons in a string context.

Once you choose a type, make sure you use the same type in all related tables. The types should match exactly, including properties such as UNSIGNED.[5] Mixing different data types can cause performance problems, and even if it doesn't, implicit type conversions during comparisons can create hard-to-find errors. These may even crop up much later, after you've forgotten that you're comparing different data types.

Choose the smallest size that can hold your required range of values, and leave room for future growth if necessary. For example, if you have a state_id column that stores US state names, you don't need thousands or millions of values, so don't use an INT. A TINYINT should be sufficient and is 3 bytes smaller. If you use this value as a foreign key in other tables, 3 bytes can make a big difference. Here we give a few tips.

---

5 If you're using the InnoDB storage engine, you may not be able to create foreign keys unless the data types match exactly. The resulting error message, "ERROR 1005 (HY000): Can't create table," can be confusing depending on the context, and questions about it come up often on MySQL mailing lists. (Oddly, you can create foreign keys between VARCHAR columns of different lengths.)

---

## Integer types

Integers are usually the best choice for identifiers because they're fast and they work with `AUTO_INCREMENT`. `AUTO_INCREMENT` is a column attribute that generates a new integer type for each new row. For example, a billing system may need to generate a new invoice for each customer. Using `AUTO_INCREMENT` means that the first invoice generated would be 1, the second 2, and so on. Be aware that you should make sure you have the right integer size for the growth of the data you expect. There has been more than one story of system downtime associated with unexpectedly running out of integers.

## ENUM and SET

The `ENUM` and `SET` types are generally a poor choice for identifiers, although they can be okay for static "definition tables" that contain status or "type" values. `ENUM` and `SET` columns are appropriate for holding information like an order's status or a product's type.

As an example, if you use an `ENUM` field to define a product's type, you might want a lookup table primary keyed on an identical `ENUM` field. (You could add columns to the lookup table for descriptive text, to generate a glossary, or to provide meaningful labels in a pull-down menu on a website.) In this case, you'll want to use the `ENUM` as an identifier, but for most purposes, you should avoid doing so.

## String types

Avoid string types for identifiers if possible, because they take up a lot of space and are generally slower than integer types.

You should also be very careful with completely "random" strings, such as those produced by `MD5()`, `SHA1()`, or `UUID()`. Each new value you generate with them will be distributed in arbitrary ways over a large space, which can slow `INSERT` and some types of `SELECT` queries:[6]

- They slow `INSERT` queries because the inserted value has to go in a random location in indexes. This causes page splits, random disk accesses, and clustered index fragmentation for clustered storage engines.

- They slow `SELECT` queries because logically adjacent rows will be widely dispersed on disk and in memory.

- Random values cause caches to perform poorly for all types of queries because they defeat locality of reference, which is how caching works. If the entire data set

---

6 On the other hand, for some very large tables with many writers, such pseudorandom values can actually help eliminate "hot spots."

is equally "hot," there is no advantage to having any particular part of the data cached in memory, and if the working set does not fit in memory, the cache will have a lot of flushes and misses.

If you do store universally unique identifier (UUID) values, you should remove the dashes or, even better, convert the UUID values to 16-byte numbers with UNHEX() and store them in a BINARY(16) column. You can retrieve the values in hexadecimal format with the HEX() function.

---

### Beware of Autogenerated Schemas

We've covered the most important data type considerations (some with serious and others with more minor performance implications), but we haven't yet told you about the evils of autogenerated schemas.

Badly written schema migration programs and programs that autogenerate schemas can cause severe performance problems. Some programs use large VARCHAR fields for everything or use different data types for columns that will be compared in joins. Be sure to double-check a schema if it was created for you automatically.

Object-relational mapping (ORM) systems (and the "frameworks" that use them) are frequently another performance nightmare. Some of these systems let you store any type of data in any type of backend data store, which usually means they aren't designed to use the strengths of any of the data stores. Sometimes they store each property of each object in a separate row, even using timestamp-based versioning, so there are multiple versions of each property!

This design may appeal to developers because it lets them work in an object-oriented fashion without needing to think about how the data is stored. However, applications that "hide complexity from developers" usually don't scale well. We suggest you think carefully before trading performance for developer productivity, and always test on a realistically large data set, so you don't discover performance problems too late.

---

## Special Types of Data

Some kinds of data don't correspond directly to the available built-in types. A good example is an IPv4 address. People often use VARCHAR(15) columns to store IP addresses. However, they are really unsigned 32-bit integers, not strings. The dotted-quad notation is just a way of writing it out so that humans can read it more easily. You should store IP addresses as unsigned integers. MySQL provides the INET_ATON() and INET_NTOA() functions to convert between the two representations. The space used shrinks from ~16 bytes for a VARCHAR(15) down to 4 bytes for an unsigned 32-bit integer. If you're concerned about readability in the database and don't want to keep using functions to view row data, remember that MySQL has views and you can use them to see your data easier.

# Schema Design Gotchas in MySQL

Although there are universally bad and good design principles, there are also issues that arise from how MySQL is implemented, and that means you can make MySQL-specific mistakes, too. This section discusses problems that we've observed in schema designs with MySQL. It might help you avoid those mistakes and choose alternatives that work better with MySQL's specific implementation.

## Too Many Columns

MySQL's storage engine API works by copying rows between the server and the storage engine in a row buffer format; the server then decodes the buffer into columns. It can be costly to turn the row buffer into the row data structure with the decoded columns. InnoDB's row format always requires conversion. The cost of this conversion depends on the number of columns. We discovered that this can become expensive when we investigated an issue with high CPU consumption for a customer with extremely wide tables (hundreds of columns), even though only a few columns were actually used. If you're planning for hundreds of columns, be aware that the server's performance characteristics will be a bit different.

## Too Many Joins

The so-called entity-attribute-value (EAV) design pattern is a classic case of a universally bad design pattern that especially doesn't work well in MySQL. MySQL has a limitation of 61 tables per join, and EAV databases require many self-joins. We've seen more than a few EAV databases eventually exceed this limit. Even at many fewer joins than 61, however, the cost of planning and optimizing the query can become problematic for MySQL. As a rough rule of thumb, it's better to have a dozen or fewer tables per query if you need queries to execute very fast with high concurrency.

## The All-Powerful ENUM

Beware of overusing ENUM. Here's an example we saw:

```
CREATE TABLE ... (
  country enum(','0','1','2',...,'31')
```

The schema was sprinkled liberally with this pattern. This would probably be a questionable design decision in any database with an enumerated value type because it really should be an integer that is foreign-keyed to a "dictionary" or "lookup" table anyway.

## The ENUM in Disguise

An ENUM permits the column to hold one value from a set of defined values. A SET permits the column to hold one or more values from a set of defined values. Sometimes these can be easy to confuse. Here's an example:

```
CREATE TABLE ...(
  is_default set('Y','N') NOT NULL default 'N'
```

That almost surely ought to be an ENUM instead of a SET, assuming that it can't be both true and false at the same time.

## NULL Not Invented Here

We wrote earlier about the benefits of avoiding NULL, and indeed, we suggest considering alternatives when possible. Even when you do need to store a "no value" fact in a table, you might not need to use NULL. Perhaps you can use zero, a special value, or an empty string instead.

However, you can take this to extremes. Don't be too afraid of using NULL when you need to represent an unknown value. In some cases, it's better to use NULL than a magical constant. Selecting one value from the domain of a constrained type, such as using −1 to represent an unknown integer, can complicate your code a lot, introduce bugs, and just generally make a total mess out of things. Handling NULL isn't always easy, but it's often better than the alternative.

Here's one example we've seen pretty frequently:

```
CREATE TABLE ... (
  dt DATETIME NOT NULL DEFAULT '0000-00-00 00:00:00'
```

That bogus all-zeros value can cause lots of problems. (You can configure MySQL's SQL_MODE to disallow nonsense dates, which is an especially good practice for a new application that hasn't yet created a database full of bad data.)

On a related topic, MySQL does index NULLs, unlike Oracle, which doesn't include nonvalues in indexes.

Now that we have covered a lot of practical advice around data types, how to choose them, and what not to do, let's move on to the other piece of good, iterative schema design: schema management.

# Schema Management

Running schema changes is one of the most common tasks a database engineer has to undertake. When you get to the stage of running dozens or hundreds of database instances with varying business contexts and evolving features, you want to be careful that applying these schema changes is not a bottleneck for the entire organization but is still being done safely and without disrupting operations. This section will cover how to think about schema change management as part of a "data store platform," what core values should guide this strategy, what tools you can introduce to enable this strategy, and how it all fits together in your larger software-delivery life cycle.

## Schema Management as Part of the Data Store Platform

If you speak with any engineering leader of a fast-growing organization, you will find that engineer velocity and the time from feature design to running in production are top of their list of things to optimize. In that context, your task as you plan managing schemas at scale is to not allow schema management to become a manual process that bottlenecks progress for the entire engineering organization on one or a few people.

### Set up your partner teams for success

As the number of teams that rely on MySQL instances in the organization grows, you want to always be the enabler of these teams' success, not the gate they need to pass through to get their work done. This applies to schema changes, too, which means you want to create a path to deploying schema changes that does not hinge on "only the database team does it."

### Integrate schema management with continuous integration

After we cover a number of tools that enable schema management at scale, we will talk about how to integrate them with CI pipelines. But right now we would like to emphasize that if you start with the premise that schema changes are going to be managed by feature teams and not just the database team, then you need to get as close in workflow as you can to how these teams already deploy code changes. Science has shown (*https://oreil.ly/hozRf*) that teams that treat schema management the same way they treat code deploys experience a more positive feature-delivery process and see improvement in the teams' velocity. We'll discuss the tools that enable that iteration with software-delivery practices in mind.

### Source control for schema changes

We all use source control for the code we deploy, right? Then why not also for what the database schema is supposed to look like? One of the very first steps to schema management at scale is making sure you have source control underpinning and tracking the changes being done. It is not only A Good Thing To Do™, but in many cases, it's required by your friendly compliance team, as you will see in Chapter 13. Let's cover some tools that enable iterating over database schemas.

For maximum value for your organization, use the same CI tool engineering uses for code deploys.

**Paid options.**  The landscape for database schema management as an enterprise tool has grown dramatically in the past few years, especially in increased support for MySQL installations. If you are looking for an off-the-shelf solution to help your organization manage schema changes, here are some things you should consider:

*Cost*
>  Cost models vary, so you should be careful if the solution you choose will charge per target (schema to manage) as that can add up quickly.

*Online schema management*
>  As of this writing, paid solutions such as Flyway (*https://flywaydb.org*) do not have a clear path to running schema changes for you in a nonblocking manner, although its competitor Liquibase (*https://www.liquibase.org*) has a well-supported plug-in for Percona's online schema change. You need to be aware of the trade-offs each vendor is deciding on your behalf and what these trade-offs mean to your availability, especially if you plan to use these vendors to manage schema changes for databases that are large in size (multiple terabytes on disk).

*Out-of-the-box integrations*
>  Most of these tools come with assumptions about what languages your in-house software is written in and therefore what hooks to provide for integration with your existing software-delivery process. If your shop is highly polyglot or in the process of changing major software languages, this could exclude some of these vendors. We will cover in the next section what to do if you need to "do it yourself" when implementing schema source control management.

**Using open source.**  If procuring a paid tool is out of reach or if you have valid reasons why none of the current solutions is a good fit for your organization, you can achieve the same outcomes using existing open source tooling and your organization's CI pipeline.

A prominent open source solution for managing schema changes in version control across multiple environments is Skeema (*https://www.skeema.io*). Skeema itself does not run the schema changes for you in production—we will cover how to do that shortly—but it is a great tool for tracking changes in a source control repository per database cluster and across multiple environments. Its CLI implementation provides a lot of flexibility when integrating with your CI solution of choice. How you integrate Skeema directly with your CI solution will require some consideration of the capabilities that CI solution has. This blog post by the team at Twilio Sendgrid (*https://oreil.ly/8YhBS*) explains how they integrated Skeema with Buildkite to achieve autonomy for feature teams looking to manage changes to their databases.

Note that however this solution integrates with your CI, it also needs access to run schema changes to all your environments, including production. This means also collaborating with your security team to make sure you are creating the correct access controls to reap the benefits of automating schema deployments using continuous integration.

 If you are already on the path of scaling your database infrastructure using Vitess, you should be aware that Vitess also manages schema changes for you. Make sure to check that specific section of the documentation.

The field for managing schema changes across environments with both an automation and compliance mindset has grown dramatically in the past few years. Here are some final takeaways for you as you make your choice:

- Stay as close as possible to the existing software-deploy tooling and workflow. You want this to be familiar to your larger engineering organization.

- Use a tool that can integrate basic linting checks against schema changes to ensure some baseline requirements are met. Your solution should automatically fail a pull request if the new table does not use the right charset or there are foreign keys if you decided you do not want to allow them.

- If you are in an organization that is polyglot and growing rapidly, make sure you are not accidentally introducing artificial bottlenecks such as one repository for all the databases and all the schema changes. Remember that the goal here is engineering team velocity.

### Running schema changes in production

Now that we have covered options to track and manage deploying schema changes for your organization, let's discuss *how* to run these changes in production without affecting the uptime of your databases or the services that rely on them.

**Native DDL statements.** MySQL introduced nonblocking schema changes in version 5.6, but in that major version, the feature came with a number of caveats that made actually using them limited to very specific schema-change types.

By the time version 8.0 became GA, support for native DDL in MySQL expanded greatly, although it is still not universal. Changes to your primary key, changes to charsets, turning on per-table encryption, and adding or removing foreign keys are all examples of schema changes you still cannot do natively with an INPLACE alter.[7] We highly recommend you get familiar through the documentation with what changes are allowed using either INPLACE or INSTANT algorithms as the preferred, native way to make schema changes in MySQL without downtime.

However, even if the change you need is technically supported by native DDL in 8.0 and beyond, if the table being changed is very large in size, you can run into rollbacks if the logfile of table changes InnoDB is internally keeping gets too large, undoing hours or days of work. Another reason you may need to use an external tool is if you have a strong desire to control the speed at which the table change happens using a throttling mechanism. This is something you can manage with the external tools we are about to discuss.

**Using external tools to run your schema change.** If you are not yet able to run the latest and greatest MySQL version with all the flexibility of the schema changes in place, you can still combine CI tooling with available open source tooling to run your schema changes in production automatically without affecting your service. Two prominent options for achieving this are Percona's pt-online-schema-change and GitHub's gh-ost. The documentation for both has all the information you need to learn how to install and use the tools, so we will focus here on how to choose which of them to use, what the major trade-offs are that you should consider, and how to improve the safety of using either tool as part of an automated schema-deploy pipeline in production.

 One thing to note: any external tool running your schema changes for you will need to make entire copies of the table you are changing. The tool merely makes the process less impactful and does not require disruptive write locks, but only native DDL in MySQL can alter table schemas without a full table copy.

The major draw for pt-online-schema-change has been its stability and how long it's been in use in the MySQL community. It primarily leverages triggers to enable changing schemas for tables of all sizes with very little impact to the database availability when switching to the new table version. But its core design also comes with trade-offs. Keep these things in mind when learning to use pt-online-schema-change to power your schema-deploy pipeline:

*Triggers have limitations*

Before MySQL 8.0, you could not have more than one trigger with the same action on the same table. What does that mean? If you have a table named sales,

---

7 See the MySQL documentation (*https://oreil.ly/nFMKg*) for more on this.

and you already need to maintain an insert time trigger on it, MySQL before 8.0 does not allow another insert trigger on that table. If you try to run a `pt-online-schema-change` schema change against it, the tool will produce an error when it attempts to add the triggers it needs to function. Although we generally highly discourage using table triggers as part of your business logic, there will still be cases where legacy choices create a constraint and this becomes part of your trade-off calculation when choosing a schema-change mechanism.

*Triggers have performance implications*

There are some excellent benchmarks by Percona (*https://oreil.ly/aGdKk*) showing the performance impact of even having triggers defined on a table. This performance penalty may be invisible to most installations, but if you happen to be running your database instances at a very high transaction-per-second throughput rate, you may need to watch the impact of the triggers introduced by `pt-online-schema-change` more closely and tune it to abort more conservatively.

*Running concurrent migrations*

Because of its use of triggers and the limitations of triggers in pre-8.0 MySQL, you will find that you cannot run multiple schema changes on the same table using `pt-online-schema-change`. This can be a minor inconvenience initially, but if you integrate the tool into a full schema-migration pipeline that's automated, it can become a bottleneck for your teams.

*Constraints around foreign keys*

Although the tool does have some level of support for schema changes with foreign keys in place, you will need to read the documentation carefully and determine which trade-off is the least impactful for your data and your transaction throughput.

`gh-ost` was created by the data engineering team at GitHub specifically as a solution for managing the schema-change process without service impact but also without using triggers at all. Instead of using triggers to track changes during the table-copy phase, it connects as a replica to one of your cluster replicas and consumes row-based replication logs as a changelog.

One thing you need to consider carefully about using `gh-ost` for schema changes is whether or not your existing database uses foreign keys. While `pt-online-schema-change` makes a solid attempt to support schema changes for tables that are the parent or child in a foreign-key relationship, it is a complex choice and full of trade-offs. (Do we sacrifice uptime for consistency? Or risk some window of possible inconsistency?) On the other hand, `gh-ost` mostly makes that choice for you and bails entirely if foreign keys exist in the table you are looking to alter. As the primary contributor on `gh-ost`, Shlomi Noach, explains in a long but very useful blog post (*https://oreil.ly/6A10o*), the use of foreign keys and online schema change tools that are ultimately still external to the database engine create an environment where trade-offs are difficult to reason about, and he proposes not using foreign keys at all if you also require online schema changes.

If you and your team are new to this task and are paving the way for CI of schema changes in your organization, we believe gh-ost is the better solution as long as you are also disciplined around not introducing foreign keys. Given its use of binary logs instead of triggers to track changes, we consider it the safer option where you don't have to worry about triggers' performance hit, it is far more agnostic to which version of MySQL you run (it can even work with statement-based replication with some caveats), and it has already been proven on large-scale deployments.

When is pt-online-schema-change the preferred option? If you are running a number of older databases where foreign keys already exist and removing them is a difficult proposal, you will find that pt-online-schema-change attempts a more expansive support for foreign keys, but you will have to carry the cognitive load of choosing the safest option for your data integrity and your uptime. Also, gh-ost leverages binary logs to do its work, so if those are inaccessible to the tool for some reason, pt-online-schema-change remains a viable option.

Ideally, someday we can all do online schema changes natively in MySQL, but that day is not here yet. Until then, the open source ecosystem has come a long way toward making schema changes a more easily automated process. Let's talk about how to put all of these tools together for a fully fleshed CI/CD pipeline for schema changes.

### A CI/CD pipeline for schema changes

Now that we have covered a number of tools, from tools that help manage schema definition versioning to tools for making the changes for you in production with minimal downtime, you can see that we have the pieces for a full continuous integration and deployment of schema changes that can remove a huge bottleneck for engineer productivity in your organization. Let's put it all together:

*Organizing your schema source control*
> First things first, you must start by separating each of your database clusters' schema definitions in a repository by itself. If the goal here is to provide flexibility for different teams to run their changes at different speeds, then it does not make sense to combine all the schema definitions of all your databases in one repository. This separation also allows each team to define different linting checks in the repository. Some teams may require a very specific character set and collation, and others are probably OK with the default. Flexibility for your partner teams here is key.

Make sure to document the workflow of how an engineer in a feature team can go from a schema change on their laptop to one that is run on all environments and runs tests before going to production. A pull-request model here can be very useful for helping each team to define what tests to run when a schema change is requested, in an automated manner, before promoting and running the change in more environments or production.

*A baseline configuration for safety*

Define a baseline configuration for your online schema change tool of choice. You are the team providing the tooling for partner teams that rely on you to give flexible, scalable, but also safe solutions. As you consider how you will implement the online schema change tool, it may be time to get opinionated about schema-design considerations that need to be part of testing schema change pull requests overall. For example, if you decide you prefer the safety of gh-ost and its trigger-free design, this will mean that you have to become a database platform free of foreign keys. Without going into the trade-offs of such a choice, if you do end up deciding "death to foreign keys," then you should make sure that is encoded in how you test your schema changes in precommit hooks or in your Skeema repository, so you can avoid accidentally introducing undesirable schema changes too far into the environment hierarchy. Similarly, you should decide on a basic configuration for your online schema change tool that provides a basic safety net for how a change runs in production. Examples of what you may want to introduce in such a configuration include maximum MySQL threads running or maximum allowed system load. Repository templates can be a powerful tool to make the right thing the easy thing when any feature team is creating a new database and wants a repository to track and manage schema changes.

*Pipeline flexibility per team*

When you organize your schema definitions in a repository per database, you allow for maximum flexibility for each team that owns that database to decide how automated or person-managed its pipeline should be. One team could be still in the iteration phase for a new product, and they are OK with a schema pull request automatically promoting as long as the defined tests pass. Another team might own a more mission-critical database and require a more cautious approach, preferring an operator to approve the pull request before the CI system can promote it to the next environment.

As you design how your organization achieves scalable schema-change deployments, keep your eye on the end goal: velocity that is coupled with safety for your growing engineering organization without the database engineering team being a bottleneck to how the company moves from ideas to features in production.

# Summary

Good schema design is pretty universal, but of course MySQL has special implementation details to consider. In a nutshell, it's a good idea to keep things as small and simple as you can. MySQL likes simplicity, and so will the people who have to work with your database. Keep these guidelines in mind:

- Try to avoid extremes in your design, such as a schema that will force enormously complex queries or tables with oodles and oodles of columns. (An oodle is somewhere between a scad and a gazillion.)

- Use small, simple, appropriate data types, and avoid NULL unless it's actually the right way to model your data's reality.

- Try to use the same data types to store similar or related values, especially if they'll be used in a join condition.

- Watch out for variable-length strings, which might cause pessimistic full-length memory allocation for temporary tables and sorting.

- Try to use integers for identifiers if you can.

- Avoid the legacy MySQL-isms, such as specifying precisions for floating-point numbers or display widths for integers.

- Be careful with ENUM and SET. They're handy, but they can be abused, and they're tricky sometimes. BIT is best avoided.

Database design is a science. If you're strongly concerned with database design, consider using dedicated source material.[8]

Also remember that your schema will evolve with both your business needs and what you learn from your users, and that means that having a robust software life cycle managing schema changes is a crucial part of making this evolution safe and scalable with your organization.

---

8 For another in-depth read, consider *Database Design for Mere Mortals* by Michael J. Hernandez (Pearson).

# CHAPTER 7

# Indexing for High Performance

*Indexes* (also called *keys* in MySQL) are data structures that storage engines use to find rows quickly. They also have several other beneficial properties that we'll explore in this chapter.

Indexes are critical for good performance and become more important as your data grows larger. Small, lightly loaded databases often perform well even without proper indexes, but as the data set grows, performance can drop very quickly.[1] Unfortunately, indexes are often forgotten or misunderstood, so poor indexing is a leading cause of real-world performance problems. That's why we put this material early in the book—even earlier than our discussion of query optimization.

Index optimization is perhaps the most powerful way to improve query performance. Indexes can improve performance by many orders of magnitude, and optimal indexes can sometimes boost performance about two orders of magnitude more than indexes that are merely "good." Creating truly optimal indexes will often require you to rewrite queries, so this chapter and the next one are closely related.

This chapter relies on using example databases, like the Sakila Sample Database (*https://oreil.ly/cIabb*), available from MySQL's website. Sakila is an example database that models a rental store, with a collection of actors, films, customers, and more.

---

1 SSDs have different performance characteristics, which we covered in Chapter 4. The indexing principles remain true, but the penalties we're trying to avoid aren't as large with SSDs as they are with conventional drives.

# Indexing Basics

The easiest way to understand how an index works in MySQL is to think about the index of a book. To find out where a particular topic is discussed in a book, you look in the index, and it tells you the page number(s) where that term appears.

In MySQL, a storage engine uses indexes in a similar way. It searches the index's data structure for a value. When it finds a match, it can find the row that contains the match. Suppose you run the following query:

```
SELECT first_name FROM sakila.actor WHERE actor_id = 5;
```

There's an index on the `actor_id` column, so MySQL will use the index to find rows whose `actor_id` is 5. In other words, it performs a lookup on the values in the index and returns any rows containing the specified value.

An index contains values from one or more columns in a table. If you index more than one column, the column order is very important because MySQL can only search efficiently on the leftmost prefix of the index. Creating an index on two columns is not the same as creating two separate single-column indexes, as you'll see.

---

### If I Use an ORM, Do I Need to Care?

The short version: yes, you still need to learn about indexing, even if you rely on an ORM tool.

ORMs produce logically and syntactically correct queries (most of the time), but they rarely produce index-friendly queries unless you use them for only the most basic types of queries, such as primary key lookups. You can't expect your ORM, no matter how sophisticated, to handle the subtleties and complexities of indexing. Read the rest of this chapter if you disagree! It's sometimes a hard job for an expert human to puzzle through all of the possibilities, let alone an ORM.

---

## Types of Indexes

There are many types of indexes, each designed to perform well for different purposes. Indexes are implemented in the storage engine layer, not the server layer. Thus, they are not standardized: indexing works slightly differently in each engine, and not all engines support all types of indexes. Even when multiple engines support the same index type, they might implement it differently under the hood. Given that this book assumes you are using InnoDB as the engine for all your tables, we will address specifically index implementations in InnoDB.

That said, let's look at the two most commonly used index types MySQL currently supports, their benefits, and their drawbacks.

---

## B-tree indexes

When people talk about an index without mentioning a type, they're probably refer-ring to a *B-tree index*, which typically uses a B-tree data structure to store its data.[2] Most of MySQL's storage engines support this index type.

We use the term *B-tree* for these indexes because that's what MySQL uses in CREATE TABLE and other statements. However, storage engines might use different storage structures internally. For example, the NDB Cluster storage engine uses a T-tree data structure for these indexes, even though they're labeled BTREE, and InnoDB uses B+ trees. The variations in the structures and algorithms are out of scope for this book, though.

The general idea of a B-tree is that all the values are stored in order, and each leaf page is the same distance from the root. Figure 7-1 shows an abstract representation of a B-tree index, which corresponds roughly to how InnoDB's indexes work.

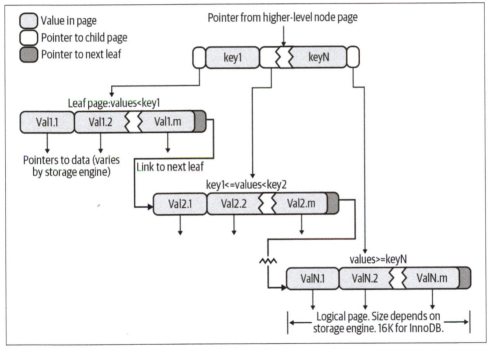

*Figure 7-1. An index built on a B-tree (technically, a B+ tree) structure*

---

2 Many storage engines actually use a B+ tree index, in which each leaf node contains a link to the next for fast range traversals through nodes. Refer to computer science literature for a detailed explanation of B-tree indexes.

A B-tree index speeds up data access because the storage engine doesn't have to scan the whole table to find the desired data. Instead, it starts at the root node (not shown in this figure). The slots in the root node hold pointers to child nodes, and the storage engine follows these pointers. It finds the right pointer by looking at the values in the node pages, which define the upper and lower bounds of the values in the child nodes. Eventually, the storage engine either determines that the desired value doesn't exist or successfully reaches a leaf page.

Leaf pages are special because they have pointers to the indexed data instead of pointers to other pages. (Different storage engines have different types of "pointers" to the data.) Our illustration shows only one node page and its leaf pages, but there might be many levels of node pages between the root and the leaves. The tree's depth depends on how big the table is.

Because B-trees store the indexed columns in order, they're useful for searching for ranges of data. For instance, descending the tree for an index on a text field passes through values in alphabetical order, so looking for "everyone whose name begins with I through K" is efficient.

Suppose you have the following table:

```
CREATE TABLE People (
  last_name varchar(50) not null,
  first_name varchar(50) not null,
  dob date not null,
  key(last_name, first_name, dob)
);
```

The index will contain the values from the last_name, first_name, and dob columns for every row in the table. Figure 7-2 illustrates how the index arranges the data it stores.

Notice that the index sorts the values according to the order of the columns given in the index in the CREATE TABLE statement. Look at the last two entries: there are two people with the same name but different birth dates, and they're sorted by birth date.

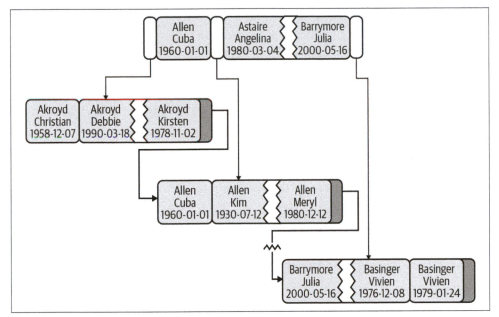

*Figure 7-2. Sample entries from a B-tree (technically, a B+ tree) index*

**Adaptive hash index.** The InnoDB storage engine has a special feature called *adaptive hash indexes*. When InnoDB notices that some index values are being accessed very frequently, it builds a hash index for them in memory on top of B-tree indexes. This gives its B-tree indexes some properties of hash indexes, such as very fast hashed lookups. This process is completely automatic, and you can't control or configure it, although you can disable the adaptive hash index altogether.

**Types of queries that can use a B-tree index.** B-tree indexes work well for lookups by the full key value, a key range, or a key prefix. They are useful only if the lookup uses a leftmost prefix of the index.[3] The index we showed in the previous section will be useful for the following kinds of queries:

*Match the full value*
> A match on the full key value specifies values for all columns in the index. For example, this index can help you find a person named Cuba Allen who was born on 1960-01-01.

---

3 This is MySQL specific, and even version specific. Some other databases can use nonleading index parts, although it's usually more efficient to use a complete prefix. MySQL might offer this option in the future; we show workarounds later in the chapter.

*Match a leftmost prefix*
> This index can help you find all people with the last name Allen. This uses only the first column in the index.

*Match a column prefix*
> You can match on the first part of a column's value. This index can help you find all people whose last names begin with J. This uses only the first column in the index.

*Match a range of values*
> This index can help you find people whose last names are between Allen and Barrymore. This also uses only the first column.

*Match one part exactly and match a range on another part*
> This index can help you find everyone whose last name is Allen and whose first name starts with the letter K (Kim, Karl, etc.). This is an exact match on last_name and a range query on first_name.

*Index-only queries*
> B-tree indexes can normally support index-only queries, which are queries that access only the index, not the row storage. We discuss this optimization in "Covering Indexes" on page 178.

Because the tree's nodes are sorted, they can be used for both lookups (finding values) and ORDER BY queries (finding values in sorted order). In general, if a B-tree can help you find a row in a particular way, it can help you sort rows by the same criteria. So our index will be helpful for ORDER BY clauses that match all the types of lookups we just listed.

Here are some limitations of B-tree indexes:

- They are not useful if the lookup does not start from the leftmost side of the indexed columns. For example, this index won't help you find all people named Bill or all people born on a certain date, because those columns are not leftmost in the index. Likewise, you can't use the index to find people whose last name *ends* with a particular letter.

- You can't skip columns in the index—that is, you won't be able to find all people whose last name is Smith and who were born on a particular date. If you don't specify a value for the first_name column, MySQL can use only the first column of the index.

- The storage engine can't optimize accesses with any columns to the right of the first range condition. For example, if your query is WHERE last_name="Smith" AND first_name LIKE 'J%' AND dob='1976-12-23', the index access will use only the first two columns in the index because the LIKE is a range condition (the server can use the rest of the columns for other purposes, though). For a column that has a limited number of values, you can often work around this by specifying equality conditions instead of range conditions.

Now you know why we said the column order is extremely important: these limitations are all related to column ordering. For optimal performance, you may need to create indexes with the same columns in different orders to satisfy your queries.

Some of these limitations are not inherent to B-tree indexes but are a result of how the MySQL query optimizer and storage engines use indexes. Some of them might be removed in the future.

### Full-text indexes

FULLTEXT is a special type of index that finds keywords in the text instead of comparing values directly to the values in the index. Full-text searching is completely different from other types of matching. It has many subtleties, such as stop words, stemming, plurals, and Boolean searching. It is much more analogous to what a search engine does than to simple WHERE parameter matching.

Having a full-text index on a column does not eliminate the value of a B-tree index on the same column. Full-text indexes are for MATCH AGAINST operations, not ordinary WHERE clause operations.

## Benefits of Indexes

Indexes enable the server to navigate quickly to a desired position in the table, but that's not all they're good for. As you've probably gathered by now, indexes have several additional benefits, based on the properties of the data structures used to create them.

B-tree indexes, which are the most common type you'll use, function by storing the data in sorted order, and MySQL can exploit that for queries with clauses such as ORDER BY and GROUP BY. Because the data is presorted, a B-tree index also stores related values close together. Finally, the index actually stores a copy of the values, so some queries can be satisfied from the index alone. Three main benefits proceed from these properties:

- Indexes reduce the amount of data the server has to examine.
- Indexes help the server avoid sorting and temporary tables.
- Indexes turn random I/O into sequential I/O.

This subject really deserves an entire book. For those who would like to dig in deeply, we recommend *Relational Database Index Design and the Optimizers* by Tapio Lahdenmaki and Mike Leach (Wiley). It explains topics such as how to calculate the costs and benefits of indexes, how to estimate query speed, and how to determine whether indexes will be more expensive to maintain than the benefits they provide.

Lahdenmaki and Leach's book also introduces a three-star system for grading how suitable an index is for a query. The index earns one star if it places relevant rows adjacent to each other, a second star if its rows are sorted in the order the query needs, and a final star if it contains all the columns needed for the query. We'll return to these principles throughout this chapter.

# Indexing Strategies for High Performance

Creating the correct indexes and using them properly is essential to good query performance. We've introduced the different types of indexes and explored their strengths and weaknesses. Now let's see how to really tap into the power of indexes.

There are many ways to choose and use indexes effectively because there are many special-case optimizations and specialized behaviors.[4] Determining what to use when and evaluating the performance implications of your choices are skills you'll learn over time. The next sections will help you understand how to use indexes effectively.

## Prefix Indexes and Index Selectivity

You can often save space and get good performance by indexing the first few characters instead of the whole value. This makes your indexes use less space, but it also makes them less *selective*. Index selectivity is the ratio of the number of distinct indexed values (the *cardinality*) to the total number of rows in the table ($\#T$), and it ranges from $1/\#T$ to 1. A highly selective index is good because it lets MySQL filter out more rows when it looks for matches. A unique index has a selectivity of 1, which is as good as it gets.

A prefix of the column is often selective enough to give good performance. If you're indexing BLOB or TEXT columns, or very long VARCHAR columns, you *must* define prefix indexes because MySQL disallows indexing their full length.

The trick is to choose a prefix that's long enough to give good selectivity but short enough to save space. The prefix should be long enough to make the index nearly as useful as it would be if you'd indexed the whole column. In other words, you'd like the prefix's cardinality to be close to the full column's cardinality.

To determine a good prefix length, find the most frequent values and compare with a list of the most frequent prefixes. There's no good table to demonstrate this in Sakila

---

4 MySQL's optimizer is a very mysterious and powerful device, and its mystery is only exceeded by its power. Due to the way it calculates optimal query planning, you should rely on using EXPLAIN in your own queries and workload to determine the most optimal strategies.

Sample Database, so we derive one from the `city` table so we have enough data to work with:

```
CREATE TABLE sakila.city_demo(city VARCHAR(50) NOT NULL);
INSERT INTO sakila.city_demo(city) SELECT city FROM sakila.city;
-- Repeat the next statement five times:
INSERT INTO sakila.city_demo(city) SELECT city FROM sakila.city_demo;
-- Now randomize the distribution (inefficiently but conveniently):
UPDATE sakila.city_demo
  SET city = (SELECT city FROM sakila.city ORDER BY RAND() LIMIT 1);
```

Now we have an example data set. The results are not realistically distributed, and we used RAND(), so your results will vary, but that doesn't matter for this exercise. First, we find the most frequently occurring cities:

```
mysql> SELECT COUNT(*) AS c, city
    -> FROM sakila.city_demo
    -> GROUP BY city ORDER BY c DESC LIMIT 10;
+-----+----------------+
| c   | city           |
+-----+----------------+
| 65  | London         |
| 49  | Hiroshima      |
| 48  | Teboksary      |
| 48  | Pak Kret       |
| 48  | Yaound         |
| 47  | Tel Aviv-Jaffa |
| 47  | Shimoga        |
| 45  | Cabuyao        |
| 45  | Callao         |
| 45  | Bislig         |
+-----+----------------+
```

Notice that there are roughly 45 to 65 occurrences of each value. Now we find the most frequently occurring city name *prefixes*, beginning with three-letter prefixes:

```
mysql> SELECT COUNT(*) AS c, LEFT(city, 3) AS pref
    -> FROM sakila.city_demo GROUP BY pref ORDER BY cc DESC LIMIT 10;
+-----+------+
| c   | pref |
+-----+------+
| 483 | San  |
| 195 | Cha  |
| 177 | Tan  |
| 167 | Sou  |
| 163 | al-  |
| 163 | Sal  |
| 146 | Shi  |
| 136 | Hal  |
| 130 | Val  |
| 129 | Bat  |
+-----+------+
```

There are many more occurrences of each prefix, so there are many fewer unique prefixes than unique full-length city names. The idea is to increase the prefix length until the prefix becomes nearly as selective as the full length of the column. A little experimentation shows that 7 is a good value:

```
mysql> SELECT COUNT(*) AS c, LEFT(city, 7) AS pref
    -> FROM sakila.city_demo GROUP BY pref ORDER BY c DESC LIMIT 10;
+-----+----------+
| c   | pref     |
+-----+----------+
| 70  | Santiag  |
| 68  | San Fel  |
| 65  | London   |
| 61  | Valle d  |
| 49  | Hiroshi  |
| 48  | Teboksa  |
| 48  | Pak Kre  |
| 48  | Yaound   |
| 47  | Tel Avi  |
| 47  | Shimoga  |
+-----+----------+
```

Another way to calculate a good prefix length is by computing the full column's selectivity and trying to make the prefix's selectivity close to that value. Here's how to find the full column's selectivity:

```
mysql> SELECT COUNT(DISTINCT city)/COUNT(*) FROM sakila.city_demo;
+-------------------------------+
| COUNT(DISTINCT city)/COUNT(*) |
+-------------------------------+
|                        0.0312 |
+-------------------------------+
```

The prefix will be about as good, on average (there's a caveat here, though), if we target a selectivity near .031. It's possible to evaluate many different lengths in one query, which is useful on very large tables. Here's how to find the selectivity of several prefix lengths in one query:

```
mysql> SELECT COUNT(DISTINCT LEFT(city, 3))/COUNT(*) AS sel3,
    -> COUNT(DISTINCT LEFT(city, 4))/COUNT(*) AS sel4,
    -> COUNT(DISTINCT LEFT(city, 5))/COUNT(*) AS sel5,
    -> COUNT(DISTINCT LEFT(city, 6))/COUNT(*) AS sel6,
    -> COUNT(DISTINCT LEFT(city, 7))/COUNT(*) AS sel7
    -> FROM sakila.city_demo;
+--------+--------+--------+--------+--------+
| sel3   | sel4   | sel5   | sel6   | sel7   |
+--------+--------+--------+--------+--------+
| 0.0239 | 0.0293 | 0.0305 | 0.0309 | 0.0310 |
+--------+--------+--------+--------+--------+
```

This query shows that increasing the prefix length results in successively smaller improvements as it approaches seven characters.

It's not a good idea to look only at average selectivity. The caveat is that the *worst-case* selectivity matters, too. The average selectivity may make you think a four- or five-character prefix is good enough, but if your data is very uneven, that could be a trap. If you look at the number of occurrences of the most common city name prefixes using a value of 4, you'll see the unevenness clearly:

```
mysql> SELECT COUNT(*) AS c, LEFT(city, 4) AS pref
    -> FROM sakila.city_demo GROUP BY pref ORDER BY c DESC LIMIT 5;
+-----+------+
| c   | pref |
+-----+------+
| 205 | San  |
| 200 | Sant |
| 135 | Sout |
| 104 | Chan |
|  91 | Toul |
+-----+------+
```

With four characters, the most frequent prefixes occur quite a bit more often than the most frequent full-length values. That is, the selectivity on those values is lower than the average selectivity. If you have a more realistic data set than this randomly generated sample, you're likely to see this effect even more. For example, building a four-character prefix index on real-world city names will give terrible selectivity on cities that begin with "San" and "New," of which there are many.

Now that we've found a good value for our sample data, here's how to create a prefix index on the column:

```
ALTER TABLE sakila.city_demo ADD KEY (city(7));
```

Prefix indexes can be a great way to make indexes smaller and faster, but they have downsides too: MySQL cannot use prefix indexes for ORDER BY or GROUP BY queries, nor can it use them as covering indexes.

A common case we've found to benefit from prefix indexes is when long hexadecimal identifiers are used. We discussed more efficient techniques of storing such identifiers in the previous chapter, but what if you're using a packaged solution that you can't modify? We see this frequently with vBulletin and other applications that use MySQL to store website sessions, keyed on long hex strings. Adding an index on the first eight characters or so often boosts performance significantly, in a way that's completely transparent to the application.

# Multicolumn Indexes

Multicolumn indexes are often very poorly understood. Common mistakes are to index many or all of the columns separately or to index columns in the wrong order.

We'll discuss column order in the next section. The first mistake, indexing many columns separately, has a distinctive signature in SHOW CREATE TABLE:

```
CREATE TABLE t (
c1 INT,
c2 INT,
c3 INT,
KEY(c1),
KEY(c2),
KEY(c3)
);
```

This strategy of indexing often results when people give vague but authoritative-sounding advice such as "create indexes on columns that appear in the WHERE clause." This advice is very wrong. It will result in one-star indexes at best. These indexes can be many orders of magnitude slower than truly optimal indexes. Sometimes when you can't design a three-star index, it's much better to ignore the WHERE clause and pay attention to optimal row order or create a covering index instead.

Individual indexes on lots of columns won't help MySQL improve performance for most queries. MySQL can cope a little with such poorly indexed tables when it employs a strategy known as *index merge*, which permits a query to make limited use of multiple indexes from a single table to locate desired rows. It can use both indexes, scanning them simultaneously and merging the results. There are three variations on the algorithm: union for OR conditions, intersection for AND conditions, and unions of intersections for combinations of the two. The following query uses a union of two index scans, as you can see by examining the Extra column:

```
mysql> EXPLAIN SELECT film_id, actor_id FROM sakila.film_actor
    -> WHERE actor_id = 1 OR film_id = 1\G
*************************** 1. row ***************************
id: 1
select_type: SIMPLE
table: film_actor
partitions: NULL
type: index_merge
possible_keys: PRIMARY,idx_fk_film_id
key: PRIMARY,idx_fk_film_id
key_len: 2,2
ref: NULL
rows: 29
filtered: 100.00
Extra: Using union(PRIMARY,idx_fk_film_id); Using where
```

MySQL can use this technique on complex queries, so you might see nested operations in the Extra column for some queries.

The index merge strategy sometimes works very well, but more commonly it's actually an indication of a poorly indexed table:

- When the server intersects indexes (usually for AND conditions), it usually means that you need a single index with all the relevant columns, not multiple indexes that have to be combined.

- When the server unions indexes (usually for OR conditions), sometimes the algorithm's buffering, sorting, and merging operations use lots of CPU and memory resources. This is especially true if not all of the indexes are very selective, so the scans return lots of rows to the merge operation.

- Recall that the optimizer doesn't account for this cost—it optimizes just the number of random page reads. This can make it "underprice" the query, which might in fact run more slowly than a plain table scan. The intensive memory and CPU usage also tends to affect concurrent queries, but you won't see this effect when you run the query in isolation. Sometimes rewriting such queries with a UNION clause is more optimal.

When you see an index merge in EXPLAIN, you should examine the query and table structure to see if this is really the best you can get. You can disable index merges with the optimizer_switch option or variable. You can also use IGNORE INDEX.

## Choosing a Good Column Order

One of the most common causes of confusion we've seen is the order of columns in an index. The correct order depends on the queries that will use the index, and you must think about how to choose the index order such that rows are sorted and grouped in a way that will benefit the query.

The order of columns in a multicolumn B-tree index means that the index is sorted first by the leftmost column, then by the next column, and so on. Therefore, the index can be scanned in either forward or reverse order to satisfy queries with ORDER BY, GROUP BY, and DISTINCT clauses that match the column order exactly.

As a result, the column order is vitally important in multicolumn indexes. The column order either enables or prevents the index from earning "stars" in Lahdenmaki and Leach's three-star system (see "Benefits of Indexes" on page 161 earlier in this chapter for more on the three-star system). We will show many examples of how this works throughout the rest of this chapter.

There is an old rule of thumb for choosing column order: place the most selective columns first in the index. How useful is this suggestion? It can be helpful in some cases, but it's usually much less important than avoiding random I/O and sorting, all things considered. (Specific cases vary, so there's no one-size-fits-all rule. That alone should tell you that this rule of thumb is probably less important than you think.)

Placing the most selective columns first can be a good idea when there is no sorting or grouping to consider, and thus the purpose of the index is only to optimize WHERE lookups. In such cases, it might indeed work well to design the index so that it filters out rows as quickly as possible, so it's more selective for queries that specify only a prefix of the index in the WHERE clause. However, this depends not only on the selectivity (overall cardinality) of the columns but also on the actual values you use to look up rows—the distribution of values. This is the same type of consideration we explored for choosing a good prefix length. You might actually need to choose the column order such that it's as selective as possible for the queries that you'll run most.

Let's use the following query as an example:

```
SELECT * FROM payment WHERE staff_id = 2 AND customer_id = 584;
```

Should you create an index on (staff_id, customer_id), or should you reverse the column order? We can run some quick queries to help examine the distribution of values in the table and determine which column has a higher selectivity. Let's transform the query to count the cardinality of each predicate in the WHERE clause:

```
mysql> SELECT SUM(staff_id = 2), SUM(customer_id = 584) FROM payment\G
*************************** 1. row ***************************
  SUM(staff_id = 2): 7992
SUM(customer_id = 584): 30
```

According to the rule of thumb, we should place customer_id first in the index because the predicate matches fewer rows in the table. We can then run the query again to see how selective staff_id is within the range of rows selected by this specific customer ID:

```
mysql> SELECT SUM(staff_id = 2) FROM payment WHERE customer_id = 584\G
*************************** 1. row ***************************
SUM(staff_id = 2): 17
```

Be careful with this technique because the results depend on the specific constants supplied for the chosen query. If you optimize your indexes for this query and other queries don't fare as well, the server's performance might suffer overall, or some queries might run unpredictably.

If you're using the "worst" sample query from a report from a tool such as *pt-query-digest*, this technique can be an effective way to see what might be the most helpful indexes for your queries and your data. But if you don't have specific samples to run, it might be better to use the old rule of thumb, which is to look at the cardinality across the board, not just for one query:

```
mysql> SELECT COUNT(DISTINCT staff_id)/COUNT(*) AS staff_id_selectivity,
    -> COUNT(DISTINCT customer_id)/COUNT(*) AS customer_id_selectivity,
    -> COUNT(*)
    -> FROM payment\G
*************************** 1. row ***************************
  staff_id_selectivity: 0.0001
customer_id_selectivity: 0.0373
              COUNT(*): 16049
```

`customer_id` has higher selectivity, so again the answer is to put that column first in the index:

```
ALTER TABLE payment ADD KEY(customer_id, staff_id);
```

As with prefix indexes, problems often arise from special values that have higher than normal cardinality. For example, we have seen applications treat users who aren't logged in as "guest" users who get a special user ID in session tables and other places where user activity is recorded. Queries involving that user ID are likely to behave very differently from other queries because there are usually a lot of sessions that aren't logged in. Sometimes system accounts cause similar problems. One application had a magical administrative account, which wasn't a real user, who was "friends" with every user of the entire website so that it could send status notices and other messages. That user's huge list of friends was causing severe performance problems for the site.

This is actually fairly typical. Any outlier, even if it's not an artifact of a poor decision in how the application is managed, can cause problems. Users who really do have lots of friends, photos, status messages, and the like can be just as troublesome as fake users.

Here's a real example we saw once on a product forum where users exchanged stories and experiences about the product. Queries of this particular form were running very slowly:

```
SELECT COUNT(DISTINCT threadId) AS COUNT_VALUE
FROM Message
WHERE (groupId = 10137) AND (userId = 1288826) AND (anonymous = 0)
ORDER BY priority DESC, modifiedDate DESC
```

This query appeared not to have a very good index, so the customer asked us to see if it could be improved. The EXPLAIN follows:

```
id: 1
select_type: SIMPLE
table: Message
type: ref
key: ix_groupId_userId
key_len: 18
ref: const,const
rows: 1251162
Extra: Using where
```

The index that MySQL chose for this query is on (`groupId`, `userId`), which would seem like a pretty decent choice if we had no information about the column cardinality. However, a different picture emerged when we looked at how many rows matched that user ID and group ID:

```
mysql> SELECT COUNT(*), SUM(groupId = 10137),
    -> SUM(userId = 1288826), SUM(anonymous = 0)
    -> FROM Message\G
*************************** 1. row ***************************
     count(*): 4142217
sum(groupId = 10137): 4092654
sum(userId = 1288826): 1288496
sum(anonymous = 0): 4141934
```

It turned out that this group owned almost every row in the table, and the user had 1.3 million rows—in this case, there simply isn't an index that can help! This was because the data was migrated from another application, and all of the messages were assigned to the administrative user and group as part of the import process. The solution to this problem was to change the application code to recognize this special-case user ID and group ID and not issue this query for that user.

The moral of this little story is that rules of thumb and heuristics can be useful, but you have to be careful not to assume that average-case performance is representative of special-case performance. Special cases can wreck performance for the whole application.

In the end, although the rule of thumb about selectivity and cardinality is interesting to explore, other factors—such as sorting, grouping, and the presence of range conditions in the query's WHERE clause—can make a much bigger difference to query performance.

## Clustered Indexes

*Clustered indexes*[5] aren't a separate type of index. Rather, they're an approach to data storage. The exact details vary among implementations, but InnoDB's clustered indexes actually store a B-tree index and the rows together in the same structure.

When a table has a clustered index, its rows are actually stored in the index's leaf pages. The term *clustered* refers to the fact that rows with adjacent key values are stored close to one another.[6] You can have only one clustered index per table because you can't store the rows in two places at once. (However, *covering indexes* allow you to emulate multiple clustered indexes; more on this later.)

Because storage engines are responsible for implementing indexes, not all storage engines support clustered indexes. We focus on InnoDB in this section, but the principles we discuss are likely to be at least partially true for any storage engine that supports clustered indexes now or in the future.

---

5 Oracle users will be familiar with the term *index-organized table*, which means the same thing.

6 This isn't always true, as you'll see in a moment.

Figure 7-3 shows how records are laid out in a clustered index. Notice that the leaf pages contain full rows, but the node pages contain only the indexed columns. In this case, the indexed column contains integer values.

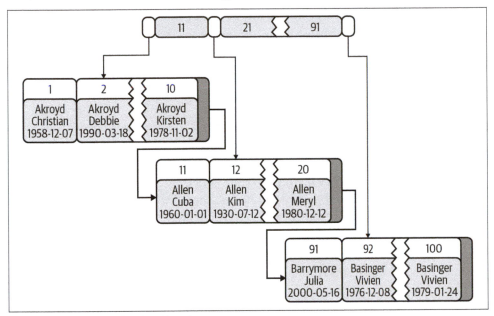

*Figure 7-3. Clustered index data layout*

Some database servers let you choose which index to cluster, but none of MySQL's built-in storage engines does at the time of this writing. InnoDB clusters the data by the primary key. That means that the "indexed column" in Figure 7-3 is the primary key column.

If you don't define a primary key, InnoDB will try to use a unique nonnullable index instead. If there's no such index, InnoDB will define a hidden primary key for you and then cluster on that. The downside of hidden primary keys is that the incremented value for these is shared across all tables that use a hidden primary key, resulting in higher mutex contention for the shared key.

Clustering data has some very important advantages:

- You can keep related data close together. For example, when implementing a mailbox, you can cluster by user_id, so you can retrieve all of a single user's messages by fetching only a few pages from disk. If you didn't use clustering, each message might require its own disk I/O.

- Data access is fast. A clustered index holds both the index and the data together in one B-tree, so retrieving rows from a clustered index is normally faster than a comparable lookup in a nonclustered index.

- Queries that use covering indexes can use the primary key values contained at the leaf node.

These benefits can boost performance tremendously if you design your tables and queries to take advantage of them. However, clustered indexes also have some disadvantages:

- Clustering gives the largest improvement for I/O-bound workloads. If the data fits in memory, the order in which it's accessed doesn't really matter, so clustering doesn't give much benefit.

- Insert speeds depend heavily on insertion order. Inserting rows in primary key order is the fastest way to load data into an InnoDB table. It might be a good idea to reorganize the table with OPTIMIZE TABLE after loading a lot of data if you didn't load the rows in primary key order.

- Updating the clustered index columns is expensive because it forces InnoDB to move each updated row to a new location.

- Tables built on clustered indexes are subject to *page splits* when new rows are inserted or when a row's primary key is updated such that the row must be moved. A page split happens when a row's key value dictates that the row must be placed into a page that is full of data. The storage engine must split the page into two to accommodate the row. Page splits can cause a table to use more space on disk.

- Clustered tables can be slower for full table scans, especially if rows are less densely packed or stored nonsequentially because of page splits.

- Secondary (nonclustered) indexes can be larger than you might expect because their leaf nodes contain the primary key columns of the referenced rows.

- Secondary index accesses require two index lookups instead of one.

The last point can be a bit confusing. Why would a secondary index require two index lookups? The answer lies in the nature of the "row pointers" the secondary index stores. Remember, a leaf node doesn't store a pointer to the referenced row's physical location; rather, it stores the row's primary key values.

That means that to find a row from a secondary index, the storage engine first finds the leaf node in the secondary index and then uses the primary key values stored there to navigate the primary key and find the row. That's double work: two B-tree navigations instead of one.[7] In InnoDB, the adaptive hash index (mentioned earlier in "B-tree indexes" on page 157) can help reduce this penalty.

### InnoDB's data layout

To better understand clustered indexes, let's see how InnoDB lays out the following table:

```
CREATE TABLE layout_test (
  col1 int NOT NULL,
  col2 int NOT NULL,
  PRIMARY KEY(col1),
  KEY(col2)
);
```

Suppose the table is populated with primary key values 1 to 10,000, inserted in random order and then optimized with OPTIMIZE TABLE. In other words, the data is arranged optimally on disk, but the rows might be in a random order. The values for col2 are randomly assigned between 1 and 100, so there are lots of duplicates.

InnoDB stores the table as shown in Figure 7-4.

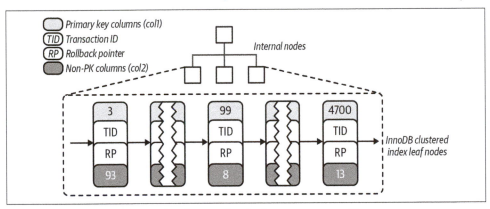

*Figure 7-4. InnoDB primary key layout for the* layout_test *table*

Each leaf node in the clustered index contains the primary key value, the transaction ID and rollback pointer InnoDB uses for transactional and MVCC purposes, and the rest of the columns (in this case, col2). If the primary key is on a column prefix, InnoDB includes the full column value with the rest of the columns.

---

7 Nonclustered index designs aren't always able to provide single-operation row lookups, by the way. When a row changes, it might not fit in its original location anymore, so you might end up with fragmented rows or "forwarding addresses" in the table, both of which would result in more work to find the row.

InnoDB's secondary index leaf nodes contain the primary key values, which serve as the "pointers" to the rows. This strategy reduces the work needed to maintain secondary indexes when rows move or when there's a data page split. Using the row's primary key values as the pointer makes the index larger, but it means InnoDB can move a row without updating pointers to it.

Figure 7-5 illustrates the col2 index for the example table. Each leaf node contains the indexed columns (in this case just col2), followed by the primary key values (col1).

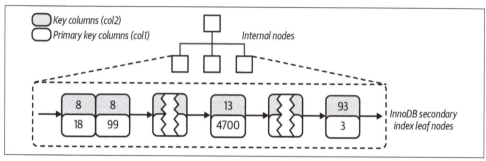

*Figure 7-5. InnoDB secondary index layout for the layout_test table*

These diagrams have illustrated the B-tree leaf nodes, but we intentionally omitted details about the nonleaf nodes. InnoDB's nonleaf B-tree nodes each contain the indexed column(s), plus a pointer to the next-deeper node (which might be either another nonleaf node or a leaf node). This applies to all B-tree indexes, clustered and secondary.

### Inserting rows in primary key order with InnoDB

If you're using InnoDB and don't need any particular clustering, it can be a good idea to define a *surrogate key*, which is a primary key whose value is not derived from your application's data. The easiest way to do this is usually with an AUTO_INCREMENT column. This will ensure that rows are inserted in sequential order and will offer better performance for joins using primary keys.

It is best to avoid random (nonsequential and distributed over a large set of values) clustered keys, especially for I/O-bound workloads. For example, using UUID values is a poor choice from a performance standpoint: it makes clustered index insertion random, which is a worst-case scenario, and does not give you any helpful data clustering.

To demonstrate, we benchmarked two cases. The first is inserting into a userinfo table with an integer ID, defined as follows:

```
CREATE TABLE userinfo (
  id int unsigned NOT NULL AUTO_INCREMENT,
  name varchar(64) NOT NULL DEFAULT '',
  email varchar(64) NOT NULL DEFAULT '',
  password varchar(64) NOT NULL DEFAULT '',
  dob date DEFAULT NULL,
  address varchar(255) NOT NULL DEFAULT '',
  city varchar(64) NOT NULL DEFAULT '',
  state_id tinyint unsigned NOT NULL DEFAULT '0',
  zip varchar(8) NOT NULL DEFAULT '',
  country_id smallint unsigned NOT NULL DEFAULT '0',
  gender ('M','F')NOT NULL DEFAULT 'M',
  account_type varchar(32) NOT NULL DEFAULT '',
  verified tinyint NOT NULL DEFAULT '0',
  allow_mail tinyint unsigned NOT NULL DEFAULT '0',
  parrent_account int unsigned NOT NULL DEFAULT '0',
  closest_airport varchar(3) NOT NULL DEFAULT '',
  PRIMARY KEY (id),
  UNIQUE KEY email (email),
  KEY country_id (country_id),
  KEY state_id (state_id),
  KEY state_id_2 (state_id,city,address)
) ENGINE=InnoDB
```

Notice the auto-incrementing integer primary key.[8]

The second case is a table named userinfo_uuid. It is identical to the userinfo table, except that its primary key is a UUID instead of an integer:

```
CREATE TABLE userinfo_uuid (
  uuid varchar(36) NOT NULL,
  ...
```

We benchmarked both table designs. First, we inserted a million records into both tables on a server with enough memory to hold the indexes. Next, we inserted three million rows into the same tables, which made the indexes bigger than the server's memory. Table 7-1 compares the benchmark results.

*Table 7-1. Benchmark results for inserting rows into InnoDB tables*

| Table | Rows | Time (sec) | Index size (MB) |
| --- | --- | --- | --- |
| userinfo | 1,000,000 | 137 | 342 |
| userinfo_uuid | 1,000,000 | 180 | 544 |
| userinfo | 3,000,000 | 1233 | 1036 |
| userinfo_uuid | 3,000,000 | 4525 | 1707 |

---

8 It's worth pointing out that this is a real table, with secondary indexes and lots of columns. If we removed these and benchmarked only the primary key performance, the difference would be even larger.

Notice that not only does it take longer to insert the rows with the UUID primary key, but the resulting indexes are quite a bit bigger. Some of that is due to the larger primary key, but some of it is undoubtedly due to page splits and resultant fragmentation as well.

To see why this is so, let's see what happened in the index when we inserted data into the first table. Figure 7-6 shows inserts filling a page and then continuing on a second page.

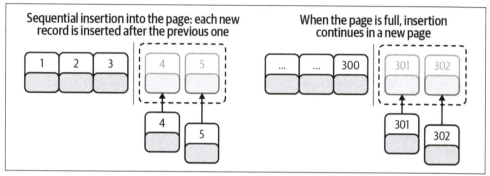

*Figure 7-6. Inserting sequential index values into a clustered index*

As Figure 7-6 illustrates, InnoDB stores each record immediately after the one before because the primary key values are sequential. When the page reaches its maximum fill factor (InnoDB's initial fill factor is only 15/16 full, to leave room for modifications later), the next record goes into a new page. Once the data has been loaded in this sequential fashion, the primary key pages are packed nearly full with in-order records, which is highly desirable. (The secondary index pages are not likely to differ, however.)

Contrast that with what happened when we inserted the data into the second table with the UUID clustered index, as shown in Figure 7-7.

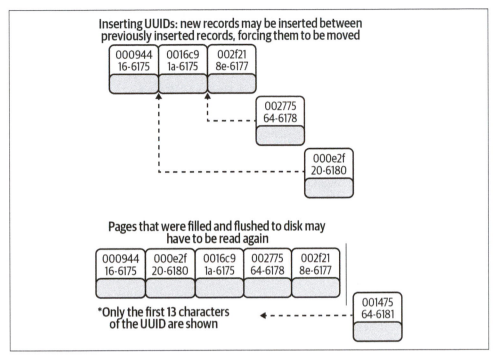

*Figure 7-7. Inserting nonsequential values into a clustered index*

Because each new row doesn't necessarily have a larger primary key value than the previous one, InnoDB cannot always place the new row at the end of the index. It has to find the appropriate place for the row—on average, somewhere near the middle of the existing data—and make room for it. This causes a lot of extra work and results in a suboptimal data layout. Here's a summary of the drawbacks:

- The destination page might have been flushed to disk and removed from the caches or might not have ever been placed into the caches, in which case InnoDB will have to find it and read it from the disk before it can insert the new row. This causes a lot of random I/O.

- When insertions are done out of order, InnoDB has to split pages frequently to make room for new rows. This requires moving around a lot of data and modifying at least three pages instead of one.

- Pages become sparsely and irregularly filled because of splitting, so the final data is fragmented.

After loading such random values into a clustered index, you should probably do an OPTIMIZE TABLE to rebuild the table and fill the pages optimally.

The moral of the story is that you should strive to insert data in primary key order when using InnoDB, and you should try to use a clustering key that will give a monotonically increasing value for each new row.

---

### When Primary Key Order Is Worse

For high-concurrency workloads, inserting in primary key order can actually create points of contention in InnoDB. The upper end of the primary key is one hot spot. Because all inserts take place there, concurrent inserts might fight over next-key locks. Another hot spot is the AUTO_INCREMENT locking mechanism; if you experience problems with that, you might be able to redesign your table or application, or configure innodb_autoinc_lock_mode. If your server version doesn't support innodb_auto inc_lock_mode, you can upgrade to a newer version of InnoDB that will perform better for this specific workload.

---

## Covering Indexes

A common suggestion is to create indexes for the query's WHERE clause, but that's only part of the story. Indexes need to be designed for the whole query, not just the WHERE clause. Indexes are indeed a way to find rows efficiently, but MySQL can also use an index to retrieve a column's data, so it doesn't have to read the row at all. After all, the index's leaf nodes contain the values they index; why read the row when reading the index can give you the data you want? An index that contains (or "covers") all the data needed to satisfy a query is called a *covering index*. It is important to note that only B-tree indexes can be used to cover indexes.

Covering indexes can be a very powerful tool and can dramatically improve performance. Consider the benefits of reading only the index instead of the data:

- Index entries are usually much smaller than the full row size, so MySQL can access significantly less data if it reads only the index. This is very important for cached workloads, where much of the response time comes from copying the data. It is also helpful for I/O-bound workloads because the indexes are smaller than the data and fit in memory better.

- Indexes are sorted by their index values (at least within the page), so I/O-bound range accesses will need to do less I/O compared to fetching each row from a random disk location. You can even OPTIMIZE the table to get fully sorted indexes, which will let simple range queries use completely sequential index accesses.

- Covering indexes are especially helpful for InnoDB tables because of InnoDB's clustered indexes. InnoDB's secondary indexes hold the row's primary key values

---

at their leaf nodes. Thus, a secondary index that covers a query avoids another index lookup in the primary key.

In all of these scenarios, it is typically much less expensive to satisfy a query from an index instead of looking up the rows.

When you issue a query that is covered by an index (an *index-covered query*), you'll see "Using index" in the Extra column in EXPLAIN.[9] For example, the sakila.inventory table has a multicolumn index on (store_id, film_id). MySQL can use this index for a query that accesses only those two columns, such as the following:

```
mysql> EXPLAIN SELECT store_id, film_id FROM sakila.inventory\G
*************************** 1. row ***************************
           id: 1
  select_type: SIMPLE
        table: inventory
   partitions: NULL
         type: index
possible_keys: NULL
          key: idx_store_id_film_id
      key_len: 3
          ref: NULL
         rows: 4581
     filtered: 100.00
        Extra: Using index
```

In most storage engines, an index can cover only queries that access columns that are part of the index. However, InnoDB can actually take this optimization a little bit further. Recall that InnoDB's secondary indexes hold primary key values at their leaf nodes. This means InnoDB's secondary indexes effectively have "extra columns" that InnoDB can use to cover queries.

For example, the sakila.actor table uses InnoDB and has an index on last_name, so the index can cover queries that retrieve the primary key column actor_id, even though that column isn't technically part of the index:

```
mysql> EXPLAIN SELECT actor_id, last_name
    -> FROM sakila.actor WHERE last_name = 'HOPPER'\G
*************************** 1. row ***************************
           id: 1
  select_type: SIMPLE
        table: actor
   partitions: NULL
         type: ref
possible_keys: idx_actor_last_name
```

---

9 It's easy to confuse "Using index" in the Extra column with "index" in the type column. However, they are completely different. The type column has nothing to do with covering indexes; it shows the query's access type, or how the query will find rows. The MySQL manual calls this the *join type*.

```
key: idx_actor_last_name
key_len: 182
ref: const
rows: 2
filtered: 100.00
Extra: Using index
```

## Using Index Scans for Sorts

MySQL has two ways to produce ordered results: it can use a sort operation, or it can scan an index in order. You can tell when MySQL plans to scan an index by looking for "index" in the type column in EXPLAIN. (Don't confuse this with "Using index" in the Extra column.)

Scanning the index itself is fast because it simply requires moving from one index entry to the next. However, if MySQL isn't using the index to cover the query, it will have to look up each row it finds in the index. This is basically random I/O, so reading data in index order is usually slower than a sequential table scan, especially for I/O-bound workloads.

MySQL can use the same index for both sorting and finding rows. If possible, it's a good idea to design your indexes so that they're useful for both tasks at once.

Ordering the results by the index works only when the index's order is exactly the same as the ORDER BY clause and all columns are sorted in the same direction (ascending or descending).[10] If the query joins multiple tables, it works only when all columns in the ORDER BY clause refer to the first table. The ORDER BY clause also has the same limitation as lookup queries: it needs to form a leftmost prefix of the index. In all other cases, MySQL uses a sort.

One case where the ORDER BY clause doesn't have to specify a leftmost prefix of the index is if there are constants for the leading columns. If the WHERE clause or a JOIN clause specifies constants for these columns, they can "fill the gaps" in the index.

For example, the rental table in the standard Sakila Sample Database has an index on (rental_date, inventory_id, customer_id):

```
CREATE TABLE rental (
  ...
  PRIMARY KEY (rental_id),
  UNIQUE KEY rental_date (rental_date,inventory_id,customer_id),
  KEY idx_fk_inventory_id (inventory_id),
  KEY idx_fk_customer_id (customer_id),
  KEY idx_fk_staff_id (staff_id),
```

---

10 If you need to sort in different directions, a trick that sometimes helps is to store a reversed or negated value.

```
...
);
```

MySQL uses the `rental_date` index to order the following query, as you can see from the lack of a filesort[11] in EXPLAIN:

```
mysql> EXPLAIN SELECT rental_id, staff_id FROM sakila.rental
    -> WHERE rental_date = '2005-05-25'
    -> ORDER BY inventory_id, customer_id\G
*************************** 1. row ***************************
    type: ref
possible_keys: rental_date
     key: rental_date
    rows: 1
   Extra: Using where
```

This works, even though the ORDER BY clause isn't itself a leftmost prefix of the index, because we specified an equality condition for the first column in the index.

Here are some more queries that can use the index for sorting. This one works because the query provides a constant for the first column of the index and specifies an ORDER BY on the second column. Taken together, those two form a leftmost prefix on the index:

```
... WHERE rental_date = '2005-05-25' ORDER BY inventory_id DESC;
```

The following query also works[12] because the two columns in the ORDER BY are a leftmost prefix of the index:

```
... WHERE rental_date > '2005-05-25' ORDER BY rental_date, inventory_id;
```

Here are some queries that *cannot* use the index for sorting.

This query uses two different sort directions, but the index's columns are all sorted ascending:

```
... WHERE rental_date = '2005-05-25' ORDER BY inventory_id DESC, customer_id ASC;
```

Here, the ORDER BY refers to a column that isn't in the index:

```
... WHERE rental_date = '2005-05-25' ORDER BY inventory_id, staff_id;
```

Here, the WHERE and the ORDER BY don't form a leftmost prefix of the index:

```
... WHERE rental_date = '2005-05-25' ORDER BY customer_id;
```

---

11 MySQL calls it a "filesort," but it doesn't always use a file on a filesystem. It only goes to disk if it cannot sort the data in memory.

12 We should note that while this can use the index for sorting, in our tests the optimizer in 8.0.25 did not use the index until we used a FORCE INDEX FOR ORDER BY condition—another reminder that the optimizer may not do what you expect, and you should always check with EXPLAIN.

This query has a range condition on the first column, so MySQL doesn't use the rest of the index:

```
... WHERE rental_date > '2005-05-25' ORDER BY inventory_id, customer_id;
```

Here, there's a multiple equality on the `inventory_id` column. For the purposes of sorting, this is basically the same as a range:

```
... WHERE rental_date = '2005-05-25' AND inventory_id IN(1,2) ORDER BY
customer_id;
```

Here's an example where MySQL could theoretically use an index to order a join but doesn't because the optimizer places the `film_actor` table second in the join:

```
mysql> EXPLAIN SELECT actor_id, title FROM sakila.film_actor
    -> INNER JOIN sakila.film USING(film_id) ORDER BY actor_id\G
+------------+------------------------------------------------+
| table      | Extra                                          |
+------------+------------------------------------------------+
| film       | Using index; Using temporary; Using filesort   |
| film_actor | Using index                                    |
+------------+------------------------------------------------+
```

One of the most important uses for ordering by an index is a query that has both an `ORDER BY` and a `LIMIT` clause.

## Redundant and Duplicate Indexes

Unfortunately, MySQL allows you to create duplicate indexes on the same column. Doing so will only return a warning, and it will not prevent you from doing this. MySQL has to maintain each duplicate index separately, and the query optimizer will consider each of them when it optimizes queries. This can affect performance and also wastes space on disk.

Duplicate indexes are indexes of the same type created on the same set of columns in the same order. You should try to avoid creating them, and you should remove them if you find them.

Sometimes you can create duplicate indexes without knowing it. For example, look at the following code:

```
CREATE TABLE test (
ID INT NOT NULL PRIMARY KEY,
A INT NOT NULL,
B INT NOT NULL,
UNIQUE(ID),
INDEX(ID)
) ENGINE=InnoDB;
```

An inexperienced user might think this identifies the column's role as a primary key, adds a UNIQUE constraint, and adds an index for queries to use. In fact, MySQL implements UNIQUE constraints and PRIMARY KEY constraints with indexes, so this actually creates three indexes on the same column! There is typically no reason to do this, unless you want to have different types of indexes on the same column to satisfy different kinds of queries.[13]

Redundant indexes are a bit different from duplicated indexes. If there is an index on (A, B), another index on (A) would be redundant because it is a prefix of the first index. That is, the index on (A, B) can also be used as an index on (A) alone. (This type of redundancy applies only to B-tree indexes.) However, an index on (B, A) would not be redundant, and neither would an index on (B), because B is not a left-most prefix of (A, B). Furthermore, indexes of different types (such as a full-text index) are not redundant to B-tree indexes, no matter what columns they cover.

Redundant indexes usually appear when people add indexes to a table. For example, someone might add an index on (A, B) instead of extending an existing index on (A) to cover (A, B). Another way this could happen is by changing the index to cover (A, ID). The ID column is the primary key, so it's already included.

In most cases, you don't want redundant indexes, and to avoid them you should extend existing indexes rather than add new ones. Still, there are times when you'll need redundant indexes for performance reasons. Extending an existing index might make it much larger and reduce performance for some queries.

For example, if you have an index on an integer column and you extend it with a long VARCHAR column, it might become significantly slower. This is especially true if your queries use the index as a covering index.

Consider the userinfo table that follows:

```
CREATE TABLE userinfo (
  id int unsigned NOT NULL AUTO_INCREMENT,
  name varchar(64) NOT NULL DEFAULT '',
  email varchar(64) NOT NULL DEFAULT '',
  password varchar(64) NOT NULL DEFAULT '',
  dob date DEFAULT NULL,
  address varchar(255) NOT NULL DEFAULT '',
  city varchar(64) NOT NULL DEFAULT '',
  state_id tinyint unsigned NOT NULL DEFAULT '0',
  zip varchar(8) NOT NULL DEFAULT '',
  country_id smallint unsigned NOT NULL DEFAULT '0',
  account_type varchar(32) NOT NULL DEFAULT '',
  verified tinyint NOT NULL DEFAULT '0',
  allow_mail tinyint unsigned NOT NULL DEFAULT '0',
  parrent_account int unsigned NOT NULL DEFAULT '0',
```

---

13 An index is not necessarily a duplicate if it's a different type of index; there are often good reasons to have KEY(col) and FULLTEXT KEY(col).

```
closest_airport varchar(3) NOT NULL DEFAULT '',
PRIMARY KEY (id),
UNIQUE KEY email (email),
KEY country_id (country_id),
KEY state_id (state_id)
) ENGINE=InnoDB
```

This table contains one million rows, and for each `state_id` there are about 20,000 records. There is an index on `state_id`, which is useful for the following query. We refer to this query as Q1:

```
SELECT count(*) FROM userinfo WHERE state_id=5;
```

A simple benchmark shows an execution rate of almost 115 queries per second (QPS) for this query. We also have a related query that retrieves several columns instead of just counting rows. This is Q2:

```
SELECT state_id, city, address FROM userinfo WHERE state_id=5;
```

For this query, the result is less than 10 QPS.[14] The simple solution to improve its performance is to extend the index to (`state_id`, `city`, `address`), so the index will cover the query:

```
ALTER TABLE userinfo DROP KEY state_id,
ADD KEY state_id_2 (state_id, city, address);
```

After extending the index, Q2 runs faster, but Q1 runs more slowly. If we really care about making both queries fast, we should leave both indexes, even though the single-column index is redundant. Table 7-2 shows detailed results for both queries and indexing strategies.

*Table 7-2. Benchmark results in QPS for SELECT queries with various index strategies*

|         | state_id only | state_id_2 only | Both state_id and state_id_2 |
|---------|---------------|-----------------|------------------------------|
| Query 1 | 108.55        | 100.33          | 107.97                       |
| Query 2 | 12.12         | 28.04           | 28.06                        |

The drawback of having two indexes is the maintenance cost. Table 7-3 shows how long it takes to insert a million rows into the table.

*Table 7-3. Speed of inserting a million rows with various index strategies*

|                                          | state_id only | Both state_id and state_id_2 |
|------------------------------------------|---------------|------------------------------|
| InnoDB, enough memory for both indexes   | 80 seconds    | 136 seconds                  |

---

14 We've used an in-memory example here. When the table is bigger and the workload becomes I/O bound, the difference between the numbers will be much larger. It's not uncommon for COUNT() queries to become one hundred or more times faster with a covering index.

As you can see, inserting new rows into the table with more indexes is slower. This is true in general: adding new indexes might have a performance impact for INSERT, UPDATE, and DELETE operations, especially if a new index causes you to hit memory limits.

The solution for redundant and duplicate indexes is simply to drop them, but first you need to identify them. You can write various complicated queries against the INFORMATION_SCHEMA tables, but there are easier techniques. You can use the *pt-duplicate-key-checker* tool included with Percona Toolkit, which analyzes table structures and suggests indexes that are duplicate or redundant.

Be careful when determining which indexes are candidates for dropping or extending. Recall that in InnoDB, an index on column (A) in our example table is really equivalent to an index on (A, ID) because the primary key is appended to secondary index leaf nodes. If you have a query such as WHERE A = 5 ORDER BY ID, the index will be very helpful. But if you extend the index to (A, B), then it really becomes (A, B, ID), and the query will begin to use a filesort for the ORDER BY portion of the query. It's good to validate your planned changes carefully with a tool such as *pt-upgrade* from Percona Toolkit.

For both cases, consider using MySQL 8.0's invisible index feature prior to removing an index. With this feature, you can issue an ALTER TABLE statement to change an index to be flagged as invisible, meaning the optimizer will ignore it when planning queries. If you discover that the index you were about to remove was important, you can easily make it visible again without having to re-create the index.

## Unused Indexes

In addition to duplicate and redundant indexes, you might have some indexes that the server simply doesn't use. These are simply deadweight, and you should consider dropping them.[15]

The best way to identify unused indexes is with performance_schema and sys, which we covered in detail in Chapter 3. The sys schema creates a view of the table_io_waits_summary_by_index_usage table that can easily tell us which indexes are unused:

```
mysql> SELECT * FROM sys.schema_unused_indexes;
+---------------+---------------+-----------------------------+
| object_schema | object_name   | index_name                  |
+---------------+---------------+-----------------------------+
| sakila        | actor         | idx_actor_last_name         |
```

---

15 Some indexes function as unique constraints, so even if an index doesn't get used for queries, it might be used to prevent duplicate values.

```
| sakila        | address       | idx_fk_city_id        |
| sakila        | address       | idx_location          |
| sakila        | payment       | fk_payment_rental     |
.. trimmed for brevity ..
```

# Index and Table Maintenance

Once you've created tables with proper data types and added indexes, your work isn't over: you still need to maintain your tables and indexes to make sure they perform well. The three main goals of table maintenance are finding and fixing corruption, maintaining accurate index statistics, and reducing fragmentation.

## Finding and Repairing Table Corruption

The worst thing that can happen to a table is corruption. All storage engines can experience index corruption due to hardware problems or internal bugs in MySQL or the operating system, although it is very rare to experience them in InnoDB.

Corrupted indexes can cause queries to return incorrect results, raise duplicate-key errors when there is no duplicated value, or even cause lockups and crashes. If you experience odd behavior—such as an error that you think shouldn't be happening—run CHECK TABLE to see if the table is corrupt. (Note that some storage engines don't support this command, and others support multiple options to specify how thoroughly they check the table.) CHECK TABLE usually catches most table and index errors.

You can fix corrupt tables with the REPAIR TABLE command, but again, not all storage engines support this. In these cases you can do a "no-op" ALTER, such as altering a table to use the same storage engine it currently uses. Here's an example for an InnoDB table:

```
ALTER TABLE <table> ENGINE=INNODB;
```

Alternatively, you can dump the data and reload it. However, if the corruption is in the system area or in the table's "row data" area instead of the index, you might be unable to use any of these options. In this case, you might need to restore the table from your backups or attempt to recover data from the corrupted files.

If you experience corruption with the InnoDB storage engine, something is seriously wrong and you need to investigate it right away. InnoDB simply shouldn't become corrupt. Its design makes it very resilient to corruption. Corruption is evidence of either a hardware problem such as bad memory or disks (likely), an administrator error such as manipulating the database files externally to MySQL (likely), or an InnoDB bug (unlikely). The usual causes are mistakes such as trying to make backups with *rsync*. There is no query you can execute—none—that you are supposed to avoid because it'll corrupt InnoDB's data. There is no hidden gun pointed at your foot. If you're corrupting InnoDB's data by issuing queries against it, there's a bug in InnoDB, and it's never your fault.

If you experience data corruption, the most important thing to do is try to determine why it's occurring; don't simply repair the data, or the corruption could return. You can repair the data by putting InnoDB into forced recovery mode with the `innodb_force_recovery` parameter; see the MySQL manual for details.

## Updating Index Statistics

When the storage engine provides the optimizer with inexact information about the number of rows a query might examine, or when the query plan is too complex to know exactly how many rows will be matched at various stages, the optimizer uses the index statistics to estimate the number of rows. MySQL's optimizer is cost based, and the main cost metric is how much data the query will access. If the statistics were never generated or if they are out of date, the optimizer can make bad decisions. The solution is to run `ANALYZE TABLE`, which regenerates the statistics.

You can examine the cardinality of your indexes with the `SHOW INDEX FROM` command. For example:

```
mysql> SHOW INDEX FROM sakila.actor\G
*************************** 1. row ***************************
        Table: actor
   Non_unique: 0
     Key_name: PRIMARY
 Seq_in_index: 1
  Column_name: actor_id
    Collation: A
  Cardinality: 200
     Sub_part: NULL
       Packed: NULL
         Null:
   Index_type: BTREE
      Comment:
*************************** 2. row ***************************
        Table: actor
   Non_unique: 1
     Key_name: idx_actor_last_name
 Seq_in_index: 1
  Column_name: last_name
    Collation: A
  Cardinality: 200
     Sub_part: NULL
       Packed: NULL
         Null:
   Index_type: BTREE
      Comment:
```

This command gives quite a lot of index information, which the MySQL manual explains in detail. We do want to call your attention to the Cardinality column, though. This shows how many distinct values the storage engine estimates are in the index. You can also get this data from the INFORMATION_SCHEMA.STATISTICS table. For example, you can write queries against the INFORMATION_SCHEMA tables to find indexes with very low selectivity. Beware, however, that on servers with a lot of data, these metadata tables can cause a lot of load on the server.

InnoDB's statistics are worth exploring more. The statistics are generated by sampling a few random pages in the index and assuming that the rest of the index looks similar. The number of pages sampled is controlled with the innodb_stats_sample_pages variable. Setting this to a value larger than the default of 8 can in theory help generate more representative index statistics, especially on very large tables, but your mileage may vary.

InnoDB calculates statistics for indexes when tables are first opened, when you run ANALYZE TABLE, and when the table's size changes significantly.

InnoDB also calculates statistics for queries against some INFORMATION_SCHEMA tables, SHOW TABLE STATUS and SHOW INDEX queries, and when the MySQL command-line client has autocompletion enabled. This can actually become a pretty serious problem on large servers with lots of data or when I/O is slow. Client programs or monitoring tools that cause sampling to occur can create a lot of locking and heavy load on the server as well as frustrate users with slow startup times. And you can't observe the index statistics without changing them because SHOW INDEX will update the statistics. You can disable the innodb_stats_on_metadata option to avoid all of these problems.

## Reducing Index and Data Fragmentation

B-tree indexes can become fragmented, which might reduce performance. Fragmented indexes can be poorly filled and/or nonsequential on disk.

By design, B-tree indexes require random disk accesses to "dive" to the leaf pages, so random access is the rule, not the exception. However, the leaf pages can still perform better if they are physically sequential and tightly packed. If they are not, we say they are *fragmented*, and range scans or full index scans can be many times slower. This is especially true for index-covered queries.

The table's data storage can also become fragmented. However, data storage fragmentation is more complex than index fragmentation. There are three types of data fragmentation:

*Row fragmentation*

This type of fragmentation occurs when the row is stored in multiple pieces in multiple locations. Row fragmentation reduces performance even if the query needs only a single row from the index.

*Intra-row fragmentation*

This kind of fragmentation occurs when logically sequential pages or rows are not stored sequentially on disk. It affects operations such as full table scans and clustered index range scans, which normally benefit from a sequential data layout on disk.

*Free space fragmentation*

This type of fragmentation occurs when there is a lot of empty space in data pages. It causes the server to read a lot of data it doesn't need, which is wasteful.

To defragment data, you can either run `OPTIMIZE TABLE` or dump and reload the data. These approaches work for most storage engines. For storage engines that don't support `OPTIMIZE TABLE`, you can rebuild the table with a no-op `ALTER TABLE`. Just alter the table to have the same engine it currently uses:

```
ALTER TABLE <table> ENGINE=<engine>;
```

# Summary

As you can see, indexing is a complex topic! The way MySQL and the storage engines access data combined with the properties of indexes make indexes a very powerful and flexible tool for influencing data access, both on disk and in memory.

Most of the time you'll use B-tree indexes with MySQL. The other types of indexes are rather more suitable for special purposes, and it will generally be obvious when you ought to use them and how they can improve query response times. We'll say no more about them in this chapter, but it's worth wrapping up with a review of the properties and uses of B-tree indexes.

Here are three principles to keep in mind as you choose indexes and write queries to take advantage of them:

- Single-row access is slow, especially on spindle-based storage. (SSDs are faster at random I/O, but this point remains true.) If the server reads a block of data from storage and then accesses only one row in it, it wastes a lot of work. It's much better to read in a block that contains lots of rows you need.

- Accessing ranges of rows in order is fast, for two reasons. First, sequential I/O doesn't require disk seeks, so it is faster than random I/O, especially on spindle-based storage. Second, if the server can read the data in the order you need it, it doesn't need to perform any follow-up work to sort it, and GROUP BY queries don't need to sort and group rows together to compute aggregates over them.

- Index-only access is fast. If an index contains all the columns that the query needs, the storage engine doesn't need to find the other columns by looking up rows in the table. This avoids lots of single-row access, which as we know from the first point is slow.

In sum, try to choose indexes and write queries so that you can avoid single-row lookups, use the inherent ordering of the data to avoid sorting operations, and exploit index-only access. This corresponds to the three-star ranking system set out in Lahdenmaki and Leach's book, mentioned at the beginning of this chapter.

It would be great to be able to create perfect indexes for every query against your tables. Unfortunately, sometimes this would require an impractically large number of indexes, and at other times there simply is no way to create a three-star index for a given query (for example, if the query is ordered by two columns, one ascending and the other descending). In these cases, you have to settle for the best you can do or pursue alternative strategies, such as denormalization or summary tables.

It's very important to be able to reason through how indexes work and to choose them based on that understanding, not on rules of thumb or heuristics such as "place the most selective columns first in multicolumn indexes" or "you should index all of the columns that appear in the WHERE clause."

How do you know whether your schema is indexed well enough? As always, we suggest that you frame the question in terms of response time. Find queries that are either taking too long or contributing too much load to the server. Examine the schema, SQL, and index structures for the queries that need attention. Determine whether the query has to examine too many rows, perform postretrieval sorting or use temporary tables, access data with random I/O, or look up full rows from the table to retrieve columns not included in the index.

If you find a query that doesn't benefit from all of the possible advantages of indexes, see if a better index can be created to improve performance. If not, perhaps a rewrite can transform the query so that it can use an index that either already exists or could be created. That's what the next chapter is about.

# Query Performance Optimization

In the previous chapters we explained schema optimization and indexing, which are necessary for high performance. But they aren't enough—you also need to design your queries well. If your queries are bad, even the best-designed schema and indexes will not perform well.

Query optimization, index optimization, and schema optimization go hand in hand. As you gain experience writing queries in MySQL, you will learn how to design tables and indexes to support efficient queries. Similarly, what you learn about optimal schema design will influence the kinds of queries you write. This process takes time, so we encourage you to refer back to these three chapters as you learn more.

This chapter begins with general query design considerations: the things you should consider first when a query isn't performing well. We then dig much deeper into query optimization and server internals. We show you how to find out how MySQL executes a particular query, and you'll learn how to change the query execution plan. Finally, we'll look at some places MySQL doesn't optimize queries well and explore query optimization patterns that help MySQL execute queries more efficiently.

Our goal is to help you understand deeply how MySQL really executes queries, so you can reason about what is efficient or inefficient, exploit MySQL's strengths, and avoid its weaknesses.

## Why Are Queries Slow?

Before trying to write fast queries, remember that it's all about response time. Queries are tasks, but they are composed of subtasks, and those subtasks consume time. To optimize a query, you must optimize its subtasks by eliminating them, making them happen fewer times, or making them happen more quickly.

In general, you can think of a query's lifetime by mentally following the query through its sequence diagram from the client to the server, where it is parsed, planned, and executed, and then back again to the client. Execution is one of the most important stages in a query's lifetime. It involves lots of calls to the storage engine to retrieve rows, as well as postretrieval operations such as grouping and sorting.

While accomplishing all these tasks, the query spends time on the network, in the CPU, and in operations like statistics, planning, locking (mutex waits), and most especially, calls to the storage engine to retrieve rows. These calls consume time in memory operations, CPU operations, and especially I/O operations if the data isn't in memory. Depending on the storage engine, a lot of context switching and/or system calls might also be involved.

In every case, excessive time may be consumed because the operations are performed needlessly, performed too many times, or are too slow. The goal of optimization is to avoid that by eliminating or reducing operations or making them faster.

Again, this isn't a complete or accurate picture of a query's life. Our goal here is to show the importance of understanding a query's life cycle and thinking in terms of where the time is consumed. With that in mind, let's see how to optimize queries.

# Slow Query Basics: Optimize Data Access

The most basic reason a query doesn't perform well is because it's working with too much data. Some queries just have to sift through a lot of data, which can't be helped. That's unusual, though; most bad queries can be changed to access less data. We've found it useful to analyze a poorly performing query in two steps:

1. Find out whether your application is retrieving more data than you need. That usually means it's accessing too many rows, but it might also be accessing too many columns.

2. Find out whether the *MySQL server* is analyzing more rows than it needs.

## Are You Asking the Database for Data You Don't Need?

Some queries ask for more data than they need and then throw some of it away. This demands extra work of the MySQL server, adds network overhead,[1] and consumes memory and CPU resources on the application server.

---

1 Network overhead is worst if the application is on a different host from the server, but transferring data between MySQL and the application isn't free even if they're on the same server.

Here are a few typical mistakes:

*Fetching more rows than needed*

One common mistake is assuming that MySQL provides results on demand, rather than calculating and returning the full result set. We often see this in applications designed by people familiar with other database systems. These developers are used to techniques such as issuing a `SELECT` statement that returns many rows, then fetching the first *N* rows and closing the result set (e.g., fetching the 100 most recent articles for a news site when they only need to show 10 of them on the front page). They think MySQL will provide them with these 10 rows and stop executing the query, but what MySQL really does is generate the complete result set. The client library then fetches all the data and discards most of it. The best solution is to add a `LIMIT` clause to the query.

*Fetching all columns from a multitable join*

If you want to retrieve all actors who appear in the film *Academy Dinosaur*, don't write the query this way:

```
SELECT * FROM sakila.actor
INNER JOIN sakila.film_actor USING(actor_id)
INNER JOIN sakila.film USING(film_id)
WHERE sakila.film.title = 'Academy Dinosaur';
```

That returns all columns from all three tables. Instead, write the query as follows:

```
SELECT sakila.actor.* FROM sakila.actor...;
```

*Fetching all columns*

You should always be suspicious when you see `SELECT *`. Do you really need all the columns? Probably not. Retrieving all columns can prevent optimizations such as covering indexes, as well as add I/O, memory, and CPU overhead for the server. Some DBAs discourage `SELECT *` universally because of this fact and to reduce the risk of problems when someone alters the table's column list.

Of course, asking for more data than you really need is not always bad. In many cases we've investigated, people tell us the wasteful approach simplifies development because it lets the developer use the same bit of code in more than one place. That's a reasonable consideration as long as you know what it costs in terms of performance. It might also be useful to retrieve more data than you actually need if you use some type of caching in your application or if you have another benefit in mind. Fetching and caching full objects might be preferable to running many separate queries that retrieve only parts of the object.

*Fetching the same data repeatedly*

If you're not careful, it's quite easy to write application code that retrieves the same data repeatedly from the database server, executing the same query to fetch it. For example, if you want to find out a user's profile image URL to display next to a list of comments, you might request this repeatedly for each comment. Or you could cache it the first time you fetch it and reuse it thereafter. The latter approach is much more efficient.

## Is MySQL Examining Too Much Data?

Once you're sure your queries *retrieve* only the data you need, you can look for queries that *examine* too much data while generating results. In MySQL, the simplest query cost metrics are:

- Response time
- Number of rows examined
- Number of rows returned

None of these metrics is a perfect way to measure query cost, but they reflect roughly how much data MySQL must access internally to execute a query and translate approximately into how fast the query runs. All three metrics are logged in the slow query log, so looking at the slow query log is one of the best ways to find queries that examine too much data.

### Response time

Beware of taking query response time at face value. Hey, isn't that the opposite of what we've been telling you? Not really. It's still true that response time is what matters, but it's a bit complicated.

Response time is the sum of two things: service time and queue time. *Service time* is how long it takes the server to actually process the query. *Queue time* is the portion of response time during which the server isn't really executing the query—it's waiting for something, such as waiting for an I/O operation to complete, waiting for a row lock, and so forth. The problem is, you can't break the response time down into these components unless you can measure them individually, which is usually hard to do. In general, the most common and important waits you'll encounter are I/O and lock waits, but you shouldn't count on it being just those two because it varies a lot. I/O and lock waits are important because they are the most detrimental to performance.

As a result, response time is not consistent under varying load conditions. Other factors—such as storage engine locks (like row locks), high concurrency, and hardware —can have a considerable impact on response times, too. Response time can also be both a symptom and a cause of problems, and it's not always obvious which is the case.

When you look at a query's response time, you should ask yourself whether the response time is reasonable for the query. We don't have space for a detailed explanation in this book, but you can actually calculate a quick upper-bound estimate

(QUBE) of query response time using the techniques explained in Tapio Lahdenmaki and Mike Leach's book *Relational Database Index Design and the Optimizers* (Wiley). In a nutshell: examine the query execution plan and the indexes involved, determine how many sequential and random I/O operations might be required, and multiply these by the time it takes your hardware to perform them. Add it all up and you have a yardstick to judge whether a query is slower than it could or should be.

### Rows examined and rows returned

It's useful to think about the number of rows examined when analyzing queries because you can see how efficiently the queries are finding the data you need. However, this is not a perfect metric for finding "bad" queries. Not all row accesses are equal. Shorter rows are faster to access, and fetching rows from memory is much faster than reading them from disk.

Ideally, the number of rows examined would be the same as the number returned, but in practice this is rarely possible. For example, when constructing rows with joins, the server must access multiple rows to generate each row in the result set. The ratio of rows examined to rows returned is usually small—say, between 1:1 and 10:1—but sometimes it can be orders of magnitude larger.

### Rows examined and access types

When you're thinking about the cost of a query, consider the cost of finding a single row in a table. MySQL can use several access methods to find and return a row. Some require examining many rows, but others might be able to generate the result without examining any.

The access method(s) appear in the `type` column in EXPLAIN's output. The access types range from a full table scan to index scans, range scans, unique index lookups, and constants. Each of these is faster than the one before it because it requires reading less data. You don't need to memorize the access types, but you should understand the general concepts of scanning a table, scanning an index, range accesses, and single-value accesses.

If you aren't getting a good access type, the best way to solve the problem is usually by adding an appropriate index. We discussed indexing in the previous chapter; now you can see why indexes are so important to query optimization. Indexes let MySQL find rows with a more efficient access type that examines less data.

For example, let's look at a simple query on the Sakila Sample Database:

```
SELECT * FROM sakila.film_actor WHERE film_id = 1;
```

This query will return 10 rows, and EXPLAIN shows that MySQL uses the `ref` access type on the `idx_fk_film_id` index to execute the query:

```
mysql> EXPLAIN SELECT * FROM sakila.film_actor WHERE film_id = 1\G
*************************** 1. row ***************************
           id: 1
  select_type: SIMPLE
        table: film_actor
   partitions: NULL
         type: ref
possible_keys: idx_fk_film_id
          key: idx_fk_film_id
      key_len: 2
          ref: const
         rows: 10
     filtered: 100.00
        Extra: NULL
```

EXPLAIN shows that MySQL estimated it needed to access only 10 rows. In other words, the query optimizer knew the chosen access type could satisfy the query efficiently. What would happen if there were no suitable index for the query? MySQL would have to use a less optimal access type, as we can see if we drop the index and run the query again:

```
mysql> ALTER TABLE sakila.film_actor DROP FOREIGN KEY fk_film_actor_film;
mysql> ALTER TABLE sakila.film_actor DROP KEY idx_fk_film_id;
mysql> EXPLAIN SELECT * FROM sakila.film_actor WHERE film_id = 1\G
*************************** 1. row ***************************
           id: 1
  select_type: SIMPLE
        table: film_actor
   partitions: NULL
         type: ALL
possible_keys: NULL
          key: NULL
      key_len: NULL
          ref: NULL
         rows: 5462
     filtered: 10.00
        Extra: Using where
1 row in set, 1 warning (0.00 sec)
```

Predictably, the access type has changed to a full table scan (ALL), and MySQL now estimates it'll have to examine 5,462 rows to satisfy the query. The "Using where" in the Extra column shows that the MySQL server is using the WHERE clause to discard rows after the storage engine reads them.

In general, MySQL can apply a WHERE clause in three ways, from best to worst:

- Apply the conditions to the index lookup operation to eliminate nonmatching rows. This happens at the storage engine layer.

- Use a covering index ("Using index" in the Extra column) to avoid row accesses, and filter out nonmatching rows after retrieving each result from the index. This happens at the server layer, but it doesn't require reading rows from the table.

- Retrieve rows from the table, then filter nonmatching rows ("Using where" in the Extra column). This happens at the server layer and requires the server to read rows from the table before it can filter them.

This example illustrates how important it is to have good indexes. Good indexes help your queries get a good access type and examine only the rows they need. However, adding an index doesn't always mean that MySQL will access and return the same number of rows. For example, here's a query that uses the COUNT()[2] aggregate function:

```
mysql> SELECT actor_id, COUNT(*)
    -> FROM sakila.film_actor GROUP BY actor_id;
+----------+----------+
| actor_id | COUNT(*) |
+----------+----------+
|        1 |       19 |
|        2 |       25 |
|        3 |       22 |
.. omitted..
|      200 |       20 |
+----------+----------+
200 rows in set (0.01 sec)
```

This query returns only 200 rows, as shown, but how many rows does it need to read? We can check this with EXPLAIN, as we talked about in the previous chapter:

```
mysql> EXPLAIN SELECT actor_id, COUNT(*)
    -> FROM sakila.film_actor GROUP BY actor_id\G
*************************** 1. row ***************************
id: 1
select_type: SIMPLE
table: film_actor
partitions: NULL
type: index
possible_keys: PRIMARY
key: PRIMARY
key_len: 4
ref: NULL
rows: 5462
filtered: 100.00
Extra: Using index
```

---

2 See "Optimizing COUNT() Queries" on page 221 later in this chapter for more on this topic.

Ouch! Reading thousands of rows only to need 200 means that we're doing much more work than necessary. An index can't reduce the number of rows examined for a query like this one because there's no WHERE clause to eliminate rows.

Unfortunately, MySQL does not tell you how many of the rows it accessed were used to build the result set; it tells you only the total number of rows it accessed. Many of these rows could be eliminated by a WHERE clause and end up not contributing to the result set. In the previous example, after removing the index on sakila.film_actor, the query accessed every row in the table and the WHERE clause discarded all but 10 of them. Only the remaining 10 rows were used to build the result set. Understanding how many rows the server accesses and how many it really uses requires reasoning about the query.

If you find that a huge number of rows were examined to produce relatively few rows in the result, you can try some more sophisticated fixes:

- Use covering indexes, which store data so that the storage engine doesn't have to retrieve the complete rows. (We discussed these in Chapter 7.)

- Change the schema. An example is using summary tables (discussed in Chapter 6).

- Rewrite a complicated query so the MySQL optimizer is able to execute it optimally. (We discuss this later in this chapter.)

# Ways to Restructure Queries

As you optimize problematic queries, your goal should be to find alternative ways to get the result you want—but that doesn't necessarily mean getting the same result set back from MySQL. You can sometimes transform queries into equivalent forms that return the same results and get better performance. However, you should also think about rewriting the query to retrieve *different* results if that provides an efficiency benefit. You might be able to ultimately do the same work by changing the application code as well as the query. In this section, we explain techniques that can help you restructure a wide range of queries and show you when to use each technique.

## Complex Queries Versus Many Queries

One important query-design question is whether it's preferable to break up a complex query into several simpler queries. The traditional approach to database design emphasizes doing as much work as possible with as few queries as possible. This approach was historically better because of the cost of network communication and the overhead of the query parsing and optimization stages.

However, this advice doesn't apply as much to MySQL because it was designed to handle connecting and disconnecting very efficiently and to respond to small, simple queries very quickly. Modern networks are also significantly faster than they used to be, reducing network latency. Depending on the server version, MySQL can run well over one hundred thousand simple queries per second on commodity server hardware and more than two thousand QPS from a single correspondent on a gigabit network, so running multiple queries isn't necessarily such a bad thing.

Connection response is still slow compared to the number of rows MySQL can traverse per second internally, though, which is counted in millions per second for in-memory data. All else being equal, it's still a good idea to use as few queries as possible, but sometimes you can make a query more efficient by decomposing it and executing a few simple queries instead of one complex one. Don't be afraid to do this; weigh the costs and go with the strategy that causes less work. We show some examples of this technique a little later in the chapter.

That said, using too many queries is a common mistake in application design. For example, some applications perform 10 single-row queries to retrieve data from a table when they could use a single 10-row query. We've even seen applications that retrieve each column individually, querying each row many times!

## Chopping Up a Query

Another way to slice up a query is to divide and conquer, keeping it essentially the same but running it in smaller "chunks" that affect fewer rows each time.

Purging old data is a great example. Periodic purge jobs might need to remove quite a bit of data, and doing this in one massive query could lock a lot of rows for a long time, fill up transaction logs, hog resources, and block small queries that shouldn't be interrupted. Chopping up the DELETE statement and using medium-size queries can improve performance considerably and reduce replication lag when a query is replicated. For example, instead of running this monolithic query:

```
DELETE FROM messages
WHERE created < DATE_SUB(NOW(),INTERVAL 3 MONTH);
```

You could do something like the following pseudocode:

```
rows_affected = 0
do {
  rows_affected = do_query(
  "DELETE FROM messages WHERE created < DATE_SUB(NOW(),INTERVAL 3 MONTH)
  LIMIT 10000")
} while rows_affected > 0
```

Deleting 10,000 rows at a time is typically a large enough task to make each query efficient and a short enough task to minimize the impact on the server[3] (transactional

---

[3] Percona Toolkit's *pt-archiver* tool makes these types of jobs easy and safe.

storage engines might benefit from smaller transactions). It might also be a good idea to add some sleep time between the DELETE statements to spread the load over time and reduce the amount of time locks are held.

## Join Decomposition

Many high-performance applications use *join decomposition*. You can decompose a join by running multiple single-table queries instead of a multitable join and then performing the join in the application. For example, instead of this single query:

```
SELECT * FROM tag
JOIN tag_post ON tag_post.tag_id=tag.id
JOIN post ON tag_post.post_id=post.id
WHERE tag.tag='mysql';
```

You might run these queries:

```
SELECT * FROM tag WHERE tag='mysql';
SELECT * FROM tag_post WHERE tag_id=1234;
SELECT * FROM post WHERE post.id in (123,456,567,9098,8904);
```

Why on earth would you do this? It looks wasteful at first glance because you've increased the number of queries without getting anything in return. However, such restructuring can actually give significant performance advantages:

- Caching can be more efficient. Many applications cache "objects" that map directly to tables. In this example, if the object with the tag mysql is already cached, the application can skip the first query. If you find posts with an ID of 123, 567, or 9098 in the cache, you can remove them from the IN() list.

- Executing the queries individually can sometimes reduce lock contention.

- Doing joins in the application makes it easier to scale the database by placing tables on different servers.

- The queries themselves can be more efficient. In this example, using an IN() list instead of a join lets MySQL sort row IDs and retrieve rows more optimally than might be possible with a join.

- You can reduce redundant row accesses. Doing a join in the application means you retrieve each row only once, whereas a join in the query is essentially a denormalization that might repeatedly access the same data. For the same reason, such restructuring might also reduce the total network traffic and memory usage.

As a result, doing joins in the application can be more efficient when you cache and reuse a lot of data from earlier queries, you distribute data across multiple servers, you replace joins with IN() lists on large tables, or a join refers to the same table multiple times.

# Query Execution Basics

If you need to get high performance from your MySQL server, one of the best ways to invest your time is in learning how MySQL optimizes and executes queries. Once you understand this, much of query optimization is a matter of reasoning from principles, and query optimization becomes a very logical process.

Let's revisit what we discussed earlier: the process MySQL follows to execute queries. Figure 8-1 shows what happens when you send MySQL a query:

1. The client sends the SQL statement to the server.

2. The server parses, preprocesses, and optimizes it into a query execution plan.

3. The query execution engine executes the plan by calling the storage engine API.

4. The server sends the result to the client.

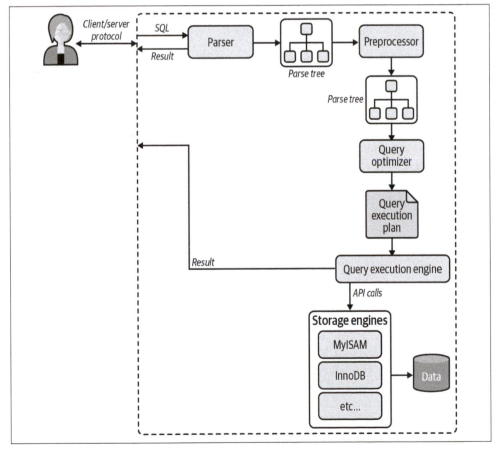

Figure 8-1. Execution path of a query

Each of these steps has some extra complexity, which we discuss in the following sections. We also explain which states the query will be in during each step. The query optimization process is particularly complex and important to understand. There are also exceptions or special cases, such as the difference in execution path when you use prepared statements; we discuss that in the next chapter.

## The MySQL Client/Server Protocol

Although you don't need to understand the inner details of MySQL's client/server protocol, you do need to know how it works at a high level. The protocol is *half-duplex*, meaning that at any given time the MySQL server can be either sending or receiving messages but not both. It also means there is no way to cut a message short.

This protocol makes MySQL communication simple and fast, but it limits it in some ways too. For one thing, it means there's no flow control; once one side sends a message, the other side must fetch the entire message before responding. It's like a game of tossing a ball back and forth: only one side has the ball at any instant, and you can't toss the ball (send a message) unless you have it.

The client sends a query to the server as a single packet of data. This is why the `max_allowed_packet` configuration variable is important if you have large queries.[4] Once the client sends the query, it doesn't have the ball anymore; it can only wait for results.

In contrast, the response from the server usually consists of many packets of data. When the server responds, the client has to receive the *entire* result set. It cannot simply fetch a few rows and then ask the server not to bother sending the rest. If the client needs only the first few rows that are returned, it either has to wait for all of the server's packets to arrive and then discard the ones it doesn't need or disconnect ungracefully. Neither is a good idea, which is why appropriate `LIMIT` clauses are so important.

Here's another way to think about this: when a client fetches rows from the server, it thinks it's *pulling* them. But the truth is, the MySQL server is *pushing* the rows as it generates them. The client is only receiving the pushed rows; there is no way for it to tell the server to stop sending rows. The client is "drinking from the fire hose," so to speak. (Yes, that's a technical term.)

Most libraries that connect to MySQL let you either fetch the whole result set and buffer it in memory or fetch each row as you need it. The default behavior is generally to fetch the whole result and buffer it in memory. This is important because until all the rows have been fetched, the MySQL server will not release the locks and other

---

4 If the query is too large, the server will refuse to receive any more data and throw an error.

resources required by the query. The query will be in the "Sending data" state. When the client library fetches the results all at once, it reduces the amount of work the server needs to do: the server can finish and clean up the query as quickly as possible.

Most client libraries let you treat the result set as though you're fetching it from the server, although in fact you're just fetching it from the buffer in the library's memory. This works fine most of the time, but it's not a good idea for huge result sets that might take a long time to fetch and use a lot of memory. You can use less memory and start working on the result sooner if you instruct the library not to buffer the result. The downside is that the locks and other resources on the server will remain open while your application is interacting with the library.[5]

Let's look at an example using PHP. Here's how you usually query MySQL from PHP:

```php
<?php
$link = mysql_connect('localhost', 'user', 'p4ssword');
$result = mysql_query('SELECT * FROM HUGE_TABLE', $link);
while ( $row = mysql_fetch_array($result) ) {
  // Do something with result
}
?>
```

The code seems to indicate that you fetch rows only when you need them, in the while loop. However, the code actually fetches the entire result into a buffer with the mysql_query() function call. The while loop simply iterates through the buffer. In contrast, the following code doesn't buffer the results because it uses mysql_unbuf fered_query() instead of mysql_query():

```php
<?php
$link = mysql_connect('localhost', 'user', 'p4ssword');
$result = mysql_unbuffered_query('SELECT * FROM HUGE_TABLE', $link);
while ( $row = mysql_fetch_array($result) ) {
  // Do something with result
}
?>
```

Programming languages have different ways to override buffering. For example, the Perl DBD::mysql driver requires you to specify the C client library's mysql_ use_result attribute (the default is mysql_buffer_result). Here's an example:

```perl
#!/usr/bin/perl
use DBI;
my $dbh = DBI->connect('DBI:mysql:;host=localhost', 'user', 'p4ssword');
my $sth = $dbh->prepare('SELECT * FROM HUGE_TABLE', { mysql_use_result => 1 });
$sth->execute();
while ( my $row = $sth->fetchrow_array() ) {
```

---

5 You can work around this with SQL_BUFFER_RESULT, which we'll see a bit later.

```
    # Do something with result
}
```

Notice that the call to `prepare()` specified to "use" the result instead of "buffering" it. You can also specify this when connecting, which will make every statement unbuffered:

```
my $dbh = DBI->connect('DBI:mysql:;mysql_use_result=1', 'user', 'p4ssword');
```

## Query States

Each MySQL connection, or *thread*, has a state that shows what it is doing at any given time. There are several ways to view these states, but the easiest is to use the `SHOW FULL PROCESSLIST` command (the states appear in the `Command` column). As a query progresses through its life cycle, its state changes many times, and there are dozens of states. The MySQL manual is the authoritative source of information for all the states, but we list a few here and explain what they mean:

*Sleep*
> The thread is waiting for a new query from the client.

*Query*
> The thread is either executing the query or sending the result back to the client.

*Locked*
> The thread is waiting for a table lock to be granted at the server level. Locks that are implemented by the storage engine, such as InnoDB's row locks, do not cause the thread to enter the `Locked` state.

*Analyzing and statistics*
> The thread is checking storage engine statistics and optimizing the query.

*Copying to tmp table [on disk]*
> The thread is processing the query and copying results to a temporary table, probably for a `GROUP BY`, for a filesort, or to satisfy a `UNION`. If the state ends with "on disk," MySQL is converting an in-memory table to an on-disk table.

*Sorting result*
> The thread is sorting a result set.

It's helpful to at least know the basic states, so you can get a sense of "who has the ball" for the query. On very busy servers, you might see a normally brief state, such as `statistics`, begin to take a significant amount of time. This usually indicates that something is wrong.

# The Query Optimization Process

The next step in the query life cycle turns a SQL query into an execution plan for the query execution engine. This has several substeps: parsing, preprocessing, and optimization. Errors (for example, syntax errors) can be raised at any point in the process. We're not trying to document the MySQL internals here, so we're going to take some liberties, such as describing steps separately even though they're often combined wholly or partially for efficiency. Our goal is simply to help you understand how MySQL executes queries so that you can write better ones.

## The parser and the preprocessor

To begin, MySQL's *parser* breaks the query into tokens and builds a "parse tree" from them. The parser uses MySQL's SQL grammar to interpret and validate the query. For instance, it ensures that the tokens in the query are valid and in the proper order, and it checks for mistakes such as quoted strings that aren't terminated.

The *preprocessor* then checks the resulting parse tree for additional semantics that the parser can't resolve. For example, it checks that tables and columns exist, and it resolves names and aliases to ensure that column references aren't ambiguous.

Next, the preprocessor checks privileges. This is normally very fast unless your server has large numbers of privileges.

## The query optimizer

The parse tree is now valid and ready for the optimizer to turn it into a query execution plan. A query can often be executed many different ways and produce the same result. The optimizer's job is to find the best option.

MySQL uses a cost-based optimizer, which means it tries to predict the cost of various execution plans and choose the least expensive. The unit of cost was originally a single random 4 KB data page read, but it has become more sophisticated and now includes factors such as the estimated cost of executing a WHERE clause comparison. You can see how expensive the optimizer estimated a query to be by running the query, then inspecting the Last_query_cost session variable:

```
mysql> SELECT SQL_NO_CACHE COUNT(*) FROM sakila.film_actor;
+----------+
| count(*) |
+----------+
|     5462 |
+----------+

mysql> SHOW STATUS LIKE 'Last_query_cost';
+-----------------+-------------+
| Variable_name   | Value       |
+-----------------+-------------+
```

```
| Last_query_cost | 1040.599000 |
+-----------------+-------------+
```

This result means that the optimizer estimated it would need to do about 1,040 random data page reads to execute the query. It bases the estimate on statistics: the number of pages per table or index, the *cardinality* (number of distinct values) of the indexes, the length of the rows and keys, and the key distribution. The optimizer does not include the effects of any type of caching in its estimates; it assumes every read will result in a disk I/O operation.

The optimizer might not always choose the best plan, for many reasons:

- The statistics could be inaccurate. The server relies on storage engines to provide statistics, and they can range from exactly correct to wildly inaccurate. For example, the InnoDB storage engine doesn't maintain accurate statistics about the number of rows in a table because of its MVCC architecture.

- The cost metric is not exactly equivalent to the true cost of running the query, so even when the statistics are accurate, the query might be more or less expensive than MySQL's approximation. A plan that reads more pages might actually be cheaper in some cases, such as when the reads are sequential so the disk I/O is faster or when the pages are already cached in memory. MySQL also doesn't understand which pages are in memory and which pages are on disk, so it doesn't really know how much I/O the query will cause.

- MySQL's idea of "optimal" might not match yours. You probably want the fastest execution time, but MySQL doesn't really try to make queries fast; it tries to minimize their cost, and as we've seen, determining cost is not an exact science.

- MySQL doesn't consider other queries that are running concurrently, which can affect how quickly the query runs.

- MySQL doesn't always do cost-based optimization. Sometimes it just follows the rules, such as "if there's a full-text MATCH( ) clause, use a FULLTEXT index if one exists." It will do this even when it would be faster to use a different index and a non-FULLTEXT query with a WHERE clause.

- The optimizer doesn't take into account the cost of operations not under its control, such as executing stored functions or user-defined functions.

- As we'll see later, the optimizer can't always estimate every possible execution plan, so it might miss an optimal plan.

MySQL's query optimizer is a highly complex piece of software, and it uses many optimizations to transform the query into an execution plan. There are two basic types of optimizations, which we call *static* and *dynamic*. *Static optimizations* can be performed simply by inspecting the parse tree. For example, the optimizer can transform the WHERE clause into an equivalent form by applying algebraic rules. Static optimizations are independent of values, such as the value of a constant in a WHERE clause. They can be performed once and will always be valid, even when the query is reexecuted with different values. You can think of these as "compile-time optimizations."

In contrast, *dynamic optimizations* are based on context and can depend on many factors, such as which value is in a WHERE clause or how many rows are in an index. They must be reevaluated each time the query is executed. You can think of these as "runtime optimizations."

The difference is important when executing prepared statements or stored procedures. MySQL can do static optimizations once, but it must reevaluate dynamic optimizations every time it executes a query. MySQL sometimes even reoptimizes the query as it executes it.[6]

Here are some types of optimizations MySQL knows how to do:

*Reordering joins*
> Tables don't always have to be joined in the order you specify in the query. Determining the best join order is an important optimization; we explain it in depth later in this chapter.

*Converting OUTER JOINs to INNER JOIN*
> An OUTER JOIN doesn't necessarily have to be executed as an OUTER JOIN. Some factors, such as the WHERE clause and table schema, can actually cause an OUTER JOIN to be equivalent to an INNER JOIN. MySQL can recognize this and rewrite the join, which makes it eligible for reordering.

*Applying algebraic equivalence rules*
> MySQL applies algebraic transformations to simplify and canonicalize expressions. It can also fold and reduce constants, eliminating impossible constraints and constant conditions. For example, the term (5=5 AND a>5) will reduce to just a>5. Similarly, (a<b AND b=c) AND a=5 becomes b>5 AND b=c AND a=5. These rules are very useful for writing conditional queries, which we discuss later in this chapter.

*COUNT(), MIN(), and MAX() optimizations*
> Indexes and column nullability can often help MySQL optimize away these expressions. For example, to find the minimum value of a column that's leftmost in a B-tree index, MySQL can just request the first row in the index. It can even do this in the query optimization stage and treat the value as a constant for the

---

6 For example, the range check query plan reevaluates indexes for each row in a JOIN. You can see this query plan by looking for "range checked for each record" in the Extra column in EXPLAIN. This query plan also increments the Select_full_range_join server variable.

rest of the query. Similarly, to find the maximum value in a B-tree index, the server reads the last row. If the server uses this optimization, you'll see "Select tables optimized away" in the EXPLAIN plan. This literally means the optimizer has removed the table from the query plan and replaced it with a constant.

*Evaluating and reducing constant expressions*

When MySQL detects that an expression can be reduced to a constant, it will do so during optimization. For example, a user-defined variable can be converted to a constant if it's not changed in the query. Arithmetic expressions are another example.

Perhaps surprisingly, even something you might consider to be a query can be reduced to a constant during the optimization phase. One example is a MIN() on an index. This can even be extended to a constant lookup on a primary key or unique index. If a WHERE clause applies a constant condition to such an index, the optimizer knows MySQL can look up the value at the beginning of the query. It will then treat the value as a constant in the rest of the query. Here's an example:

```
mysql> EXPLAIN SELECT film.film_id, film_actor.actor_id
    -> FROM sakila.film
    -> INNER JOIN sakila.film_actor USING(film_id)
    -> WHERE film.film_id = 1\G
*************************** 1. row ***************************
          id: 1
 select_type: SIMPLE
       table: film
  partitions: NULL
        type: const
possible_keys: PRIMARY
         key: PRIMARY
     key_len: 2
         ref: const
        rows: 1
    filtered: 100.00
       Extra: Using index
*************************** 2. row ***************************
          id: 1
 select_type: SIMPLE
       table: film_actor
  partitions: NULL
        type: index
possible_keys: NULL
         key: PRIMARY
     key_len: 4
         ref: NULL
        rows: 5462
    filtered: 10.00
       Extra: Using where; Using index
```

MySQL executes this query in two steps, which correspond to the two rows in the output. The first step is to find the desired row in the film table. MySQL's optimizer knows there is only one row because there's a primary key on the film_id column and it has already consulted the index during the query optimization stage to see how many rows it will find. Because the query optimizer has a known quantity (the value in the WHERE clause) to use in the lookup, this table's ref type is const.

In the second step, MySQL treats the film_id column from the row found in the first step as a known quantity. It can do this because the optimizer knows that by the time the query reaches the second step, it will know all the values from the first step. Notice that the film_actor table's ref type is const, just as the film table's was.

Another way you'll see constant conditions applied is by propagating a value's constantness from one place to another if there is a WHERE, USING, or ON clause that restricts the values to being equal. In this example, the optimizer knows that the USING clause forces film_id to have the same value everywhere in the query; it must be equal to the constant value given in the WHERE clause.

*Covering indexes*

MySQL can sometimes use an index to avoid reading row data when the index contains all the columns the query needs. We discussed covering indexes at length in the previous chapter.

*Subquery optimization*

MySQL can convert some types of subqueries into more efficient alternative forms, reducing them to index lookups instead of separate queries.

*Early termination*

MySQL can stop processing a query (or a step in a query) as soon as it fulfills the query or step. The obvious case is a LIMIT clause, but there are several other kinds of early termination. For instance, if MySQL detects an impossible condition, it can abort the entire query. You can see this in the following example:

```
mysql> EXPLAIN SELECT film.film_id FROM sakila.film WHERE film_id = -1;
*************************** 1. row ***************************
id: 1
select_type: SIMPLE
table: NULL
partitions: NULL
type: NULL
possible_keys: NULL
key: NULL
key_len: NULL
ref: NULL
rows: NULL
```

```
    filtered: NULL
    Extra: Impossible WHERE
```

This query stopped during the optimization step, but MySQL can also terminate execution early in some other cases. The server can use this optimization when the query execution engine recognizes the need to retrieve distinct values or to stop when a value doesn't exist. For example, the following query finds all movies without any actors:[7]

```
SELECT film.film_id
FROM sakila.film
LEFT OUTER JOIN sakila.film_actor USING(film_id)
WHERE film_actor.film_id IS NULL;
```

This query works by eliminating any films that have actors. Each film might have many actors, but as soon as it finds one actor, it stops processing the current film and moves to the next one because it knows the WHERE clause prohibits outputting that film. A similar "Distinct/not-exists" optimization can apply to certain kinds of DISTINCT, NOT EXISTS(), and LEFT JOIN queries.

*Equality propagation*

MySQL recognizes when a query holds two columns as equal—for example, in a JOIN condition—and propagates WHERE clauses across equivalent columns. For instance, in the following query:

```
SELECT film.film_id
FROM sakila.film
INNER JOIN sakila.film_actor USING(film_id)
WHERE film.film_id > 500;
```

MySQL knows that the WHERE clause applies not only to the film table but to the film_actor table as well because the USING clause forces the two columns to match.

If you're used to another database server that can't do this, you might have been advised to "help the optimizer" by manually specifying the WHERE clause for both tables, like this:

```
... WHERE film.film_id > 500 AND film_actor.film_id > 500
```

This is unnecessary in MySQL. It just makes your queries harder to maintain.

---

7 We agree, a movie without actors is strange, but the Sakila Sample Database lists no actors for *Slacker Liaisons*, which it describes as "A Fast-Paced Tale of a Shark and a Student Who Must Meet a Crocodile in Ancient China."

IN() *list comparisons*

In many database servers, IN() is just a synonym for multiple OR clauses because the two are logically equivalent. Not so in MySQL, which sorts the values in the IN() list and uses a fast binary search to see whether a value is in the list. This is $O(\log n)$ in the size of the list, whereas an equivalent series of OR clauses is $O(n)$ in the size of the list (i.e., much slower for large lists).

The preceding list is woefully incomplete because MySQL performs more optimizations than we could fit into this entire chapter, but it should give you an idea of the optimizer's complexity and intelligence. If there's one thing you should take away from this discussion, it's *don't preemptively try to outsmart the optimizer*. You might end up just defeating it or making your queries more complicated and harder to maintain for zero benefit. In general, you should let the optimizer do its work.

Of course, as smart as the optimizer is, there are times when it doesn't give the best result. Sometimes you might know something about the data that the optimizer doesn't, such as a fact that's guaranteed to be true because of application logic. Also, sometimes the optimizer doesn't have the necessary functionality, such as hash indexes; at other times, as mentioned earlier, its cost estimates might prefer a query plan that turns out to be more expensive than an alternative.

If you know the optimizer isn't giving a good result and you know why, you can help it. Some of the options are to add a hint to the query,[8] rewrite the query, redesign your schema, or add indexes.

### Table and index statistics

Recall the various layers in the MySQL server architecture, which we illustrated in Figure 1-1. The server layer, which contains the query optimizer, doesn't store statistics on data and indexes. That's a job for the storage engines because each storage engine might keep different kinds of statistics (or keep them in a different way).

Because the server doesn't store statistics, the MySQL query optimizer has to ask the engines for statistics on the tables in a query. The engines provide the optimizer with statistics such as the number of pages per table or index, the cardinality of tables and indexes, the length of rows and keys, and key distribution information. The optimizer can use this information to help it decide on the best execution plan. We see how these statistics influence the optimizer's choices in later sections.

---

8  See both "Index Hints" and "Optimizer Hints" in the MySQL manual for version-specific details on what hints are available and how to use them.

### MySQL's join execution strategy

MySQL uses the term *join* more broadly than you might be used to. In sum, it considers every query a join—not just every query that matches rows from two tables, but every query, period (including subqueries and even a `SELECT` against a single table). Consequently, it's very important to understand how MySQL executes joins.

Consider the example of a `UNION` query. MySQL executes a `UNION` as a series of single queries whose results are spooled into a temporary table, then read out again. Each of the individual queries is a join, in MySQL terminology, and so is the act of reading from the resulting temporary table.

MySQL's join execution strategy used to be simple: it treated every join as a nested-loop join. This means MySQL runs a loop to find a row from a table, then runs a nested loop to find a matching row in the next table. It continues until it has found a matching row in each table in the join. It then builds and returns a row from the columns named in the `SELECT` list. It tries to build the next row by looking for more matching rows in the last table. If it doesn't find any, it backtracks one table and looks for more rows there. It keeps backtracking until it finds another row in some table, at which point it looks for a matching row in the next table, and so on.[9]

As of version 8.0.20, block nested-loop joins are no longer used; instead, a hash join (*https://oreil.ly/WdIQm*) has replaced it. This makes the join process perform as fast as, or faster, than before, especially if one of the sets of data can live in memory.

### The execution plan

MySQL doesn't generate bytecode to execute a query, as many other database products do. Instead, the query execution plan is actually a tree[10] of instructions that the query execution engine follows to produce the query results. The final plan contains enough information to reconstruct the original query. If you execute `EXPLAIN EXTENDED` on a query, followed by `SHOW WARNINGS`, you'll see the reconstructed query.[11]

Any multitable query can conceptually be represented as a tree. For example, it might be possible to execute a four-table join as shown in Figure 8-2.

---

9 As we show later, MySQL's query execution isn't quite this simple; there are many optimizations that complicate it.

10 You can see this by using `EXPLAIN FORMAT=TREE` ... before your statement.

11 The server generates the output from the execution plan. It thus has the same semantics as the original query but not necessarily the same text.

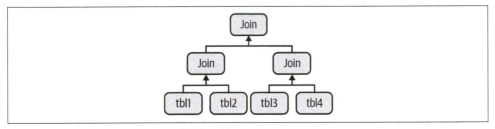

Figure 8-2. One way to join multiple tables

This is what computer scientists call a *balanced tree*. This is not how MySQL executes the query, though. As we described in the previous section, MySQL always begins with one table and finds matching rows in the next table. Thus, MySQL's query execution plans always take the form of a *left-deep tree*, as in Figure 8-3.

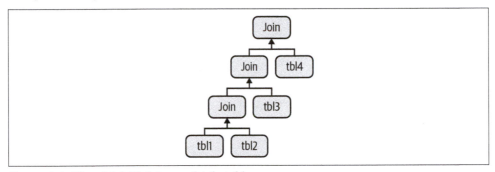

Figure 8-3. How MySQL joins multiple tables

### The join optimizer

The most important part of the MySQL query optimizer is the *join optimizer*, which decides the best order of execution for multitable queries. It is often possible to join the tables in several different orders and get the same results. The join optimizer estimates the cost for various plans and tries to choose the least expensive one that gives the same result.

Here's a query whose tables can be joined in different orders without changing the results:

```
SELECT film.film_id, film.title, film.release_year, actor.actor_id,
actor.first_name, actor.last_name
FROM sakila.film
INNER JOIN sakila.film_actor USING(film_id)
INNER JOIN sakila.actor USING(actor_id);
```

You can probably think of a few different query plans. For example, MySQL could begin with the film table, use the index on film_id in the film_actor table to find actor_id values, and then look up rows in the actor table's primary key. Oracle users might phrase this as "the film table is the driver table into the film_actor table, which is the driver for the actor table." This should be efficient, right? Now let's use EXPLAIN to see how MySQL wants to execute the query:

```
*************************** 1. row ***************************
          id: 1
 select_type: SIMPLE
       table: actor
  partitions: NULL
        type: ALL
possible_keys: PRIMARY
         key: NULL
     key_len: NULL
         ref: NULL
        rows: 200
    filtered: 100.00
       Extra: NULL
*************************** 2. row ***************************
          id: 1
 select_type: SIMPLE
       table: film_actor
  partitions: NULL
        type: ref
possible_keys: PRIMARY,idx_fk_film_id
         key: PRIMARY
     key_len: 2
         ref: sakila.actor.actor_id
        rows: 27
    filtered: 100.00
       Extra: Using index
*************************** 3. row ***************************
          id: 1
 select_type: SIMPLE
       table: film
  partitions: NULL
        type: eq_ref
possible_keys: PRIMARY
         key: PRIMARY
     key_len: 2
         ref: sakila.film_actor.film_id
        rows: 1
    filtered: 100.00
       Extra: NULL
```

This is quite a different plan from the one suggested in the previous paragraph. MySQL wants to start with the actor table (we know this because it's listed first in the EXPLAIN output) and go in the reverse order. Is this really more efficient? Let's find out. The STRAIGHT_JOIN keyword forces the join to proceed in the order specified in the query. Here's the EXPLAIN output for the revised query:

```
mysql> EXPLAIN SELECT STRAIGHT_JOIN film.film_id...\G
*************************** 1. row ***************************
  id: 1
  select_type: SIMPLE
  table: film
  partitions: NULL
  type: ALL
  possible_keys: PRIMARY
  key: NULL
  key_len: NULL
  ref: NULL
  rows: 1000
  filtered: 100.00
  Extra: NULL
*************************** 2. row ***************************
  id: 1
  select_type: SIMPLE
  table: film_actor
  partitions: NULL
  type: ref
  possible_keys: PRIMARY,idx_fk_film_id
  key: idx_fk_film_id
  key_len: 2
  ref: sakila.film.film_id
  rows: 5
  filtered: 100.00
  Extra: Using index
*************************** 3. row ***************************
  id: 1
  select_type: SIMPLE
  table: actor
  partitions: NULL
  type: eq_ref
  possible_keys: PRIMARY
  key: PRIMARY
  key_len: 2
  ref: sakila.film_actor.actor_id
  rows: 1
  filtered: 100.00
  Extra: NULL
```

This shows why MySQL wants to reverse the join order: doing so will enable it to examine fewer rows in the first table.[12] In both cases, it will be able to perform fast indexed lookups in the second and third tables. The difference is how many of these indexed lookups it will have to do. Placing film first will require about one thousand probes (see the rows field) into film_actor and actor, one for each row in the first

---

12 Strictly speaking, MySQL doesn't try to reduce the number of rows it reads. Instead, it tries to optimize for fewer page reads. But a row count can often give you a rough idea of the query cost.

table. If the server scans the `actor` table first, it will have to do only two hundred index lookups into later tables. In other words, the reversed join order will require less backtracking and rereading.

This is a simple example of how MySQL's join optimizer can reorder queries to make them less expensive to execute. Reordering joins is usually a very effective optimization. There are times when it won't result in an optimal plan, though, and for those times you can use `STRAIGHT_JOIN` and write the query in the order you think is best—but such times are rare. In most cases, the join optimizer will outperform a human.

The join optimizer tries to produce a query execution plan tree with the lowest achievable cost. When possible, it examines all potential combinations of subtrees, beginning with all one-table plans.

Unfortunately, a join over *n* tables will have *n*-factorial combinations of join orders to examine. This is called the *search space* of all possible query plans, and it grows very quickly: a 10-table join can be executed up to 3,628,800 different ways! When the search space grows too large, it can take far too long to optimize the query, so the server stops doing a full analysis. Instead, it resorts to shortcuts such as "greedy" searches when the number of tables exceeds the limit specified by the `opti mizer_search_depth` variable (which you can change if necessary).

MySQL has many heuristics, accumulated through years of research and experimentation, that it uses to speed up the optimization stage. This can be beneficial, but it can also mean that MySQL might (on rare occasions) miss an optimal plan and choose a less optimal one because it's trying not to examine every possible query plan.

Sometimes queries can't be reordered, and the join optimizer can use this fact to reduce the search space by eliminating choices. A `LEFT JOIN` is a good example, as are correlated subqueries (more about subqueries later). This is because the results for one table depend on data retrieved from another table. These dependencies help the join optimizer reduce the search space by eliminating choices.

### Sort optimizations

Sorting results can be a costly operation, so you can often improve performance by avoiding sorts or by performing them on fewer rows.

When MySQL can't use an index to produce a sorted result, it must sort the rows itself. It can do this in memory or on disk, but it always calls this process a *filesort*, even if it doesn't actually use a file.

If the values to be sorted will fit into the sort buffer, MySQL can perform the sort entirely in memory with a *quicksort*. If MySQL can't do the sort in memory, it performs it on disk by sorting the values in chunks. It uses a quicksort to sort each chunk and then merges the sorted chunks into the results.

There are two filesort algorithms:

*Two passes (old)*

Reads row pointers and ORDER BY columns, sorts them, and then scans the sorted list and rereads the rows for output.

The two-pass algorithm can be quite expensive because it reads the rows from the table twice and the second read causes a lot of random I/O.

*Single pass (new)*

Reads all the columns needed for the query, sorts them by the ORDER BY columns, and then scans the sorted list and outputs the specified columns.

It can be much more efficient, especially on large I/O-bound data sets, because it avoids reading the rows from the table twice and trades random I/O for more sequential I/O. However, it has the potential to use a lot more space because it holds all the desired columns from each row, not just the columns needed to sort the rows. This means fewer tuples will fit into the sort buffer, and the filesort will have to perform more sort merge passes.

MySQL might use much more temporary storage space for a filesort than you'd expect because it allocates a fixed-size record for each tuple it will sort. These records are large enough to hold the largest possible tuple, including the full length of each VARCHAR column. Also, if you're using utf8mb4, MySQL allocates 4 bytes for each character. As a result, we've seen cases where poorly optimized schemas caused the temporary space used for sorting to be many times larger than the entire table's size on disk.

When sorting a join, MySQL might perform the filesort at two stages during the query execution. If the ORDER BY clause refers only to columns from the first table in the join order, MySQL can filesort this table and then proceed with the join. If this happens, EXPLAIN shows "Using filesort" in the Extra column. In all other circumstances—such as a sort against a table that's not first in the join order or when the ORDER BY clause contains columns from more than one table—MySQL must store the query's results into a temporary table and then filesort the temporary table after the join finishes. In this case, EXPLAIN shows "Using temporary; Using filesort" in the Extra column. If there's a LIMIT, it is applied after the filesort, so the temporary table and the filesort can be very large.

## The Query Execution Engine

The parsing and optimizing stage outputs a query execution plan, which MySQL's query execution engine uses to process the query. The plan is a data structure; it is not executable bytecode, which is how many other databases execute queries.

In contrast to the optimization stage, the execution stage is usually not all that complex: MySQL simply follows the instructions given in the query execution plan. Many of the operations in the plan invoke methods implemented by the storage engine interface, also known as the *handler API*. Each table in the query is represented by an instance of a handler. If a table appears three times in the query, for example, the server creates three handler instances. Although we glossed over this before, MySQL actually creates the handler instances early in the optimization stage. The optimizer uses them to get information about the tables, such as their column names and index statistics.

The storage engine interface has lots of functionality, but it needs only a dozen or so "building-block" operations to execute most queries. For example, there's an operation to read the first row in an index and one to read the next row in an index. This is enough for a query that does an index scan. This simplistic execution method makes MySQL's storage engine architecture possible, but it also imposes some of the optimizer limitations we've discussed.

 Not everything is a handler operation. For example, the server manages table locks. The handler might implement its own lower-level locking, as InnoDB does with row-level locks, but this does not replace the server's own locking implementation. As explained in Chapter 1, anything that all storage engines share is implemented in the server, such as date and time functions, views, and triggers.

To execute the query, the server just repeats the instructions until there are no more rows to examine.

## Returning Results to the Client

The final step in executing a query is to reply to the client. Even queries that don't return a result set still reply to the client connection with information about the query, such as how many rows it affected.

The server generates and sends results incrementally. As soon as MySQL processes the last table and generates one row successfully, it can and should send that row to the client. This has two benefits: it lets the server avoid holding the row in memory, and it means the client starts getting the results as soon as possible.[13] Each row in the result set is sent in a separate packet in the MySQL client/server protocol, although protocol packets can be buffered and sent together at the TCP protocol layer.

---

13 You can influence this behavior if needed—for example, with the SQL_BUFFER_RESULT hint. See "Optimizer Hints" in the official MySQL manual for more information.

# Limitations of the MySQL Query Optimizer

MySQL's approach to query execution isn't ideal for optimizing every kind of query. Fortunately, there are only a limited number of cases where the MySQL query optimizer does a poor job, and it's usually possible to rewrite such queries more efficiently.

## UNION Limitations

MySQL sometimes can't "push down" conditions from the outside of a UNION to the inside, where they could be used to limit results or enable additional optimizations.

If you think any of the individual queries inside a UNION would benefit from a LIMIT or if you know they'll be subject to an ORDER BY clause once combined with other queries, you need to put those clauses inside each part of the UNION. For example, if you UNION together two tables and LIMIT the result to the first 20 rows, MySQL will store both tables into a temporary table and then retrieve just 20 rows from it:

```
(SELECT first_name, last_name
 FROM sakila.actor
 ORDER BY last_name)
UNION ALL
(SELECT first_name, last_name
 FROM sakila.customer
 ORDER BY last_name)
LIMIT 20;
```

This query will store 200 rows from the actor table and 599 from the customer table into a temporary table and then fetch the first 20 rows from that temporary table. You can avoid this by adding LIMIT 20 redundantly to each query inside the UNION:

```
(SELECT first_name, last_name
 FROM sakila.actor
 ORDER BY last_name
 LIMIT 20)
UNION ALL
(SELECT first_name, last_name
 FROM sakila.customer
 ORDER BY last_name
 LIMIT 20)
LIMIT 20;
```

Now the temporary table will contain only 40 rows. In addition to the performance improvement, you'll probably need to correct the query: the order in which the rows are retrieved from the temporary table is undefined, so there should be an overall ORDER BY just before the final LIMIT.

## Equality Propagation

Equality propagation can have unexpected costs sometimes. For example, consider a huge IN() list on a column the optimizer knows will be equal to some columns on other tables, due to a WHERE, ON, or USING clause that sets the columns equal to one another.

The optimizer will "share" the list by copying it to the corresponding columns in all related tables. This is normally helpful because it gives the query optimizer and execution engine more options for where to actually execute the IN() check. But when the list is very large, it can result in slower optimization and execution. There's no built-in workaround for this problem at the time of this writing—you'll have to change the source code if it's a problem for you. (It's not a problem for most people.)

## Parallel Execution

MySQL can't execute a single query in parallel on many CPUs. This is a feature offered by some other database servers, but not MySQL. We mention it so that you won't spend a lot of time trying to figure out how to get parallel query execution on MySQL!

## SELECT and UPDATE on the Same Table

MySQL doesn't let you SELECT from a table while simultaneously running an UPDATE on it. This isn't really an optimizer limitation, but knowing how MySQL executes queries can help you work around it. Here's an example of a query that's disallowed, even though it is standard SQL. The query updates each row with the number of similar rows in the table:

```
mysql> UPDATE tbl AS outer_tbl
    -> SET c = (
    -> SELECT count(*) FROM tbl AS inner_tbl
    -> WHERE inner_tbl.type = outer_tbl.type
    -> );
ERROR 1093 (HY000): You can't specify target table 'outer_tbl'
for update in FROM clause
```

To work around this limitation, you can use a derived table because MySQL materializes it as a temporary table. This effectively executes two queries: one SELECT inside the subquery and one multitable UPDATE with the joined results of the table and the subquery. The subquery opens and closes the table before the outer UPDATE opens the table, so the query will now succeed:

```
mysql> UPDATE tbl
    -> INNER JOIN(
    -> SELECT type, count(*) AS c
    -> FROM tbl
```

```
-> GROUP BY type
-> ) AS der USING(type)
-> SET tbl.c = der.c;
```

# Optimizing Specific Types of Queries

In this section, we give advice on how to optimize certain kinds of queries. We've covered most of these topics in detail elsewhere in the book, but we wanted to make a list of common optimization problems that you can refer to easily.

Most of the advice in this section is version dependent, and it might not hold for future versions of MySQL. There's no reason why the server won't be able to do some or all of these optimizations itself someday.

## Optimizing COUNT() Queries

The COUNT() aggregate function, and how to optimize queries that use it, is probably one of the top 10 most-misunderstood topics in MySQL. You can do a web search and find more misinformation on this topic than we care to think about.

Before we get into optimization, it's important that you understand what COUNT() really does.

### What COUNT() does

COUNT() is a special function that works in two very different ways: it counts *values* and *rows*. A value is a non-NULL expression (NULL is the absence of a value). If you specify a column name or other expression inside the parentheses, COUNT() counts how many times that expression has a value. This is confusing for many people, in part because values and NULL are confusing. If you need to learn how this works in SQL, we suggest a good book on SQL fundamentals. (The internet is not necessarily a good source of accurate information on this topic.)

The other form of COUNT() simply counts the number of rows in the result. This is what MySQL does when it knows the expression inside the parentheses can never be NULL. The most obvious example is COUNT(*), which is a special form of COUNT() that does not expand the * wildcard into the full list of columns in the table, as you might expect; instead, it ignores columns altogether and counts rows.

One of the most common mistakes we see is specifying column names inside the parentheses when you want to count rows. When you want to know the number of rows in the result, you should always use COUNT(*). This communicates your intention clearly and avoids poor performance.

### Simple optimizations

A commonly asked question is how to retrieve counts for several different values in the same column with just one query, to reduce the number of queries required. For example, say you want to create a single query that counts how many items have each of several colors. You can't use an OR (e.g., SELECT COUNT(color = 'blue' OR color = 'red') FROM items;) because that won't separate the different counts for the different colors. And you can't put the colors in the WHERE clause (e.g., SELECT COUNT(*) FROM items WHERE color = 'blue' AND color = 'red';) because the colors are mutually exclusive. Here is a query that solves this problem:[14]

```
SELECT SUM(IF(color = 'blue', 1, 0)) AS blue,SUM(IF(color = 'red', 1, 0))
AS red FROM items;
```

And here is another that's equivalent, but instead of using SUM(), it uses COUNT() and ensures that the expressions won't have values when the criteria are false:

```
SELECT COUNT(color = 'blue' OR NULL) AS blue, COUNT(color = 'red' OR NULL)
AS red FROM items;
```

### Using an approximation

Sometimes you don't need an accurate count, so you can just use an approximation. The optimizer's estimated rows in EXPLAIN often serve well for this. Just execute an EXPLAIN query instead of the real query.

At other times, an exact count is much less efficient than an approximation. One customer asked for help counting the number of active users on his website. The user count was cached and displayed for 30 minutes, after which it was regenerated and cached again. This was inaccurate by nature, so an approximation was acceptable. The query included several WHERE conditions to ensure that it didn't count inactive users or the "default" user, which was a special user ID in the application. Removing these conditions changed the count only slightly but made the query much more efficient. A further optimization was to eliminate an unnecessary DISTINCT to remove a filesort. The rewritten query was much faster and returned almost exactly the same results.

### More complex optimizations

In general, COUNT() queries are hard to optimize because they usually need to count a lot of rows (i.e., access a lot of data). Your only other option for optimizing within MySQL itself is to use a covering index. If that doesn't help enough, you need to make changes to your application architecture. Consider an external caching system such

---

14 You can also write the SUM() expressions as SUM(color = 'blue'), SUM(color ='red').

as *memcached*. You'll probably find yourself faced with the familiar dilemma, "fast, accurate, and simple: pick any two."

## Optimizing JOIN Queries

This topic is actually spread throughout most of the book, but we'll mention a few highlights:

- Make sure there are indexes on the columns in the ON or USING clauses. Consider the join order when adding indexes. If you're joining tables A and B on column c and the query optimizer decides to join the tables in the order B, A, you don't need to index the column on table B. Unused indexes are extra overhead. In general, you need to add indexes only on the second table in the join order, unless they're needed for some other reason.
- Try to ensure that any GROUP BY or ORDER BY expression refers only to columns from a single table, so MySQL can try to use an index for that operation.
- Be careful when upgrading MySQL because the join syntax, operator precedence, and other behaviors have changed at various times. What used to be a normal join can sometimes become a cross product, a different kind of join that returns different results, or even invalid syntax.

## Optimizing GROUP BY with ROLLUP

A variation on grouped queries is to ask MySQL to do super aggregation within the results. You can do this with a WITH ROLLUP clause, but it might not be as well optimized as you need. Check the execution method with EXPLAIN, paying attention to whether the grouping is done via filesort or temporary table; try removing the WITH ROLLUP and see if you get the same group method. You might be able to force the grouping method with the hints we mentioned earlier in this section.

Sometimes it's more efficient to do super aggregation in your application, even if it means fetching many more rows from the server. You can also nest a subquery in the FROM clause or use a temporary table to hold intermediate results and then query the temporary table with a UNION.

The best approach might be to move the WITH ROLLUP functionality into your application code.

## Optimizing LIMIT and OFFSET

Queries with LIMITs and OFFSETs are common in systems that do pagination, nearly always in conjunction with an ORDER BY clause. It's helpful to have an index that supports the ordering; otherwise, the server has to do a lot of filesorts.

A frequent problem is having a high value for the offset. If your query looks like LIMIT 10000, 20, it is generating 10,020 rows and throwing away the first 10,000 of them, which is very expensive. Assuming all pages are accessed with equal frequency, such queries scan half the table on average. To optimize them, you can either limit how many pages are permitted in a pagination view or try to make the high offsets more efficient.

One simple technique to improve efficiency is to do the offset on a covering index, rather than the full rows. You can then join the result to the full row and retrieve the additional columns you need. This can be much more efficient. Consider the following query:

```
SELECT film_id, description FROM sakila.film ORDER BY title LIMIT 50, 5;
```

If the table is very large, this query is better written as follows:

```
SELECT film.film_id, film.description
FROM sakila.film
INNER JOIN (
SELECT film_id FROM sakila.film
ORDER BY title LIMIT 50, 5
) AS lim USING(film_id);
```

This "deferred join" works because it lets the server examine as little data as possible in an index without accessing rows and then, once the desired rows are found, join them against the full table to retrieve the other columns from the row. A similar technique applies to joins with LIMIT clauses.

Sometimes you can also convert the limit to a positional query, which the server can execute as an index range scan. For example, if you precalculate and index a position column, you can rewrite the query as follows:

```
SELECT film_id, description FROM sakila.film
WHERE position BETWEEN 50 AND 54 ORDER BY position;
```

Ranked data poses a similar problem but usually mixes GROUP BY into the fray. You'll almost certainly need to precompute and store ranks.

The problem with LIMIT and OFFSET is really the OFFSET, which represents rows the server is generating and throwing away. If you use a sort of cursor to remember the position of the last row you fetched, you can generate the next set of rows by starting from that position instead of using an OFFSET. For example, if you want to paginate through rental records starting from the newest rentals and working backward, you can rely on the fact that their primary keys are always increasing. You can fetch the first set of results like this:

```
SELECT * FROM sakila.rental
ORDER BY rental_id DESC LIMIT 20;
```

This query returns rentals 16049 through 16030. The next query can continue from that point:

```
SELECT * FROM sakila.rental
WHERE rental_id < 16030
ORDER BY rental_id DESC LIMIT 20;
```

The nice thing about this technique is that it's very efficient no matter how far you paginate into the table.

Other alternatives include using precomputed summaries or joining against redundant tables that contain only the primary key and the columns you need for the ORDER BY.

## Optimizing SQL_CALC_FOUND_ROWS

Another common technique for paginated displays is to add the SQL_ CALC_ FOUND_ROWS hint to a query with a LIMIT, so you'll know how many rows would have been returned without the LIMIT. It might seem that there's some kind of "magic" happening here, whereby the server predicts how many rows it would have found. But unfortunately, the server doesn't really do that; it can't count rows it doesn't actually find. This option just tells the server to generate and throw away the rest of the result set instead of stopping when it reaches the desired number of rows. That's very expensive.

A better design is to convert the pager to a "next" link. Assuming there are 20 results per page, the query should then use a LIMIT of 21 rows and display only 20. If the 21st row exists in the results, there's a next page, and you can render the "next" link.

Another possibility is to fetch and cache many more rows than you need—say, 1,000 —and then retrieve them from the cache for successive pages. This strategy lets your application know how large the full result set is. If it's fewer than 1,000 rows, the application knows how many page links to render; if it's more, the application can just display "more than 1,000 results found." Both strategies are much more efficient than repeatedly generating an entire result and discarding most of it.

Sometimes you can also just estimate the full size of the result set by running an EXPLAIN query and looking at the rows column in the result (hey, even Google doesn't show exact result counts!). If you can't use these tactics, using a separate COUNT(*) query to find the number of rows can be much faster than SQL_CALC_FOUND_ROWS, if it can use a covering index.

## Optimizing UNION

MySQL always executes UNION queries by creating a temporary table and filling it with the UNION results. MySQL can't apply as many optimizations to UNION queries as you might be used to. You might have to help the optimizer by manually "pushing down" WHERE, LIMIT, ORDER BY, and other conditions (i.e., copying them, as appropriate, from the outer query into each SELECT in the UNION).

It's important to always use UNION ALL, unless you need the server to eliminate duplicate rows. If you omit the ALL keyword, MySQL adds the distinct option to the temporary table, which uses the full row to determine uniqueness. This is quite expensive. Be aware that the ALL keyword doesn't eliminate the temporary table, though. MySQL always places results into a temporary table and then reads them out again, even when it's not really necessary (for example, when the results could be returned directly to the client).

## Summary

Query optimization is the final piece in the interlocking puzzle of schema, index, and query design to create high-performance applications. To write good queries, you need to understand schemas and indexing, and vice versa.

Ultimately, it is still about response time and understanding how queries execute so that you can reason about where the time is consumed. With the addition of a few things such as the parsing and optimization process, this is just the next step in understanding how MySQL accesses tables and indexes, which we discussed in the previous chapter. The extra dimension that emerges when you start studying the interplay between queries and indexes is how MySQL accesses one table or index based on the data that it finds in another one.

Optimization always requires a three-pronged approach: stop doing things, do them fewer times, and do them more quickly.

# Replication

MySQL's built-in replication is the foundation for building large, high-performance applications on top of MySQL, using the so-called "scale-out" architecture. Replication lets you configure one or more servers as replicas of another server, keeping their data synchronized with the source copy. This is not just useful for high-performance applications—it is also the cornerstone of many strategies for high availability, scalability, disaster recovery, backups, analysis, data warehousing, and numerous other tasks.

In this chapter, our focus is less on what each feature is and more on when to use it. The official MySQL documentation (*https://dev.mysql.com/doc*) is exceptionally detailed at explaining what features like semisynchronous replication, multisource replication, and so on are, and you should refer to this documentation when setting up these features.

---

### A Note on Terminology

Long-time users of MySQL will be familiar with the terminology *master* and *slave* as it relates to replication. These terms have since been replaced with *source* and *replica*. This book attempts to maintain the new wording to align with this change. Some older versions of MySQL still contain those replaced terms, so refer to the MySQL manual as needed.

---

## Replication Overview

The basic problem replication solves is keeping data synchronized among database instances within the same topology. It does this by writing events that modify data or data structure to a log on a source server. Replica servers can then read the events from the log on the source and replay them. This creates an asynchronous process, one where the replica's copy of data is not guaranteed to be up-to-date at any given instant. Replica lag—the delay between real time and what is represented on the replica—has no upper bound. Large queries can make the replica fall seconds, minutes, or even hours behind the source.

MySQL's replication is mostly backward compatible—that is, a newer server can usually be a replica of an older server without trouble. However, older versions of the server are often unable to act as replicas of newer versions: they might not understand new features or SQL syntax the newer server uses, and there might be differences in the file formats replication uses. For example, you can't replicate from a MySQL 5.6 source to a MySQL 5.5 replica. It's a good idea to test your replication setup before upgrading from one major or minor version to another, such as from 5.6 to 5.7 or 5.7 to 8.0. Upgrades within a minor version, such as from 5.7.34 to 5.7.35, are expected to be compatible; read the release notes to find out exactly what changed from version to version.

Replication is relatively good for scaling reads, which you can direct to a replica, but it's not a good way to scale writes unless you design it right. Attaching many replicas to a source simply causes the writes to be done many times, once on each replica. The entire system is limited to the number of writes the weakest part can perform.

Here are some of the more common uses for replication:

*Data distribution*

MySQL's replication is usually not very bandwidth intensive, although, as you'll see later, the row-based replication can use much more bandwidth than the more traditional statement-based replication. You can also stop and start replication at will. Thus, it's useful for maintaining a copy of your data in a geographically distant location, such as a different data center or cloud region. The distant replica can even work with a connection that's intermittent (intentionally or otherwise). However, if you want your replicas to have very low replication lag, you'll need a stable, low-latency link.

*Scaling read traffic*

MySQL replication can help you distribute read queries across several servers, which works very well for read-intensive applications. You can do basic load balancing with a few simple code changes. On a small scale, you can use simplistic approaches such as hardcoded hostnames or round-robin DNS (which points a single hostname to multiple IP addresses). You can also take more sophisticated approaches. Standard load-balancing solutions, such as network load-balancing products, can work well for distributing reads among MySQL servers.

*Backups*

> Replication is a valuable technique for helping with backups. However, a replica is neither a backup nor a substitute for backups.

*Analytics and reporting*

> Using a dedicated replica for reporting/analytics (online analytical processing, or OLAP) queries is a good strategy for isolating that load away from what your business needs to serve external customer requests. Replication is a way to power that isolation.

*High availability and failover*

> Replication can help avoid making MySQL a single point of failure in your application. A good failover system involving replication can help reduce downtime significantly.

*Testing MySQL upgrades*

> It's common practice to set up a replica with an upgraded MySQL version and use it to ensure that your queries work as expected before upgrading every instance.

## How Replication Works

Before we get into the details of setting up replication, let's quickly look at how MySQL actually replicates data. In this explanation, we're covering the simplest replication topology, a single source and a single replica.

At a high level, replication is a simple three-part process:

1. The source records changes to its data in its binary log as "binary log events."

2. The replica copies the source's binary log events to its own local relay log.

3. The replica replays the events in the relay log, applying the changes to its own data.

Figure 9-1 illustrates the most basic form of replication in more detail.

This replication architecture decouples the processes of fetching and replaying events on the replica, which allows them to be asynchronous—that is, the I/O thread can work independently of the SQL thread.

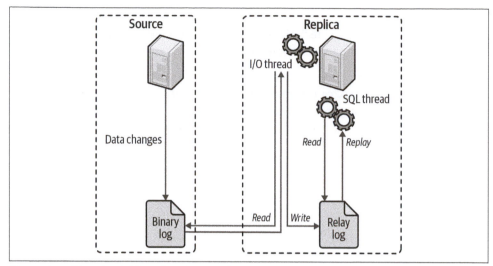

*Figure 9-1. How MySQL replication works*

# Replication Under the Hood

Now that we've refreshed you on the replication basics, let's dive deeper into it. Let's take a look at how replication really works, see what strengths and weaknesses it has as a result, and examine some more advanced options for replication configuration.

## Choosing Replication Format

MySQL offers three different binary log formats for replication: statement-based, row-based, and mixed. These are controlled with the binlog_format configuration parameter, which controls how the data is written to the binary log.

Statement-based replication works by recording the query that changed the data on the source. When the replica reads the event from the relay log and executes it, it is reexecuting the actual SQL query that the source executed. The main draw for this format is that it is simple and compact. A query that updates large amounts of data can be a few dozen bytes in the binary log. The largest downside to statement-based is that it generally has problems with nondeterministic queries. Consider a statement that deletes one hundred rows of a one-thousand-row table with no ORDER BY clause. If the rows are ordered differently between source and replica, you may delete a different one hundred rows on each, leading to inconsistencies.

Row-based replication writes events to the binary log that indicate how the row has changed. This sounds very simplistic, but it's a big change from statement-based because it's deterministic. With row-based, you can look at the binary log and see exactly what rows changed and what the values became. With statement-based, the

SQL is interpreted at execution time, and whatever rows the server found at execution time are what get changed. The drawback to row-based is that writing the events for row data changes for every row affected can increase the size of the binary log dramatically.

The mixed method attempts to combine the best of both worlds, using statement-based format as the default and only switching to row-based when it needs to. We say "attempts" because while it tries really hard, it has a lot of conditions[1] to meet for when to write each, and this leads to unpredictable events in the binary log. We take the opinion that binary log data should be one or the other, not a mix of both.

Our recommendation is to stick with row-based replication unless you have an express need to use statement-based temporarily. Row-based provides the safest method of replicating your data.

## Global Transaction Identifiers

Until MySQL 5.6, a replica had to keep track of what binary logfile and log position it was reading from when connecting to a source. For example, a replica connected to an upstream source and read data from `binlog.000002` at position 2749. As the replica read in events from that binary log, it advanced the position each time. Then, disaster struck! The source has crashed and you had to rebuild the data from a backup. The question became: how could you reattach your replica if the binary logs started over again? This was a fairly complicated process of reading events and determining where to attach to. If you made a mistake and went too early, you might duplicate events, and if too late, you skipped events. Either way, it was very easy to attach a replica incorrectly.

To solve this, MySQL added an alternate method for tracking replication positions: global transaction identifiers (GTIDs). With GTIDs, every transaction that a source server commits is assigned a unique identifier. This identifier is a combination of the `server_uuid`[2] and an incrementing transaction number. When the transaction is written to the binary log, the GTID is also written with it. From our refresher earlier in the chapter, you'll remember that a replica copies the binary log event into its local relay log and uses the SQL thread to apply changes to the local copy. When the SQL thread commits a transaction, it records the GTID as being completed as well.

---

1 As expected, we refer you to the manual to make sure you see the latest in how MIXED mode works with different types of SQL statements.

2 Note that `server_uuid` is different from the similarly named `server_id`. The `server_id` parameter is a user-defined value that you designate for your server whereas `server_uuid` is generated the first time MySQL starts if it does not detect the file *auto.cnf*.

To better illustrate this, let's use an example. Suppose our source server has just been set up and has no data in it—not even a database created. On this source server, our `server_uuid` was also generated to be `b9acac5a-7bbe-11eb-a043-42010af8001a`. We've done the same to our replica, and used the appropriate commands to instruct our replica to use the source server for replication.

On our source server, we would need to create a new database:

```
CREATE DATABASE misc;
```

This event will be written to the binary log so that our replica can also create the database. In the binary log, we would see a single event identified by the GTID:

```
b9acac5a-7bbe-11eb-a043-42010af8001a:1
```

As the replica server applies this event, it remembers that it has completed transaction `b9acac5a-7bbe-11eb-a043-42010af8001a:1`.

In our contrived example, let's say that we stop MySQL on our replica at this point. It has committed a single transaction. If our source continues to take writes, our transaction list will continue to grow: 2, 3, 4, 5, and so on. When we start our replica back up,[3] it knows that it has already seen transaction 1, and can begin with processing transaction 2.

GTIDs solve one of the more painful parts of running MySQL replication: dealing with logfiles and positions. We strongly recommend that you always enable GTIDs for your databases following the guide in the official MySQL documentation.

## Making Replication Crash Safe

Although GTIDs solved the logfile and position problem, a number of other problems also plagued administrators of MySQL. Later in this chapter, we'll touch on the common failure modes; however, before that, there are a few configuration settings that can greatly improve your experience using replication.

To minimize the chances for replication to break, we recommend setting the following:

`innodb_flush_log_at_trx_commit = 1`
> Although not strictly a replication setting, this ensures that logs are written and synchronized to disk at each transaction. This is the full ACID-compliant setting and will go the furthest toward protecting your data—even with replication. This is because binary log events are committed first and then the transaction will be

---

[3] This assumes you used the `SOURCE_AUTO_POSITION = 1` option when issuing the `CHANGE REPLICATION SOURCE TO` command, which you should typically always do.

committed and flushed to disk. Setting this to 1 will increase disk write operations while ensuring your data is durable.

`sync_binlog = 1`

This variable controls how often MySQL synchronizes the binary log data to disk. Setting this value to 1 means before every transaction. This protects against losing transactions in the event of a server crash. Just like the previous setting, this will increase disk writes.

`relay_log_info_repository = TABLE`

MySQL replication used to rely on files on disk to track replication position. This meant that transactions completed by replication had to synchronize to disk as a second step. If a crash happened between a transaction commit and the synchronization, the file on disk would have the incorrect file and position in it. That information has moved into InnoDB tables within MySQL itself, allowing replication to update both the transaction and the relay log information within the same transaction. This creates an atomic action and aids in crash recovery.

`relay_log_recovery = ON`

Simply put, `relay_log_recovery` throws away all local relay logs when a crash is detected and fetches the missing data from the source. This ensures that any corruption or incomplete relay logs on disk that may have happened in a crash are recoverable. This setting also eliminates the need for using `sync_relay_log` as, in the event of a crash, the relay logs are deleted. There's no need to spend extra operations synchronizing them to disk.

# Delayed Replication

In some scenarios, it can be advantageous to have a delayed replica in your topology. This strategy can be used to keep data online and running but keep it consistently behind real time by many hours or days. This is configured with the `CHANGE REPLICA` `TION SOURCE TO` statement and the `SOURCE_DELAY` option.

Imagine you're working with a large amount of data and there was an accidental change: a table was dropped. it might take you several hours to restore that from backup. With a time-delayed replica, you can find the GTID of the `DROP TABLE` statement and catch replication up to the point just prior to that table being dropped. This often can lead to much faster remediation times.

Nothing comes without trade-offs, though. While delayed replication can be tremendously useful in mitigating certain data-loss scenarios, it also brings complexity to many other operational aspects. If you decide you need to use delayed replication, you should also consider how to properly exclude this delayed replica from being a source node candidate (if your write failover is automated, this is even more important), how you monitor replication, and how that handles this special replica. These are just a few of the added complexities you should address when introducing delayed replicas.

## Multithreaded Replication

One of the historical challenges with replication was that, while you could take parallel writes on your source, your replicas were single threaded. Modern MySQL versions offer multithreaded replication (see Figure 9-2) where you can run multiple SQL applier threads to apply changes from the relay log locally.

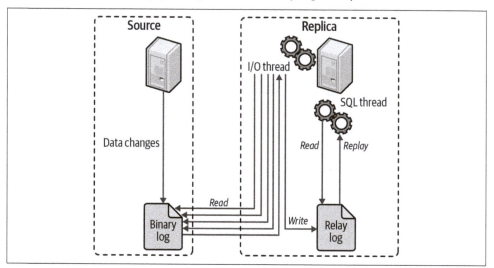

*Figure 9-2. Multithreaded replication setup*

There are two modes for multithreaded replication: DATABASE and LOGICAL_CLOCK. The DATABASE option uses multiple threads to update different databases; no two threads will update the same database at the same time. This method works well if you spread your data across multiple databases in MySQL and update them consistently and concurrently. The other option, LOGICAL_CLOCK, allows parallel updates against the same database as long as they are part of the same binary log group commit.

---

### What Is a Binary Log Group Commit?

To best explain this, we're going to use an excellent analogy by Morgan Tocker: (*https://oreil.ly/WiSps*) the example of a single ferry trying to ship passengers from point A to point B.

In MySQL 5.0, the ferry will pick up the next passenger in line from point A and transfer them to point B. The trip between A and B takes about a 10-minute return

---

trip, so it's possible that several new passengers will arrive while the ferry is in transit. That doesn't matter; when the ferry arrives back at point A, it will only pick up the very next passenger in line.

In MySQL 5.6, the ferry will pick up all passengers from the line at point A and then transfer them to point B. Each time it returns to point A to pick up new passengers, it will collect everyone who is waiting and transfer them across to point B.

This is measurably better performance in real-life situations where many passengers tend to arrive while waiting for the ferry to arrive back at point A, and the trip between A and B tends to take some time. It is not so measurable in naive benchmarks that run in a single thread.

MySQL 5.7 and later behave similarly to 5.6 in that it will pick up all waiting passengers from point A and transfer them to point B, but with one notable enhancement!

When the ferry arrives back at point A to pick up waiting passengers, it can be configured to wait just a little bit longer with the knowledge that new passengers will likely arrive. For example: if you know the trip between point A and point B is 10 minutes in duration, why not wait an extra 30 seconds at point A before departing? This may save you on round trips and improve the overall number of passengers that can be transported.

The configuration variables for artificial delay are `binlog_group_commit_sync_delay` (delay in microseconds) and `binlog_group_commit_sync_no_delay_count` (number of transactions to wait for before deciding to abort waiting).

In this example passengers are obviously transactions, and the ferry is an expensive `fsync()` operation. It's important to note that there is just one ferry in operation (a single set of ordered binary logs), so being able to tune this provides a nice level of advanced configuration.

In most cases, you can simply turn this feature on and see immediate benefit by setting `replica_parallel_workers` to a nonzero value. If you are operating on a single database, you will also need to change `replica_parallel_type` to LOGICAL_CLOCK. Since multithreaded replication uses a coordinator thread, there will be some overhead for that thread managing the states of all other threads. In addition, ensure that your replicas run with `replica_preserve_commit_order` so that committing out of order won't cause issues. See the "Gaps" section of the official documentation (*https://oreil.ly/Tjb28*) for a detailed explanation of why this is important.

There are two ways you can determine the optimal `replica_parallel_workers` value. The imprecise method would be to stop replication and then measure how long it takes to catch up using differing amounts of threads until you find the optimal setting. This is flawed because it assumes a consistent number of data manipulation language (DML) statements are being sent over replication and that they all perform relatively the same. In practice, this is hardly true.

The more precise method would be to look at how busy each of the applier threads are for your workload to determine how much parallelism you are getting. To do this, we need to enable performance schema consumers and instruments, allow it to collect some information, and then review the results.

To start, we need to enable the following:[4]

```
UPDATE performance_schema.setup_consumers SET ENABLED = 'YES'
WHERE NAME LIKE 'events_transactions%';

UPDATE performance_schema.setup_instruments SET ENABLED = 'YES', TIMED = 'YES'
WHERE NAME = 'transaction';
```

Allow replication to process events for a time period. Ideally, you would look at this during your heaviest write workloads or any time you see replication lag increasing:

```
mysql> USE performance_schema;
events_transactions_summary_by_thread_by_event_name.thread_id AS THREAD_ID,
events_transactions_summary_by_thread_by_event_name.count_star AS COUNT_STAR
FROM events_transactions_summary_by_thread_by_event_name
WHERE
events_transactions_summary_by_thread_by_event_name.thread_id IN (SELECT
replication_applier_status_by_worker.thread_id
FROM replication_applier_status_by_worker);
+-----------+------------+
| THREAD_ID | COUNT_STAR |
+-----------+------------+
|   1692957 |      23413 |
|   1692958 |       7150 |
|   1692959 |       1568 |
|   1692960 |        291 |
|   1692961 |         46 |
|   1692962 |          9 |
+-----------+------------+
6 rows in set (0.00 sec)
```

This query will help you identify how many transactions are processed by each thread. As we can see from the results on this sample workload, our optimal usage is somewhere between three and four threads, and anything over that is used very little.

---

4 Performance Schema consumers and instruments cause MySQL to collect additional data about its internals, which can use additional CPU. As a reminder, you should always test how changes like this will affect production workloads in a safe environment beforehand.

## Semisynchronous Replication

When you enable semisynchronous replication, every transaction that your source commits must be acknowledged as received by at least one replica.[5] The acknowledgment confirms that the replica received it and successfully wrote it to its own relay log (but not necessarily applied it to the local data).

Since each transaction must wait on the response from other nodes, this feature adds additional latency to every transaction that your server does. This means you need to consider the trade-off involved.

One very important thing to note here is that if no replicas acknowledge the transaction during the time frame, MySQL reverts to its standard asynchronous replication. It will not fail the transaction. This really helps illustrate that semisynchronous replication is not a tool to prevent data loss but rather a building block for a larger set of tooling that allows you to have more resilient failover.

Given the fallback to asynchronous, we struggled to find a good use case for why you would enable this. The logical use case would be to confirm that, in the event of a network partition, an isolated source isn't still writing data while partitioned from its replicas. Unfortunately, that source will just revert back to asynchronous and keep accepting writes. For that reason, we'd recommend not relying on this for any data integrity.

## Replication Filters

Replication-filtering options let you replicate just part of a server's data, which is much less of a good thing than you might think. There are two kinds of replication filters: those that filter events out of the binary log on the source and those that filter events coming from the relay log on the replica. Figure 9-3 illustrates the two types.

The options that control binary log filtering are `binlog_do_db` and `binlog_ignore_db`. You should not enable these, as we'll explain in a moment, unless you think you'll enjoy explaining to your boss why the data is gone permanently and can't be recovered.

On the replica, the `replicate_*` options filter events as the replication SQL thread reads them from the relay log. You can replicate or ignore one or more databases, rewrite one database to another database, and replicate or ignore tables based on LIKE pattern-matching syntax.

---

5 The number of replicas required is a configurable option (`rpl_semi_sync_source_wait_for_rep lica_count`). With wider topologies, you may consider requiring two or even three acknowledgments before completing the original transaction.

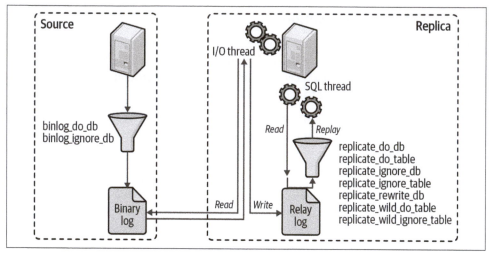

*Figure 9-3. Replication-filtering options*

The most important thing to understand about these options is that the *_do_db and *_ignore_db options, both on the source and on the replica, do not work as you might expect. You might think they filter on the object's database name, but they actually filter on the current default database—that is, if you execute the following statements on the source:

```
USE test;
DELETE FROM sakila.film;
```

The *_do_db and *_ignore_db parameters will filter the DELETE statement on test, not on sakila. This is not usually what you want, and it can cause the wrong statements to be replicated or ignored. The *_do_db and *_ignore_db parameters have uses, but they're limited and rare, and you should be very careful with them. If you use these parameters, it's very easy for replication to get out of sync or fail.

The binlog_do_db and binlog_ignore_db options don't just have the potential to break replication; they also make it impossible to do point-in-time recovery from a backup. For most situations, you should never use them.

In general, replication filters are a problem waiting to happen. For example, suppose you want to prevent privilege changes from propagating to replicas, a fairly common goal. (The desire to do this should probably tip you off that you're doing something wrong; there are probably other ways to accomplish your real goal.) Replication filters on the system tables will certainly prevent GRANT statements from replicating, but they will prevent events and routines from replicating, too. Such unforeseen consequences are a reason to be careful with filters. It may be a better idea to prevent specific statements from being replicated, usually with SET SQL_LOG_BIN=0, although that practice has its own hazards. In general, you should use replication filters very carefully and only if you really need them because they make it so easy to break replication and cause problems that will manifest when least convenient, such as during disaster recovery.

That being said, there can be specific situations where replication filters are beneficial. Perhaps you created multiple databases users_1, users_2, users_3, and users_4, and now performance on your server is too impacted. By restoring a backup and attaching replication, you can prepare to move the queries for users_3 and users_4 to another server. This works perfectly fine, except that you still have users_1 and users_2 on your new database. At some point, you'll have to drop the data that may be affecting performance. Consider this alternative. You restore your backup and then drop users_1 and users_2. Then you configure a replication rule to ignore users_1 and users_2 and complete replication setup. Now you're only processing events for users_3 and users_4 on your new server. Once you're caught up on replication, you're good to take production traffic.

The filtering options are well documented in the MySQL manual, so we won't repeat the details here.

# Replication Failover

At the beginning of the chapter, we mentioned that replication is the cornerstone of high availability, among other things. Having a copy of your data continuously updated in another location makes it much easier to recover from catastrophe than going to backup. More than that, there will be times you simply need to do some maintenance that involves restarting MySQL.

In this section, we want to talk about the right ways to promote a replica to become the source node. It's easy to get wrong, and getting it wrong can lead to data issues and extended downtime. We want to clarify that "promoting a replica" and "failing over" are synonymous. They both mean the act of demoting a source from taking writes and promoting a replica to the source role.

A much more detailed explanation of how to handle this is in the official MySQL documentation, under the "Switching Sources During Failover" section, but given how important this is to get right, we wanted to touch on it at least at some level.

## Planned Promotions

The most common reason for a promotion is some kind of maintenance event, including security patching, kernel updates, and even just restarting MySQL, as there are a few configuration options that require a restart. This type of promotion is referred to as a *controlled* or *planned promotion*.

To perform this promotion successfully, you want to accomplish the following steps:

1. Determine which replica you are going to promote. This is often the replica you are sure has all the data. That is your target.

2. Check the lag to make sure that you are within a few seconds.

3. Stop taking writes on your source by setting `super_read_only`.[6]

4. Wait until replication is in sync with your target. Compare GTIDs to be sure.

5. Unset `read_only` on target.

6. Switch application traffic to the target.

7. Repoint all replicas to the new source, including the demoted one. This is trivial with GTIDs and `AUTO_POSITION=1`.

## Unplanned Promotions

On a long enough timeline, every system fails, either as a result of software or hardware. When this happens on a source server where writes are happening, it can have a big impact on the user experience. Most applications will simply return an error, leaving the user to retry themselves. This is a case where an *unplanned promotion* is needed.

Since you do not have a live source to check, this is an abbreviated planned promotion, where you choose which replica based on data that was already replicated:

1. Determine which replica you are going to promote. This is often the replica you are sure has all the data. This is your target.

2. Unset `read_only` on target.

3. Switch application traffic to the target.

4. Repoint all replicas to the new source, including the demoted one when it returns to service. This is trivial with GTIDs.

You should also ensure that when your former source comes back online, it defaults to `super_read_only` enabled. This will help prevent any accidental writes.

## Trade-Offs of Promotion

We are compelled to point out that sometimes your first reaction to downtime is to failover. Because it is more difficult to know how much data may be missing from the target, it can sometimes be a better strategy to *not* failover.

---

6 Setting `super_read_only` implicitly enables `read_only`. Conversely, disabling `read_only` implicitly disables `super_read_only`. There's no reason for you to enable or disable both variables at the same time during this process.

An unplanned promotion is not a very practiced event—that is, you don't do it very often. When you are called upon to do it, you may need to look up documentation to make sure you don't miss a step. You also have to inspect other replicas to verify which is the likely candidate. All of this takes time. In some cases, it may simply be faster for you to wait for your server or MySQL process to come back online. The advantage of this is that if you followed the steps for ACID compliance in Chapter 5, you didn't lose any data, and your replicas will pick up where things left off.

# Replication Topologies

You can set up MySQL replication for almost any configuration of sources and replicas. Many complex topologies are possible, but even the simple ones can be very flexible. A single topology can have many different uses. The variety of ways you can use replication could easily fill its own book.

All of this flexibility means you can easily design a topology that is unmaintainable. We highly recommend you keep your replication topology as simple as possible while still meeting your needs. With that said, we recommend two possible strategies that should cover nearly every use case. You may have valid reasons for deviating from these, but make sure you ask yourself if you're still solving the right problems when you go more complex.

## Active/Passive

In an active/passive topology, you direct all reads and writes to a single source server. Additionally, you maintain a small number of passive replicas that do not actively serve any application traffic. The primary reason for choosing this model is when you don't want to worry about replication lag. Since all reads go to the source, you prevent any read-after-write problems that an application may not tolerate.

Figure 9-4 shows this arrangement with multiple replicas.

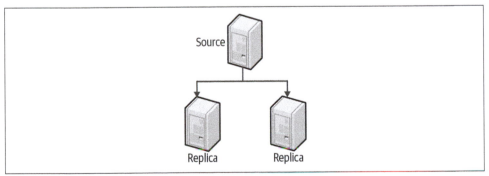

*Figure 9-4. A source with multiple replicas*

### Configuration

In this topology, we expect that the source and replicas are identical configurations in terms of CPU, memory, and so forth. Over a long enough period, you will need to fail over from the current running source to one of the replicas, either for maintenance, software upgrade or patching, or even a hardware failure. By having the same hardware and software configuration on replicas, you ensure that you can sustain the traffic capacity and throughput as before you failed over.

### Redundancy

In a physical hardware environment, you really want $n+2$ redundancy for at least three total servers. In the event of a hardware failure, you still have one additional server for failover. You can also use one of the replicas as a backup server if you are uncomfortable or unable to take backups on your source.

In a cloud environment, you can get away with $n+1$ redundancy for two total servers if your data is small enough or you can copy the data easily. Otherwise, $n+2$ is needed. If you go the $n+1$ route, the dynamic provisioning nature of cloud providers can make this easier to manage. For maintenance events like patching, it's easier to provision a third replica on demand, perform any necessary actions on it (like upgrading the kernel or applying a security update), and then replace the other replica. Then you fail over and repeat the process on the former source. The goal is to keep a replica ready to be the target of a failover at all times.

In either case, you can place one of these replicas in a geographically distant location, although you will have to pay attention to replication lag and ensure that it is usable. Replicas should be recoverable and any data loss within guidelines that you establish. We talk about this in "Defining Recovery Requirements" on page 259 in Chapter 10.

### Caveats

By choosing this model, you are explicitly binding your read scaling to the capacity of a single server. If you hit a read scaling limit, you will have to evolve beyond this topology—likely into the active/read pool configuration—or you will have to leverage sharding to reduce reads on the source.

## Active/Read Pool

In an active/read pool configuration, you direct all writes to the source. Reads can be sent to either the source server or the read pool, depending upon application needs. A read pool allows you to scale reads horizontally for read-intensive applications. At some point, the horizontal scaling will fall off due to the demand of replication on the source.

Figure 9-5 shows this arrangement with a single source and a replica pool.

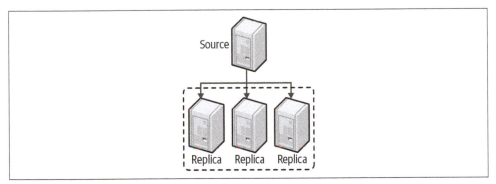

*Figure 9-5. A source with a read pool*

## Configuration

Ideally, you want an identical configuration between the source and at least one, preferably two, of the replicas in the read pool. Again, you will at some point need to fail over to one of those replicas, and it should have enough capacity to keep up with your traffic.

If you see this pool growing over time, you may optimize for cost and use a different configuration for some of the members. If that's the case, try to look at traffic weighting as a way to balance traffic across them. If you have 32 cores for the failover targets and 8 cores for other replicas, try to send four times more traffic to the 32-core node to ensure you get utilization.

## Redundancy

The number of servers you have in this pool should meet the requirements previously given, meaning at least one server can act as a failover target. Beyond that, you need enough nodes to accommodate your read traffic, plus a small buffer for node failures. With reads, your most likely indicator of utilization will be CPU, and as such, target somewhere between 50%–60% utilization per node in the pool. As CPU increases, it spends more time context switching between work and latency increases. Try to find the right balance between latency and utilization that meets your application expectations.

## Caveats

When you use a read pool, your application must have some tolerance for stale reads. You will never be able to guarantee that a write you complete on the source has already been replicated to a replica. You may also need a way to depool nodes that fall too far behind on replication.

The size of the read pool also has an impact on how much administration you have to do and when you should look at automation. A 16-node pool will mean that you have to do kernel updates or security patching 16 times. Automating this task to gracefully depool a node, perform patching, reboot, and repool will reduce the amount of work you do by hand in the future.

## Discouraged Topologies

By using either of the two recommendations we've given in this chapter, you keep your topology simple and easy to understand. There are a number of other suggestions from earlier editions of this book, or perhaps you anecdotally heard about how another company's topology is set up. We call out some of these here as discouraged because they come with more risk and complexity than we like to see.

### Dual source in active-active mode

*Dual source replication* (also known as *bidirectional replication*) involves two servers, each configured as both a source and a replica of the other—in other words, a pair of cosources. Figure 9-6 shows the setup.

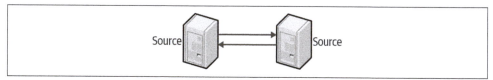

*Figure 9-6. Dual source in active-active mode*

At first glance, this doesn't look any different than active/passive with two servers, except that replication is already configured in the opposite direction. The real danger is when you explicitly send write traffic to both sides, hence the active/active part.

Active/active is *very* difficult to do correctly. Some strategies involve choosing which side to send to based on even/odd hashing. This ensures that reads-after-write are consistent for the same row, but queries that include rows that are canonical on the other side may not be consistent. Said more plainly, reading rows with ID 1, 3, and 5 from one side will always be consistent. What about a query that reads ID 1–6? Where do you send that query? What if an update exists on the other side that is not reflected on this one due to replication lag?

You also need to carefully balance capacity. In a cosource scenario, each server is the other server's replica and the most likely target of the failover. You have to plan your capacity in a way that ensures that when you shift traffic from one side to the other, you do not run out of CPU. You're also failing over and introducing an entirely different working set of data. The InnoDB buffer pool now churns, removing entries to make room for the new hot set of data.

Take our advice and stay away from this one. It may feel like you're getting "use" out of a passive server by having it handle traffic instead of sitting idle. You'll end up introducing data inconsistencies into the application and always be on edge that you don't have enough capacity to failover. Once you lose your failover strategy, you've lost resilience.

### Dual source in active-passive mode

There's a variation on dual source in active-active mode that avoids the pitfalls we just discussed. The main difference is that one of the servers is a read-only "passive" server, as shown in Figure 9-7.

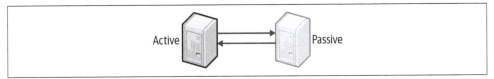

*Figure 9-7. Dual source in active-passive mode*

There's really nothing wrong with this setup on the surface. The only way it differs from our recommendation for active/passive is that replication has been preconfig-ured back to the other server. This only works in a two-server configuration. If you run more than two servers, you'll need to decide which node is the best target for a failover. Preconfiguring replication only ties you directly to one and doesn't give you flexibility in an outage situation.

We maintain that setting up replication is an easy, automatable step as part of the replication-failover process we talked about before. This is an unnecessary configura-tion that only invites confusion.

### Dual sources with replicas

Mashing up things even more, we can add one or more replicas to each cosource, as shown in Figure 9-8.

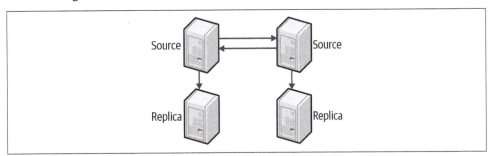

*Figure 9-8. Dual source topology with replicas*

This maintains most of the problems with dual source in active-active, the most important being how you route traffic. It resolves the concerns about capacity planning and buffer pool churn in a failover. You have additional steps in a failover to point one of the sources to a newly promoted replica on top of it.

We're definitely against this as well, largely for the data access concerns. Cosources only lead to trouble.

### Ring replication

*Ring replication* has three or more sources where each server is a replica of the server before it in the ring and a source of the server after it, as shown in Figure 9-9. This topology is also called *circular replication*.

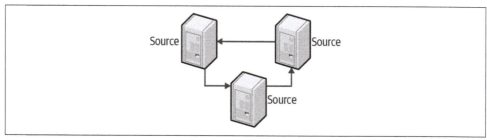

*Figure 9-9. A replication ring topology*

If any server in this topology goes offline, your topology is broken and updates stop flowing around the ring. There are attached replica variations of this, where each source in Figure 9-9 has a dedicated replica to swap in. That still means the ring is broken until you promote a replica into the former position.

This topology is the opposite of simple and has no advantages.

### Multisource replication

While keeping your replication topology simple is important, there may be situations where you need to use more advanced features to handle one-off functions. Suppose you built a brand-new video upload and viewing site, which is now becoming popular. One of your early design decisions was to separate data about videos and data about users into two separate database clusters. As you've grown, you find yourself wanting to merge them back together in queries. You can accomplish this with multisource replication to bring back both data sets together in a replica, as shown in Figure 9-10.

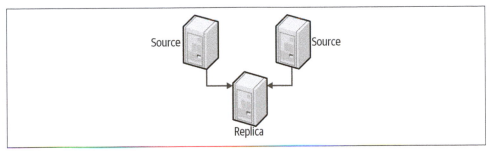

*Figure 9-10. Multisource replication*

This functionality is built off a concept called *replication channels*. In the preceding example, you would need a third cluster for MySQL. This new third cluster would have two replication channels created: one for the video data and one for the user data. Once you've loaded and replicated data, you could take a very brief downtime where you freeze writes to the two sources and push your code to switch reading and writing to the new combined database. Voila, you've now merged two databases into one.

Before we move on, there's one important limitation to know about: you cannot configure a replica to use multisource replication multiple times against the same source.

This topology is very much intended for special-use circumstances. We cite it as discouraged only in the case where you build a permanent topology around this concept. Using it temporarily to merge data is still an acceptable use case with the end goal to go back to one of our two recommendations.

# Replication Administration and Maintenance

With a small amount of data and a consistent write workload, it's unlikely that you'll be called upon to look at replication lag or worse, replication breaking, very often. Most databases tend to grow in size over time, and with that growth will come maintenance.

## Monitoring Replication

Replication increases the complexity of MySQL monitoring. Although replication actually happens on both the source and the replica, most of the work is done on the replica, and that is where the most common problems occur. Are all the replicas working? Has any replica had errors? How far behind is the slowest replica? Out of the box, MySQL provides most of the information you need to answer these questions, but automating the monitoring process and making replication robust is left up to you.

When setting up replication monitoring, there are a few items that we consider most important to observe:

*Replication requires disk space on both source and replica*
> As seen earlier in Figure 9-1, replication uses both binary logs on the source and relay logs on the replicas. If there is no free disk space on the source, transactions will be unable to complete and will begin timing out. If the same condition happens on a replica, MySQL behaves a little more gracefully by pausing replication and waiting for free disk space. You'll want to monitor both for available disk space to ensure continued operation.

*Replication should be monitored for state and for errors*
> Although replication has been a long-standing feature and is very robust, external factors like network issues, data inconsistencies, and data corruption can cause it to break. Because of this, it's ideal to monitor for whether replication threads are running and if not, look into what the latest error is to determine what your next step should be. We cover more about how to troubleshoot specific problems in "Replication Problems and Solutions" on page 251.

*Delayed replication should be delayed as expected*
> Since we mentioned delayed replication earlier, it's advisable to set up monitoring to ensure that delayed replicas are in fact delayed by the correct amount of time. Too long of a delay might make it much more time consuming to use. If the delay is too little—or even worse, not delayed at all—the delayed copy may be of no use to you if you need it.

## Measuring Replication Lag

One of the most common things you'll need to monitor is how far behind the source a replica is running. Although the Seconds_behind_source column in SHOW REPLICA STATUS theoretically shows the replica's lag, in fact it's not always accurate, for a variety of reasons:

- The replica calculates Seconds_behind_source by comparing the server's current timestamp to the timestamp recorded in the binary log event, so the replica can't even report its lag unless it is processing a query.

- The replica will usually report NULL if the replication threads aren't running.

- Some errors (for example, mismatched max_allowed_packet settings between the source and replica or an unstable network) can break replication and/or stop the replication threads, but Seconds_behind_source will report 0 rather than indicating an error.

- The replica sometimes can't calculate the lag even if the replication processes are running. If this happens, the replica might report either 0 or NULL.

- A very long transaction can cause the reported lag to fluctuate. For example, if you have a transaction that updates data, stays open for an hour, and then commits, the update will go into the binary log an hour after it actually happened. When the replica processes the statement, it will temporarily report that it is an hour behind the source, and then it will jump back to zero seconds behind.

The solution to these problems is to ignore Seconds_behind_source and monitor replica lag with something you can observe and measure directly. The best solution is a heartbeat record, which is a timestamp that you update once per second on the source. To calculate the lag, you can simply subtract the heartbeat from the current timestamp on the replica. This method is immune to all the problems we just mentioned, and it has the added benefit of creating a handy timestamp that shows at what point in time the replica's data is current. The pt-heartbeat script, included in Percona Toolkit, is the most popular implementation of a replication heartbeat.

A heartbeat has other benefits, too. The replication heartbeat records in the binary log are useful for many purposes, such as disaster recovery in otherwise hard-to-solve scenarios.

None of the lag metrics we just mentioned gives a sense of how long it will take for a replica to actually catch up to the source. This depends on many factors, such as how powerful the replica is and how many write queries the source continues to process. See the subsection "Excessive Replication Lag" in the "Replication Problems and Solutions" section for more on that topic.

## Determining Whether Replicas Are Consistent with the Source

In a perfect world, a replica would always be an exact copy of its source, minus any replication delay. But in the real world, discrepancies can be introduced into replicas. Some possible causes are:

- Accidental writes to the replica
- Using dual source replication with both sides taking writes
- Nondeterministic queries and statement-based replication
- MySQL crashes while you run in a less-than-durable mode (see Chapter 5 for durability configurations)
- Bugs in MySQL

We suggest the following rules:

*Always run your replicas with* `super_read_only` *enabled*

Using `read_only` prevents users without the SUPER privilege from being able to write, but this won't prevent your DBAs from running a DELETE or ALTER without realizing they're on the replica. The `super_read_only` setting only allows replication to write and is the safest way to run replicas.

*Use row-based replication or deterministic statements*

Despite having situations where it will use a much larger amount of disk space, row-based replication is the most consistent way to replicate data. This is because it includes the exact row data changing for every entry.

Consider the following with statement-based replication:

```
DELETE FROM users WHERE last_login_date <= NOW() LIMIT 10;
```

What happens when there are one thousand users in this table that match the WHERE clause? MySQL will use the natural order in the table to only delete the first 10 rows. The natural order of the table may be different on replicas, so a different set of 10 rows may be affected. Statements run in the future that modify or delete the rows based on `last_login_date` may or may not exist. This can cause an inconsistency with the data.

The best way to write this would be to use an ORDER BY to make the row order deterministic:

```
DELETE FROM users WHERE last_login_date <= NOW() ORDER BY user_id
LIMIT 10;
```

With this statement, as long as the data is consistent between source and replica, the same 10 rows will be deleted.

*Do not try to write to multiple servers in a replication topology at the same time*

This includes using cosources with writes on both sides or ring replication. The most practical replication topology is to use one source, taking all your writes, and one or more replicas, optionally taking reads.

Last, we highly recommend that if you encounter any replication errors, you use the strategies (*https://oreil.ly/DlYzR*) in the official MySQL documentation for rebuilding the replica.

# Replication Problems and Solutions

The simple implementation of MySQL replication makes it easy to set up yet also means there are many ways to stop, confuse, and otherwise disrupt it. Earlier in this chapter, we talked about crash-safe replication and rules to help keep your source and replicas in sync. This section discusses common problems, how they manifest themselves, and how you can solve or even prevent them.

## Binary Logs Corrupted on the Source

If the binary log is corrupted on the source, you'll have no choice but to rebuild your replicas. Skipping over the corrupted entry will skip some transactions, which would no longer be processed by your replicas.

## Nonunique Server IDs

This is one of the more elusive problems you might encounter with replication. If you accidentally configure two replicas with the same server ID, they might seem to work just fine if you're not watching closely. But if you watch their error logs or watch the source with a tool like *innotop*, you'll notice something very odd.

On the source, you'll see only one of the two replicas connected at any time. (Usually, all replicas are connected and replicating all the time.) On the replica, you'll see frequent disconnect and reconnect error messages in the error log but no mention of a misconfigured server ID.

Depending on the MySQL version, the replicas might replicate correctly but slowly, or they might not actually replicate correctly—any given replica might miss binary log events or even repeat them, causing duplicate key errors (or silent data corruption). You can also cause problems on the source because of the increased load from the replicas fighting among themselves. And if replicas are fighting one another badly enough, the error logs can become enormous in a very short time.

The only solution to this problem is to be careful when setting up your replicas. You might find it helpful to create a canonical list of replica-to-server ID mappings so that you don't lose track of which ID belongs to each replica. If your replicas live entirely within one network subnet, you can choose unique IDs by using the last octet of each machine's IP address.

## Undefined Server IDs

If you don't define the server ID, MySQL will appear to set up replication with `CHANGE REPLICATION SOURCE TO` but will not let you start the replica:

```
mysql> START REPLICA;
ERROR 1200 (HY000): The server is not configured as replica; fix in config file
or with CHANGE REPLICATION SOURCE TO
```

This error is especially confusing if you've just used `CHANGE REPLICATION SOURCE TO` and verified your settings with `SHOW REPLICA STATUS`. You might get a value from `SELECT @@server_id`, but it's just a default. You have to set the value explicitly.

## Missing Temporary Tables

Temporary tables are handy for some uses, but unfortunately, they're incompatible with statement-based replication. If a replica crashes or if you shut it down, any temporary tables the replica thread was using disappear. When you restart the replica, any further statements that refer to the missing temporary tables will fail.

The best approach here is to use row-based replication. The second-best approach is to name your temporary tables consistently (prefix with `temporary_`, for example) and use replication rules to skip replicating them entirely.

## Not Replicating All Updates

If you misuse `SET SQL_LOG_BIN=0` or don't understand the replication filtering rules, your replica might not execute some updates that have taken place on the source. Sometimes you want this for archiving purposes, but it's usually accidental and has bad consequences.

For example, suppose you have a `replicate_do_db` rule to replicate only the `sakila` database to one of your replicas. If you execute the following commands on the source, the replica's data will become different from the data on the source:

```
mysql> USE test;
mysql> UPDATE sakila.actor ...
```

Other types of statements can even cause replication to fail with an error because of nonreplicated dependencies.

## Excessive Replication Lag

Replication lag is a frequent problem. No matter what, it's a good idea to design your applications to tolerate some lag on the replicas. Here are some common approaches to reducing replication lag:

*Multithreaded replication*

Ensure you're using multithreaded replication and you've looked at tuning the various options as per the manual for how to get the most efficiency from it.

*Use sharding*

While it seems like a cop-out answer, using sharding techniques to spread writes across multiple sources is a very effective strategy. The long-standing rule of thumb for MySQL has been: scale reads with replicas, scale writes with sharding.

*Temporarily lower durability*

Purists will disagree, but there may be times when you've exhausted all tuning and tweaking and sharding is not a viable option because of either effort or design issues. If your replication lag is largely due to write operation limitations, you can temporarily set `sync_binlog=0` and `innodb_flush_log_at_trx_com mit=0` to boost replication speed.

If you go this last route, you should be very, very careful. You should only do this on your replica, and if your replica is also where you take backups, changing these settings may make it impossible for you to recover from a backup.[7] Also, if your replica crashes during this reduced durability, you will likely have to rebuild from your source. Lastly, if you do this manually, it's terribly easy to forget to set the durability back. Ensure you have good monitoring or have scripted some way to set durability again.

One possible strategy would be to watch the `Seconds_behind_source` value from the `SHOW REPLICA STATUS` command, and when it exceeds a certain value, trigger an action that does the following:

1. Ensure that the server is a nonwritable replica, likely by verifying that `super_read_only` is enabled.

2. Change the settings for `sync_binlog` and `innodb_flush_log_at_trx_commit` to reduce write operations.

3. Periodically check `SHOW REPLICA STATUS` for the value of `Seconds_ behind_ source`.

4. When below an acceptable threshold, revert the settings back to their durable nature.

---

7 This is typically true in cases where you may use LVM snapshots or a cloud-based disk snapshot approach to backups.

## Oversized Packets from the Source

Another hard-to-trace problem in replication can occur when the source's `max_allowed_packet` size doesn't match the replica's. In this case, the source can log a packet the replica considers oversized, and when the replica retrieves that binary log event, it might suffer from a variety of problems. These include an endless loop of errors and retries or corruption in the relay log.

## No Disk Space

Replication can indeed fill up your disks with binary logs, relay logs, or temporary files, especially if you do a lot of `LOAD DATA INFILE` queries on the source and have `log_replica_updates` enabled on the replica. The more a replica falls behind, the more disk space it is likely to use for relay logs that have been retrieved from the source but not yet executed. You can prevent these errors by monitoring disk usage and setting the `relay_log_space` configuration variable.

## Replication Limitations

MySQL replication can fail or get out of sync, with or without errors, just because of its inherent limitations. A fairly large list of SQL functions and programming practices simply won't replicate reliably (we've mentioned many of them in this chapter). It's hard to ensure that none of these finds a way into your production code, especially if your application or team is large.

Another issue is bugs in the server. We don't want to sound negative, but many major versions of the MySQL server have historically had bugs in replication, especially in the first releases of the major version. New features, such as stored procedures, have usually caused more problems.

For most users, this is not a reason to avoid new features. It's just a reason to test carefully, especially when you upgrade your application or MySQL. Monitoring is also important; you need to know when something causes a problem.

MySQL replication is complicated, and the more complicated your application is, the more careful you need to be. However, if you learn how to work with it, it works quite well.

# Summary

MySQL replication is the Swiss Army knife of MySQL's built-in capabilities, and it increases MySQL's range of functionality and usefulness dramatically. It is probably one of the key reasons why MySQL became so popular so quickly, in fact.

Although replication has many limitations and caveats, it turns out that most of them are relatively unimportant or easy for most users to avoid. Many of the drawbacks are simply special-case behaviors of advanced features that most people won't use but are very helpful for the minority of users who need them.

When it comes to replication, your motto should be to keep it simple. Don't do anything fancy, such as using replication rings or replication filters, unless you really need to. Use replication simply to mirror an entire copy of your data, including all privileges. Keeping your replicas identical to the source in every way will help you avoid many problems.

# Backup and Recovery

If you don't plan for backups up front, you might later find that you've ruled out some of the best options. For example, you might set up a server and then wish for LVM so that you can take filesystem snapshots—but it's too late. You also might not notice some important performance impacts of configuring your systems for backups. And if you don't plan for and practice recovery, it won't go smoothly when you need to do it.

We won't cover all parts of a well-designed backup and recovery solution in this chapter—just the parts that are relevant to MySQL. Here are some points we decided not to include here but that you should still absolutely be including in your overall backup and recovery strategy:

- Security (access to the backup, privileges to restore data, and whether the files need to be encrypted)
- Where to store the backups, including how far away from the source they should be (on a different disk, a different server, or offsite) and how to move the data from the source to the destination
- Retention policies, auditing, legal requirements, and related subjects
- Storage solutions and media, compression, and incremental backups
- Storage formats
- Monitoring and reporting on your backups
- Backup capabilities built into storage layers or particular devices, such as prefabricated file servers

Before we begin, let's clarify some key terms. First, you'll often hear about so-called *hot*, *warm*, and *cold* backups. People generally use these terms to denote a backup's impact: "hot" backups aren't supposed to require any server downtime, for example. The problem is that these terms don't mean the same things to everyone. Some tools even use the word *hot* in their names but definitely don't perform what we consider to be hot backups. We try to avoid these terms and instead tell you how much a specific technique or tool interrupts your server.

Two other confusing words are *restore* and *recover*. We use them in specific ways in this chapter. *Restoring* means retrieving data from a backup and either loading it into MySQL or placing the files where MySQL expects them to be. *Recovery* generally means the entire process of rescuing a system, or part of a system, after something has gone wrong. This includes restoring data from backups as well as all the steps necessary to make a server fully functional again, such as restarting MySQL, changing the configuration, warming up the server's caches, and so on.

To many people, recovery just means fixing corrupted tables after a crash. This is not the same as recovering an entire server. A storage engine's crash recovery reconciles its data and logfiles. It makes sure the datafiles contain only the modifications made by committed transactions, and it replays transactions from the logfiles that have not yet been applied to the datafiles. This might be part of the overall recovery process, or even part of making backups. However, it's not the same as the recovery you might need to do after an accidental DROP TABLE, for example. Depending on the issue you are recovering from, the actions you take for recovery may be vastly different.

Lastly, there are two main types of backups: raw and logical. *Raw backups*—sometimes called *physical*[1] *backups*—refer to a copy of files from a filesystem. *Logical backups* refer to the SQL statements needed to reconstruct the data.

# Why Backups?

Here are a few reasons that backups are important:

*Disaster recovery*

Disaster recovery is what you do when hardware fails, a nasty bug corrupts your data, or your server and its data become unavailable or unusable for some other reason. You need to be ready for everything from someone accidentally connecting to the wrong server doing an ALTER TABLE, to the building burning down, to a malicious attacker or a MySQL bug. Although the odds of any particular disaster striking are fairly low, taken together they add up.

---

1 Raw backups may also be unintuitively referred to as *physical backups* with the idea you're moving the physical files to your backup destination. We say "unintuitive" because the file itself isn't physical at all!

---

*People changing their minds*

You'd be surprised how often people intentionally delete data and then want it back.

*Auditing*

Sometimes you need to know what your data or schema looked like at some point in the past. You might be involved in a lawsuit, for example, or you might discover a bug in your application and need to see what the code used to do (sometimes just having your code in version control isn't enough).

*Testing*

One of the easiest ways to test on realistic data is to refresh a test server periodically with the latest production data. If you're making backups, it's easy: just restore the backup to the test server.

Check your assumptions. For example, do you assume your shared hosting provider is backing up the MySQL server provided with your account? You might be surprised. Many hosting providers don't back up MySQL servers at all, and others just do a file copy while the server is running, which probably creates a corrupt backup that's useless.

# Defining Recovery Requirements

If all goes well, you'll never need to think about recovery. But when you do, the best backup system in the world won't help if you never tested recovering it. You'll need a great recovery system.

Unfortunately, it's easier to make your backup systems work smoothly than it is to build good recovery processes and tools. Here's why:

- Backups come first. You can't recover unless you've first backed up, so your attention naturally focuses on backups when building a system.

- Backups are automated with scripts and jobs. It's easy to spend time fine-tuning the backup process, often without thinking of it. Five-minute tweaks to your backup process might not seem important, but are you applying the same attention to recovery, day in and day out?

- Backups are routine, but recovery is usually a crisis situation.

- Security gets in the way. If you're doing offsite backups, you're probably encrypting the backup data or taking other measures to protect it. You know how damaging it would be for your data to be compromised, but how damaging is it when nobody can unlock your encrypted volume to recover your data or when you need to extract a single file from a monolithic encrypted file?

- One person can plan, design, and implement backups. That person might not be available when disaster strikes. You need to train several people and plan for coverage, so you're not asking an unqualified person to recover your data.

There are two Big Important Requirements that are helpful to consider when you're planning your backup and recovery strategy. These are the *recovery point objective (RPO)* and the *recovery time objective (RTO)*. If you notice, these sound very similar to the SLOs we discussed in Chapter 2. They define how much data you're comfortable losing and how long you're comfortable waiting to get it back. Try to answer the following types of questions when defining your RPO and RTO:

- How much data can you lose without serious consequences? Do you need point-in-time recovery, or is it acceptable to lose whatever work has happened since your last regular backup? Are there legal requirements?

- How fast does recovery have to be? What kind of downtime is acceptable? What impacts (e.g., partial unavailability) can your application and users accept, and how will you build in the capability to continue functioning when those scenarios happen?

- What do you need to recover? Common requirements are to recover a whole server, a single database, a single table, or just specific transactions or statements.

It's a good idea to document the answers to these questions, and indeed your entire backup policy, as well as the backup procedures.

---

### Backup Myth #1: "My Replica Is My Backup"

This is a mistake we see quite often. A replica is not a backup. Neither is a RAID array. To understand why, consider this: will they help you get back all your data if you accidentally execute DROP DATABASE on your production database? RAID and replication don't pass even this simple test. Not only are they not backups, they're not a substitute for backups. Nothing but backups fill the need for backups.

---

# Designing a MySQL Backup Solution

Backing up MySQL is harder than it looks. At its most basic, a backup is just a copy of the data, but your application's needs, MySQL's storage engine architecture, and your system configuration can make it difficult to make a copy of your data.

Before we go into great detail on all of the available options, we want to recommend:

- Raw backups are practically a must-have for large databases: logical backups are simply too slow and resource intensive, and recovery from a logical backup takes way too long. Snapshot-based backups, Percona XtraBackup, and MySQL Enterprise Backup are the best options. For small databases, logical backups can work nicely.

- Keep several backup generations.

- Extract logical backups (probably from the raw backups) periodically.

- Keep binary logs for point-in-time recovery. Set `expire_logs_days` long enough to recover from at least two generations of raw backups so that you can create a replica and start it from the running source without applying any binary logs to it. Back up your binary logs independently of the expiry setting, and keep them in the backup long enough to recover from at least the most recent logical backup.

- Monitor your backups and backup processes independently from the backup tools themselves. You need external verification that they're OK.

- Test your backups and recovery process by going through the entire recovery process. Measure the resources needed for recovery (CPU, disk space, wall-clock time, network bandwidth, etc.).

- Think hard about security. What happens if someone compromises your server— can they then get access to the backup server too, or vice versa?

Knowing your RPO and RTO will guide your backup strategy. Do you need point-in-time recovery capability, or is it enough to recover to last night's backup and lose whatever work has been done since then? If you need point-in-time recovery, you can probably make a regular backup and ensure that the binary log is enabled, so you can restore that backup and recover to the desired point by replaying the binary log.

Generally, the more you can afford to lose, the easier it is to do backups. If you have very strict requirements, it's harder to ensure you can recover everything. There are also different flavors of point-in-time recovery. A "soft" point-in-time recovery requirement means you'd like to be able to re-create your data so that it's "close enough" to where it was when the problem happened. A "hard" requirement means you can never tolerate the loss of a committed transaction, even if something terrible happens (such as the server catching fire). This requires special techniques, such as keeping your binary log on a separate SAN volume or using Distributed Replicated Block Device (DRBD) disk replication.

## Online or Offline Backups?

If you can get away with it, shutting down MySQL to make a backup is the easiest, safest, and overall best way to get a consistent copy of the data with minimal risk of corruption or inconsistency. If you shut down MySQL, you can copy the data without any complications from things like dirty buffers in the InnoDB buffer pool or other caches. You don't need to worry about your data being modified while you're trying to back it up, and because the server isn't under load from the application, you can make the backup more quickly.

However, taking a server offline is more expensive than it might seem. As a result, you'll almost certainly need to design your backups so that they don't require the production server to be taken offline. Depending on your consistency requirements, though, making a backup while the server is online can still mean interrupting service significantly.

Here are some performance-related factors to consider when you're planning backups:

*Backup time*

> How long does it take to make the backup and copy the backup to the destination?

*Backup load*

> How much does copying the backup to the destination affect the server's performance?

*Recovery time*

> How long does it take to copy your backup image from its storage location to the MySQL server, replay binary logs, and so on?

The biggest trade-off is backup time versus backup load. You can often improve one at the other's expense; for example, you can prioritize the backup at the expense of causing more performance degradation on the server.

You can also design your backups to take advantage of load patterns. For instance, if your server is only 50% loaded for eight hours during the night, you can try to design your backups to load the server less than 50% and still complete within eight hours. You can accomplish this in many ways: for example, you can use *ionice* and *nice* to prioritize the copy or compression operations, use different compression levels, or compress the data on the backup server instead of the MySQL server. You can also use *lzo* or *pigz* for faster compression. You can use `O_DIRECT` or `fadvise()` to bypass the operating system's cache for the copy operations, so they don't pollute the server's caches. Tools such as Percona XtraBackup and MySQL Enterprise Backup also have throttling options, and you can use *pv* with the `--rate-limit` option to limit the throughput of scripts you write yourself.

# Logical or Raw Backups?

As mentioned earlier, there are two major ways to back up MySQL's data: with a *logical backup* (also called a *dump*) and by copying the *raw files*. A logical backup contains the data in a form that MySQL can interpret either as SQL or as delimited text.[2] The raw files are the files as they exist on disk.

Each type of backup has advantages and disadvantages.

## Logical backups

Logical backups have the following advantages:

- They're normal files you can manipulate and inspect with editors and command-line tools such as *grep* and *sed*. This can be very helpful when restoring data or when you just want to inspect the data without restoring.

- They're simple to restore. You can just pipe them into *mysql* or use *mysqlimport*.

- You can back up and restore across the network—that is, on a different machine from the MySQL host.

- They can work for cloud-based MySQL systems, where you have no access to the underlying filesystem.

- They can be very flexible because *mysqldump*—the tool most people prefer to use to make them—can accept lots of options, such as a WHERE clause to restrict which rows are backed up.

- They're independent of the storage engine. Because you create them by extracting data from the MySQL server, they abstract away differences in the underlying data storage.[3]

- They can help avoid data corruption. If your disk drives are failing and you copy the raw files, you'll get an error and/or make a partial or corrupt backup, and unless you check the backup, you won't notice it and it'll be unusable later. If the data MySQL has in memory is not corrupt, you can sometimes get a trustworthy logical backup when you can't get a good raw file copy.

Logical backups have their shortcomings, though:

---

2 Logical backups produced by *mysqldump* are not always text files. SQL dumps can contain many different character sets and can even include binary data that's not valid character data at all. Lines can be too long for many editors, too. Still, many such files will contain data a text editor can open and read, especially if you run *mysqldump* with the `--hex-blob` option.

3 Keep in mind that while the data that is dumped is engine independent, the storage engine features may not be compatible. For example, you couldn't dump an InnoDB database with foreign key relationships defined and expect the foreign keys to work in an engine that doesn't implement them.

- The server has to do the work of generating them, so they use more CPU cycles.

- Logical backups can be bigger than the underlying files in some cases.[4] The ASCII representation of the data isn't always as efficient as the way the storage engine stores the data. For example, an integer requires 4 bytes to store, but when written in ASCII, it can require up to 12 characters. You can often compress the files effectively and get a smaller backup, but this uses more CPU resources, resulting in a longer recovery time. (Logical backups are typically smaller than raw backups if there are a lot of indexes.)

- Dumping and restoring your data isn't always guaranteed to result in the same data. Floating-point representation problems, bugs, and so on can cause trouble, though this is rare.

- Restoring from a logical backup requires MySQL to load and interpret the statements, convert them to the storage format, and rebuild indexes, all of which is very slow.

The biggest disadvantages are really the cost of dumping the data from MySQL and the cost of loading data back in via SQL statements. If you use logical backups, it is essential to test the time required for restoring the data.

### Raw backups

Raw backups have the following benefits:

- Raw file backups simply require you to copy the desired files somewhere else for backup. The raw files don't require any extra work to generate.

- Raw backups are very portable across platforms, operating systems, and MySQL versions. (Logical dumps are, too. We're simply pointing this out to alleviate any concerns you might have.)

- It can be faster to restore raw backups because the MySQL server doesn't have to execute any SQL or build indexes. If you have InnoDB tables that don't fit entirely in the server's memory, it can be much faster to restore raw files—an order of magnitude or more. In fact, one of the scariest things about logical backups is their unpredictable restore time.

Here are some disadvantages of raw backups:

- InnoDB's raw files are often far larger than the corresponding logical backups. The InnoDB tablespace typically has lots of unused space. Quite a bit of space is

---

4 In our experience, logical backups are generally smaller than raw backups, but they aren't always.

also used for purposes other than storing table data (the insert buffer, the rollback segment, etc.).

- Raw backups are not always portable across platforms, operating systems, and MySQL versions. Filename case sensitivity and floating-point formats are places where you might encounter trouble. You might not be able to move files to a system whose floating-point format is different (however, the vast majority of processors use the IEEE floating-point format).

Raw backups are generally easier and much more efficient.[5] You should not rely on raw backups for long-term retention or legal requirements, though; you must make logical backups at least periodically.

Don't consider a backup (especially a raw backup) to be good until you've tested it. For InnoDB, that means starting a MySQL instance and letting InnoDB recovery run, then running CHECK TABLES. You can skip this or just run *innochecksum* on the files, but we don't recommend it.

We suggest a blend of the two approaches: make raw copies, then start a MySQL server instance with the resulting data and run *mysqlcheck*. Then, at least periodically, dump the data with *mysqldump* to get a logical backup. This gives you the advantages of both approaches without unduly burdening the production server during the dump. It's especially convenient if you have the ability to take filesystem snapshots: you can take a snapshot, copy the snapshot to another server and release it, then test the raw files and perform a logical backup.

## What to Back Up

Your recovery requirements will dictate what you need to back up. The simplest strategy is to just back up your data and table definitions, but this is a bare-minimum approach. You generally need a lot more to recover a server for use in production. Here are some things you might consider including with your MySQL backups:

*Nonobvious data*

Don't forget data that's easy to overlook: your binary logs and InnoDB transaction logs, for example. Ideally, you should back up the entire data directory for MySQL together.

*Code*

A modern MySQL server can store a lot of code, such as triggers and stored procedures. If you back up the mysql database, you'll back up much of this code, but then it will be hard to restore a single database in its entirety because some of the

---

5 It's worth mentioning that raw backups can be more prone to errors; it's hard to beat the simplicity of *mysqldump*.

"data" in that database, such as stored procedures, will actually be stored in the `mysql` database.

*Server configuration*

If you have to recover from a real disaster—say you're building a server from scratch in a new data center after an earthquake—you'll appreciate having the server's configuration files included in the backup.

*Selected operating system files*

As with the server configuration, it's important to back up any external configuration that is essential to a production server. On a Unix server, this might include your *cron* jobs, user and group configurations, administrative scripts, and *sudo* rules.

These recommendations quickly translate into "back up everything" in many scenarios. If you have a lot of data, however, this can get expensive, and you might have to be smarter about how you do your backups. In particular, you might want to back up different data into different backups. For example, you can back up data, binary logs, and operating system and system configuration files separately.

## Incremental and Differential Backups

A common strategy for dealing with too much data is to do regular incremental or differential backups. The difference might be a little confusing, so let's clarify the terms: a *differential backup* is a backup of everything that has changed since the last full backup, whereas an *incremental backup* contains everything that has changed since the last backup of any type.

For example, suppose that you do a full backup every Sunday. On Monday, you do a differential backup of everything that has changed since Sunday. On Tuesday, you have two choices: you can back up everything that's changed since Sunday (differential), or you can back up only the data that has changed since Monday's backup (incremental).

Both differential and incremental backups are partial backups: they generally don't contain a full data set, because some data almost certainly hasn't changed. Partial backups are often desirable for their savings in overhead on the server, backup time, and backup space. Some partial backups don't really reduce the overhead on the server, though. Percona XtraBackup and MySQL Enterprise Backup, for example, still scan every block of data on the server, so they don't save a lot of overhead, although they do save a bit of wall-clock time, lots of CPU time for compression, and, of course, disk space.[6]

You can get pretty fancy with advanced backup techniques, but the more complex your solution is, the more risky it's likely to be. Beware of hidden dangers, such as multiple generations of backups that are tightly coupled to one another, because if one generation contains corruption, it can invalidate all of the others, too.

Here are some advanced backup ideas:

- Use the incremental backup features of Percona XtraBackup or MySQL Enterprise Backup.

- Back up your binary logs. You can also use FLUSH LOGS to begin a new binary log after each backup, then back up only new binary logs.

- If you have "lookup" tables that contain data such as lists of month names in various languages or abbreviations for states or regions, it can be a good idea to place them into a separate database, so you don't have to back them up all the time. An even better option would be to move these to code instead of a database.

- Don't back up rows that haven't changed. If a table is INSERT-only, such as a table that logs hits to a web page, you can add a TIMESTAMP column and back up only rows that have been inserted since the last backup. This works best in conjunction with *mysqldump*.

- Don't back up some data at all. Sometimes this makes a lot of sense—for example, if you have a data warehouse that's built from other data and is technically redundant, you can merely back up the data you used to build the warehouse instead of the data warehouse itself. This can be a good idea even if it's very slow to "recover" by rebuilding the warehouse from the original files. Avoiding the backups can add up over time to much greater savings than the potentially faster recovery time you'll gain by having a full backup. You can also opt not to back up some temporary data, such as tables that hold website session data.

- Back up everything, but send it to a destination that has data deduplication features, such as a ZFS filer.

The drawbacks of incremental backups include increased recovery complexity, increased risk, and a longer recovery time. If you can do full backups, we suggest that you do so for simplicity's sake.

---

6 A "true" incremental backup feature for Percona XtraBackup is in progress. It will be able to back up the blocks that have changed without needing to scan every block.

Regardless, you definitely need to do full backups occasionally; we suggest at least weekly. You can't expect to recover from a month's worth of incremental backups. Even a week is a lot of work and risk.

# Replication

The biggest advantage to backing up from a replica is that it doesn't interrupt the source or place extra load on it. This is a good reason to set up a replica server, even if you don't need it for load balancing or high availability. If money is a concern, you can always use the backup replica for other purposes, such as reporting—as long as you don't write to it and thus change the data you're trying to back up. The replica doesn't have to be dedicated to backups; it just has to be able to catch up to the source in time to make your next backup in the event that its other roles make it fall behind in replication at times.

When you make a backup from a replica, it's very wise to use GTIDs, as mentioned in Chapter 9. This avoids having to save all the information about the replication processes, such as the replica's position relative to the source. This is useful for cloning new replicas, reapplying binary logs to the source to get point-in-time recovery, promoting the replica to a source, and more. Also be sure that no temporary tables are open if you stop your replica because they might keep you from restarting replication.

As we mentioned in "Delayed Replication" on page 233 in Chapter 9, intentionally delaying replication on one of your replicas can be very useful for recovering from some disaster scenarios. Suppose you delay replication by an hour. If an unwanted statement runs on the source, you have an hour to notice it and stop the replica before it repeats the event from its relay log. You can then promote the replica to source and replay some relatively small number of log events, skipping the bad statements. This can be much faster than the point-in-time recovery technique we discuss later.

> The replica might not have the same data as the source. Many people assume replicas are exact copies of their source, but in our experience, data mismatches on replicas are common, and MySQL has no way to detect this problem. The only way to detect it is with a tool like Percona Toolkit's *pt-table-checksum*. The best way to prevent this is to use the super_read_only flag to ensure that only replication can write to replicas.
>
> Having a replicated copy of your data might help protect you from problems like disk meltdowns on the source, but there's no guarantee. Replication is *not* a backup.

# Managing and Backing Up Binary Logs

Your server's binary logs are one of the most important things you can back up. They are necessary for point-in-time recovery, and because they're usually smaller than your data, they're easier to back up frequently. If you have a backup of your data at some point and all the binary logs since then, you can replay the binary logs and "roll forward" changes made since the last full backup.

MySQL uses the binary log for replication, too. That means that your backup and recovery policy often interacts with your replication configuration. It's a good idea to back up binary logs frequently. If you can't afford to lose more than 30 minutes' worth of data, back them up at least every 30 minutes.

You'll need to decide on a log-expiration policy to keep MySQL from filling your disk with binary logs. How large your logs grow depends on your workload and the logging format (row-based logging results in larger log entries). We suggest you keep logs as long as they're useful, if possible. Keeping them is helpful for setting up replicas, analyzing your server's workload, auditing, and point-in-time recovery from your last full backup. Consider all of these needs when you decide how long you want to keep your logs.

A common setup is to use the `binlog_expire_logs_seconds` variable to tell MySQL to purge logs after a while. You should not remove these files by hand.

The `binlog_expire_logs_seconds` setting takes effect upon server startup or when MySQL rotates the binary log, so if your binary log never fills up and rotates, the server will not purge older entries. It decides which files to purge by looking at their modification times, not their contents.

# Backup and Recovery Tools

A variety of good and not-so-good backup tools are available. For raw backups, we recommend Percona XtraBackup. It's open source, widely used, and well documented. For logical backups, we prefer *mydumper*. Although *mysqldump* ships with MySQL, its single-threaded nature can make for some very long backup and restore times out of the box. *mydumper* has parallelism built in, which can make it much faster to get a logical backup.

## MySQL Enterprise Backup

This tool is part of a MySQL Enterprise subscription from Oracle. Using it does not require stopping MySQL, setting locks, or interrupting normal database activity (although it will cause some extra load on your server). It supports features like compressed backups, incremental backups, and streaming backups to another server. It is the "official" backup tool for MySQL.

## Percona XtraBackup

Percona XtraBackup is quite similar to MySQL Enterprise Backup in many ways, but it's open source and free. It supports features like streaming, incremental, compressed, and multithreaded (parallel) backup operations. It also has a variety of special features to reduce the impact of backups on heavily loaded systems.

Percona XtraBackup works by "tailing" the InnoDB logfiles in a background thread, then copying the InnoDB datafiles. This is a slightly involved process, with special checks to ensure that data is copied consistently. When all the datafiles are copied, the log-copying thread finishes, too. The result is a copy of all the data but at different points in time. The logs can now be applied to the datafiles, using InnoDB's crash recovery routines, to bring all of the datafiles into a consistent state. This is referred to as the *prepare* process. Once prepared, the backup is fully consistent and contains all committed transactions as of the ending point of the file-copy process. All of this happens completely externally to MySQL, so it doesn't need to connect to or access MySQL in any way.

## mydumper

Several current and former MySQL engineers created *mydumper* (*https://oreil.ly/i3AXj*) as a replacement for *mysqldump*, based on their years of experience. It is a multithreaded (parallel) backup and restore tool set for MySQL with a lot of nice features. Many people will probably find the speed of multithreaded backups and restores to be this tool's most attractive feature.

## mysqldump

Most people use the programs that ship with MySQL, so despite its shortcomings, the most common choice for creating logical backups of data and schemas is *mysqldump*. Refer to the official manual for details on how to use this tool.

# Backing Up Data

As with most things, there are better and worse ways to actually make a backup—and the obvious ways are sometimes not so good. The trick is to maximize your network, disk, and CPU capacity to make backups as fast as possible. This is a balancing act, and you'll have to experiment to find the "sweet spot."

## Logical SQL Backups

Logical SQL dumps are what most people are familiar with because they're what *mysqldump* creates by default. For example, dumping a small table with the default options will produce the following (abridged) output:

```
$ mysqldump test t1
-- [Version and host comments]
/*!40101 SET @OLD_CHARACTER_SET_CLIENT=@@CHARACTER_SET_CLIENT */;
-- [More version-specific comments to save options for restore]
--
-- Table structure for table `t1`
--

DROP TABLE IF EXISTS `t1`;
/*!40101 SET @saved_cs_client = @@character_set_client */;
/*!50503 SET character_set_client = utf8mb4 */;
CREATE TABLE `t1` (
 `a` int NOT NULL,
 PRIMARY KEY (`a`)
) ENGINE=InnoDB DEFAULT CHARSET=utf8mb4 COLLATE=utf8mb4_0900_ai_ci;
/*!40101 SET character_set_client = @saved_cs_client */;
--
-- Dumping data for table `t1`
--
LOCK TABLES `t1` WRITE;
/*!40000 ALTER TABLE `t1` DISABLE KEYS */;
INSERT INTO `t1` VALUES (1);
/*!40000 ALTER TABLE `t1` ENABLE KEYS */;
UNLOCK TABLES;
/*!40103 SET TIME_ZONE=@OLD_TIME_ZONE */;
/*!40101 SET SQL_MODE=@OLD_SQL_MODE */;
-- [More option restoration]
```

The dump file contains both the table structure and the data, all written out as valid SQL commands. The file begins with comments that set various MySQL options. These are present either to make the restore work more efficiently or for compatibility and correctness. Next, you can see the table's structure and then its data. Finally, the script resets the options it changed at the beginning of the dump.

The dump's output is executable for a restore operation. This is convenient, but *mysqldump*'s default options aren't great for making a huge backup.

*mysqldump* is not the only tool that can make SQL logical backups. You can also create them with *mydumper* or *phpMyAdmin*, for example. What we'd really like to point out here is not so much problems with any particular tool but rather the shortcomings of doing monolithic SQL logical backups in the first place. Here are the main problem areas:

*Schema and data stored together*
> Although this is convenient if you want to restore from a single file, it makes things difficult if you need to restore only one table or want to restore only the data. You can alleviate this concern by dumping twice—once for data, once for schema—but you'll still have the next problem.

*Huge SQL statements*
> It's a lot of work for the server to parse and execute all of the SQL statements. This is a very slow way to load data.

*A single huge file*
> Most text editors can't edit large files or files with very long lines. Although you can sometimes use command-line stream editors, such as *sed* or *grep*, to pull out the data you need, it's preferable to keep the files small.

*Logical backups are expensive*
> There are more efficient ways to get data out of MySQL than fetching it from the storage engine and sending it over the client/server protocol as a result set.

As you can see, logical backups can be difficult to make work for your environment. If you need to use logical backups, we strongly recommend that you look at *mydumper* to avoid the single-threaded nature and spend time measuring the impact on your database as you perform the backup.

## Filesystem Snapshots

Filesystem snapshots are a great way to make online backups. Snapshot-capable filesystems can create a consistent image of their contents at an instant in time, which you can then use to make a backup. Snapshot-capable filesystems and appliances include FreeBSD's filesystem, the ZFS filesystem, GNU/Linux's LVM, and many SAN systems and file-storage solutions, such as NetApp storage appliances. Some of the remotely attached disk options available in cloud providers offer disk snapshotting as well.

Don't confuse a snapshot with a backup. Taking a snapshot is simply a way of reducing the time for which locks must be held; after releasing the locks, you must copy the files to the backup. In fact, you can optionally take snapshots on InnoDB without even acquiring locks. We'll show you two ways to use LVM to make backups of an all-InnoDB system, with your choice of minimal or zero locking.

---

### Backup Myth #2: "My Snapshot Is My Backup"

A snapshot, whether it's an LVM, ZFS, or SAN snapshot, isn't a real backup because it doesn't contain a full copy of your data. Because snapshots are copy-on-write, they contain only the differences between the live copy of the data and the data at the point in time when the snapshot happened. If an unmodified block becomes corrupt in the live copy of the data, there's no good copy of that block that you can use for recovery, and every snapshot sees the same corrupted block that the live volume does. Use snapshots to "freeze" your data while you take a backup, but don't rely on the snapshot itself as a backup.

---

A snapshot can be a great way to make a backup for specific uses. One example is as a fallback in case of a problem during an upgrade. You can take a snapshot, upgrade, and, if there's a problem, just roll back to the snapshot. You can do the same thing for any operation that's uncertain and risky, such as altering a huge table (which will take an unknown amount of time).

## How LVM snapshots work

LVM uses copy-on-write technology to create a snapshot—that is, a logical copy of an entire volume at an instant in time. It's a little like MVCC in a database, except it keeps only one old version of the data.

Notice we didn't say a *physical* copy. A logical copy appears to contain all the same data as the volume you snapshotted, but initially it contains no data. Instead of copying the data to the snapshot, LVM simply notes the time at which you created the snapshot, then it reads the data from the original volume when you request it from the snapshot. So the initial copy is basically an instantaneous operation, no matter how large a volume you're snapshotting.

When something changes the data in the original volume, LVM copies the affected blocks to an area reserved for the snapshot before it writes any changes to them. LVM doesn't keep multiple "old versions" of the data, so additional writes to blocks that are changed in the original volume don't require any further work for the snapshot. In other words, only the first write to each block causes a copy-on-write to the reserved area.

Now, when you request these blocks in the snapshot, LVM reads the data from the copied blocks instead of from the original volume. This lets you continue to see the same data in the snapshot without blocking anything on the original volume. Figure 10-1 depicts this arrangement.

The snapshot creates a new logical device in the /dev directory, and you can mount this device just as you would mount any other.

You can theoretically snapshot an enormous volume and consume very little physical space with this technique. However, you need to set aside enough space to hold all the blocks you expect to be updated in the original volume while you hold the snapshot open. If you don't reserve enough copy-on-write space, the snapshot will run out of space, and the device will become unavailable. The effect is like unplugging an external drive: any backup job that's reading from the device will fail with an I/O error.

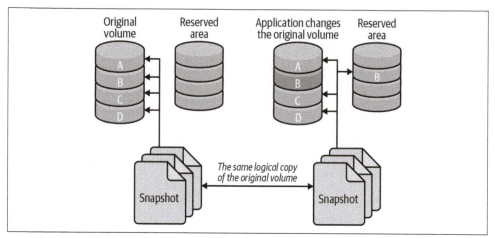

*Figure 10-1. How copy-on-write technology reduces the size needed for a volume snapshot*

### Prerequisites and configuration

It's almost trivial to create a snapshot, but you need to ensure that your system is configured in such a way that you can get a consistent copy of *all* the files you want to back up at a single instant in time. First, make sure your system meets these conditions:

- All InnoDB files (InnoDB tablespace files and InnoDB transaction logs) must be on a single logical volume (partition). You need absolute point-in-time consistency, and LVM can't take consistent snapshots of more than one volume at a time. (This is an LVM limitation; some other systems do not have this problem.)

- If you need to back up the table definitions too, the MySQL data directory must be in the same logical volume. If you use another method to back up table definitions, such as a schema-only backup into your version control system, you might not need to worry about this.

- You must have enough free space in the volume group to create the snapshot. How much you need will depend on your workload. When you set up your system, leave some unallocated space so that you'll have room for snapshots later.

LVM has the concept of a *volume group*, which contains one or more logical volumes. You can see the volume groups on your system as follows:

```
$ vgs
  VG #PV #LV #SN Attr   VSize   VFree
  vg  1   4   0 wz--n- 534.18G 249.18G
```

This output shows a volume group that has four logical volumes distributed across one physical volume, with about 250 GB free. The vgdisplay command gives more detail if you need it. Now let's take a look at the logical volumes on the system:

```
$ lvs
LV VG Attr LSize Origin Snap% Move Log Copy%
home vg -wi-ao 40.00G
mysql vg -wi-ao 225.00G
tmp vg -wi-ao 10.00G
var vg -wi-ao 10.00G
```

The output shows that the mysql volume has 225 GB of space. The device name is */dev/vg/mysql*. This is just a name, even though it looks like a filesystem path. To add to the confusion, there's a symbolic link from the file of the same name to the real device node at */dev/mapper/vg-mysql*, which you can see with the ls and mount commands:

```
$ ls -l /dev/vg/mysql
lrwxrwxrwx 1 root root 20 Sep 19 13:08 /dev/vg/mysql -> /dev/mapper/vg-mysql
# mount | grep mysql
/dev/mapper/vg-mysql on /var/lib/mysql
```

Armed with this information, you're ready to create a filesystem snapshot.

### Creating, mounting, and removing an LVM snapshot

You can create the snapshot with a single command. You just need to decide where to put it and how much space to allocate for copy-on-write. Don't hesitate to use more space than you think you'll need. LVM doesn't use the space you specify right away; it just reserves it for future use, so there's no harm in reserving lots of space, unless you need to leave space for other snapshots at the same time.

Let's create a snapshot just for practice. We'll give it 16 GB of space for copy-on-write, and we'll call it backup_mysql:

```
$ lvcreate --size 16G --snapshot --name backup_mysql /dev/vg/mysql
Logical volume "backup_mysql" created
```

 We deliberately called the volume backup_mysql instead of mysql_backup so that tab completion would be unambiguous. This helps avoid the possibility of tab completion causing you to delete the mysql volume group accidentally.

Now let's see the newly created volume's status:

```
$ lvs
LV VG Attr LSize Origin Snap% Move Log Copy%
backup_mysql vg swi-a- 16.00G mysql 0.01
home vg -wi-ao 40.00G
```

```
mysql vg owi-ao 225.00G
tmp   vg -wi-ao 10.00G
var   vg -wi-ao 10.00G
```

Notice that the snapshot's attributes are different from the original device's and that the display shows a little extra information: its origin and how much of the allocated 16 GB is currently being used for copy-on-write. It's a good idea to monitor this as you make your backup, so you can see if the device is getting full and is about to fail. You can monitor your device's status interactively or with a monitoring system, such as Nagios:

```
$ watch 'lvs | grep backup'
```

As you saw from the output of mount earlier, the mysql volume contains a filesystem. That means the snapshot volume does too, and you can mount and use it just like any other filesystem:

```
$ mkdir /tmp/backup
$ mount /dev/mapper/vg-backup_mysql /tmp/backup
$ ls -l /tmp/backup
total 188880
-rw-r-----. 1 mysql mysql 56 Jul 30 22:16 auto.cnf
-rw-r-----. 1 mysql mysql 475 Jul 30 22:31 binlog.000001
-rw-r-----. 1 mysql mysql 156 Jul 30 22:31 binlog.000002
-rw-r-----. 1 mysql mysql 32 Jul 30 22:31 binlog.index
-rw-------. 1 mysql mysql 1676 Jul 30 22:16 ca-key.pem
-rw-r--r--. 1 mysql mysql 1120 Jul 30 22:16 ca.pem
-rw-r--r--. 1 mysql mysql 1120 Jul 30 22:16 client-cert.pem
-rw-------. 1 mysql mysql 1676 Jul 30 22:16 client-key.pem
... omitted ...
```

This is just for practice, so we'll unmount and remove the snapshot now with the lvremove command:

```
$ umount /tmp/backup
$ rmdir /tmp/backup
$ lvremove --force /dev/vg/backup_mysql
  Logical volume "backup_mysql" successfully removed
```

## Lock-free InnoDB backups with LVM snapshots

When you run MySQL 8+ with only InnoDB tables, using GTIDs and full ACID-compliant mode, making a backup is incredibly easy. While MySQL is running, simply take a snapshot, mount the snapshot, and then copy the files to your backup location. There's no need to lock any files, capture any output, or do anything special. Restoring the files from one of these backups will perform InnoDB crash recovery, and the GTID settings will already know which transactions have been processed.

### Planning for LVM backups

The most important thing to plan for is allocating enough space for the snapshot. We take the following approach:

- Remember that LVM needs to copy each modified block to the snapshot only once. When MySQL writes a block in the original volume, it copies the block to the snapshot, then makes a note of the copied block in its exception table. Future writes to this block will not cause any further copies to the snapshot.

- If you use only InnoDB, consider how InnoDB writes data. Because it writes all data twice, at least half of InnoDB's write I/O goes to the doublewrite buffer, log-files, and other relatively small areas on disk. These reuse the same disk blocks over and over, so they'll have an initial impact on the snapshot, but after that, they'll stop causing writes to the snapshot.

- Next, estimate how much of your I/O will be writing to blocks that haven't yet been copied to the snapshot, as opposed to modifying the same data again and again. Be generous with your estimate.

- Use *vmstat* or *iostat* to gather statistics on how many blocks your server writes per second.

- Measure (or estimate) how long it will take to copy your backup to another location: in other words, how long you need to keep the LVM snapshot open.

Let's suppose you've estimated that half of your writes will cause writes to the snapshot's copy-on-write space, and your server writes 10 MB per second. If it takes an hour (3,600 seconds) to copy the snapshot to another server, you will need $1/2 \times 10$ MB $\times 3,600$ or 18 GB of space for the snapshot. Err on the side of caution and add some extra space as well.

Sometimes it's easy to calculate how much data will change while you keep the snapshot open.

### Other uses and alternatives

You can use snapshots for more than just backups. For example, as mentioned previously, they can be a useful way to take a "checkpoint" just before a potentially dangerous action. Some systems let you promote the snapshot to the original filesystem. This makes it easy to roll back to the point at which you took the snapshot.

Filesystem snapshots aren't the only way to get an instantaneous copy of your data, either. Another option is a RAID split: if you have a three-disk software RAID mirror, for example, you can remove one disk from the mirror and mount it separately. There's no copy-on-write penalty, and it's easy to promote this kind of "snapshot" to be the source's copy if necessary. After adding the disk back to the RAID set, however, it will have to be resynced. There's no free lunch, sadly.

## Percona XtraBackup

XtraBackup is one of the most popular solutions for backing up MySQL, and for good reason. It is very configurable, including ways to back up compressed, encrypted files.

### How XtraBackup works

InnoDB is a crash-safe storage engine. If MySQL experiences a crash, it uses a crash recovery mode, which is based on redo logs, to bring your data back online correctly. Percona XtraBackup is based on this design. When you take a backup with Percona XtraBackup, it records the log sequence number (LSN) and uses that to perform crash recovery on your backed-up files. It also incorporates locking at specific points to ensure that data about replication is consistent with the data. For a more detailed explanation, refer to the XtraBackup documentation (*https://oreil.ly/8JWIB*).

Here's a sample XtraBackup process:

```
$ xtrabackup --backup --target-dir=/backups/

xtrabackup version 8.0.25-17 based on MySQL server 8.0.25 Linux (x86_64)
(revision id: d27028b)
Using server version 8.0.25-15
210821 17:01:40 Executing LOCK TABLES FOR BACKUP…
```

Up to here, we can see that XtraBackup has determined the running version of MySQL. This helps it determine what capabilities it has and how it should back up files. In our case, the LOCK TABLES FOR BACKUP command is available and is how XtraBackup will get a lock on tables:

```
210821 17:01:41 [01] Copying ./ibdata1 to /backups/ibdata1
210821 17:01:41 [01] ...done
210821 17:01:41 [01] Copying ./sys/sys_config.ibd to /backups/sys/sys_config.ibd
210821 17:01:41 [01] ...done
210821 17:01:41 [01] Copying ./test/t1.ibd to /backups/test/t1.ibd
210821 17:01:41 [01] ...done
210821 17:01:41 [01] Copying ./foo/t1.ibd to /backups/foo/t1.ibd
210821 17:01:41 [01] ...done
210821 17:01:41 [01] Copying ./sakila/actor.ibd to /backups/sakila/actor.ibd
210821 17:01:41 [01] ...done
```

XtraBackup is now copying the files from the source to destination:

```
210821 17:01:42 Finished backing up non-InnoDB tables and files
210821 17:01:42 Executing FLUSH NO_WRITE_TO_BINLOG BINARY LOGS
210821 17:01:42 Selecting LSN and binary log position from p_s.log_status
210821 17:01:42 [00] Copying /var/lib/mysql/binlog.40 to /backups/binlog.04
up to position 156
210821 17:01:42 [00] ...done
210821 17:01:42 [00] Writing /backups/binlog.index
210821 17:01:42 [00] ...done
```

```
210821 17:01:42 [00] Writing /backups/xtrabackup_binlog_info
210821 17:01:42 [00] ...done
```

Once finished copying files, it collects replication information:

```
210821 17:01:42 Executing FLUSH NO_WRITE_TO_BINLOG ENGINE LOGS...
xtrabackup: The latest check point (for incremental): '35005805'
xtrabackup: Stopping log copying thread at LSN 35005815.
210821 17:01:42 >> log scanned up to (35005825)
Starting to parse redo log at lsn = 35005460
210821 17:01:43 Executing UNLOCK TABLES
210821 17:01:43 All tables unlocked
```

Now XtraBackup has determined the latest checkpoint for InnoDB. This will help it apply the writes that happened during the backup. It releases the previous LOCK TABLES FOR BACKUP command with UNLOCK TABLES:

```
210821 17:01:43 [00] Copying ib_buffer_pool to /backups/ib_buffer_pool
210821 17:01:43 [00] ...done
210821 17:01:43 Backup created in directory '/backups/'
MySQL binlog position: filename 'binlog.000004', position '156'
210821 17:01:43 [00] Writing /backups/backup-my.cnf
210821 17:01:43 [00] ...done
210821 17:01:43 [00] Writing /backups/xtrabackup_info
210821 17:01:43 [00] ...done
xtrabackup: Transaction log of lsn (35005795) to (35005835) was copied.
210821 17:01:44 completed OK!
```

The last steps are to record the LSN, copy over a buffer pool dump, and write out the final files. One is a copy of the *my.cnf* file, and the *xtrabackup_info* file contains metadata about the backup, like the MySQL UUID, versions of the server, and XtraBackup.

## Example usage

We've highlighted some basic recipes for how to use XtraBackup in common ways, but a few notes before that:

- Your MySQL installation should be secured with a password. Make sure you use the --user and --password options to specify an account with enough permissions to make backups.

- XtraBackup is also very verbose in its output. We've trimmed the output to highlight the most important parts of each use case.

- As always, review the official manual for Percona XtraBackup before running any commands here, as syntax and options may change. Even though we're not aware of any data loss associated with this tool, you should test on a nonproduction backup before trying with your critical data.

**Basic backup to directory.**   The first method we want to show is how you can use Xtra-Backup to make a full backup of your data into another directory. This allows you to choose what you do with the data afterward, which could be another disk, a directory on the same disk, or a mounted file share on a larger backup server. Keep in mind, doing this kind of full backup will require the appropriate space available to copy the files.

Here is the most basic usage for XtraBackup, specifying the mode (backup) and where to back up the files (`target-dir`):

```
$ xtrabackup --backup --target-dir=/backups/
```

Once you execute, the output will look similar to that under "How XtraBackup works" on page 278. If successful, the */backups* directory will contain a complete copy of your data.

**Streaming backup.**   Copying all files into a new directory may not be the most ideal use case. Sometimes it's easier to keep multiple backups in a directory. This is where the streaming-backup option can be useful. Streaming allows you to write the backup out as a single file:

```
$ xtrabackup --backup --stream=xbstream > /backups/backup.xbstream
```

In this usage, we've still specified the `backup` mode and removed the `target-dir` option, since output will be to `STDOUT`. We then redirected it to a file.

Note that you could also use a Bash shell command with date to include the time-stamp in the output filename, like this:

```
$ xtrabackup --backup --stream=xbstream > /backups/backup-$(date +%F).xbstream
```

This will run through the entire backup process as before, with <STDOUT> being used as the destination. The contents will be written to the *xbstream* file in */backups*.

**Backup with compression.**   As we noted previously, you'll need to have enough space to make an entire copy of your datafiles or enough space for the single *xbstream* file. One common option to ease the space requirement is to use the compression feature of XtraBackup:

```
$ xtrabackup --backup --compress --stream=xbstream > /backups/backup-
compressed.xbstream
```

You will notice that instead of showing "Streaming" for each table, it now reports "Compressing and streaming." In our testing, we had loaded the Sakila Sample Database and observed a 94 MB uncompressed *xbstream* file turn into a 6.5 MB compressed one.

**Backup with encryption.**   The last example we want to cover is using encryption as part of your backup strategy. Using encryption will use more CPU, and your backup process will take longer; however, this could be an acceptable trade-off given that a backup is an easy target to get a lot of data with one file. We're again using the backup mode and streaming, but we're using `encrypt` with a cipher and `encrypt-key-file` to point to where the key is:

```
$ xtrabackup --backup --encrypt=AES256 --encrypt-key-
file=/safe/key/location/encrypt.key --stream=xbstream > /backups/backup-
encrypted.xbstream
```

Our output changed again, indicating "Encrypting and streaming" for each file.

Note that you can also use `--encrypt-key` and specify it on the command line. We discourage doing this because the key will be exposed in the process list or as part of the */proc* filesystem on Linux.

**Other important flags.**   One of the aspects you'll want to pay attention to is how long it takes your backup to complete. To help with this, take a look at the `--parallel` and `-compress-threads` options. Using these will increase the CPU usage but should reduce the overall time it takes to back up. Encryption also has a similar parallelization option.

If you have a large number of databases and tables, look at `--rsync` to optimize the file-copy process.

# Recovering from a Backup

How you recover your data depends on how you backed it up. You might need to take some or all of the following steps:

1. Stop the MySQL server.
2. Take notes on the server's configuration and file permissions.
3. Move the data from the backup into the MySQL data directory.
4. Make configuration changes.
5. Change file permissions.
6. Restart the server with limited access, and wait for it to start fully.
7. Reload logical backup files.
8. Examine and replay binary logs.
9. Verify what you've restored.
10. Restart the server with full access.

We demonstrate how to do each of these steps as needed in the following sections. We also add notes specific to certain backup methods or tools in sections about those methods or tools later in this chapter.

 If there's a chance you'll need the current versions of your files, *don't replace them with the files from the backup*. For example, if your backup includes the binary logs and you need to replay binary logs for point-in-time recovery, don't overwrite the current binary logs with older copies from the backup. Rename them or move them elsewhere if necessary.

During recovery, it's often important to make MySQL inaccessible to everything except the recovery process. We like to start MySQL with the `--skip-networking` and `--socket=/tmp/mysql_recover.sock` options to ensure that it is unavailable to existing applications until we've checked it and brought it back online. This is especially important for logical backups, which are loaded in pieces.

## Restoring Logical Backups

If you're restoring logical backups instead of raw files, you need to use the MySQL server itself to load the data back into the tables, as opposed to using the operating system to simply copy files into place.

Before you load that dump file, however, take a moment to consider how large it is, how long it'll take to load, and anything you might want to do before you start, such as notifying your users or disabling part of your application. Disabling binary logging might be a good idea, unless you need to replicate the restoration to a replica: a huge dump file is hard enough for the server to load, and writing it to the binary log adds even more (possibly unnecessary) overhead. Loading huge files also has consequences for some storage engines. For example, it's not a good idea to load 100 GB of data into InnoDB in a single transaction because of the huge rollback segment that will result. You should load in manageable chunks and commit the transaction after each chunk.

There are two kinds of restoration you might do, which correspond to the two kinds of logical backups you can make.

If you have a SQL dump, the file will contain executable SQL. All you need to do is run it. Assuming you backed up the Sakila Sample Database and schema into a single file, the following is a typical command you might use to restore it:

```
$ mysql < sakila-backup.sql
```

You can also load the file from within the *mysql* command-line client with the `SOURCE` command. Although this is mostly a different way of doing the same thing, it makes some things easier. For example, if you're an administrative user in MySQL, you can turn off binary logging of the statements you'll execute from within your client connection and then load the file without needing to restart the MySQL server:

```
SET SQL_LOG_BIN = 0;
SOURCE sakila-backup.sql;
SET SQL_LOG_BIN = 1;
```

If you use SOURCE, be aware that an error won't abort a batch of statements, as it will by default when you redirect the file into *mysql*.

If you compressed the backup, don't separately decompress and load it. Instead, decompress and load it in a single operation. This is much faster:

```
$ gunzip -c sakila-backup.sql.gz | mysql
```

What if you want to restore only a single table (for example, the actor table)? If your data has no line breaks, it's not hard to restore the data if the schema is already in place:

```
$ grep 'INSERT INTO `actor`' sakila-backup.sql | mysql sakila
```

Or, if the file is compressed:

```
$ gunzip -c sakila-backup.sql.gz | grep 'INSERT INTO `actor`'| mysql sakila
```

If you need to create the table as well as restore the data and you have the entire database in a single file, you'll have to edit the file. This is why some people like to dump each table into its own file. Most editors can't deal with huge files, especially if they're compressed. Besides, you don't want to actually edit the file itself; you just want to extract the relevant lines, so you'll probably have to do some command-line work. It's easy to use *grep* to pull out only the INSERT statements for a given table, as we did in the previous commands, but it's harder to get the CREATE TABLE statement. Here's a *sed* script that extracts the paragraph you need:

```
$ sed -e '/./{H;$!d;}' -e 'x;/CREATE TABLE `actor`/!d;q' sakila-backup.sql
```

That's pretty cryptic, we admit. If you have to do this kind of work to restore data, your backups are poorly designed. With a little planning, it's possible to prevent a situation in which you're panicked and trying to figure out how *sed* works. Just back up each table into its own file, or, better yet, back up the data and schema separately.

## Restoring Raw Files from Snapshot

Restoring raw files tends to be pretty straightforward, which is another way of saying there aren't many options. This can be a good or a bad thing depending on your recovery requirements. The usual procedure is simply to copy the files into place.

If you're restoring a traditional InnoDB setup, where all tables are stored in a single tablespace, you'll have to shut down MySQL, copy or move the files into place, and then restart. You also need to ensure that InnoDB's transaction logfiles match its tablespace files. If the files don't match—for example, if you replace the tablespace files but not the transaction logfiles—InnoDB will refuse to start. This is one reason it's crucial to back up the transaction log along with the datafiles.

If you're using the InnoDB file-per-table feature (`innodb_file_per_table`), InnoDB stores the data and indexes for each table in an *.ibd* file. You can back up and restore individual tables by copying these files, and you can do it while the server is running, but it's not very simple. The individual files are not independent from InnoDB as a whole. Each *.ibd* file has internal information that tells InnoDB how the file is related to the main (shared) tablespace. When you restore such a file, you have to tell InnoDB to "import" the file.

There are many restrictions on this process, which you can read about in the MySQL manual section on using per-table tablespaces. The biggest is that you can only restore a table to the server from which you backed it up. It's not impossible to back up and restore tables in this configuration, but it's trickier than you might think.

All this complexity means that restoring raw files can be very tedious, and it's easy to get it wrong. A good rule of thumb is that the harder and more complex your recovery procedure becomes, the more you need to protect yourself with logical backups as well. It's always a good idea to have a logical backup, in case something goes wrong and you can't convince MySQL to use your raw backups.

## Restoring with Percona XtraBackup

In the section "How XtraBackup works" on page 278, we mentioned that it uses InnoDB's crash-recovery process to take safe backups. This means that for us to use files that were backed up with XtraBackup, we need to go through additional steps.

If you used a streaming backup, you'll need to unpack the *xbstream* file first. For *xbstream*, you can use the `xbstream` command to extract:

```
$ xbstream -x < backup.xbstream
```

This will extract all files to your current location, or you can use the `-C` option to change to a specific directory beforehand. If you used compression or encryption, you can use similar options to reverse the process. For a compressed file, use `--decompress`, and for encryption, use `--decrypt` while specifying the `--encrypt-key-file` location:

```
$ xbstream -x --decompress < backup-compressed.xbstream

$ xbstream -x --decrypt --encrypt-key-file=/safe/key/location/encrypt.key
  < backup-encrypted.xbstream
```

Once complete, the next step is to prepare the files. Preparing is the process that actually performs the crash-recovery actions and ensures that you're recovering all data:

```
$ xtrabackup --prepare --target-dir=/restore
```

 If you're not using streaming mode, you can perform the prepare phase after you make the backup. This will result in backing up a prepared backup and reduce the amount of work you need to do when it comes time to restore.

Once completed and successful, you're now ready to use these files to start MySQL:

```
$ xtrabackup --move-back --target-dir=/restore
```

 You can use the --copy-back or --move-back flags with xtra backup to copy or move the files into place correctly.

XtraBackup will automatically detect your data-dir variable from your MySQL installation and move the files to the correct location.

## Starting MySQL After Restoring Raw Files

There are a few things you'll need to do *before* you start the MySQL server you're recovering.

The first and most important thing, and one of the easiest to forget, is to check your server's configuration and make sure the restored files have the correct owner and permissions before you try to start the MySQL server. These attributes must be exactly right, or MySQL might not start. The attributes vary from system to system, so check your notes to see exactly what you'll need to set. You typically want the *mysql* user and group to own the files and directories, which you want to be readable and writable by that user and group but no others.

We also suggest watching the MySQL error log while the server starts. On a Unix-style system, you can watch the file like this:

```
$ tail -f /var/log/mysql/mysql.err
```

The exact location of the error log will vary. Once you're monitoring the file, you can start the MySQL server and watch for errors. If all goes well, you'll have a nicely recovered server once MySQL starts.

Watching the error log is even more important in newer MySQL versions. Even if the server seems to start without trouble, you should run `SHOW TABLE STATUS` in each database, then check the error log again.

## Summary

Everyone knows that they need backups, but not everyone realizes that they need recoverable backups. There are many ways to design backups that contradict your recovery requirements. To help avoid this problem, we suggest that you define and document your RPO and RTO, and use those requirements when choosing a backup system.

It's also important to test recovery on a routine basis and ensure that it works. It's easy to set up *mysqldump* and let it run every night without realizing that your data has grown over time to the point where it might take days or weeks to import again. The worst time to find out how long your recovery will take is when you actually need it. A backup that completes in hours can literally take weeks to restore, depending on your hardware, schema, indexes, and data.

Don't fall into the trap of thinking that a replica is a backup. It's a less intrusive source for taking a backup, but it's not a backup. The same is true of your RAID volume, SAN, and filesystem snapshots. Make sure that your backups can pass the `DROP TABLE` test (or the "I got hacked" test), as well as the test of losing your data center. And if you take backups from a replica, be sure that your replicas are consistent by rebuilding them from your source and enforcing `super_read_only` from that point forward.

Hands down, our preferred way to take backups is to use Percona XtraBackup for raw backups and *mydumper* for logical backups. Both techniques let you take nonintrusive binary (raw) backups of your data, which you can then verify by starting a *mysqld* instance and checking the tables. Sometimes you can even kill two birds with one stone: test recovery every single day by restoring the backup to your development or staging server. You can also dump the data from that instance to create a logical backup. We also like to back up binary logs and to keep enough generations of backups and binary logs that we can perform recovery or set up a new replica even if the most recent backup is unusable.

# Scaling MySQL

Running MySQL in a personal project, or even in a young company, is very different from running it in a business with an established market and "hockey stick growth." In a high-velocity business setting, traffic can grow orders of magnitude year over year, the environment becomes more complex, and the accompanying data needs accelerate rapidly. Scaling up MySQL is very different from other types of servers largely because of the stateful nature of the data. Compare this to a web server, where the widely accepted model of adding more behind a load balancer is typically all you need to do.

In this chapter, we explain what scaling means and walk you through the different axes where you may need to scale. We explore why read scaling is essential and show you how to accomplish it safely, with strategies like queuing for making scaling writes more predictable. Finally, we cover sharding data sets to scale writes using tools like ProxySQL and Vitess. By the end of this chapter, you should be able to identify what seasonal pattern your system has, how to scale reads, and how to scale writes.

## What Is Scaling?

*Scaling* is the system's ability to support growing traffic. The criteria for whether a system scales well or scales poorly can be measured by cost and simplicity. If it is excessively expensive or complicated to increase your system's ability to scale, you likely will expend significantly more effort remediating this as you hit limitations.

*Capacity* is a related concept. The system's capacity is the amount of work it can perform in a given amount of time.[1] However, capacity must be qualified. The system's maximum throughput is not the same as its capacity. Most benchmarks measure a system's maximum throughput, but you can't push real systems that hard. If you do, performance will degrade, and response times will become unacceptably large and variable. We define the system's actual capacity as the throughput it can achieve while still delivering acceptable performance.

Capacity and scalability are independent of performance. You can compare it to cars on a highway:

- The system is the highway and all the lanes and cars in it.
- Performance is how fast the cars are.
- Capacity is the number of lanes times the maximum safe speed.
- Scalability is the degree to which you can add more cars and more lanes without slowing traffic.

In this analogy, scalability depends on factors like how well the interchanges are designed, how many cars have accidents or break down, and whether the cars drive at different speeds or change lanes a lot—but generally, scalability does not depend on how powerful the cars' engines are. This is not to say that performance doesn't matter, because it does. We're just pointing out that systems can be scalable even if they aren't high performance.

From the 50,000-foot view, scalability is the ability to add capacity by adding resources.

Even if your MySQL architecture is scalable, your application might not be. If it's hard to increase capacity for any reason, your application isn't scalable overall. We previously defined capacity in terms of throughput, but it's worth looking at capacity from the same 50,000-foot view. From this vantage point, capacity simply means the ability to handle load, and it's useful to think of load from several different angles:

*Quantity of data*
   The sheer volume of data your application can accumulate is one of the most common scaling challenges. This is particularly an issue for many of today's web applications, which never delete any data. Social networking sites, for example, typically never delete old messages or comments.

---

1 In the physical sciences, work per unit of time is called *power*, but in computing, "*power*" is such an overloaded term that it's ambiguous and we avoid it. However, a precise definition of *capacity* is the system's maximum power output.

*Number of users*

Even if each user has only a small amount of data, if you have a lot of users, it adds up—and the data size can grow disproportionately faster than the number of users. Many users generally means more transactions too, and the number of transactions might not be proportional to the number of users. Finally, many users (and more data) can mean increasingly complex queries, especially if queries depend on the number of relationships among users. (The number of relationships is bounded by $(N \times (N - 1)) / 2$, where $N$ is the number of users.)

*User activity*

Not all user activity is equal, and user activity is not constant. If your users suddenly become more active—because of a new feature they like, for example—your load can increase significantly. User activity isn't just a matter of the number of page views, either. The same number of page views can cause more work if the part of the site that requires a lot of work to generate becomes more popular. Some users are much more active than others, too: they might have many more friends, messages, or photos than the average user.

*Size of related data sets*

If there are relationships among users, the application might need to run queries and computations on entire groups of related users. This is more complex than just working with individual users and their data. Social networking sites often face challenges due to popular groups or users who have many friends.

Scaling challenges can come in many forms. In the next section, we talk about how to determine where your bottleneck is and what you can do about it.

# Read- Versus Write-Bound Workloads

One of the first things you should examine when thinking about scaling your database architecture is whether you are scaling a *read-bound* workload or a *write-bound* workload. A read-bound workload is one where the amount of read traffic (SELECT) is overwhelming the capacity of your server. A write-bound workload overwhelms the capacity of your server to serve DML (INSERT, UPDATE, DELETE). Understanding which you are hitting involves understanding your workload.

## Understanding Your Workload

A database workload is many things. First, it's your capacity, or as we mentioned before, the measure of work over time. For databases, this usually boils down to queries per second. One definition of workload could be how many QPS the system can perform. Don't be disillusioned by this, however. One thousand QPS at 20% CPU doesn't always mean you can add four thousand more QPS. Not every query is created equal.

Queries come in all forms: reads, writes, primary key lookups, subqueries, joins, bulk inserts, and so forth. Each has a cost associated with it. This cost is measured in CPU time, or latency. When a query waits longer on a disk to return information, that time is added to the cost.[2] It is important to understand the capacity of your resources. How many CPUs do you have, what are the read and write IOPS and throughput limitations of your disk, and what network throughput do you have? Each of these will have their own influence on latency, which directly relates to your workload.

A workload is the blend of all types of queries and their latencies. It would be more fair to say that, if we process one thousand QPS at 20% CPU, we can add four thousand more QPS *as long as their latencies are the same*.[3] If we introduce four thousand more queries and we hit a disk IOPS bottleneck, the latency of all reads goes up.

If the only metrics you have access to are basic system ones, like CPU, memory, and disk, it can be nearly impossible to understand which of these you are hitting. You will want to determine what your read versus write performance is. We provided an example of this in "Examining Read Versus Write Performance" on page 62 in Chapter 3. Using that example, you can determine the latency of reads versus writes. If you trend these numbers over time, you can see if your read or write latencies are increasing and, consequently, where you might be bound.

## Read-Bound Workloads

Assume that, when you began designing your product, you took the shortcut of using one source host for all database traffic. Adding more application nodes may scale the clients serving requests but will ultimately be capped by the ability of your one-source database host to respond to these read requests. The primary indicator of this is CPU utilization. High CPU means the server is spending all of its time processing queries. The higher CPU utilization gets, the more latency you will see in queries. This isn't the only indicator, however. You can also see heavy disk read IOPS or throughput, indicating that you are going to disk very often or for large numbers of rows read from disk.

You can initially improve this by adding indexes, optimizing queries, and caching data you can cache. Once you run out of improvements, you will be left with a read-bound workload and this is where scaling read traffic using replicas comes in. We will discuss later in this chapter how to scale your reads using read replica pools, how to run health checks for these pools, and what pitfalls to avoid when you start using that architecture.

---

2 We're choosing to ignore the complexities of multiple CPUs and context switching for simplicity's sake in this explanation.

3 This is still not entirely accurate because as CPU approaches 100%, latency increases, and you will not be able to add four thousand more queries.

## Write-Bound Workloads

You may also be encountering a write-bound load. Here are some examples of a write-bound database load:

- Perhaps signups are growing exponentially.
- It is peak ecommerce season, and sales are growing, along with the number of orders to track.
- It is election season, and you have a lot of campaign communication going out.

All of these are business use cases that lead to exponentially more database writes that you now have to scale. Again, a single-source database, even if you can scale it vertically for some time, can only go so far. When the bottleneck is the write volume, you have to start thinking about ways to split your data so that you can accept writes in parallel on separate subsets. We will talk about how to shard for write scaling later in this chapter as well.

It's logical at this point to ask, "What if I'm seeing both types of growth?" It is important to inspect your schema closely and identify whether there is a subset of tables growing faster in reads versus another subset growing in write needs. Trying to scale a database cluster for both at the same time is asking for a lot of pain and incidents. We recommend separating tables in different functional clusters to scale reads and writes independently; this is a prerequisite for scaling read traffic with read pools far more effectively.

Now that you have determined whether you have a read- or write-bound load, we discuss how you can help guide this functional splitting of data in an effective manner.

# Functional Sharding

Splitting your data based on its "function" in the business is a context-heavy task that requires a deep understanding of what the data is. This goes hand in hand with popular software architecture paradigms like service-oriented architecture (SOA) and microservices. Not all functional approaches are created equal, and in a hyperbolic example, if you were to put each table in its own "functional" database, you could definitely make everything worse through too much fragmentation.

How do you approach splitting your large monolith/mixed concerns database into a sensible set of smaller clusters that help the business scale? Here are some guidelines to keep in mind:

- Do not split based on the structure of the engineering team. That will always change at some point.

- Do split tables based on business function. Tables that power account signups can be separate from tables that host existing customer settings, and tables that power a new feature should start off in their own database.

- Do not shy away from tackling spots where separate business concerns have been intermingled in the data and you need to advocate for not just data separation but also application refactoring and introducing API access across those boundaries. A common example we have seen is mixing customer identity with customer billing.

It is normal that at first there will be tables that clearly have their own business function and access pattern and therefore are an easy target for splitting off to a separate cluster, but that separation will get more nuanced as you get further along.

Now that we have split data in a thoughtful manner based on business function, let's talk about how to scale for read-bound loads using replica read pools.

## Scaling Reads with Read Pools

Replicas in a cluster can serve more than one purpose. First and foremost, they are candidates for failing over writes, either in a planned or unplanned manner, when the current source needs to be taken out of service for any reason. But since these replicas are also constantly running updates to match the data in the source, you can use them to serve read requests as well.

In Figure 11-1, we start by getting a visual of what this new setup with read replica pools looks like.

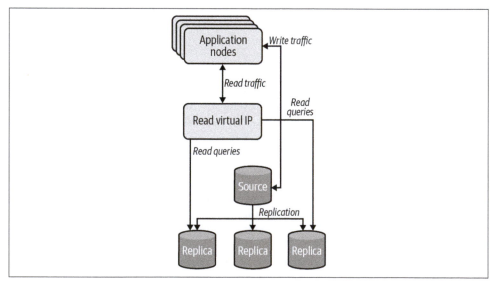

*Figure 11-1. Application nodes using a virtual IP to access read replicas*

For the sake of simplicity, we will pretend application nodes still fulfill write requests by directly connecting to the source database. We will later cover how connecting to the source node can scale better. Note, though, that the same application nodes connect to a virtual IP, which acts as a middle layer between them and the read replicas. This is a *replica read pool*, and this is how you spread the growing read load to more than one host. You may also note that not all replicas are in the pool. That is a common way to prevent different read workloads from affecting one another. If you have reporting processes or your backup process tends to consume all of the disk I/O resources and cause replication lag, you can leave out one or more replica nodes to fulfill those tasks and exclude it from the read pool that serves customer-facing traffic. Alternatively, you can augment your load balancer health check with a replication check that automatically removes the backup node that is behind from the pool and reintroduces it when it is caught up. The flexibility of turning your read replicas into interchangeable resources grows significantly when there is a single point the application talks to for reads and you can manage these resources seamlessly without impact on your customers.

Now that there is more than one database host serving read requests, there are a few things to consider for smooth production sailing:

- How do you route traffic to all these read replicas?
- How do you evenly distribute the load?
- How do you run health checks and remove unhealthy or lagged replicas to avoid serving stale data?
- How do you avoid accidentally removing all of the nodes, causing more damage to the application traffic?
- How do you manually remove a server proactively for maintenance?
- How do you add newly provisioned servers to your load balancer?
- What automated checks are in place to avoid adding a newly provisioned node to the load balancer before it is ready?
- Is your definition of "ready for a new node" specific enough?

A very common way to manage these read pools is to use a load balancer to run a virtual IP that acts as an intermediary for all traffic meant to go to the read replicas. Technologies for doing this include HAProxy, a hardware load balancer if you self-host, or a network load balancer if you are running in a public cloud environment. In the case of using HAProxy, all application hosts will connect to that one "frontend," and HAProxy takes care of directing those requests to one of the read replicas defined in the backend. Here is a sample HAProxy config file that defines a virtual IP frontend and maps that to multiple read replicas as a backend pool:

```
global
  log 127.0.0.1 local0 notice
  user haproxy
  group haproxy

defaults
  log global
  retries 2
  timeout connect 3000
  timeout server 5000
  timeout client 5000

listen mysql-readpool
  bind 127.0.0.1:3306
  mode tcp
  option mysql-check user haproxy_check
  balance leastconn
  server mysql-1 10.0.0.1:3306 check
  server mysql-2 10.0.0.2:3306 check
```

Typically, you use configuration management to auto populate such a file. There are a few things to note in this configuration. Balancing between your pool nodes with *leastconn* is the recommended way in MySQL. Random balancing such as *roundrobin* in times of elevated load will not help you use the hosts that are not overloaded. Make sure you have the proper database user created on your MySQL instances to run this health check, or else all your nodes will be marked unhealthy.

Tooling that facilitates sharding, such as Vitess and ProxySQL, can also act like a load balancer. We'll cover these tools toward the end of the chapter.

## Managing Configuration for Read Pools

Now that you have a "gate" between the application nodes and your replicas, you need a way to easily manage the nodes included, or not included, in this read pool using your load balancer of choice. You do not want this to be a manually managed configuration. You are already on a trajectory of scaling to lots of database instances, and managing configuration files manually will lead to mistakes, slower response times, and host failures, and it simply does not scale.

Service discovery is a good option to use here for automatically discovering what hosts can be in this list. This may mean deploying a service-discovery solution as part of your tech stack or relying on a managed service-discovery option at your cloud provider, if that is available. The important thing to be careful with here is to be very specific on the criteria that make a read replica qualify for this read pool. Ideally, you exclude the source node and potentially one or more replicas dedicated for reporting. But maybe you need something even more complex where the replicas are further segmented to serve different application read loads? We recommend at minimum three nodes per pool of replicas serving a specific purpose in addition to your backup/reporting server and the source node.

Whether you run your own service discovery[4] or use something offered by your cloud provider, you should be aware of the guarantees of that service. Here are some things to consider, whether you will be running service discovery or working with a team on it:

- How soon can it detect the failure of a host?
- How fast does that data propagate?
- When there is a database instance failure, how will the configuration refresh on your load balancer?
- Does the change of database members happen as a background process, or will it require severing existing connections?
- What happens if service discovery itself is down? Does that impair any new database connections or only impair making changes to load-balancer membership? Can you make changes manually at that point?

With flexibility comes complexity, and you must balance the two for optimal outcomes in production when failures happen. Your job here is to always tether your decisions to what SLIs and SLOs are being pursued and not to achieve a mythical 100% uptime goal.

Now that you know how to populate the configurations and update them as hosts come and go, it's time to talk about how to run health checks for the members of a replica read pool.

## Health Checks for Read Pools

At this point, you will need to consider what the acceptable criteria that deem a read replica healthy and ready to accept read traffic from the application are. These criteria can be as simple as "the database process is up and running, the port responds" but can become more complex, such as "the database is up, and replication lag needs to be no more than 30 seconds, and read queries need to be running at a latency no higher than 100 ms."

Check the state of the variables `read_only` and `super_read_only` to make sure that all the members in the read pool of your load balancer are actually replicas.

---

4 The most commonly used and our recommendation is Consul by Hashicorp (*https://www.consul.io*).

Deciding how far to take these health checks should be a conversation with your application developer teams so that everyone understands and aligns on what behavior they expect when reading from the database. Here are some questions to ask the team that can help guide this decision process:

- How much data staleness is acceptable? If the data returned is a few minutes old, what does that affect?
- What is the maximum acceptable query latency for the application?
- What, if any, retry logic exists for read queries, and if it exists, is it exponential backoff?
- Do we already have an SLO for the application? Does that SLO extend to query latency or only address uptime?
- How does the system behave in the absence of this data? Is that degradation acceptable? If so, for how long?

In many cases, you will be fine using only a port check to confirm the MySQL process is live and can accept connections. This means that as long as the database is running, it will be part of that pool and serving requests.

However, sometimes you may need something more sophisticated because the data set involved is critical enough that you do not want to serve it when replication lags more than a few seconds or if replication is not running at all. For these scenarios, you can still use a read pool but augment the health check with an HTTP check. The way this works is that your load balancer of choice will run a command (usually a script) and, based on the response code, will determine if the node is healthy or not. In HAProxy, for example, the backend would have lines of code like this:

```
option httpchk GET /check-lag
```

This line means that for every host in the read pool, the load balancer will call the path /check-lag using a GET call and inspect the response code. That path runs a script that holds the logic as to how much lag is acceptable. The script compares existing lag status with that threshold and, depending on that, the load balancer either considers the replica healthy or not.

 Even though health checks are a powerful tool, be careful using those with complex logic (such as the lag check described previously), and make sure you have a plan for what to do if all replicas in the pool fail the health checks. You can have a static "fallback" pool that brings all the nodes back in for certain global failures (e.g., the entire cluster is lagged) to avoid accidentally breaking all read requests. For more detail on how one company has implemented this, see this post on the GitHub blog (*https://oreil.ly/ zyjA4*).

# Choosing a Load-Balancing Algorithm

There are many different algorithms to determine which server should receive the next connection. Each vendor uses different terminology, but this list should provide an idea of what's available:

*Random*

> The load balancer directs each request to a server selected at random from the pool of available servers.

*Round-robin*

> The load balancer sends requests to servers in a repeating sequence: A, B, C, A, B, C, and so on.

*Fewest connections*

> The next connection goes to the server with the fewest active connections.

*Fastest response*

> The server that has been handling requests the fastest receives the next connection. This can work well when the pool contains a mix of fast and slow machines. However, it's very tricky with SQL when the query complexity varies widely. Even the same query can perform very differently under different circumstances, such as when it's served from the query cache or when the server's caches already contain the needed data.

*Hashed*

> The load balancer hashes the connection's source IP address, which maps it to one of the servers in the pool. Each time a connection request comes from the same IP address, the load balancer sends it to the same server. The bindings change only when the number of machines in the pool does.

*Weighted*

> The load balancer can combine and add weight to several of the other algorithms. For example, you might have single- and dual-CPU machines. The dual-CPU machines are roughly twice as powerful, so you can tell the load balancer to send them an average of twice as many requests.

The best algorithm for MySQL depends on your workload. The least-connections algorithm, for example, might flood new servers when you add them to the pool of available servers before their caches are warmed up.

You'll need to experiment to find the best performance for your workload. Be sure to consider what happens under extraordinary circumstances as well as in the day-to-day norm. It is in those extraordinary circumstances—for example, during times of high query load, when you're doing schema changes, or when an unusual number of servers go offline—that you can least afford something going terribly wrong.

We've described only instant-provisioning algorithms here, which don't queue connection requests. Sometimes algorithms that use queuing can be more efficient. For example, an algorithm might maintain a given concurrency on the database server, such as allowing no more than $N$ active transactions at the same time. If there are too many active transactions, the algorithm can put a new request in a queue and serve it from the first server that becomes "available" according to the criteria. Some connection pools support queuing algorithms.

Now that we have covered how to scale your read load and how to health-check it, it's time to discuss scaling writes. Before looking for how to scale the writes directly, you can look at places where queuing can make the write traffic growth more manageable. Let's discuss how queuing can help scale your write performance.

# Queuing

Scaling your application layer becomes a lot more complex when scaling write transactions with a data store that favors consistency over availability by design. More application nodes writing to the one source node will lead to a database system more susceptible to lock timeouts, deadlocks, and failed writes to have to retry. All this will ultimately lead to customer-facing errors or unacceptable latencies.

Before looking into sharding the data, which we discuss next, you should examine the write hotspots in your data and consider whether all the writes are truly required to persist to the database actively. Can some of them be placed into a queue and written to the database within an acceptable time frame?

Let's say you have a database that stores large data sets of customer historical data. Customers occasionally send API requests to retrieve this data, but you also need to support an API to delete this data. You can plausibly serve read API calls from a growing number of replicas, but what about deletes? The HTTP RFC allows for a response code, "202 Accepted." You can return that, place the request in a queue (e.g., Apache Kafka or Amazon Simple Queue Service), and process these requests at the pace that doesn't lead to overloading the database directly with delete calls.

This is obviously not the same as a 200 response code that implies the request has been instantaneously fulfilled. This is a common spot where negotiation with your product team is crucial for making the guarantees of the API plausible and achievable. The difference between the 200 and 202 response codes is all the engineering work of sharding this data to support a lot more parallel writes.

One important design choice to make if you do apply queuing to a write load is to determine up front the desired time frame within which these calls are expected to be fulfilled after being placed in queue. Monitoring the growth of the time a request spends in a queue is going to be your metric for when this strategy has run its course and you really need to start splitting this data set to support more parallel write load. You can do that using sharding, which we discuss next.

# Scaling Writes with Sharding

If you cannot manage write traffic growth with optimized queries and queuing writes, then sharding is your next option.

*Sharding* means splitting your data into different, smaller database clusters so that you can execute more writes on more source hosts at the same time. There are two different kinds of sharding or partitioning you can do: functional partitioning and data sharding.

*Functional partitioning*, or division of duties, means dedicating different nodes to different tasks. An example of this might be putting user records on one cluster and their billing on a different cluster. This approach allows each cluster to scale independently. A surge in user registrations might put a strain on the user cluster. With separate systems, your billing cluster is less loaded, allowing you to bill customers. Conversely, if your billing cycle is the first of the month, you can run that knowing you won't be affecting user registration.

*Data sharding* is the most common and successful approach for scaling today's very large MySQL applications. You shard the data by splitting it into smaller pieces, or shards, and storing them on different nodes.

Most applications shard only the data that needs sharding—typically, the parts of the data set that will grow very large. Suppose you're building a blogging service. If you expect 10 million users, you might not need to shard the user registration information because you might be able to fit all of the users (or the active subset of them) entirely in memory. If you expect 500 million users, on the other hand, you should probably shard this data. The user-generated content, such as posts and comments, will almost certainly require sharding in either case because these records are much larger and there are many more of them.

Large applications might have several logical data sets that you can shard differently. You can store them on different sets of servers, but you don't have to. You can also shard the same data multiple ways, depending on how you access it.

Be wary when planning to "only shard what needs sharding." That concept needs to include not just the data that is growing rapidly but also the data that logically belongs with it and will regularly be queried at the same time. If you are sharding based on a user_id field but there is a set of other smaller tables that join on that same user_id in a majority of queries, it makes sense to shard all these tables together so that you can keep a majority of your application queries against one shard at a time and avoid cross database joins.

# Choosing a Partitioning Scheme

The most important challenge with sharding is finding and retrieving data. How you find data depends on how you shard it. There are many ways to do this, and some are better than others.

The goal is to make your most important and frequent queries touch as few shards as possible (remember, one of the scalability principles is to avoid crosstalk between nodes). The most critical part of that process is choosing a partitioning key (or keys) for your data. The partitioning key determines which rows should go onto each shard. If you know an object's partitioning key, you can answer two questions:

- Where should I store this data?
- Where can I find the data I need to fetch?

We'll show you a variety of ways to choose and use a partitioning key later. For now, let's look at an example. Suppose we do as MySQL's NDB Cluster does and use a hash of each table's primary key to partition the data across all the shards. This is a very simple approach, but it doesn't scale well because it frequently requires you to check all the shards for the data you want. For example, if you want user 3's blog posts, where can you find them? They are probably scattered evenly across all the shards because they're partitioned by the primary key, not by the user. Using a primary key hash makes it simple to know where to store the data, but it might make it harder to fetch it, depending on which data you need and whether you know the primary key.

You always want your queries localized to one shard. When sharding your data horizontally, you want to *always* avoid having to query across shards to accomplish a task. Joining data across shards will add complexity to your application layer and eats away at the benefit of sharding the data in the first place. The worst case with sharded data sets is when you have no idea where the desired data is stored so that you need to scan every shard to find it.

A good partitioning key is usually the primary key of a very important entity in the database. These keys determine the unit of sharding. For example, if you partition your data by a user ID or a client ID, the unit of sharding is the user or client.

A good way to start is to diagram your data model with an entity-relationship diagram or an equivalent tool that shows all the entities and their relationships. Try to lay out the diagram so that the related entities are close together. You can often inspect such a diagram visually and find candidates for partitioning keys that you'd otherwise miss. Don't just look at the diagram, though; consider your application's queries as well. Even if two entities are related in some way, if you seldom or never join on the relationship, you can break the relationship to implement the sharding.

Some data models are easier to shard than others, depending on the degree of connectivity in the entity-relationship graph. Figure 11-2 depicts an easily sharded data model on the left and one that's difficult to shard on the right.

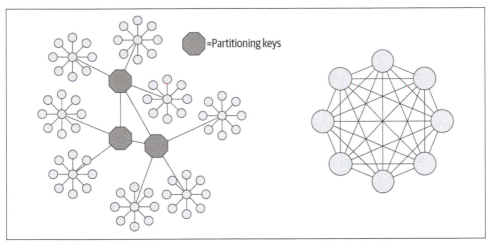

*Figure 11-2. Two data models, one easy to shard and the other difficult[5]*

The data model on the left is easy to shard because it has many connected subgraphs consisting mostly of nodes with just one connection and you can "cut" the connections between the subgraphs relatively easily. The model on the right is hard to shard because there are no such subgraphs. Most data models, luckily, look more like the lefthand diagram than the righthand one.

When choosing a partitioning key, try to pick something that lets you avoid cross-shard queries as much as possible but also makes shards small enough that you won't have problems with disproportionately large chunks of data. You want the shards to end up uniformly small, if possible, and if not, at least small enough that they're easy to balance by grouping different numbers of shards together. For example, if your application is US only and you want to divide your data set into 20 shards, you probably shouldn't shard by state because California has such a huge population. But you could shard by county or telephone area code, because even though those won't be uniformly populated, there are enough of them that you can still choose 20 sets that will be roughly equally populated in total, and you can choose them with an affinity that helps avoid cross-shard queries.

---

5 Thanks to the HiveDB project and Britt Crawford for contributing these elegant diagrams.

## Multiple Partitioning Keys

Complicated data models make data sharding more difficult. Many applications have more than one partitioning key, especially if there are two or more important "dimensions" in the data. In other words, the application might need to see an efficient, coherent view of the data from different angles. This means you might need to store at least some data twice within the system.

For example, you might need to shard your blogging application's data by both the user ID and the post ID because these are two common ways the application looks at the data. Think of it this way: you frequently want to see all posts for a user and all comments for a post. Sharding by user doesn't help you find comments for a post, and sharding by post doesn't help you find posts for a user. If you need both types of queries to touch only a single shard, you'll have to shard both ways.

Just because you need multiple partitioning keys doesn't mean you'll need to design two completely redundant data stores. Let's look at another example: a social networking book-club website where the site's users can comment on books. The website can display all comments for a book as well as all books a user has read and commented on.

You might build one sharded data store for the user data and another for the book data. Comments have both a user ID and a post ID, so they cross the boundaries between shards. Instead of completely duplicating comments, you can store the comments with the user data. Then you can store just a comment's headline and ID with the book data. This might be enough to render most views of a book's comments without accessing both data stores, and if you need to display the complete comment text, you can retrieve it from the user data store.

## Querying Across Shards

Most sharded applications have at least some queries that need to aggregate or join data from multiple shards. For example, if the book-club site shows the most popular or active users, it must by definition access every shard. Making such queries work well is the most difficult part of implementing data sharding because what the application sees as a single query needs to be split up and executed in parallel as many queries, one per shard. A good database abstraction layer can help ease the pain, but even then such queries are so much slower and more expensive than in-shard queries that aggressive caching is usually necessary as well.

You will know that the sharding scheme you chose was a good one if the cross-shard queries become outliers instead of norms. You should strive to make your queries as simple as possible and contained within one shard. For those cases where some cross-shard aggregation is needed, we recommend you make that part of the application logic.

Cross-shard queries can also benefit from summary tables. You can build them by traversing all the shards and storing the results redundantly on each shard when they're complete. If duplicating the data on each shard is too wasteful, you can consolidate the summary tables onto another data store so that they're stored only once.

Nonsharded data often lives in the global node, with heavy caching to shield it from the load.

Some applications use essentially random sharding where consistent data distribution is important or when there is no good partitioning key. A distributed search application is a good example. In this case, cross-shard queries and aggregation are the norm, not the exception.

Querying across shards isn't the only thing that's harder with sharding. Maintaining data consistency is also difficult. Foreign keys won't work across shards, so the normal solution is to check referential integrity as needed in the application or use foreign keys within a shard because internal consistency within a shard might be the most important thing. It's possible to use XA transactions (*https://oreil.ly/Z5gSe*), but this is uncommon in practice because of the overhead.

You can also design clean-up processes that run intermittently. For example, if a user's book-club account expires, you don't have to remove it immediately. You can write a periodic job to remove the user's comments from the per-book shard, and you can build a checker script that runs periodically and makes sure the data is consistent across the shards.

Now that we have explained the different ways you can split your data across multiple clusters and how to choose a partitioning key, let's cover two of the most popular open source tools that can help facilitate both sharding and partitioning.

## Vitess

Vitess is a database-clustering system for MySQL. It originated within YouTube, then became PlanetScale, a separate product and company cofounded by Jiten Vaidya and Sugu Sougoumarane.

Vitess enables a number of features:

- Horizontal sharding support, including sharding the data
- Topology management
- Source node failover management
- Schema change management
- Connection pooling
- Query rewriting

Let's explore Vitess's architecture and its components.

## Vitess architecture overview

Figure 11-3 is a diagram from Vitess's website showing the different parts of its architecture.

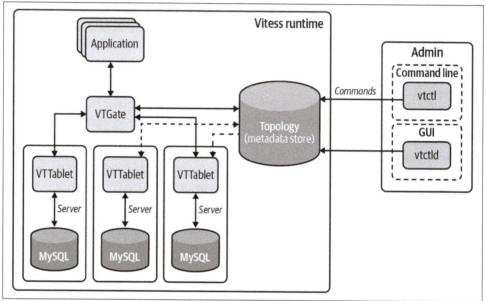

*Figure 11-3. Vitess architecture diagram (adapted from vitess.io)*

Here are some terms you need to know:

*Vitess pod*
> The general encapsulation of a set of databases and the Vitess-related pieces that support sharding, topology management, management of schema changes, and application access to those databases.

*VTGate*
> The service that controls access to the database instances for applications and operators trying to manage topology, add nodes, or shard some of the data. It is akin to the load balancer in the architecture described previously.

*VTTablet*
> The agent running on each database instance managed by Vitess. It can receive database management commands from operators and execute them on the operators' behalf.

*Topology (metadata store)*
> Holds the inventory of database instances managed by Vitess in a given pod as well as accompanying information.

*vtctl*
> The command-line tool to make operational changes to a Vitess pod.

*vtctld*
> A graphical interface for the same management operations.

Vitess's architecture starts with a consistent topology store that holds definitions for all the clusters, MySQL instances, and *vtgate* instances. This consistent metadata store plays a crucial role in managing topology changes. When an operator wants to make a change to the topology of a cluster managed by Vitess, it really sends commands through a service called *vtctl* to that data store, which then sends the component operations of that command to *vtgate*.

Vitess offers database operators that can deploy the *vtgate* layer and the metadata store in Kubernetes. Having its control plane in a platform like Kubernetes increases its resilience to single points of failure.

One of Vitess's greatest strengths is its philosophy about how to scale MySQL (*https:// oreil.ly/5QKCD*), which includes the following:

*A preference for using smaller instances*
> Split your data functionally, horizontally, or both. But smaller instances make for a smaller blast radius when failures happen.

*Replication and automated write failover to increase resilience*
> Vitess does not promise "100% online writes" through multiwriter node tricks. Instead, it automates write failover and, during that failover, manages both the topology change and application access to the database nodes to make the write downtime as short as possible.

*Durability using semisync replication*
> Vitess strongly recommends semisync replication (as opposed to the default asynchronous) to ensure that writes are always persisted by more than one node in the database layer before acknowledging them to the application. This is a crucial trade-off in latency for the sake of guaranteed durability that pays its dividends when Vitess needs to failover the writer host in an unplanned manner.

These architectural principles can help sustain exponential growth in your business traffic with a lot more resilience in the database layer of your infrastructure. And you should heed many of these best practices regardless of whether you specifically use Vitess or another solution as part of your architecture.

### Migrating your stack to Vitess

Vitess is an opinionated platform for running the database layer and is not a drop-in solution. Therefore, you need to plan thoughtfully how implementing such a transition would happen before you adopt it as the access layer for your database.

Specifically, be sure to consider the following migration steps as you evaluate Vitess as a possible solution:

1. *Test and document the latency you're introducing to the overall system.*
   Introducing a complex stack like Vitess to an application stack will definitely add some amount of latency, especially when you consider the enforcement of semi-sync replication. Make sure this trade-off is well documented and explicitly communicated so that your downstream dependencies are making informed decisions when building SLOs that rely on this database architecture.

2. *Use the canary deployment model (https://oreil.ly/ldtnN).*
   During the transition in production, you can configure *vttablet* as "externally managed." This allows for both *vttablet* and direct connections to the database server as you slowly ramp up the connection change through your application node fleet.

3. *Start sharding.*
   Once all the application layer access is through *vtgate/vttablet* and not directly to MySQL, you can start using the full feature set of Vitess to split tables off in new clusters, shard data horizontally for more write throughput, or simply add replicas for more read load capacity.[6]

Vitess is a powerful database access and management product that has come a long way from its early days at Google. It has proven its ability to enable dramatic growth and a resilient database infrastructure. However, this power and flexibility come at a cost of added complexity. Vitess is not as simple as a load balancer passing through traffic, and you should weigh the needs of the business with the cost of introducing and maintaining a database management tool as complex as Vitess.

## ProxySQL

ProxySQL is written specifically for the MySQL protocol and released with a General Public License (GPL). René Cannaò, a DBA who has consulted for many companies and a long-time MySQL contributor, is the primary author. It is now a full-fledged company that offers paid support and development contracts of the ProxySQL product.

---

6 This deployment strategy is explained in detail by Morgan Tocker in a talk at Kubecon 2019 (*https://www.youtube.com/watch?v=OCS45iy5v1M*).

Let's dig into some details about its architecture, configuration patterns, use cases, and features.

## ProxySQL architecture overview

You can use ProxySQL as a layer in between any application code and MySQL instances. ProxySQL provides a session-aware, MySQL-protocol-based interface for applications to interact with the databases. Instead of applications opening connections directly to the database instances, ProxySQL opens them on the applications' behalf.

This design makes the proxy seem invisible to the application nodes. Its session awareness allows for moving these connections between MySQL instances without downtime. This is especially useful when you are dealing with applications that you are no longer investing in because you can now utilize features in ProxySQL without needing to make any changes to code that you may not feel confident changing.

ProxySQL also provides powerful connection pooling. Connections opened by applications to ProxySQL are separate from the connections ProxySQL opens to database instances it is configured to connect to. This separation allows for protecting the database instances from sudden traffic spikes in the application layer.

When you have the ability to manage client-side connections separately from how many connections actually are made to the database, you introduce flexibility you did not have before. You can now scale out the application node pool without having to worry that it will increase connection load to the database beyond what you want to support. This allows for diverse scenarios of application and business needs, as we will explain in the common patterns when using ProxySQL.

## Configuring ProxySQL

ProxySQL uses a configuration file for startup but maintains its runtime configuration both in memory and in an embedded SQLite file that you can access directly and query using an admin interface.

ProxySQL's admin interface allows you to issue commands to change the running configuration, then dump that new configuration out to disk for persistence using MySQL commands. This allows you to make zero-downtime changes to a running ProxySQL instance. You can also use this admin interface to make automated changes issued by your configuration management or automated failover scripts. You can see in Figure 11-4 how your architecture would generally leverage both ProxySQL and service discovery to provide a robust access layer for services.

It's important to note that while we show ProxySQL as one object in this diagram, we strongly recommend in production environments leveraging its clustering mechanism and deploying multiple instances in a given stack. Never run a single point of failure (SPoF).

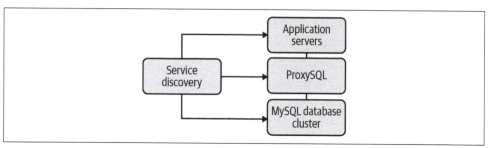

*Figure 11-4. The interaction between application nodes, ProxySQL, and service discovery (adapted from a diagram by Bill Sickles)*

ProxySQL has independent and hierarchical health checking for databases it connects to. Based on the results of these health checks, ProxySQL adds or removes hosts or adjusts traffic weights. You can specify replication-lag thresholds, time to connect successfully, and connection retries on failure, among many other configuration options, to control how much fault tolerance is acceptable within the context of your service and application needs. These configuration options allow ProxySQL to react accurately to unresponsive hosts by either temporarily removing backend databases and then repeating the health check later, or fully removing the struggling backend member until an operator is involved.

### Using ProxySQL for sharding

ProxySQL is very useful for a number of sharding topologies. While it does not bring automation to the actual splitting of the data the way Vitess does, it can be a great lightweight middle layer that is sharding aware and can route your application connections accordingly. Let's cover the different ways you can use it to be a routing layer to your shards.

**Sharding by user.**   If your data is split functionally or by business function in different database clusters and different application fleets accessing these clusters, you should also be using entirely different database credentials for each of these applications. ProxySQL can leverage this user parameter to route traffic to entirely separate backend database pools for either writes or reads.

You can configure such routing in ProxySQL by running these commands against its admin interface, then saving the change to its disk configuration file:

```
INSERT INTO mysql_users
(username, password, active, default_hostgroup, comment)
VALUES
('accounts', 'shard0_pass', 1, 0, 'Routed to the accounts shard'),
('transactions', 'shard1_pass', 1, 1, 'Routed to the transactions shard'),
('logging', 'shard2_pass', 1, 2, 'Routed to the logging shard');

LOAD MYSQL USERS RULES TO RUNTIME;
SAVE MYSQL USERS RULES TO DISK;
```

 Always make sure you are keeping ProxySQL's runtime configuration and on-disk configuration in sync to avoid nasty surprises when a ProxySQL process restarts.

This adds the convenience of also logging all operations done by these users for compliance without causing any load on the database. You will see in Chapter 13 that we also recommend separate database users for compliance reasons, and therefore this design aligns with some compliance goals as well.

**Sharding by schema.**  Another way you can use ProxySQL to support sharded data sets is using schema names as the rule to manage the traffic routing. Here is an example of how you would define that in ProxySQL's configuration:

```
INSERT INTO mysql_query_rules (rule_id, active, schemaname,
destination_hostgroup, apply)
VALUES
(1, 1, 'shard_0', 0, 1),
(2, 1, 'shard_1', 1, 1),
(3, 1, 'shard_2', 2, 1);

LOAD MYSQL QUERY RULES TO RUNTIME;
SAVE MYSQL QUERY RULES TO DISK;
```

Note that this configuration can be used for either horizontal sharding or functional sharding as long as you name your schemas properly.

A final important recommendation we have when using ProxySQL in this manner is to make sure to use its native clustering feature, which ensures that a critical configuration table like mysql_rules is synced to all the ProxySQL nodes in the cluster, providing redundancy in your middleware layer.

## Other benefits of using ProxySQL

Let's discuss some common patterns where using ProxySQL can help alleviate common issues in fast-growing environments.

In many applications, "open more connections to the database" is a pattern we commonly see when query latency starts to climb. However, in practice this can lead to outages[7] and tends to leave a lot of connections idle, consuming resources but not doing any work. When you open more connections by the application layer directly to the database, the amount of resources the database server spends on connection management also increases. This snowballs into thousands of connections overwhelming already overloaded database instances. All of this activity leads to prolonged downtimes, cascading failures in multiple microservices, and extended customer-facing impact.

ProxySQL's connection-management architecture helps shield the database layer from unexpected application peaks by opening to the database only the number of connections that can do work. ProxySQL can reuse those connections for different client-side requests. This behavior maximizes the work that a single connection to the database servers can do, which in turn reduces the number of resources managing connections and allows for more efficient use of the database server's memory resources.

### Other notable features in ProxySQL

ProxySQL has a number of other features that stand out in a general-use application proxy:

- Query routing based on port, user, or simply a regex match
- TLS support on both the frontend application connections and backend connections to databases
- Support for various MySQL flavors, such as AWS Aurora, Galera Cluster, and Clickhouse
- Connection mirroring
- Result set caching
- Query rewrites
- Audit log

You can read about the extensive feature set of ProxySQL (which goes well beyond sharding support) by visiting its documentation (*https://oreil.ly/PTZFW*).

ProxySQL is a powerful tool you can use for scaling out your application with proper performance protections for the database layer and with added features that support all sorts of business needs (like compliance, security rules, etc.). If your company is

---

7 For more information, see the Wikipedia entry on the thundering herd problem (*https://oreil.ly/YOtAt*).

finding itself on a high-growth trajectory with a robust mix of new and less-new services sharing database resources, it can be a powerful tool for safely continuing that growth. ProxySQL provides an easy-to-deploy abstraction that can be more sophisticated than HAProxy but with less up-front investment in infrastructure and complexity. However, it also does not offer some of the more advanced features found in Vitess, such as automated sharding of data sets, management of schema changes, and VReplication (*https://oreil.ly/k2J7R*), which is a powerful tool for enabling extract, transform, load (ETL) pipelines and changing data streams.

## Summary

Scaling MySQL is a journey. You should come out of this chapter more prepared to assess your scaling needs and understand how to scale reads, how to scale writes, and how to make your traffic growth more predictable by adding queuing to your architecture. You should also now understand sharding to scale writes and all the complex decisions that come with it.

Before you dive into scalability bottlenecks, make sure you've optimized your queries, checked your indexes, and have a solid configuration for MySQL. This may buy you the necessary time to plan a better long-term strategy. Once optimized, focus on determining whether you are read- or write-bound, and then consider what strategies work best to solve any immediate issues. When planning your solution, make sure you consider how to set yourself up for long-term scalability.

For read-bound workloads, our recommendation is to move to read pools unless replication lag is an impossible problem to overcome. If lag is an issue or if your problem is write-bound, you need to consider sharding as your next step.

# MySQL in the Cloud

In all likelihood, you won't have much control over whether you move to a cloud provider or even which one your organization ultimately adopts. What you can control is how you build your database environment. There are two directions you can take: managed MySQL or building on VMs. Managed MySQL tends to be more hands-off, but it's usually more expensive and gives you less control. Building on a VM means you get a lot more flexibility in how you build and how to observe your platform, but it requires more time and operational overhead.

In this chapter, we'll outline the major options for managed MySQL and how they can be useful to you. We'll also explain how to get started building a VM option, including selecting the right specs and disk types, and we will cover the operational complexities (like host reboots) you have to prepare for when running MySQL on VMs in a cloud.

 We will not cover bugs in cloud-provider offerings. These offerings are ever-evolving products, so we recommend you keep up-to-date with dynamic sources like newsletters or bug boards rather than a point-in-time reference such as this book.

## Managed MySQL

Offerings for managed MySQL among cloud providers bring a lot of convenience to teams looking to reduce the cognitive load of operating MySQL as their product grows and their feature set expands. Every public cloud has its own interpretation of what a managed SQL database should look like and how it should work. Amazon Web Services (AWS) offers a few flavors of Aurora MySQL (we discuss these in detail shortly), Google Cloud Platform (GCP) has Cloud SQL, and so on, with almost all public cloud providers offering something similar.

The key appeal of managed solutions is that they provide an accessible database setup without needing to get deep into MySQL specifics. With a few clicks or a `terraform apply`, you can have a database online with a replica and scheduled backups, and you're all ready to go. This can be a very attractive option for companies or teams that want to get started quickly.

On the other hand, with managed MySQL you lack a lot of visibility and control. You do not have access to the operating system or the filesystem, and you are restricted in how much you can do within the process itself. You can't inspect anything else about the system other than what the cloud provider gives you. In most cases, if you experience an issue, you're relegated to opening a support ticket and waiting for a response. You can't set up any advanced topologies, and your backup and restore methods are limited to what the cloud provider offers.

It is worth noting that many of these cloud offerings give you a *MySQL-compatible* data store. This is a data store that has a SQL interface but with internal workings that may be entirely different from the Oracle MySQL that this book focuses on. We will cover general trade-offs and how each managed solution is different to help you choose the option that fits your team and business needs best.

## Amazon Aurora for MySQL

Aurora MySQL is a MySQL-compatible hosted database. Aurora's most appealing selling point is that it separates compute from storage, which allows them to scale separately and more flexibly. Aurora manages a number of operational tasks that you would normally take care of, such as performing snapshot backups, managing fast schema changes, audit logging, and managing replication within a single region.

---

### A Note on Compatibility

When Amazon says "MySQL compatible," you have to confirm which major version of MySQL is intended in that phrase. None of the hosted solutions in Aurora is MySQL 8.0 compatible, for example, and some of the older ones are only compatible with MySQL 5.6. If you are considering moving from self-managed MySQL to Amazon Aurora MySQL, be sure to note this in application testing before moving production data.

---

There are also different offerings of Aurora MySQL. We'll briefly cover the differences between these offerings.

The standard Aurora offering is long-running compute instances where you choose an instance class (just like when running your own MySQL), and you get attached storage that internally replicates to six copies.

As of this writing, Aurora fast DDL is considered by AWS a "lab mode" feature. If you are reading this and that is still the case, we recommend you refer to Chapter 6 to learn more about online schema-change options with tools external to your database.

It is important to note that replication within an Aurora cluster is entirely proprietary to Amazon and is not the replication we know and use in Oracle MySQL. Since all Aurora instances in a cluster share the same storage layer to access data, replication within a cluster is done using block storage.[1] Aurora, however, does support writing binary logs in the format we are familiar with in a community server for teams who wish to replicate data from an Aurora cluster to another cluster or for any other purpose of binary logs, such as change data captures.[2]

If you are looking to put any mission-critical databases on Aurora, we strongly recommend you also consider using Amazon's RDS Proxy to manage how your application will communicate with Aurora. In situations where you know there is potential for new connection storms from the application side, RDS Proxy can come in very handy in not letting that new connection volume affect the database.

Since Aurora MySQL's appearance on the scene in 2015, AWS has expanded the options of Aurora MySQL that you can leverage to meet a larger swath of use cases and business needs:

*Aurora Serverless*
 The serverless offering of Aurora MySQL removes the long-running compute and leverages Amazon's serverless platform to serve the compute layer of your database. This gives you a lot of cost flexibility if your workload does not need to run constantly.

---

1 If you really want to know the details of that architecture, we highly recommend the SIGMOD paper (*https://oreil.ly/hhFhU*) the Aurora team published in 2017.

2 Change data capture is a design pattern in data architecture that is used to determine when data has changed and transfer that change across domains and systems. For more reading on this, we highly recommend Chapter 11 of *Designing Data-Intensive Applications* by Martin Kleppman (O'Reilly).

*Aurora Global Database*

This is Aurora's solution for those who need their data available in multiple geographic regions but don't want to use binary log replication to manually manage getting data changes from a primary cluster to clusters in other regions. Note that this comes with trade-offs, and you should always refer back to Amazon's documentation to make sure you are accepting the right ones.

*Aurora Multi-Master*

Multi-Master is a special flavor of Aurora clusters that can accept writes on more than one compute node at the same time. It is intended as a highly available solution where write availability in a single region is the highest priority. Note that Aurora Multi-Master comes with its own set of limitations. For starters, as of this writing it runs a MySQL 5.6 server core, which precludes you from using a number of features. There is a maximum number of nodes allowed in a cluster, and you cannot mix Multi-Master and Global Database in the same deployment. We consider Aurora Multi-Master a very opinionated solution for the availability and consistency choices you have at every data store and application interaction, and we recommend you think carefully about your stated constraints and trade-offs before choosing it.

AWS continues to make updates and improvements to its managed relational database offerings, so we will avoid going into the deep details of feature differences between the Aurora flavors. Figure 12-1, however, does provide a flowchart to help you see generically which type of Aurora might be best suited for your needs and at what trade-offs.

Figure 12-1 gives you a basic decision tree to help you decide among Aurora options. The important takeaway is that, although Aurora has a number of options, there are always trade-offs. For example, you cannot achieve both multiwriter high availability and cross-regional subsecond replication. But you *can* use the offerings to present these trade-offs and drive difficult product discussions about which is the most important: write availability or regional replication.

Aurora is not the only managed MySQL offering by a cloud provider. GCP has its own offering.

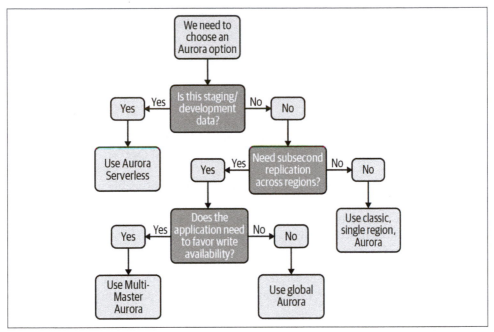

*Figure 12-1. A flowchart to help you choose which flavor of Aurora is suitable for your needs*

## GCP Cloud SQL

Cloud SQL is GCP's managed MySQL offering. A core difference between this offering and AWS's is that it runs the community server but with certain features disabled specifically to allow for the multitenancy and managed aspect of the product. Here are some of the things you cannot use with Cloud SQL even though it runs the community server:

- SUPER privilege is disabled.
- Loading plug-ins are disabled.[3]
- Some clients are also disabled, such as *mysqldump* and *mysqlimport*.

Similar to AWS's offering, you cannot get SSH access to the instances.

---

3 Cloud SQL does offer its own solution for audit logging (*https://oreil.ly/RM7MW*) to support compliance needs.

On the other hand, there are a number of operational tasks that Cloud SQL manages for you:

- Native high-availability support. Failovers are automated using a configuration option.
- Native encryption of the data at rest.
- Flexibly managed upgrades using multiple methods. Note that ultimately these maintenance windows involve some downtime (similarly to AWS Aurora), and it is your responsibility to balance that with application SLOs.[4]

As we mentioned at the beginning of this chapter, you are probably not going to have a choice of which cloud provider to build these databases in, so you are more likely going to need to know what the managed option from the cloud provider chosen for you offers and how to work with it—or to make the case for moving to using VMs directly instead of managed MySQL.

Now that we have covered managed relational database options and the intricacies of those choices, let's talk about the slightly more complex path: running MySQL on cloud-hosted VMs.

# MySQL on Virtual Machines

The features of managed MySQL can be very attractive for those who want to get up and going quickly, so why would someone choose to run their own? Running MySQL on a VM is just like running it on bare metal. You get complete and total control over all operational aspects. You can run your primary MySQL in a single region but set up replicas in other regions for disaster-recovery purposes—or run a time-delayed replica. You can also tailor your backup method to be the most optimal for your workload. If performance degrades or you experience issues, you have full control over the operating system and filesystem, allowing you to do any introspection you want.

## Machine Types in Cloud

As discussed in Chapter 4, the number of CPU cores and available RAM for MySQL have a direct impact on the performance of MySQL. The downside of choosing specific hardware specs for a data center is that they cannot be changed very easily. If you have a 56-core, 512 GB RAM machine racked, you certainly can reduce the installed

---

4 For more information, see "Minimizing the Impact of Maintenance" (*https://oreil.ly/3kNIh*) in the Cloud SQL documentation.

RAM—but you already paid for it, so unless you can reuse the RAM elsewhere, you may have overspent on hardware.

Optimizing the machine specs for your workload is much easier when you use a cloud provider. The major cloud providers allow you to choose a machine spec that sets ranges of virtual CPUs (vCPUs), the amount of RAM available, and networking and disk limitations. With this comes the ability to resize the VMs as your workload changes. This could mean that if you experience peak traffic over a specific time of year—like a holiday season—you can temporarily increase your machine specs to account for that. Once traffic patterns dip back down, you can resize them smaller again. This flexibility is why many people move to the cloud.

## Choosing the Right Machine Type

If you're already on a cloud provider, choosing a machine is fairly trivial. If you're running into a vCPU, memory, or network bottleneck, you can find the appropriate machine type to overcome it and resize. If you're making a move from a data center, though, it can be tricky to determine the right configuration up front.

### CPU

In Chapter 4, we talked about how to select the right CPUs for your workload. When you transition to the cloud, most of that guidance still holds true. Remember that with cloud providers, you're getting *virtual* CPUs, not physical CPUs. This means that the CPU is not exclusively yours. It may be shared with other tenants on the same physical host. In all likelihood, you'll see more variation on latency and utilization than you would on your own exclusive server.

If you're migrating from physical machines to a cloud provider, it can also be tricky to estimate your CPU usage. We have had success using the following formula for vCPU count: (Core Count × 95% Total CPU Usage) × 2.

For example, suppose you have a 40-core server in a data center. Over the last 30 days, the peak CPU usage was 30%. How many cores do you need to run this in a cloud provider at 50% utilization? Using the preceding formula, we would estimate 24 cores. If your chosen cloud provider does not offer a 24-core machine type, consider rounding up to the nearest type or determining whether your provider offers custom machine types.[5]

---

5 Be mindful that custom machine types may cost more than predetermined machine types. When working at large numbers of instances, it's always important to consider cost when choosing your sizing.

As CPU usage or core count increases, so does context switching: the act of switching tasks on the CPU. Because of this, you do not want to run at 100% CPU capacity because you will waste a lot of time switching between threads. This will manifest itself as latency for your queries. We recommend a target of 50% typical utilization, with peaks up to 65%–70%. If you sustain 70% CPU or greater, you will likely see latency increase, and you should consider adding more CPUs.

Also pay attention to the CPU chip family, if that's an option. If you're running a high-traffic web application, you may want to ensure that you have a much later generation of chip available. Likewise, if you are looking at backend data processing where older, slightly slower CPU chip families could be fine, that could possibly be a cost savings.

### Memory

As discussed in Chapters 1 and 4, RAM can greatly influence MySQL performance.

Choose whatever machine spec best fits your needs for your working set of data, while erring on the side of too much RAM instead of not enough.

### Network performance

While CPU and memory sizing are the most important parts of choosing a machine type, make sure you also review the available network performance limitations to ensure that you don't starve your applications. For example, if you have a batch process that will read large amounts of data, you may find that you exhaust your bandwidth on a smaller machine type.

It's worth noting that network egress between cloud zones and regions usually has a cost associated with it. This can come as a surprise when setting up replicas, but we still think it's important to place replicas in separate zones for redundancy purposes.

## Choosing the Right Disk Type

Although machine types are generally dynamic, the selection you make for data storage will likely be your most complicated decision. Once you've chosen a disk type and started to use it for data, moving to another disk type becomes difficult. Typically, you'd need to mount a second disk and copy the data over. It's not impossible to correct, but it certainly is more involved than just a quick reboot to add more CPUs.

Picking the correct disk type is also highly context sensitive to what workload you expect to run. Highly read-intensive workloads will benefit from more memory over disk performance because memory access is orders of magnitude faster. If your working set is larger than your InnoDB buffer pool, you will always end up going to disk to read some data. Write-intensive workloads will always go to disk, and that's where most people will start to see their first disk bottlenecks.

## Attachment types

The first decision to make is whether you go with locally attached disks or network-attached disks. Locally attached disks have the benefit of offering incredibly high performance and consistent throughput but are also vulnerable to data loss. This is because they are treated as disks for ephemeral data only. If the hardware running your VM with locally attached data crashes, you could lose all your data on the local disk. Likewise, in some circumstances, even shutting down the instance can mean that when you start it up again, you're on a different host machine and empty disks. Locally attached disks typically do not have any replication or RAID behind them. A host-level disk failure could cause you to lose your data. If you go this route, we recommend strongly considering using software RAID to at least minimize the chances of data loss. See our discussion on RAID in Chapter 4 for more information.

By contrast, network-attached disks go the other way, offering redundancy and reliability over performance. That's not to say that the performance on a network-attached disk is bad—it's just not as performant as local. Your network-attached disk may experience stalls where a locally attached disk may not. You can also typically achieve much higher throughput and IOPS numbers locally.

Cloud providers provide convenient backup or snapshot tooling when using network-attached disks. These work fine for MySQL use, assuming you have ACID-compliant settings[6] configured and your backup solution is properly designed. You can take a disk snapshot at any point and recover it through normal crash recovery with no issues.

You can also use disk snapshotting to make replicas *extremely* fast, even on disk sizes in the many terabytes. By doing this, you minimize the amount of replication lag that needs to catch up before the replica can be usable.

Note that if you use a locally attached disk instead of a network-attached one, you'll need to solve how to back up your data yourself with LVM or a third-party tool like XtraBackup. See Chapter 10 for a more thorough discussion of backups.

The last note on attachment types is that cloud providers do not offer something like a write cache (battery or flash backed) as one might see from a RAID card on hardware.

---

6 As a reminder, these are `innodb_flush_log_at_trx_commit=1` and `sync_binlog=1`.

### SSD versus HDD

By and large, you'll want to use SSDs for everything—especially your MySQL data volume. If you find yourself particularly tight on budget, you can explore HDDs as a cheaper option for the boot disk. In our experimentation, we found that an SSD booted two to three times faster than an HDD. If the boot time matters, particularly in an outage or reboot scenario, stick with SSD all the way.

### IOPS and throughput

Another complicated factor is determining your IOPS and throughput requirements. You should have a good understanding, both historical and forward looking, for what each of these requirements looks like before choosing what kind of disk you need.

If you are migrating from an existing workload, ideally you already have historical disk-use metrics for these that will allow you to best choose your disk. If not, you can use *pt-diskstats* (*https://oreil.ly/GRdGx*), from the Percona Toolkit package, to collect metrics for a day to measure peaks.

For new databases, invest some time to see how intensive the application will be. Even something as basic as understanding your read-to-write ratio can help. If all else fails, find a good middle ground between performance and cost, and set an expectation that you may need to adjust later.

## Additional Tips

If you choose to run your own MySQL on VM, you will be responsible for a lot more than a managed service. You'll need to do things like disk sizing, backups, and so forth on your own. Here are a few tips to consider if you go this route.

### Dealing with host reboots

Your VM is really just running on someone else's hardware. As much as we don't like it, hardware can and does fail, and when that happens, your VM will immediately terminate. If configured, your VM will then begin booting back up on another host. If this happens while you are serving production traffic, especially on a source node taking writes, it can be a disruption to your users.

There are no magic solutions that will let you avoid this—you just have to deal with it. You tend to have two options if this happens: initiate a failover process to a replica (covered in "Replication Failover" on page 239 in Chapter 9), or wait for the source to come back online. Dealing with an unplanned promotion can be very tricky. Our advice is to just allow the server to come back online and replication to reattach itself naturally.

You can make this process easier to cope with by following these suggestions:

- Use an SSD boot disk to allow rebooting as fast as possible. Often systems are back online in less than five minutes.

- Suppress any host down on-call notifications you have for up to five minutes to allow the system to reboot fully and become healthy.

- If a source server was rebooted, you may be able to code an option to turn off the read_only flag dynamically, allowing writes to continue without human intervention. This works well when coupled with the *crond* @reboot option, which will run a script at system startup. The only caveat is that you need to be able to query a system to determine if the system should be taking writes.

- Maximize communication by automatically sending emails or chat messages to teams or channels that may need to be aware of the disruption. "The host FQDN has gone down unexpectedly and should be back online in five minutes" may be enough to stop people from messaging you or even paging you.

### Separate operating system and MySQL data

Regardless of whether you choose locally attached or network-attached, we recommend keeping your operating system and MySQL data separate for these reasons:

- Disk snapshots will be limited to just MySQL data and won't contain any operating system information.

- In the case of a network-attached disk, you can disconnect and reconnect a disk to another machine easily.

- Also for network-attached disks, you can upgrade or replace your operating system without having to recopy data onto the filesystem.

Also consider where you put specific files, like the MySQL process ID file, any log-files, and the socket file. We recommend these stay with the operating system, although the logs could possibly stay on the data disk.

### Backing up binary logs

Send your binary logs to a bucket. Set life-cycle controls on the bucket to purge old files automatically after a certain time period elapses. Likewise, prevent deletion of files before a certain time period or disallow deletion altogether.

Don't forget to think about security here. Leaving this bucket open for the world to read can be a nightmare waiting to happen. Controlling who can read or delete this data is essential to maintaining a secure backup strategy. Consider allowing all database machines to write but none of them to read or delete. Control reads and deletes separately from a restricted account, machine, or both.

### Auto-extend your disks

With network-attached disks, you pay for the amount of space *provisioned*, not used. This can mean that it is wasteful to leave a large amount of provisioned but unused space on your MySQL data disks. One way you can optimize this would be to target a much higher percentage of disk space usage, like 90%, but how do you mitigate the risk of running out of disk space?

Cloud providers typically have an API call available to extend your disk size. With a little bit of code, you can determine if your servers are going over the 90% disk-full mark and call that API to extend the disks. This can also reduce the likelihood of getting paged for a server that is close to running out of disk space. Overall, this process can make a sizable difference in how much you spend on provisioned disk space.

We'll share a few warnings about this, however:

- Think about how frequently you should run the code that looks for used disk space percentage. You need to figure out, based on the disk's throughput, how long a process would take to fill the remaining disk completely. Your code should run more frequently than that.

- If your process runs away and keeps extending the disk without limits, you could wake up to a 64 TB volume. This might be a costly surprise when it comes time to pay the provider's bill.

- This disk extension API call can cause the disk to stall briefly. Be sure you test this under load to ensure it doesn't adversely affect your users.

## Summary

If you work in one of the thousands of companies that run in public clouds, you have many options when it comes to how to run your databases. As a database engineer, you will be asked which managed solution to use, whether to use managed relational database solutions at all, and what the trade-offs are for each choice. The most important thing to keep in mind when giving your input in these discussions is that there is no free lunch. Every one of your options comes with a set of trade-offs. The most useful thing you can do is to frame these trade-offs in the context of how your business operates and what maturity stage it is in to help guide your organization toward the best fit. We hope this chapter has helped you come to these conversations with an ability to compare the trade-offs at hand with the needs of your company.

# Compliance with MySQL

The role of database engineering teams is of interest to many internal business stakeholders. As we have covered already, you have to plan not just for performance and uptime but also for infrastructure cost, disaster recovery, and all sorts of compliance needs.

Your job is not limited to managing this data while the business is running. You also need to help the business protect the data and certify for regulatory certifications that are either legally required or critical for business. You have to understand the business goals for fulfilling these needs and include these requirements in all data architecture design, including how you automate operational tasks, manage access, and convert administrative tasks into code that automates such tasks.

This chapter covers the different types of compliance certifications a business may pursue and various database-specific concerns they have. We help explain how to design for different compliance needs and discuss how access logging can be a crucial part of filling compliance requirements. Finally, we cover data sovereignty as an emerging concern for data architecture practices in all types of businesses.

 This chapter does not seek to give you legal advice. We are looking to help you manage compliance needs when you are running a large number of databases and how to design for compliance early on. When looking for advice on how to properly fulfill specific controls, you should always consult with your company's legal team.

# What Is Compliance?

Governance, risk management, and compliance (GRC) are the tenets, processes, and laws that guide how a business assesses and prioritizes risk to its assets and how it adheres to laws that govern the processing and transfer of personal or health data it might be using to power its product. Early-stage startups commonly do not have many compliance needs as they find their product market fit. As the business grows, however, you will begin running into a number of regulations. Some regulations need to apply to all of a business's data, whereas some can be scoped to specific parts.

A regularly used term in the context of compliance is *controls*. Controls are processes and rules that a company internally defines and practices to reduce the chances of an unwanted risk outcome.

Let's introduce some of the compliance regulations you should know about. Later, we cover architectural changes that can help make fulfilling these various requirements more manageable.

## Service Organization Controls Type 2

Service Organization Controls Type 2 (SOC 2) (*https://oreil.ly/PwWBg*) is a set of compliance controls that service organizations can use to report on their practices relevant to security, availability, processing integrity, confidentiality, and privacy. Database engineers in organizations looking to be SOC 2 certified will need to have well-established practices around database change management, backup and restore procedures, and managing access to database instances.

## Sarbanes–Oxley Act

The Sarbanes–Oxley Act (SOX) of 2002 (*https://oreil.ly/qHAN0*) is a law that all companies that become publicly traded have to comply with. It is intended to protect investors by improving the accuracy and reliability of corporate disclosures made pursuant to the securities laws and for other purposes. For an engineering organization, SOX duties require proving that databases containing revenue-impacting data are only accessed by those who have a need to and that any changes to this data are logged and the changes are for documented reasons.

If you are a publicly traded company, SOX control 404 is a legally required control that you have to be familiar with and fulfill. It aims to guarantee with evidence that the financials reported by a company are backed by data access and change management practices that accurately attribute the services rendered to the revenue collected and provide an audit trail for any changes to such data.

## Payment Card Industry Data Security Standard

The Payment Card Industry Data Security Standard (PCI DSS) (*https://oreil.ly/V6GBh*) is a standard required of all financial institutions handling credit card data. Its intent is to protect credit card holders' data from being leaked and used in fraudulent transactions.

An important aspect of PCI-DSS control when it comes to your work as a database engineer is managing access to cardholder data. It means you will need to consider that control in your architecture to make sure that card data is managed separately. We will discuss how you can achieve that later in this chapter when we cover separation of roles.

## Health Insurance Portability and Accountability Act

The Health Insurance Portability and Accountability Act (HIPAA) of 1996 (*https://oreil.ly/fKeQd*) is a US regulation designed to protect the privacy of health-related data of individuals when collected and processed by health providers, health plans, or their business associates. This law applies to data defined as electronic personal health information (ePHI). Organizations offering products that require HIPAA compliance will need their database engineers to implement controls such as access controls for ePHI, encryption of all ePHI, and activity logging whenever ePHI is accessed.

## Federal Risk and Authorization Management Program

For companies operating in the US and looking to generate business with US government entities, the Federal Risk and Authorization Management Program (FedRAMP) (*https://oreil.ly/ZVQqq*) is a certification offered by the federal government to qualify businesses for being cloud providers for federal entities. It is a collection of standards required to be eligible to take on federal entities as customers. These standards include configuration management, access controls, security assessments, and audits of access and changes to data.

## General Data Protection Regulation

General Data Protection Regulation (GDPR) is a European Union regulation introduced in 2016 to govern how personally identifiable information on EU persons is stored and managed by entities that act as data processors, regardless of where they are headquartered. It introduced the first steps of managing data privacy, such as requiring consent before collecting private data, setting limits on access to that private data across a processor's organization, and providing a legal avenue for individuals to request that their data be purged from the systems of any data processor that may have collected it through their online activity. This is known as the individual's "right to be forgotten."

## Schrems II

In 2020, a case between the EU and Facebook's Ireland entity was ruled on by the EU justice court. The ruling, commonly known as *Schrems II* (*https://oreil.ly/4wqAm*) signaled widespread impact on all US companies that operate and collect data on EU persons.

Privacy Shield (*https://oreil.ly/I9lPC*) was the legal standing US companies had been operating under in the EU for years. The Schrems ruling declared it insufficient to protect the privacy of EU persons when their data is collected by US company entities in the EU. At the core of that cancellation is the ruling by the EU justice court that Privacy Shield is not sufficient to guarantee that EU persons will not be surveilled by the US government through US legal means (namely using a mechanism provided by the Foreign Intelligence Surveillance Act (*https://oreil.ly/hthsk*) of 1978, or FISA), and that therefore, personally identifiable data on EU persons collected by US entities must remain in the EU and not cross into US assets or be accessible by US persons.

The ruling makes it more complex to reason about data architecture in comparison to the initial version of GDPR. Due to how recent this ruling was made, enforcement remains an unknown quantity. This situation leaves each business to determine how much of the data it collects and processes is in scope and in what way. It's safe to assume that Schrems II will be coming for the applications and data infrastructure you run if you have any current or future customers in Europe.

# Building for Compliance Controls

As you can see, the world of regulatory compliance of businesses and, by consequence, the data the business uses to operate is vast, and controls can be numerous depending on the goal of each law or the certification your business needs. The good news is that there is plenty of room for the same work to cover more than one control, allowing for efficiency and more consistent practices when managing the infrastructure. You do, however, need to understand which of these controls are required for the business and for what purpose. Once your company grows to a size where it needs to start implementing any subset of these regulatory compliance controls, you will become the person who gets to present evidence of compliance to different kinds of auditors. Understanding what each control is aimed at will go a long way toward presenting the right kind of evidence to make the audits easier.

Building for compliance is an ongoing process that cannot be easily "added on" when needed. A lot of the architectural advice presented in this chapter (separation of roles, tracking changes, and so forth) is the sort of thing you should be thinking about and advocating for once your company is past the "still finding market fit" stage. These are practices that will set your business up for success by the time compliance becomes a real need and not just a "nice to have."

## Secrets Management

Before we discuss how to manage secrets, let's first align on what things in your infrastructure might fall under that definition:

- Password strings for applications to interact with databases
- Password strings for support staff/operators to manage the database instances
- API tokens that can access/modify data
- SSH private keys
- Certificate keys

A core ability you need in your organization to facilitate a lot of security controls is a way to manage secrets securely and separately from managing your configuration. You need a way of delivering and rotating sensitive data like database access credentials, whether it is for use by applications or teams, for the purposes of reporting.

If you run your applications and databases in a cloud environment, we highly recommend you find out the preferred secrets management solution for that cloud provider before looking to build your own. You will need something that provides at minimum a level of encryption that is acceptable by National Institute of Standards and Technology (NIST) standards[1] because that is required for a number of regulations, including HIPAA and FedRAMP.

If your cloud provider does not have an acceptable solution for secret management, you may have to host your own. This might be a new endeavor for your organization and will require a more broad effort than is in scope for this book.

Whether you use a managed solution or end up needing to run your own, be aware of the complexity this secret management solution brings to your architecture. The goal of this solution is to manage secrets, not to be a single point of failure for your product. Clearly written trade-offs explaining what happens when the secret management

---

1 For more information on these standards, start a conversation with your friendly information security team or grab the *NIST Cybersecurity Framework* (*https://oreil.ly/s7XOJ*) pocket guide from O'Reilly.

solution is available will come in handy. An explicit conversation in advance with both your legal team and security organization about what secrets are cached and in what ways will help avoid misaligned expectations later.

Often, decisions made by a company in its early development days that were based on convenience need to be wound back well before planning for compliance controls. You should be prepared to explain to your leadership why this work is important in the context of improving your security posture and reducing risk.

### Do not share users

Do not share database credentials across services. This is the type of decision that pays off in orders of magnitude if you have a database accidentally leak and you now have to assess the blast radius of how many parts of the application stack and processes have to get a new database credential pair. As a database engineer, it is common to join a startup where folks have taken the seemingly convenient shortcut of "all the code uses the same pair to access the database." Believe us: this is a very expensive shortcut, and your future self will thank you if you limit the access of each database user to just the service it needs.

Now that we've covered this basic but crucial fundamental practice, let's talk about things to consider when choosing a solution to store database credentials or secrets in general.

### Do not check production database credentials in code repositories

This may seem obvious, but it is something that keeps happening as we see in plenty of postsecurity incident reports from companies both large and small. It is important to keep a humble mindset about this and don't assume that this mistake is unlikely in your organization. A trust-but-verify approach will go a long way toward preventing future pain. Scanning code repositories for potential secret strings before a pull request is merged is a common practice (and something that hosted repo services like GitHub can do for you). If that is not something your organization is already thinking about, you may need to become an advocate for this need. Remember that compliance and security are needed for the organization as a whole, and although not everything can or should be done by the database team, you are a stakeholder in how the engineering organization at large talks about these priorities.

These practices are fundamental to starting off your compliance and security posture on the right foot. They will make a number of the operations we are about to cover when using secret management all the more straightforward and will further reduce risk to the business if there is ever a need to make an urgent change.

Let's talk about the trade-offs in choosing a secret management solution.

## Choosing a secret management solution

Choosing a secret management solution is going to rely on what environment you run in and what can most easily integrate with not just the databases but also the application stack. There will always be trade-offs between convenience and meeting all your needs. So you need to be clear with all stakeholders (some of whom are not in engineering) on what the limitations are and what the trade-offs for availability or resilience are. Some of these trade-offs that you should consider as you check what your cloud (or private) infrastructure can offer include the following:

*Space limitations*
> A number of cloud-provided secret management solutions make assumptions about how *long* a secret is, which can lead to surprises if you want to store something longer than a database user and password pair. If your compliance controls require also treating longer text strings as secrets (such as SSH keys or private certificates for SSL), you should check into the maximum size you can store on a given key. One of the land mines some organizations stumble on later is that as the secret footprint grows, a new and different secret management solution is needed to accommodate longer secrets. Now they have to deal with either migrating (which can affect uptime) or managing tooling and integrations with two separate secret solutions, which comes with its own complexity.

*Secret rotation*
> If you run in a public cloud and can use their hosted secret management solution, there is good news for you: all three major cloud offerings as of this writing offer some method of automating the rotation of secrets along with versioning to make the transition to new secrets seamless for your services. However, if your secret management solution of choice does not support rotating secrets, then you need to plan for how you will do that both as a planned change (for example, you may have a control that requires that database credentials rotate on a cadence) or as an unplanned emergency change (for instance, someone accidentally checked a database password in a public repository). How do you do this without affecting your running applications? That depends to a large extent on how you deliver configuration changes to running applications and what your deployment pipeline operates. This is the general idea of how to orchestrate it. This change is a deployment. Even if your applications access database credentials as a configuration line, you still need to propagate this configuration change to all of your fleet and typically also orchestrate a restart without affecting availability of the service as a whole.

*Regional availability*
> Consider that your secret management solution is not just for storing secrets but also for delivering them. If you are to avoid a known bad practice like storing secrets in code, you need your application to be able to retrieve the secrets it

needs to handle requests at runtime. This means you now have to think about how these secrets will be retrieved, what happens if your application cannot access the secret management service, and what failure modes this new dependency introduces. If you are responsible for applications that need to run in many geographical regions, the regional capabilities of your secret management solution become another thing to consider. Does the solution by your cloud provider automatically replicate secrets to other regions? Or do you have to build that capability?

## Separation of Roles and Data

An important goal of these regulatory laws is the separation of data based on the risk it presents for either the business or its customers in case of a leak. This is the concept of *least privilege*, both for human access and application code access. This separation allows for more appropriate controls and tracking of changes depending on what the data is and what risk is associated with it.

### Sharding for compliance reasons

One axis that may force a specific separation of data sets into dedicated clusters is having different compliance requirements with very different controls. Let's say you are a marketing communications provider that is creating a new, separate product with an emphasis on health-care tech. The data that is currently in use was not health related and was not subject to a number of legal requirements. Once the business makes this entry into health technology, you now have a subset of customers and their data where your company carries the legal burden of being a processor of personal health information (PHI). In that scenario, it makes sense to develop the new product from the get-go in dedicated data storage so that you can more appropriately apply HIPAA compliance controls without adding undue burden on the existing data set and its dependent applications.

### Separate database users

As your product grows more complex and the tech stack that supports it follows suit, you will start having more than one application with data access. It is very important to start well-controlled data access controls early in your organization by not sharing the same database access credentials across multiple code bases. Security incidents and accidental leaks of credentials are events that happen to all sorts of companies regardless of size, and when they do, you will be well served to have the leaked secrets impact a known and isolated blast radius of your business operations as you scramble to rotate that secret.

# Tracking Changes

A number of compliance regulations come with controls around tracking changes: changes to subsets of your data that affect financial reporting, changes to your systems that generate invoices, and how these changes are reviewed, tested, and tracked. One of the obvious first spots where this kind of compliance control becomes pertinent is the database. As you work for a business with expanding compliance responsibilities, processes like "how a schema change gets reviewed, applied, and tracked in production" need more rigor and planning than simply "an engineer logs on the source node in production and makes a change." This is far less of a burden if you prepare by planning alongside your internal audit team or compliance team for how to handle audits.

The goal here is to avoid annual audits from becoming a major disruptive event where the team is scrambling to collect evidence for the audit team. Instead, if you make some changes to how these normal business operations work, you can have "baked in" evidence that is far simpler to collect and use for audits. You will see in this section a recurring theme around producing structured logs from everything. This is intentional. It goes a long way toward making all sorts of changes trackable in the same manner, and that consistency helps the business achieve its audit needs with far less disruption. You can see how this all comes together in Figure 13-1.

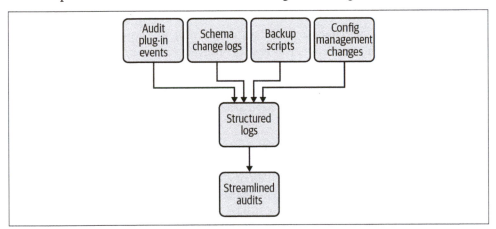

*Figure 13-1. Examples of different operational tasks all sending structured logs to one place, making audits easier*

Let's look at different types of changes to database systems and how to automate compliance tracking for them.

## Data access logging

Many compliance controls ask that you maintain logs of changes or access to specific data sets. This can be for the purposes of tracking changes to financial data or for regulations such as PCI or HIPAA where the data is sensitive enough that all access needs to be tracked.

You can address this need directly at the database level by leveraging either Percona's audit log plug-in (*https://oreil.ly/0SJa0*) if you run Percona's fork or the equivalent MySQL Enterprise Audit plug-in (*https://oreil.ly/2tanA*) if you run MySQL Community Server. The benefit here is that you now can track changes at the last hop before data changes, especially if you are in an environment where changes to the database can happen via multiple paths.

**Undesirable options for tracking changes.** You may ask, "Why not use triggers to track any changes to the tables I care about?" This is definitely an approach we have seen in the past, but it is not recommended. Here are some reasons we discourage using triggers for this:

- Triggers are known to present a write performance hit, which will affect you at the worst possible time.
- Triggers amount to storing business logic in the database, which is not recommended.
- Storing code in the database will likely circumvent any process for testing, staging, and deploying that code. It is easy for triggers to become an unexpected surprise for your team during incidents.
- Triggers can only support tracking write actions. It is a solution that cannot expand to track read access if the need arises.

Let's see how you would use the Percona audit log plug-in and how to tune it.

**Installing and tuning Percona audit logs.** Percona's audit log plug-in ships as part of Percona's MySQL fork but is not installed or enabled by default. You can install it by running the following command on your instances as part of the bootstrap process of any new instance:

```
INSTALL PLUGIN audit_log SONAME 'audit_log.so';
SHOW PLUGINS;
```

The second command lists the running plug-ins and should confirm that the audit log plug-in is, in fact, now running as part of the server process. Besides turning it on, you also need to determine how you will ingest its output. This is where the real planning happens.

The audit log plug-in by Percona allows you to define what statement verbs you need to track. This allows for flexibility to meet various controls without committing to a lot of noise in your audit logs that are irrelevant to what you care about. Make sure you review its documentation to properly configure that variable as needed.

One of the flexible advantages of the plug-in is that you can have it installed but not actually monitoring queries.[2] This can be useful if you are still working on how to ingest its output and need to turn it off and on without uptime impact. But with that flexibility comes complexity. Besides managing the configuration variables that come with the audit log plug-in, you also need to monitor that it is running at all times. If this is a critical function for the business, it means it is worth monitoring. Since the plug-in can be disabled on the fly without a server restart, you need more than just checking the on disk *my.cnf* file to confirm that it is doing what it needs to be doing. Your best bet is to use shell queries to parse out the current state of the plug-in and confirm that it is, in fact, monitoring queries. Here are two sample single liners to check for each of these:

```
# Single liner to check that the audit log plugin is active
$ mysql -e "show plugins" | grep -w audit_log | grep -iw active

# Single liner to check that the plugin policy is actually monitoring queries
$ mysqladmin variables | grep -w audit_log_policy | grep -iw queries
```

These examples assume that you are only looking to monitor queries. You will need to edit the check if you also expect to use the plug-in to track logins.

**Ingesting and using audit plug-in logs.**   As you can see, there is a lot of flexibility with the audit log plug-in, but it also only produces audit events for you. It is on you to determine the best way to ingest these logs, have them in a place where they can be easily searched and analyzed, and reasonably discover anomalies in them without it being a major burden. The plug-in can simply dump the output to local files, but that can increase the risk of causing outages by filling up your database host disks with these logs.

A more complex option is to use the plug-in's ability to send its output to `rsyslog`, a common Unix log management utility, and from there use `rsyslog` to forward all these events to your organization's structured logging platform of choice. This option is appealing as it brings this data into the same place where your organization already does structured log storage, which lowers the barrier for stakeholders outside the database team to be able to see, search, and analyze these events. Keep in mind, though, that using `rsyslog` for log forwarding in this manner will require you to become familiar with how it works. Make sure you decide and document in an

---

2 See the plug-in documentation (*https://oreil.ly/gwqc2*) for more on this.

intentional manner how `rsyslog` for this data stream is configured.[3] It is quite possible there are a number of default configurations in `rsyslog` that are not helpful to your desired outcome, and it is on you to do the due diligence to find these and change them accordingly.

 Make sure to document how the audit log plug-in output is stored, even if temporarily, on database hosts. If the shipping method for these files slows down, the impact of buffering the events in the plug-in can affect the performance of the database server itself. This failure state is hard to debug because its only symptom is queries executing slower. Plan chaos testing for the entire pipeline of these logs with resilience in mind.

The Percona audit log plug-in is a powerful tool that can help you fulfill a number of compliance controls. In our experience, it is a far more performant solution than using triggers, and it integrates well with configuration management and structured logging software, making for a solution that is effective across a number of stakeholder teams.

### Version control for schema changes

Chapter 6 covered different strategies and tools that facilitate running schema changes at scale. Let's talk about the compliance concerns these strategies enable.

Using version control to both track and run your schema changes comes with built-in tracking of who requested a change, who reviewed and approved it, and how it ran in production. This is also a good reason to use a separate repository per database cluster. As the database footprint in your company grows, you will find that not all databases are created equal. Some will need more rigor for compliance (for example, databases that hold financial data), and some power product experiments that are not as critical. When it comes time for an audit, having the change record for each data set and cluster available will be a huge convenience.

This separation of data and cluster schema management based on compliance needs also makes it easier to control who can submit or approve schema changes in your version control management of choice. It is common when running a business audit to need to justify who can make changes to the databases. Having a smaller circle of human operators that *can* make changes to this data keeps with least-privilege security principles.

---

3  As a start, here is an entire page on "reliable log forwarding" (*https://oreil.ly/76e9K*).

### Database user management

Changes to databases are not limited to schema changes. You also need to manage database users and their granular privileges in a manner that is trackable and repeatable. Let's find out how you can meet some common compliance controls that address database access controls.

**Use configuration management.**   A simple way to make database user tracking compliant is to leverage the same process you use to make database configuration changes compliant. You manage it all in a configuration management repository and use source control, a pull request process, and peer review to provide the evidence that all changes to the database users are done in a manner that can be audited and tracked.

**Plan for credential rotation.**   Whether for unplanned security incidents or because you have a control that requires rotating credentials on a schedule, you need to have a plan for how to rotate database users without affecting your application uptime. This likely means changing both the username and password string used by applications. If you are not yet running the latest and greatest major version with dual password support, here are the steps you should employ to rotate database credentials in an application in production without affecting the service uptime:

1. Introduce a new username/password pair in the database first.

2. Test that the new credentials have the same access privileges the old ones have. Ideally, you do this automatically as part of deploying the new credentials by comparing SHOW GRANTS and confirming the privileges are identical.

3. Create an application deployment that replaces the credentials in your application configuration.

4. Restart all instances of this service to make sure the new pair is in use.

5. Drop the old username and password pair.

This process should work the same whether the change is routine or urgent because of a credential leak or a security risk. Since the latter is not an event you can control or entirely prevent from happening, you will be best served to have this process automated, or at least well documented in a runbook and done routinely, so it is not a scary fire-drill situation for your team when it happens unexpectedly.

Rotating database user passwords in MySQL used to be a complex orchestrating endeavor to accomplish without affecting availability. MySQL 8.0.14 introduced dual password support, which, in conjunction with password expiration policy support, makes doing the right thing far easier operationally.

**Retire database users not in use.** Any database user not in use that remains active on your instances is a security liability you do not need. It is important to audit the database users active on your instances regularly, compared to what is configured on your applications, and drop any users not actively in use by any applications.

When fulfilling compliance needs for your company, you will come to see that a lot of those compliance controls require the organization to track any and all changes to certain assets. These controls are typical in reports like SOC 2, which we described earlier in this chapter, where the primary concern is providing evidence of data integrity and security.

There are a few ways to find out if a defined database user is in use or not. We covered Performance Schema extensively in Chapter 3 as a way to inspect server performance. There is a `users` table in Performance Schema that stores historical information about users that have connected to the server. This historical tracking goes as far back as the life of the server process or the maximum size allowed for this table, whichever happens first. Since the table tracks users that *have* connected, not ones that have *not,* you will need to loop over known users and see if any do not appear in this table as the signal that they might not be in use anymore.

Here is a query to enable that instrument in Performance Schema:

```
mysql> UPDATE performance_schema.setup_instruments
    -> SET ENABLED='YES' WHERE NAME='memory/sql/user_conn';
Query OK, 1 rows affected (0.00 sec)
Rows matched: 1 Changed: 1 Warnings: 0
```

Once you have that enabled, the table to find this information is `performance_schema.users`.

If you use an audit-logging solution for compliance controls, such as Percona's plug-in that we mentioned previously, you can use these logs to determine whether a user has connected to the instances within a given number of weeks.

Regardless of which way you determine this, it is recommended to set a policy where "after six months of inactivity, a database user that has not connected will be removed." This is a practice that will help prevent having access that is not needed and is now a liability.

The databases you help manage are going to be in scope for controls that require this level of diligence. As your company matures and starts considering becoming more compliant, you will need to have a story for how you will show evidence that changes to the databases in production are reviewed and tracked before they are applied. The other thing that compliance controls will focus on is proving your ability to restore data and service when a catastrophic event happens. For that, we need to go over to backups and restores and see how they fit in.

## Backup and Restore Procedures

Chapter 10 covers the different kinds of backups. Backups are obviously important. They can be tremendously helpful in incidents but also are a key part of many compliance controls. In most SOC 2 implementations, you will have controls for both creating and testing the backups (but you should also test your backups anyway). As the number of database clusters you manage grows, you will quickly find that you cannot continue doing processes like backup and backup tests manually, or even report on success and failure by manually reading logfiles.

You need to cover some requirements when assessing how you will manage backups for compliance reasons:

- You need to automate the process of backups.
- You need the backup process to alert you if it fails.
- You need to automate tests of the backups.
- Failed tests of backups should also be events you can track somewhere.

Next we discuss how to schedule backups and backup tests.

### Running automated backups and backup tests

To fulfill these requirements, you need a mechanism that does not just run scheduled jobs (such as *crond* in Linux systems) but that can run on a schedule and also has the ability to send events to your monitoring system and your ticketing system to both alert on failure and track the failure for audits later. One way you can do this is by running backups and backup tests as a monitoring check,[4] but backups can take a while to run, especially if you have some database instances sized in the terabytes. Running backups as a monitoring item can work as long as the monitoring system you are about to use for running your backup tasks can handle checks that can run for periods that are much longer than the typical few seconds. So make sure that your team running the monitoring system is aware of this use case.

If your monitoring system cannot handle this kind of use case, then make sure you have some method to leave behind "bread crumbs" to track that a backup has happened and finished successfully and that a backup test has happened and also finished successfully. One such bread crumb can be a file with a timestamp in it that your backup process edits at the end of every backup or backup test run as proof that the task happened and was completed. Once that bread crumb is in place, you can use the monitoring system to do the much faster check that the bread crumb exists.

---

4 In the blog post "Using Sensu for DBA tasks" (*https://oreil.ly/Meunp*), you can see some examples of making tasks like backups a part of your database monitoring solution.

In all these strategies, what you want to have, and what your SOC 2 control requires, is a track record of backups finishing successfully as well as of any failed backups, showing that they were turned into properly tracked work items.

### Centralized logs for backups and backup tests

You may also be asked to show logs proving the successful completion of backups and backup test processes. You would be well served to prepare for such an audit item by using a centralized logging solution you can ship logs to for continuity. Remember that the solutions we build for these business needs should assume servers are easily and repeatedly replaceable, not bespoke. So local logfiles on a random instance are not ideal if you ever retire that machine and replace it before the next audit. You want any business-related assets, such as logs of the backup process, to be in a centralized location that anyone with the right access policies can access.

### Disaster-recovery planning through backups

Also as part of SOC 2 is the requirement to have proper disaster-recovery planning. This means proof that you test any backups that your system produces, you have tracking of when these tests fail and that the failure was corrected, and, ideally, that you have an idea of how long disaster recovery of data takes. This last part requires tracking metrics for how long a test of a backup takes. Chapter 2 mentioned database instance size as a metric for determining whether it is getting too large for backup recovery within an intended objective time. The way to make this a self-improving cycle is to make your backup and scripts that test the backups also send metrics of how long each takes. This way, you have per-database cluster metrics of how long backups take and how long restoring and testing those backups take. You now have a way to track whether any given set of data is getting too large for what the business expects in terms of MTTR. If you are, then you have the data to either prioritize the work to split the data set down to an acceptable size or revisit the business SLA for recovery.

An important final note about backups: your security stakeholders will need access to both the live databases and the backups to be controlled. Make sure that your backup setup in your favorite cloud provider does not default to permissive access controls for backup buckets. Many security breaches happen not through breaching the live infrastructure, but through backups leaking from a storage bucket somewhere.

# Summary

Compliance is a wide-ranging world of policy and controls as well as interpretations of each. It affects not just how you run databases in your business but also the legal, finance, and IT departments, and even how you deploy changes to your software. This chapter focused on how each common type of compliance regulation affects your duties as a database engineer specifically. We then covered different practices and architectural decisions that can be affected by these regulations, which you also need to consider.

Broadly, the best way to get ahead of control-related nightmares is to plan early. Separate your application users, plan a credential rotation strategy, and ensure that your passwords are always stored encrypted—never as plain text. Ensure that before you need to start logging access to the database, you have a logging pipeline you can trust. Lastly, you want schema changes to be controlled and logged.

The goal of this chapter has not been to overwhelm you with thinking about all these controls across your entire infrastructure at once, but to make the task of providing evidence for the parts that are in scope for each regulation easier and as automated or simple to put together as possible. Ultimately, these controls are meant to protect the business and your customers' privacy. Having a strong grasp on what each control aims to achieve will make this important task more manageable for you and your team as your company grows and enters wider markets.

# Upgrading MySQL

Upgrading is a trade-off between stability[1] and features. You should consider this when choosing to upgrade. One of the best parts about using MySQL is its wide installation base. This means you get the benefit of so many other people testing and using MySQL. If you upgrade to too new of a version, you may unknowingly introduce a bug or regression into your environment. If you stay too far behind, you may be experiencing nonobvious bugs or won't be able to take advantage of a feature that has been optimized for performance.

## Why Upgrade?

Deciding to go forward with a version upgrade can be a risky process. It usually involves backing up all your data, testing the changes, and then running the upgrade process. Before we go into the details, it's important to understand why you might want to upgrade.

There are a number of reasons to upgrade:

*Security vulnerabilities*
> It has become less likely over the years, but it is still possible that people discover security vulnerabilities in MySQL. You or your security team may assess these and determine that you should perform an upgrade.

---

1 Stewart Smith, a long-time MySQL community member, famously coined the dot-20 rule: "[The rule] is that a piece of software is never really mature until a dot-20 release." While this isn't a hard-and-fast rule, it does highlight the trade-off between new releases and stability.

*Known bugs*

When encountering an unknown or unexplainable behavior in production, we recommend finding what version of MySQL you're running and then read the release notes for the subsequent versions to the latest. It is entirely possible you'll discover the situation you're experiencing is actually a software bug in MySQL. If your issue is covered, you may find the need to upgrade MySQL.

*Newer features*

MySQL doesn't always adhere to a strict major/minor/point release strategy with respect to how features are added. Many people may expect that a point release (e.g., 8.0.21 to 8.0.22) would only contain bug fixes, and a minor version change (8.0 to 8.1) would include minor features. Oracle often releases new features in minor point releases that may have an impact on your workload. This strategy is a double-edged sword and why you should read all of the release notes before upgrading.

*MySQL end-of-life support*

Oracle sets end-of-life (EOL) time frames for MySQL. In general, it is advisable to stay within a supported version so that, at a minimum, security fixes are still supported.

Now that we have covered the various factors that are part of your decision to upgrade and to which specific version, let's discuss the process for planning and safely completing an upgrade.

# Upgrade Life Cycle

Once you've made the decision that upgrading is the right step for you, you'll typically take the following steps:

1. Read the release notes for the version, including any minor changes.

2. Read the upgrade notes in the official documentation.

3. Perform testing of the new version.

4. Finally, upgrade your servers.

The release notes will often have important information like new features, changes, or deprecated features, and usually a list of bugs that have been fixed. The upgrade notes give you a detailed overview of how to perform the upgrade, and they call your attention to any important information that you need to know before continuing.

In addition, you should also have a plan for what to do if you introduce issues, like a query begins performing poorly, or worse, you begin experiencing a crashing bug. For all major and minor version changes (e.g., 8.0 down to 5.7 or 5.7 down to 5.6), the only way to downgrade is to restore a backup from before you upgraded. This makes upgrading especially risky, so be sure you have a plan.

 It's important to note that since MySQL 8.0, you cannot downgrade point release versions either. For example, once you are running 8.0.25, you cannot downgrade to 8.0.24 without exporting all of your data and reimporting.

# Testing Upgrades

Once you've read the release and upgrade notes, you should have a good understanding of any concerns or areas of focus for testing. The next step would be to test how this new version will behave with your workload. You'll also want to verify you've reviewed your configuration files. Newer versions of MySQL often rename variables or deprecate them entirely.

Testing is a tricky step to accomplish, and each of the methods has caveats. Given the risk we cited before about downgrading, you should employ as many of these methods as are feasible prior to upgrading.

## Development Environment Testing

Hopefully, you have a development environment for your data. This is a great place to begin your testing, either on a shared development database or on a standalone one for you. The main goal of using this is to surface any obvious issues with syntax. Most development environments do not contain the same size production data, so it can be difficult to run accurate testing. For example, you may run your commonly used queries and see that they're fine because they access only 10 rows in a table. When you go to production, with 10 million rows in the same table, you may see a regression.

## Production Mirror

Another option would be to create a copy of your production data and send a copy of your SQL traffic to it. This method was showcased in a blog post on Etsy's Code As Craft blog (*https://oreil.ly/yByfy*). In short, you have a second copy of your production database, cease using replication, and upgrade MySQL on the copy. Once complete, send traffic to both your live production system *and* the copy using a combination of *tcpdump* and *pt-query-digest*. Your application is still using only the production system for live traffic while the copy with the upgraded version can give you performance metrics and surface errors in syntax.

## Replica

If your topology has read replicas and you have the ability to depool the replica, you could consider upgrading one of the replicas first. This would allow you to see how your read traffic performs with an actual production workload. If you observe errors or regressions, you can depool the replica and make adjustments. The downside of this method is that you cannot test performance or write traffic.

## Tooling

Percona Toolkit offers the tool *pt-upgrade*, which takes an input of queries, runs them against two different targets, and produces a report telling you about any differences in row counts, row data, or errors. Since it can take many different types of input (slow query log, general query log, binary logs), it can be a good option to get additional test coverage.

The best way to use this would be to first collect the queries you are most interested in, with either the slow query log or the binary log. Then set up two identical systems, upgrade only one of them to your new version, and run *pt-upgrade* against both to see the differences.

# Upgrading at Scale

Upgrading MySQL is very straightforward and is covered thoroughly in the official MySQL documentation. In brief, if you're doing an in-place upgrade, you'll stop MySQL, replace the binaries, start MySQL, and then run the `mysql_upgrade` script.

This can be repetitive if you're doing this on a fleet of hundreds of MySQL servers. Our suggestion would be to automate this as much as possible. One way you can do this is with Ansible.

Here's a suggested skeleton process for performing safe upgrades that you can use as a guide to build an Ansible playbook, if you choose to:

1. *Verify target.*

   The very first thing you want to do is prevent any accidental upgrades of production systems. If you have a system that you can query to determine whether a database is actively taking traffic, this is the place to check it. If you followed our advice from Chapter 5, you should be using the `read_only` flag to prevent unexpected writes to your replicas. This can serve as a good alternative if you don't have a system that you can check. If a server is writable, chances are you don't want to upgrade it since it may be taking production writes. You can also use this step to verify that you haven't already upgraded the server. This allows you to run the playbook against it later and it will take no action.

2. *Set downtime.*
   Hopefully, your systems are being monitored. The next step involves setting some form of downtime or alert suppression so that you don't get paged for the step where MySQL is restarted on the new version.

3. *Other preconditions.*
   If you have any other dependent services, like a configuration management tool or other monitoring tools that will generate errors while MySQL is offline, now is a good time to shut them down.

4. *Remove old packages.*
   Our preferred method is to completely remove any installed packages for MySQL at this point. This helps avoid any conflicting packages for major versions (5.7 to 8.0).

5. *Install new packages.*
   Next, you'll want to install the new packages onto your system.

6. *Start* mysqld.
   Start the mysqld service.

7. *Run* mysql_upgrade.
   If older than MySQL 8.0,[2] run the mysql_upgrade process. As a special note, if you run MySQL with super_read_only like we recommend, you'll want to set it to OFF for the mysql_upgrade step.

8. *Restart* mysqld.
   We prefer to give a clean restart to mysqld at this point. This will ensure that it starts up correctly with the upgraded files and that your configuration files are also working.

9. *Verify you can connect.*
   Simply connect and run a SELECT 1 to ensure that MySQL is up and working.

10. *Restore any disabled services.*
    If you turned off any configuration management or monitoring tools, enable them again.

11. *Clear downtime.*
    Take your server out of downtime so you can observe if there are any that failed the upgrade process.

---

2 MySQL 8.0 moved the mysql_upgrade process into the startup of the server itself. There is no need to run this as an additional step.

With this process, you're able to point your runbook at any server and only upgrade the nonupgraded nodes that are not taking traffic.

## Summary

There are many reasons for upgrading MySQL, the most compelling being fixes to a bug you are actively experiencing or being able to leverage a new feature. For example, MySQL 8.0 introduced a feature for InnoDB where columns can be added instantly—no need to rebuild the entire table. This type of feature enhancement can be a huge time saver for companies that perform a high volume of ALTER TABLE .. ADD COLUMN statements. The effort you put into working through a safe upgrade process will eventually pay itself back in time saved performing those column add statements as well as an improved developer experience.

Major version upgrades can be daunting, however. You should absolutely put a lot of effort into testing your upgrades for any adverse effects. Typically, you want to check for any query latency deviations or new errors as a result of an upgrade. Once you gain confidence, roll things out slowly and have a rollback process.

Lastly, if you have a large fleet of servers to manage, consider investing heavily in automating the process as best as possible. Automation can make the upgrade process easily repeatable and more time efficient than logging in to each server directly, and it runs a slightly lower chance of typos and accidental downtime from being on the wrong server.

# MySQL on Kubernetes

If you have been working in tech at all in the past five years, you very likely have heard of Kubernetes, work with teams that run Kubernetes, or have watched a lot of conference talks or read a lot of blog posts that explain Kubernetes. If your organization runs its own Kubernetes clusters, you will at some point get asked whether running MySQL on them too is a good idea. And on the surface it seems like a reasonable path to take. Managing many Kubernetes clusters is a complex task that typically needs dedicated human resources, and it is reasonable for your organization to want to leverage that expertise for more than only stateless workloads. But there are good reasons to explore running MySQL on Kubernetes and not so good reasons to do so. Let's demystify some of the FUD (fear, uncertainty, doubt) around running MySQL on Kubernetes here.

## Provisioning Resources with Kubernetes

Before Kubernetes reached peak tech popularity, a lot of companies either built entirely bespoke tech stacks for provisioning and managing VMs and bare metal servers or glued together open source projects that did smaller parts of the life cycle of a resource. Then came Kubernetes as a more complete ecosystem for managing both compute and storage resources, and the prospect of using it as the provisioning stack to rule them all has become more and more appealing. Yet stateful loads such as MySQL remained behind and left out of that added value because the common wisdom had been "you can't run databases on containers."

## Carefully Scope Your Goal

The important thing to keep in mind is "What specific value do we want to get back here?" Kubernetes is powerful for stateless loads because it brings elasticity and efficiency of compute resources. However, it is reasonable to scope down the win when looking at a unified provisioning stack to "we only want to use Kubernetes to provision and configure the systems for database resources." This means you need to be clear up front that the database workloads that will be provisioned with Kubernetes will be managed separately from stateless workloads, will require different operator skill sets, and will handle container failure differently.

## Choose Your Control Plane

There are various MySQL operators in the wild now, but the choice of which is the best will be mostly a consequence of what you decide as the scope of your Kubernetes management of MySQL. Will you need an operator that does it all: provisioning, failover, and managing connecting to the databases? Or will you simply use Kubernetes as a provisioning stack and use other means to manage databases after they are in service? Decide early on what you expect from your control plane, as that will drive a lot of the finer operability details.

## The Finer Details

Once you have decided to start provisioning MySQL resources using Kubernetes, you need to get agreement across your organization on what size data is appropriate for this solution. Remember that this is now a new operating model for running a relational database, and on this less-paved road, everything gets more complex as it gets bigger. Here are some important items to consider as you collaborate with your Kubernetes engineering team (hopefully, you have a dedicated team for this) on how to support stateful workloads:

- What maximum data set size for a single database instance will be supported?
- Will you be mounting volumes to containers and managing container recovery separately from the data mounts? Or will the data be part of the container?
- What maximum query throughput is going to be supported? How will you manage resources?
- How will you ensure Kubernetes nodes running database workloads are dedicated to that and not shared with stateless, more elastic, workloads?
- What control plane will you use for running the database instances? Is it Kubernetes native?
- How will backups work? What's the restore process?
- How will you control and safely roll out configuration changes and MySQL upgrades?
- How will you upgrade your Kubernetes clusters themselves without causing disruption?

Being on the same page with your partner Kubernetes engineering team on how this solution will work will go a long way toward having well-established SLOs for feature teams looking to use this solution and in properly communicating what it solves and what the teams still have to solve on their own.

Our advice with running MySQL on Kubernetes is to invest in learning a control plane that is already vetted and proven in the Kubernetes ecosystem, like Vitess. But also crawl before you try to run. MySQL should not be the first guinea pig for running workloads on Kubernetes in your organization. Always prove viability and learn the sharp edges as a team with stateless workloads first before attempting to run more complex use cases like MySQL. As you determine the best initial use cases for adoption, start with small data sets (databases that are only a few gigabytes on disk) and with less mission-critical data sets to get your team, the Kubernetes team, and the feature teams familiar with the new operational model of running stateful workloads on Kubernetes with less risk to the business.[1]

Running stateful workloads on Kubernetes has been maturing for the past few years and continues to do so with critical contributions from companies that have invested significant engineering hours into making it a more plausible reality, but it is still in its infancy compared to running on VMs directly, and you will find that a slow and careful approach to adoption is what pays off in the long run. Especially consider what the failure modes look like with MySQL on Kubernetes and ask yourself: if everything goes wrong, how will I put this back together again? Will I lose data? Make sure you have an answer.

# Summary

Kubernetes is one of the fastest growing infrastructure platforms in tech right now and for good reason. The engineer velocity it enables and the rich ecosystem that is supported by the cloud native foundation make it an appealing investment for companies. But you should consider decisions like running MySQL on Kubernetes through the lens of risk and reward to your team and your company. Make sure you have a shared understanding of where stateful services like data stores are in your organization's Kubernetes journey. It is understandable to want to leverage existing investment in Kubernetes for all workloads, but that needs to be well balanced against your data store layer's stability needs.

---

[1] For an excellent "from the trenches" conference talk about running database workloads on Kubernetes, we recommend "The Container Operator's Manual" (*https://oreil.ly/TVD6c*) keynote, by Alice Goldfuss.

# Index

## A

access control lists (ACLs), 138
access methods, 195
ACID (atomicity, consistency, isolation, and durability), 7
active/passive replication topology, 241-242
active/read pool replication topology, 242
adaptive hash indexes, 159
algebraic transformations, 207
ALTER TABLE statement, 11
Amazon Aurora, 314-316
analytics and reporting, 229
ANALYZE TABLE command, 187
ANSI SQL standard, 8, 11
architecture
    concurrency control, 3-6
    data files structure, 16
    InnoDB engine, 16-18
    multiversion concurrency control, 13-15
    MySQL logical architecture, 1-3
    replication, 15
    transactions, 6-13
asynchronous replication, 237
atomic data definition changes, 18
atomicity, consistency, isolation, and durability (ACID), 7
attached disks, 321
auditing, 259
authentication, 2
auto-extending disks, 324
auto-generated schemas, 144
auto-increment space, tracking, 33
AUTOCOMMIT mode, 11
autoscaling, 45

AUTO_INCREMENT locking mechanism, 178
availability
    availability time by nines, 22
    definition of term, 26
    monitoring, 25
    using replication for high availability, 229
averages, avoiding in metrics, 38

## B

B-tree indexes
    basics of, 157
    benefits of, 161
    limitations of, 160
    query types using, 159
    reducing index and data fragmentation, 188
backup and recovery
    adjusting MTTR target and, 34
    backing up data
        filesystem snapshots, 272-277
        logical SQL dumps, 270-272
        Percona XtraBackup, 278-281
    building for compliance controls, 339-340
    defining recovery requirements, 259
    designing MySQL backup solution
        incremental and differential backups, 266
        knowing your RPO and RTO, 261
        logical or raw backups, 263-265
        online or offline backups, 261
        recommendations for, 260
        replication, 268
        soft versus hard requirements, 261
        what to back up, 265
    key terms, 257

## V

VARBINARY string type, 130
VARCHAR string type, 128-131
variables, examining, 66-69, 108 (see also configuration settings)
variables, versus options, 101
variables_by_thread table, 67
variables_info table, 69
virtual machines (see cloud offerings)
Vitess, 149, 303-306
vmstat, 90
vmstat tool, 92-95

## W

warm backups, 257
wear leveling, 79
WHERE clause, 196
whole numbers, 127

WITH ROLLUP clause, 223
working sets (of data), 77
workloads
    disk type selection and, 320
    read- versus write-bound workloads, 289
    read-bound workloads, 290
    understanding workloads, 289
    write-bound workloads, 291
worst-case selectivity, 165
write amplification, 79
write locks, 4-6, 12
write-ahead logging, 10, 77
write-bound workloads, 291

## X

XFS filesystem, 89, 97
XtraBackup, 270, 278-281, 284, 286

## About the Authors

**Silvia Botros** is a Software Architect at Twilio. During her time at SendGrid, she helped build the database platform that supports sending billions of emails, support other products, and drive datastore designs from inception to production.

**Jeremy Tinley** is a Senior Staff Systems Engineer at Etsy, with over 20 years of MySQL experience. Throughout his career, he has managed tens of thousands of MySQL instances with an eye toward availability, reliability, and operational efficiency.

## Colophon

The animal on the cover of *High Performance MySQL* is a sparrow hawk (*Accipiter nisus*), a small woodland member of the falcon family found in Eurasia and North Africa. Sparrow hawks have a long tail and short wings; males are bluish-gray with a light brown breast, and females are more brown-gray and have an almost fully white breast. Males are normally somewhat smaller (11 inches) than females (15 inches).

Sparrow hawks live in coniferous woods and feed on small mammals, insects, and birds. They nest in trees and sometimes on cliff ledges. At the beginning of the summer, the female lays four to six white eggs, blotched red and brown, in a nest made in the boughs of the tallest tree available. The male feeds the female and their young.

Like all hawks, the sparrow hawk is capable of bursts of high speed in flight. Whether soaring or gliding, the sparrow hawk has a characteristic flap-flap-glide action; its large tail enables the hawk to twist and turn effortlessly in and out of cover.

Many of the animals on O'Reilly's covers are endangered; all of them are important to the world.

The cover illustration is by Karen Montgomery, based on an antique line engraving from Lydekker's *The Royal Natural History*. The cover fonts are Gilroy Semibold and Guardian Sans. The text font is Adobe Minion Pro; the heading font is Adobe Myriad Condensed; and the code font is Dalton Maag's Ubuntu Mono.

# O'REILLY®

## There's much more where this came from.

Experience books, videos, live online training courses, and more from O'Reilly and our 200+ partners—all in one place.

Learn more at oreilly.com/online-learning

Milton Keynes UK
Ingram Content Group UK Ltd.
UKHW050020230924
448644UK00003B/11

9 781492 080510